SUN SIGN BOOK

Printed in the United States of America
Typography property of Llewellyn Worldwide, Ltd.

ISBN: 0-56718-901-6

Cover design by Christopher Wells

Forecasts: Gloria Star
Contributing Writers:
Edward A. Helin, Ninah Kessler,
Barbara Koval, Vince Ploscik,
Kim Rogers-Gallagher, Jackie Cavalero Slevin,
Gloria Star, Noel Tyl, Joyce C. Wehrman

Editor: Connie Hill

Published by
LLEWELLYN WORLDWIDE, LTD.
P.O. Box 64383-901
St. Paul, MN 55164-0383

1995

DECEMBER 1994						
S	M	T	W	T	F	S
				1	2	3
4	5	6	7	8	9	10
11	12	13	14	15	16	17
18	19	20	21	22	23	24
25	26	27	28	29	30	31

JANUARY 1995						
S	M	T	W	T	F	S
1	2	3	4	5	6	7
8	9	10	11	12	13	14
15	16	17	18	19	20	21
22	23	24	25	26	27	28
29	30	31				

FEBRUARY 1995						
S	M	T	W	T	F	S
			1	2	3	4
5	6	7	8	9	10	11
12	13	14	15	16	17	18
19	20	21	22	23	24	25
26	27	28				

MARCH 1995						
S	M	T	W	T	F	S
			1	2	3	4
5	6	7	8	9	10	11
12	13	14	15	16	17	18
19	20	21	22	23	24	25
26	27	28	29	30	31	

APRIL 1995						
S	M	T	W	T	F	S
						1
2	3	4	5	6	7	8
9	10	11	12	13	14	15
16	17	18	19	20	21	22
23	24	25	26	27	28	29
30						

MAY 1995						
S	M	T	W	T	F	S
	1	2	3	4	5	6
7	8	9	10	11	12	13
14	15	16	17	18	19	20
21	22	23	24	25	26	27
28	29	30	31			

JUNE 1995						
S	M	T	W	T	F	S
				1	2	3
4	5	6	7	8	9	10
11	12	13	14	15	16	17
18	19	20	21	22	23	24
25	26	27	28	29	30	

JULY 1995						
S	M	T	W	T	F	S
						1
2	3	4	5	6	7	8
9	10	11	12	13	14	15
16	17	18	19	20	21	22
23	24	25	26	27	28	29
30	31					

AUGUST 1995						
S	M	T	W	T	F	S
		1	2	3	4	5
6	7	8	9	10	11	12
13	14	15	16	17	18	19
20	21	22	23	24	25	26
27	28	29	30	31		

SEPTEMBER 1995						
S	M	T	W	T	F	S
					1	2
3	4	5	6	7	8	9
10	11	12	13	14	15	16
17	18	19	20	21	22	23
24	25	26	27	28	29	30

OCTOBER 1995						
S	M	T	W	T	F	S
1	2	3	4	5	6	7
8	9	10	11	12	13	14
15	16	17	18	19	20	21
22	23	24	25	26	27	28
29	30	31				

NOVEMBER 1995						
S	M	T	W	T	F	S
			1	2	3	4
5	6	7	8	9	10	11
12	13	14	15	16	17	18
19	20	21	22	23	24	25
26	27	28	29	30		

DECEMBER 1995						
S	M	T	W	T	F	S
					1	2
3	4	5	6	7	8	9
10	11	12	13	14	15	16
17	18	19	20	21	22	23
24	25	26	27	28	29	30
31						

JANUARY 1996						
S	M	T	W	T	F	S
	1	2	3	4	5	6
7	8	9	10	11	12	13
14	15	16	17	18	19	20
21	22	23	24	25	26	27
28	29	30	31			

FEBRUARY 1996						
S	M	T	W	T	F	S
				1	2	3
4	5	6	7	8	9	10
11	12	13	14	15	16	17
18	19	20	21	22	23	24
25	26	27	28	29		

TABLE OF CONTENTS

New Concepts for the Signs of the Zodiac   6
Understanding the Basics of Astrology   9
Ascendant Tables   14

FORECASTS FOR 1995   **17**
  Symbol Guide   18
  Aries   19
  Taurus   41
  Gemini   63
  Cancer   85
  Leo   107
  Virgo   129
  Libra   151
  Scorpio   173
  Sagittarius   195
  Capricorn   217
  Aquarius   239
  Pisces   261

FEATURES   **283**
  About our authors   284
  The Way It Will Be   285
    by BarbaraKoval
  Fitness from the Stars   301
    by Ninah Kessler
  "Getting to Node You"—Astrology's   315
  Hidden Grip in Relationships
    by Noel Tyl

Sun-Moon Concept Chart 330

The 1995 Eclipses 331
  by Vince Plosik

Insights into Children's Needs through the Zodiac 341
  by Gloria Star

Gambling and Astrology 365
  by Edward A. Helin

And the Race is On . . . 381
  by Joyce C. Wehrman

Why Astrology Works 383
  by Jackie Cavalero Slevin

Pluto Enters Sagittarius: Three Degrees of Change 391
  by Kim Rogers-Gallagher

Signs of the Presidents 406

New Headliners Close the Millennium 407
  by Noel Tyl

Astrological Dictionary 420

PRODUCTS AND SERVICES **421**

Gloria Star

The sign descriptions, yearly and monthly horoscopes for *Sun Signs 1995* are all written by Gloria Star. A professional astrologer for 20 years, she is an internationally renowned consultant, author and teacher. In addition to writing the *Sun Sign Book* for Llewellyn since 1990, she is the author of *Optimum Child: Developing Your Child's Fullest Potential through Astrology* (Llewellyn 1987) and a contributing author of *Houses: Power Places in the Horoscope* (Llewellyn 1990), *How to Manage the Astrology of Crisis* (Llewellyn 1993), and *Astrology's Special Measurements* (Llewellyn 1994).

Gloria is active within the astrological community, has served on the faculty of the United Astrology Congress (UAC) since its inception in 1986, and has lectured for groups and conferences throughout North America. She is a member of the Advisory Board for the National Council for Geocosmic Research (NCGR) and has served on the Steering Committee for the Association for Astrological Networking (AFAN) from 1990 through 1994 and is the Editor of the AFAN Newsletter. She makes her home in the shoreline township of Clinton, Connecticut with her husband, Richard, and son, Chris.

NEW CONCEPTS
FOR THE SIGNS OF THE ZODIAC

Aries	♈	The Initiator
Taurus	♉	The Maintainer
Gemini	♊	The Questioner
Cancer	♋	The Nurturer
Leo	♌	The Loyalist
Virgo	♍	The Modifier
Libra	♎	The Judge
Scorpio	♏	The Catalyst
Sagittarius	♐	The Adventurer
Capricorn	♑	The Pragmatist
Aquarius	♒	The Reformer
Pisces	♓	The Visionary

New Concepts for the Signs of the Zodiac

The signs of the zodiac represent characteristics and traits which indicate how energy operates within our lives. The signs tell the story of human evolution and development, and are all necessary to form the continuum of whole life experience. In fact, within your own personal astrological chart, all twelve signs are indicated!

Although the traditional metaphors for the twelve signs (e.g. "Aries, The Ram") are always functional, these alternative concepts for each of the twelve signs are indicative of the gradual unfolding of the human spirit.

Aries. The Initiator, is the first sign of the zodiac and encompasses the primary concept of getting things started. This fiery ignition and bright beginning can prove to be the thrust necessary for new life. But The Initiator can also appear before a situation is ready for new change and create disruption!

Taurus. The Maintainer, sustains what Aries has begun and brings stability and focus into the picture, yet there can also be a tendency to try to maintain something in its current state without allowing for new growth!

Gemini. The Questioner, seeks to determine if alternatives are possible—and offers diversity to the processes Taurus has brought into stability. Yet questioning can also lead to distraction, subsequently scattering energy and diffusing focus.

Cancer. The Nurturer, provides the qualities necessary for growth and security and encourages a deepening awareness of the emotional needs. Yet this same nurturance can stifle individuation if it becomes smothering.

Leo. The Loyalist, directs and centralizes the experiences Cancer feeds. This quality is powerfully targeted toward self-awareness, but can be short sighted. Hence,

7

The Loyalist can hold steadfastly to viewpoints or feelings which inhibit new experiences.

Virgo. The Modifier, analyzes the situations Leo brings to light and determines possibilities for change. Even though this change may be in the name of improvement, it can lead to dissatisfaction with the self if not directed in harmony with higher needs.

Libra. The Judge, is constantly comparing everything to be sure that a certain level of rightness and perfection is presented. However, The Judge can present possibilities which are harsh and seem to be cold or without feeling.

Scorpio. The Catalyst, steps into the play of life to provide the quality of alchemical transformation. The Catalyst can stir the brew just enough to create a healing potion, or may get things going to such a powerful extent that they boil out of control.

Sagittarius. The Adventurer, moves away from Scorpio's dimension to seek what lies beyond the horizon. The Adventurer continually looks for possibilities which answer the ultimate questions, but may forget the pathway back home.

Capricorn. The Pragmatist, attempts to put everything into its rightful place and find ways to make life work out "right." Although The Pragmatist can teach lessons of practicality and determination, when short-sighted, can become highly self-righteous.

Aquarius. The Reformer, looks for ways to take what Capricorn has built and bring it up to date. Yet there is also a tendency to scrap the original in favor of a new plan which may not have the stable foundation necessary to operate effectively.

Pisces. The Visionary, brings mysticism and imagination and challenges the soul to move into the realm beyond the physical plane into what might be. The Visionary can pierce the veil, returning enlightened to the physical world. The challenge is to avoid getting lost within the illusion of an alternate reality.

Understanding the Basics of Astrology

Gloria Star

Astrology is an ancient and continually evolving system used to clarify your identity and your needs. Your astrological chart—which is calculated using the date, time, and place of your birth—contains many factors which symbolically represent needs, expression, and experiences which make up the whole YOU. A professional astrologer interprets this symbolic picture, offering you an accurate portrait of your personality.

The chart itself, your horoscope, is a symbol of the individual as a complete person. Generally, a natal (or birth) horoscope is drawn on a circular wheel. The wheel is divided into twelve segments, called the Houses. Each of the twelve houses represents a different facet of the individual, much like the facets of a brilliantly cut stone. Your houses indicate the different environments in which you live your life and express yourself (e.g. home, school, work, institutions) and also represent the different relationships of your life (e.g. parents, friends, lovers, children, partners). In each environment, you show a different facet of yourself. At home, you may represent yourself quite differently than you would on the job. Additionally, in each relationship you will project a different part of yourself. Parents rarely see the side we show to our intimate friends.

Within the circle and inside the houses are placed the symbols for the planets, Sun and Moon. Each of these represent energy. You experience and express the energy of the Sun, Moon, and planets in specific ways. Refer to the table on the following page for quick reference.

Sun	The Ego Self, Willpower
Moon	The Subconscious Self, Habits
Mercury	Communication, The Intellect
Venus	Emotional Expression, Love, Appreciation, Artistry
Mars	Physical Drive, Assertiveness, Anger
Jupiter	Philosophy, Ethics, Generosity
Saturn	Discipline, Focus, Responsibility
Uranus	Individuality, Rebelliousness
Neptune	Imagination, Sensitivity, Compassion
Pluto	Transformation, Healing, Regeneration

The way you use each of these energies is up to you. The planets in your chart do not make you do anything!

The Twelve Signs of the Zodiac indicate the characteristics and traits which further define your personality and needs. Each sign has positive and negative forms of expression. The basic meaning of each of the signs is explained in the corresponding sections ahead. One thing to keep in mind: you have all twelve signs somewhere in your chart! But those signs which are strongly emphasized by the planets have greater emphasis. The Sun, Moon and planets are placed within a certain degree of a sign according to their position at the time of your birth. The qualities of a sign, combined with the energy of a planet, indicate how you might be most likely to use that energy and the best ways to develop that energy. The signs add color, emphasis and dimension to the energy of your personality.

The signs are also placed at the cusps, or dividing lines, of each of the houses. The influence of the signs upon the houses is much the same as their influence upon the Sun, Moon and planets. The basic indicator of the house would be influenced or shaped by the quality of the sign on the cusp of that house. When you view the horoscope, you will notice that there appear to be four distinctive angles dividing the wheel of the chart. The line which divides the chart into a top and bottom half represents the horizon. In most cases, the left side of this horizon is called the Ascendant. The zodiac sign on the Ascendant is your Rising sign. This point in the chart shows the mask of your personality, and indicates the way others are likely to view you.

In a nutshell, the Sun, Moon, or planet indicate what the energy is, much like the actor in a drama. The sign shows how the energy works, like the role the actor plays in a drama. The house indicates where the energy operates, like the setting or scene of a play. On a psychological level, the Sun represents who you think you are, the Ascendant, who others think you are, and the Moon shows your innerself.

In addition, astrologers also study the geometric relationships between the Sun, Moon, and planets to one another. These geometric angles are called "aspects." Aspects further define the strengths, weaknesses, and challenges within your physical, mental, emotional, and spiritual Self. Sometimes, particular patterns also appear within an astrological chart. These patterns also have meaning.

To understand cycles for any given point in time, astrologers study several factors. One commonly used technique is called the transit. The term transit refers to the position of a planet at a given time. Using the positions of the planets, Sun, and Moon for any given date, an astrologer compares that position to your birth horoscope. The transit indicates an activation of energy in a particular area of your chart. The *Sun Sign Book* is written using the technique of transits.

As you can see, your Sun sign is only one factor among many which describes who you are, but it is a powerful one! As the symbol of the ego self, the Sun in your chart shows your drive to be noticed as a significant human being. Most people can easily relate to the concepts associated with their Sun sign, since it is tied to the ego or sense of personal identity.

Using This Book

The horoscopes in the following section are based upon the sign the Sun was in at the time of your birth. Al-

11

though we can examine a number of your needs and life situations from this information, there are many other factors which a professional astrologer would explore to help you guide your life. If you would like more information to accompany the guidelines in this book, you might appreciate the personalized, more detailed insights you'll receive from a competent professional astrologer.

I've described the year's major challenges and opportunities for every Sun sign in the "Year Ahead" section. The first part of the section applies to all individuals born under the influence of the sign. In addition, I've included information for specific birth dates that will help you understand the inner process of change you'll be experiencing during 1995. The cycles described in this section illustrate your fundamental themes for the year ahead. Consider these ideas as underlying principles that will be present throughout the entire year. These cycles comprise your major challenges and opportunities relating to your personal identity. Blend these ideas with the information you find in the monthly forecast section for your Sun sign and Ascendant.

To best use the information in the monthly forecasts, you'll want to determine your Ascendant, or Rising sign. If don't know your Ascendant, the Ascendant Tables (following this description) will help you determine your rising sign. They are most accurate for those born in the Western Hemisphere between 60-130 degrees longitude (e.g. the Continental United States). These tables are only an approximation, but can be used as a good rule of thumb. Your exact Ascendant may vary from the tables according to your time and place of birth. Once you've approximated your Ascending sign using the tables or determined your Ascendant by having your chart calculated, you'll know two significant factors in your astrological chart. Read the monthly forecast sections for both your Sun and Ascendant to gain the most useful information.

Your "Rewarding and Challenging Days" sections indicate times when you'll feel more centered ("Rewarding") or out of balance ("Challenging"). The Rewarding Days are not the only times you can perform well, but you're likely to feel better integrated! These days support your expression of individual identity. During the Challenging Days, take some extra time to center yourself by meditating or using other techniques which help you feel more objective.

These guidelines, although highly useful, cannot incorporate all the factors influencing your current life situation. However, you can use this information as a form of objective awareness about the way the current cycles are affecting you at an ego level. Realize that the power of astrology is even more useful when you have a complete chart and professional guidance.

The Year 1995 at a Glance

An exciting change occurs during 1995 with the planets Uranus and Pluto each changing signs. Uranus enters its sign of natural affinity, Aquarius, marking a period of increasing technological, intellectual and collective focus. The information SuperHighway is a likely reality during Uranus' transit in its own sign (lasting into the year 2003). In fact, we should see even greater innovations which have not yet come into form! Pluto's ingress into Sagittarius marks a cycle which will last into the year 2008. It is likely that educational, religious, and philosophical issues will undergo significant alteration and transformation during Pluto's transit in Sagittarius. With two long cycles beginning near the same time, there should definitely be some reshaping in our lives on planet Earth.

To take advantage of this period of physical, spiritual, and emotional shifting, you may have to be more honest about your own individual needs — but not in a negatively selfish form. Our interactive lives with one another and with the other life forms on our planet need love and care. Even if we are not aware of alien life forms walking among us, we may, ourselves, feel a bit alien during this year. Find ways to use this sense of change in consciousness within your relationships. But most especially, determine how to become the best expression of all that you are.

Enjoy a spectacular year!

Gloria Star

Your Ascendant is the following if your time of birth was:

If your Sun Sign is:	6 to 8 am	8 to 10 am	10 am to Noon	Noon to 2 pm	2 to 4 pm	4 to 6 pm
Aries	Taurus	Gemini	Cancer	Leo	Virgo	Libra
Taurus	Gemini	Cancer	Leo	Virgo	Libra	Scorpio
Gemini	Cancer	Leo	Virgo	Libra	Scorpio	Sagittarius
Cancer	Leo	Virgo	Libra	Scorpio	Sagittarius	Capricorn
Leo	Virgo	Libra	Scorpio	Sagittarius	Capricorn	Aquarius
Virgo	Libra	Scorpio	Sagittarius	Capricorn	Aquarius	Pisces
Libra	Scorpio	Sagittarius	Capricorn	Aquarius	Pisces	Aries
Scorpio	Sagittarius	Capricorn	Aquarius	Pisces	Aries	Taurus
Sagittarius	Capricorn	Aquarius	Pisces	Aries	Taurus	Gemini
Capricorn	Aquarius	Pisces	Aries	Taurus	Gemini	Cancer
Aquarius	Pisces	Aries	Taurus	Gemini	Cancer	Leo
Pisces	Aries	Taurus	Gemini	Cancer	Leo	Virgo

If your Sun Sign is:	6 to 8 pm	8 to 10 pm	10 pm to Midnight	Midnight to 2 am	2 to 4 am	4 to 6 am
Aries	Scorpio	Sagittarius	Capricorn	Aquarius	Pisces	Aries
Taurus	Sagittarius	Capricorn	Aquarius	Pisces	Aries	Taurus
Gemini	Capricorn	Aquarius	Pisces	Aries	Taurus	Gemini
Cancer	Aquarius	Pisces	Aries	Taurus	Gemini	Cancer
Leo	Pisces	Aries	Taurus	Gemini	Cancer	Leo
Virgo	Aries	Taurus	Gemini	Cancer	Leo	Virgo
Libra	Taurus	Gemini	Cancer	Leo	Virgo	Libra
Scorpio	Gemini	Cancer	Leo	Virgo	Libra	Scorpio
Sagittarius	Cancer	Leo	Virgo	Libra	Scorpio	Sagittarius
Capricorn	Leo	Virgo	Libra	Scorpio	Sagittarius	Capricorn
Aquarius	Virgo	Libra	Scorpio	Sagittarius	Capricorn	Aquarius
Pisces	Libra	Scorpio	Sagittarius	Capricorn	Aquarius	Pisces

1. Find your Sun Sign (left column);
2. Determine correct approximate time of birth column;
3. Line up your Sun Sign with birth time to find ascendant.

PLANETARY ASSOCIATIONS

Sun: Authority figures, favors, advancement, health, success, display, drama, promotion, fun, matters related to Leo and the 5th House.

Moon: Short trips, women, children, the public, domestic concerns, emotions, fluids, matters related to Cancer and the 4th House.

Mercury: Communications, correspondence, phone calls, computers, messages, education, students, travel, merchants, editing, writing, advertising, signing contracts, siblings, neighbors, kin, matters related to Gemini, Virgo, and the 3rd and 6th Houses.

Venus: Affection, relationships, partnerships, alliances, grace, beauty, harmony, luxury, love, art, music, social activity, marriage, decorating, cosmetics, gifts, income, matters related to Taurus, Libra, and the 2nd and 7th Houses.

Mars: Strife, aggression, sex, physical energy, muscular activity, guns, tools, metals, cutting, surgery, police, soldiers, combat, confrontation, matters related to Aries, Scorpio, and the 1st and 8th Houses.

Jupiter: Publishing, college education, long-distance travel, foreign interests, religion, philosophy, forecasting, broadcasting, publicity, expansion, luck, growth, sports, horses, the law, matters related to Sagittarius, Pisces, and 9th and 12th House issues.

Saturn: Structure, reality, the laws of society, limits, obstacles, tests, hard work, endurance, real estate, dentists, bones, teeth, matters related to Capricorn, Aquarius, and the 10th and 11th Houses.

Uranus: Astrology, the New Age, technology, computers, modern gadgets, lecturing, advising, counseling, inventions, reforms, electricity, new methods, originality, matters related to Aquarius and the 11th House.

Neptune: Mysticism, music, creative imagination, dance, illusion, sacrifice, service, oil, chemicals, paint, drugs, anesthesia, sleep, religious experience, matters related to Pisces and the 12th House.

Pluto: Probing, penetration, goods of the dead, investigation, insurance, taxes, others' money, loans, the masses, the underworld, transformation, death, matters related to Scorpio and the 8th House.

LLEWELLYN'S 1995

SUN SIGN BOOK

SUN SIGN
FORECASTS

for

1995

Sign	Glyph	Dates	Ruler	Element	Quality	Nature
Aries	♈	Mar 21–Apr 20	Mars	Fire	Cardinal	Barren
Taurus	♉	Apr 20–May 21	Venus	Earth	Fixed	Semi-Fruitful
Gemini	♊	May 21–June 22	Mercury	Air	Mutable	Barren
Cancer	♋	June 22–July 23	Moon	Water	Cardinal	Fruitful
Leo	♌	July 23–Aug 23	Sun	Fire	Fixed	Barren
Virgo	♍	Aug 23–Sept 23	Mercury	Earth	Mutable	Barren
Libra	♎	Sept 23–Oct 23	Venus	Air	Cardinal	Semi-Fruitful
Scorpio	♏	Oct 23–Nov 22	Pluto	Water	Fixed	Fruitful
Sagittarius	♐	Nov 22–Dec 22	Jupiter	Fire	Mutable	Barren
Capricorn	♑	Dec 22–Jan 21	Saturn	Earth	Cardinal	Semi-Fruitful
Aquarius	♒	Jan 21–Feb 20	Uranus	Air	Fixed	Barren
Pisces	♓	Feb 20–Mar 21	Neptune	Water	Mutable	Fruitful

ARIES
The Ram

March 21 to April 20

Element: Fire

Quality: Cardinal

Polarity: Masculine/Yang

Planetary Ruler: Mars

Meditation: "I actively pursue the fulfillment of my destiny"

Gemstone: Diamond

Power Stones: Ruby, carnelian, bloodstone

Key Phrase: "I am"

Glyph: Ram's head

Anatomy: Head and face

Colors: Red and white

Animal: Ram

Myths/Legends: Jason & the Golden Fleece, Artemis

House Association: 1st

Opposite Sign: Libra

Flower: Geranium

Key Word: Initiative

Positive Expression:
Self-reliant
Incisive
Assertive
Courageous
Energetic
Daring
Innovative
Intrepid
Inspiring
Exuberant
Exciting

Misuse of Energy:
Reckless
Combative
Abrasive
Rash
Impatient
Careless
Childish
Belligerent
Incomplete
Blunt

♈ ARIES ♈

Your Ego's Strengths and Weaknesses

As "The Initiator" of the zodiac, you're always in the process of getting things started. Your courageous spirit gladly takes on new challenges, and you may find yourself alone in the lead while others are still waiting for a signal to move! Your daring energy can be inspiring, and leads you to "boldly go where none has gone before."

Your identity is forged through the drive and power of your ruling planet, Mars, whose energy represents the power to take action. It is through this energy that you show positive assertiveness and can build strength. But while you're busy forging ahead, others may experience your exuberance as abrasive. You can avoid negative confrontation and instead inspire more admiration from others by simply increasing your awareness of the effect your actions and words can have upon others.

By using your ability to continually create new ideas and options for yourself, you may feel inspired in a world filled with despair or apathy. You're hungry for a life of passion and power, but may forget to take time to enjoy what you've created or to revitalize yourself before you reach a point of exhaustion. Your excitement for life keeps you ever-youthful, and you continually create an exceptional reality for yourself and others.

Your Career Development

To hold your interest, a career must keep you busy and active, and you may decide to pursue an option which keeps you both physically challenged and mentally alert. A career in athletics, coaching, fire-fighting, dancing, police work, or the military may have strong appeal. Occupations in the travel industry, beauty and hair-design, jewelry-making, auto design or mechanics, masonry, welding, or metal-working may hold your interest. You're a natural salesperson. You need a job which gives you plenty of room to exercise your independence and try some new ideas.

Your Approach to Romance

The thrill of pursuit, the passion in the moment of conquest—these elements spur your sense of romance. It's more likely that you'll be the pursuer in the chase, since waiting for the other person to act can try your (limited) patience. But do watch your passion, since the shy types can easily feel overwhelmed by your exuberance. In order to stay interested over the long-term, you'll need to feel that you have plenty of room to move, or you're likely to move on! Your ideal mate will enjoy your playfulness and desire to expose the reaches of the unexplored.

As a fire sign, you need a partner who understands your volatility and who knows how to stand on his or her own. Another Aries can be stimulating, but the two of you need a little time apart to keep the flames from burning out of control. Leo's fire is a constant warmth and comfort, but be sure not to fail in your loyalty, and the fiery, flirtatious, fun-loving antics of Sagittarius can be truly invigorating.

Taurus' sensual appetites are quite appealing, but you may become irritated with their slower pace. The diversity of Gemini challenges your mind, and you'll both enjoy your battles of wits. Although you enjoy the protective feeling of Cancer at home, you'll run into trouble if you fail to show up for dinner on time! As a working partner, Virgo can be excellent and may have strong appeal, but you may feel pressured by their expectations.

Enticed by your provocative opposite, Libra, you can feel you've met your match, but may find their demands for refinement difficult to satisfy all the time. An intense relationship with Scorpio definitely lights your fire, but your flame may wane if they try to overpower you with control games. And while Capricorn provides intrigue, your passion can cool in the face of all those rules and commitments. There may be a natural ease with independent Aquarius, whose friendship and support offer plenty of room for your individual expression. With Pisces, you can forgive a sense of not quite knowing where you stand, since you may feel a deep bond of friendship and closeness once you drop your barriers.

Your Use of Power

When you're beginning something new, you know your strongest feeling of power— engine at full throttle, all systems go! You shine in positions of leadership and can be a powerful motivator of others, but in many instances, the responsibilities which come with power can dampen your spirit unless you can find fresh ways of approaching these responsibilities and see them as a means to gain even greater autonomy.

You have the power to get things moving again when everyone else has come to a grinding halt, although you can become domineering or selfish when faced with inaction on the part of others. Remember your tendency to "unintentionally" run rough-shod over another, leaving trauma or hurt feelings in your wake. An uncooperative or defensive backlash from others can result if you continue merrily on your way, not realizing the responses others have to you and your actions.

You have chosen the path of self-knowledge, which can only come from exploring both the outside world and the inner path to your True Self. And as you continue this exploration, your light shines brightly, illuminating a path of possibilities when others have lost their way.

Famous Aries

Oleg Cassini, Richard Chamberlain, Eric Clapton, Francis Ford Coppolla, Aretha Franklin, J. William Fulbright, Leeza Gibbons, Eric Idle, Walt Frazier, Thomas Jefferson, Shirley Jones, Marcel Marceau, Reba McIntyre, Leonard Nimoy, Dennis Quaid, Al Unser, Jr., Billy Dee Williams

THE YEAR AHEAD FOR ARIES

This year marks an important cycle of reaching beyond your current life circumstances and expanding your horizons. Many of your old attitudes about yourself, your needs, and your life choices may also be changing and dissolving, since your connection to your inner self is more marked now. You're paving the way for several years of positive personal self-expression, and may feel an increased clarity in your insight toward future possibilities.

A sharpening of your intuitive insights may lead to you taking risks in your life choices which can be positively inspiring, but you are also primed to remove any unnecessary psychological or physical baggage in order to move ahead as far as you can. Jupiter transits in your Solar 9th House throughout the year, a cycle which encourages you to explore and expand your philosophical attitudes, ethical stances, and need to connect with your higher mind. This period can stimulate a desire to increase your knowledge or expertise in an area through study, teaching, or writing, but this is also an exciting cycle for travel, involvement in cultural affairs and discovery of what lies beyond your own backyard. You may not feel particularly inclined toward hard work, since your underlying feeling is to take it easy and enjoy the ride. But if you do have particular aims or goals, focusing the power of Jupiter trine to your Sun can help you reach further and progress more quickly. In fact, there are other aspects involved which may require you to apply yourself or lose a significant opportunity!

You may feel that many of your plans for action seem to be delayed or thwarted in some way, and that your physical energy and drive are not quite up to their usual spark in the first quarter of this year. Your planetary ruler, Mars, will be in its cycle of retrograde from January 2 through March 24, and reaches its aphelion (its position of greatest distance from the Sun in its orbit) on March 14. It may not be until after the Vernal Equinox on March 20 that you begin to feel as though your life is moving in the direction you want it to go, and at the pace you prefer! You can still use this cycle in early 1995 to successfully finish projects, tie up those loose ends, make plans, and get organized for action.

The Solar Eclipses this year emphasize your finances and material concerns, but also mark a period of increased awareness of the best ways to use all your resources (including time and physical energy). It's critical for you now to uncover and truly appreciate your value as a person. You may also find it easier to acknowledge the contributions and worth of significant others in your life, particularly if you have a partner.

If you were born from March 20–24, you're feeling the powerful stimulation of insight and understanding which can be the result of Uranus and Pluto transiting in strong aspect to your Sun. Pluto is trine your Sun from January through May, and again during November and December. This cycle is usually accompanied by a feeling of increased self-awareness, and can be a time of significant healing and revitalization. If you're considering making far-reaching changes in your work or profession, this is an exceptional time to take the steps which will make those changes a reality. Use the energy of Uranus transiting in sextile to your Sun from March through June to emphasize your talents and unique abilities. Many times, circumstances change during this cycle which open a pathway which was previously closed to you. You simply have to be sufficiently aware to take the right steps on a newly illumined path. With the energy of both of these planets working to support change and growth, you can move further, faster than in the past. Take the time to get in touch with your inner and Higher Self. Determine for yourself the things which are more important to you, and use this time to develop those aspects of your life. Also remember that you may not be able to take all the vestiges of your previous existence with you. Those things which are no longer in harmony with your growth are definitely dissolving, and you're learning how it feels to be free.

For those born from March 25–April 7, the supportive energy of Jupiter transiting in trine aspect to your Sun brings a period of expansion and opportunity. This cycle can bring many blessings, and frequently indicates

24

a period of reaping the rewards from the efforts you have previously put forth. During this cycle of accumulation, you may draw to yourself circumstances which are more comfortable and may also see improvements in your relationships as a result of developing greater tolerance and understanding. This is an excellent time to share your good fortune with those you love, to offer yourself— through using your resources, talents or abilities— and widen your sphere of influence. Concentrate on developing some humility during this cycle, since this energy can also stimulate a feeling of exaggerated self-importance!

You're feeling an undercurrent of separation from many elements of your past this year if you were born from March 28–April 16. The energy of Saturn transiting in semisextile to your Sun stimulates an increased sense of realistic perception, and may also put you closely in touch with all the things you've accumulated that have become excessive or unnecessary. Review your relationships for attitudes and interactions which seem out of place. Perhaps you have been hanging on to immature attitudes which have infringed upon your forward progress, especially in your intimate relationships or career development. Becoming real is sometimes painful, since you have to release those Peter Pan ideas and determine the best ways to become responsible for yourself and your needs. Your reward comes from finding a way to incorporate that vitality, youthfulness, and innovation into your life in ways which help you feel more substantial. You are more likely to lose those freedoms you so deeply cherish if you cannot find a way to secure them as a true part of yourself!

If you were born from April 11–7, you may be feeling a bit confused about the nature of reality while Neptune transits in square aspect to your Sun. Sorting through this period requires diligence and effort on your part, since it is all too easy to become lost in misguided delusions. You're also more willing to forgive, and if you've been feeling guilty, remorseful, or ashamed of yourself, this is the perfect time to relinquish those blocking emotions and forgive yourself so you can go on with your life. Things which may have once seemed insignificant may now take on an entirely different meaning. You're gaining a new level of awareness of yourself and your surroundings, but may feel that you're in foreign territory. To incorporate these new dimensions takes time and exploration. The difficulties during this cycle result from getting involved in circumstances, belief systems, or relationships which you cannot see clearly. Seek advice from trusted sources. Make daily contact with your inner self to be sure you know what you're feeling, and wait a while to determine whether or not you're willing to make long-lasting commitments to these new realities, since many of them are illusory, while others are the prelude to what can become a whole new world.

Your sense of rebelliousness and determination to be yourself are strongly marked if you were born from April 15–20, while Uranus transits in square to your Sun. This year marks a cycle of breakthrough, but can also signify a period of breaking away from life circumstances, relationships, or attitudes which have stifled your self-expression and personal growth. The difficulty is in determining boundaries, since it may seem that the best avenue of expression is to throw it all out and start over again. Before you toss your old life into the dumpster, take some time to carefully determine your needs. You may just need to eliminate part of your old self! Negative attitudes of stubborn independence can also be emphasized now, and others may accuse you of being unfeeling or selfish. Certainly, the most significant part of this cycle is letting go and moving forward, but what you're really needing now is to let go of those expressions and situations which are in the way. If any of those are coming from you, you have the greatest power now to do an about-face and take a good look in the mirror. It's time to be all that you truly wish to be and to remove the masks.

If you were born from April 15–20, you're also feeling a deep sense of discontent with some elements of your life. Pluto's transit in quincunx to your Sun is like that itch you can't quite reach. You know something's out of place, but may have to go carefully and slowly or try unusual methods to get yourself or your life just the way you want it. Now is a great time to get involved in introspective analysis, therapeutic counseling, or self-improvement. But it's also the time to look at your deeper emotional needs and to become more intimately aware of yourself, your relationships, and your underlying motivations. Watch your physical health, since this is a time when the body tends to experience a purging of old toxic material. If you persist in adding more toxins to your body, your system can feel sluggish and overwhelmed. Try this one on for size: It's time to get clear!

Tools to Make a Difference

Your mind may be more active than usual this year, and finding positive outlets for your ideas can be positively illuminating! Keeping a journal or some record of your thoughts may offer the opportunity to express some unique ideas, but could also lead to solutions to some of your deeper questions. If you write or work in a profession which requires sharing ideas, take every opportunity to teach, train, or inspire others.

Even though this may be a highly active year, you still need to concentrate on maintaining a connection with your inner self. Active approaches to inner awareness, through martial arts, hatha yoga, running, or dancing may give you the time to clear your mind and open more to yourself. Every action and each thought are manifested in some element of your life, and the sense of control you need to achieve now might be enhanced by simply becoming more aware of the direct link between cause and effect!

Use the concept of crystalline clarity when you feel distracted or overwrought. Envision a small, crystal-clear form of yourself. Imagine that you can hold this small self in the palm of your hands. Send warmth, energy and love to this being. Then, bring this image of yourself deep into the center of your heart. Know that you are also held just as securely in the heart of Divine Wisdom.

Affirmation for the Year

"I am inspired by truth to walk the path
toward my own enlightenment."

27

ACTION TABLES FOR ARIES

These dates reflect the best (but not the only) times for success and ease in these activities according to your Sun Sign.

Change Residence	July 10–25
Request a Raise	Mar. 31
Begin a Course of Study	May 29, Dec. 21
Visit a Doctor	Mar. 14–Apr. 1; Aug. 10–29
Start a Diet	Jan. 19–20; Feb 16–17; Mar. 15–16; Apr. 11–12; May 9–10; June 5–6; July 2–3, 30–31; Aug. 26–27; Sep. 22–23; Oct. 19–21; Nov. 16–17; Dec. 13–14
Begin a Romance	July 27–28
Join a Club	Jan. 30–31
Seek Employment	Jan. 1–5; Aug. 10–28; Dec. 12–31
Take a Vacation	Jan. 26–27; Feb. 22–23; Mar. 21–22; Apr. 18–19; May 15–16; June 11–12; July 9–10; Aug. 5–6; Sep. 1–2, 29–30; Oct. 26–27; Nov. 23–24; Dec. 20–21
Change Your Wardrobe	July 26–Aug. 9
End a Relationship	Apr. 15
Seek Professional Advice	Jan. 21–22; Feb. 18–19; Mar. 17–18; Apr. 13–15; May 11–12; June 7–8; July 4–6; Aug. 1–2, 28–29; Sep. 24–25; Oct. 22–23; Nov. 18–19; Dec. 16–17
Have a Makeover	Mar. 31–Apr. 1
Obtain a Loan	Jan. 24–25; Feb. 20–21; Mar. 19–20; Apr. 16–17; May 13–14; June 9–10; July 7–8; Aug. 3–4, 30–31; Sep. 27–28; Oct. 24–25; Nov. 20–21; Dec. 18–19

PRIMARY FOCUS

This is a month of high-level, diverse action. Broaden your cultural interests or spend some extra time reading or studying. Community or club activities also figure prominently.

HEALTH AND FITNESS

Take a lively approach to exercise and also concentrate on building up your resistance. Seek options which are entertaining and also provide sound training after the 22nd.

ROMANCE AND RELATIONSHIPS

Reaching toward a deeper level of intimacy from the 1st–6th may require a gentler approach to sexual sharing. You may find just the spark you need to enliven a love relationship or seek a new love interest while traveling or through educational pursuits after the 7th. New pursuits fare best from the 1st–15th, and you're more likely to prefer sharing quiet time at home during the Full Moon on the 16th. Overall, this is a socially active month when friends and family alike may delight in your entertaining antics.

FINANCE AND CAREER

Undercurrents of conflict may not be readily apparent in your career, but if you look carefully, you may find that petty jealousies or different political or philosophical opinions can threaten the stability of your career position. Bring differences out into the open on the 17th–18th to clear the air. Investments and long-range financial plans show success from the 14th–26th.

OPPORTUNITY OF THE MONTH

Outreach in your career is especially promising from the 11th–19th. But watch for delays after the 26th, when Mercury moves into its retrograde cycle.

Rewarding Days: 3, 7, 8, 12, 13, 17, 18, 26, 27, 30
Challenging Days: 1, 6, 10, 15, 16, 21, 22, 23, 28, 29

AFFIRMATION FOR THE MONTH:
"I am alert, awake, and mindful."

PRIMARY FOCUS

Promising career developments offer a chance to use your talents more effectively than in the past. Stay alert to the need to draw the lines between business and pleasure!

HEALTH AND FITNESS

Pushing past your limits will definitely affect your energy level. Pace yourself, and find enjoyable ways to build your vitality. If it's not fun, you may not be interested!

ROMANCE AND RELATIONSHIPS

The extra time you want to spend on romantic pursuits may be gobbled up by career activities. But if you're a busy volunteer, these circumstances are a more likely culprit. Reevaluate your priorities and make some adjustments in your schedule. Romance can be powerful during the Full Moon on the 15th, although you may run into some philosophical differences with your lover. Be wary of new love interests after the 19th, when you may be seeking an escape from the ordinary and lose track of your real needs.

FINANCE AND CAREER

To stabilize career opportunities, get back in touch with groups or individuals who have shown support in the past. From the 1st–16th, concentrate on clearing the way and completing tasks already begun. Make sure to clarify misunderstandings, and watch a tendency to jump to conclusions before you have all the facts from the 23rd–28th. Strive to satisfy the more conservative side.

OPPORTUNITY OF THE MONTH

Even though you may be eager to try a new approach, working with the established order is your quickest route to success. Learn how the system operates before you try to change it!

Rewarding Days: 3, 4, 5, 8, 13, 14, 22, 23, 27
Challenging Days: 1, 7, 11, 12, 18, 19, 24, 25

AFFIRMATION FOR THE MONTH
"I am creating future possibilities by remaining aware of the power of the present moment."

PRIMARY FOCUS

Friends benefit every aspect of your life, and may provide new opportunities in career growth in addition to bringing a more effective tie to your community. Rewards from your career grow.

HEALTH AND FITNESS

Time for physical activity still needs a high priority to help you stay on top of stress levels. Time in contemplation or reflection is important after the 14th.

ROMANCE AND RELATIONSHIPS

An active love life helps you stay in touch with your feelings, but be sure you're also aware of your needs! The New Moon on the 1st emphasizes growth in spiritual awareness, and you may need to seek feedback from others who share your beliefs and ideals. Conflicts between friends and lovers are possible mid-month, but friends can also be supportive if you're uncertain about a love relationship. Regardless of what others say, you must determine your true needs and take action to satisfy them on the 31st.

FINANCE AND CAREER

Your financial prospects brighten considerably from the 2nd–28th. An advisor might offer positive insights about the best ways to manage your funds, although it's a good idea to investigate any speculative options before you jump into them. Impulsive spending from the 1st–4th or 14th–20th may lead to regret. Work behind the scenes brings positive results from the 20th–26th, although you may be less than enthusiastic about the job.

OPPORTUNITY OF THE MONTH

Take the lead from the 12th–14th, when your actions open the way to long-term successful commitments.

Rewarding Days: 3, 4, 8, 13, 14, 21, 22, 26, 30, 31
Challenging Days: 1, 6, 10, 11, 15, 17, 18, 24, 25

AFFIRMATION FOR THE MONTH
"I listen to my inner voice and respect
my intuitive insights."

PRIMARY FOCUS

Powerful progress on the personal horizon results from clearer communication and more direct action on your part. Surround yourself with people and situations that inspire your generosity.

HEALTH AND FITNESS

Building endurance and strength are easier now, although you may also need to take some time early in the month to relax and release tension. Find activities which show your best abilities.

ROMANCE AND RELATIONSHIPS

Draw the line between fantasy and reality by active pursuit of your love interest. The Lunar Eclipse on the 15th stimulates deeper realizations about your relationship choices. By the time of the Solar Eclipse on the 29th, you're finding better ways to embrace your own power and worth. Determine what you really want—because now you can make it happen!

FINANCE AND CAREER

Business travel, conferences, and presentations offer a special chance to advance in your profession from the 2nd–17th. You can continue this influence beyond the 17th, but only if you have something truly substantial to offer. Watch your own competitive nature, since your needs for attention can create confrontation with others. Capitalize on your uniqueness this month, since your ticket to stardom is in standing apart from the crowd.

OPPORTUNITY OF THE MONTH

You're in an exceptional position to take advantage of quickly changing circumstances in your career on the 10th. Go for it!

Rewarding Days: 4, 5, 9, 10, 18, 19, 22, 26, 27
Challenging Days: 2, 7, 8, 14, 15, 20, 21, 29

AFFIRMATION FOR THE MONTH
"I cherish all that is special about myself."

PRIMARY FOCUS

Allow time and room for creative expression, which may also be the key to your financial success this month. Build a strong communication network with influential groups and individuals.

HEALTH AND FITNESS

Mars continues its transit in Aries, and can boost your energy, but pace yourself to avoid burning out too quickly. Avoid extreme risks from the 13th–21st.

ROMANCE AND RELATIONSHIPS

Now's the time to pursue the one you adore with delightful results, but watch a tendency to move too quickly from the 10th through the Full Moon on the 14th, when your passion could be overwhelming. A more casual pace from the 10th–20th could lead to the understanding interaction you desire by the time of the New Moon on the 29th. (Patience may be a virtue after all!) Financial disputes can spoil the mood with your partner from the 18th–22nd unless you're both willing to admit to your honest concerns. Confess!

FINANCE AND CAREER

Improvement in money matters results from direct efforts on your part to illustrate your value to your employer or customers. Take the risk of exposing your real talents and abilities from the 3rd–15th, while Venus transits in Aries with strong support from Jupiter. Be careful in spending or investments from the 12th–18th, when you may be tempted by something that isn't what it seems.

OPPORTUNITY OF THE MONTH

Take advantage of Mercury's retrograde cycle beginning the 24th to follow-up on unfulfilled promises.

Rewarding Days: 1, 2, 6, 7, 15, 16, 19, 24, 25, 29, 30
Challenging Days: 4, 5, 11, 12, 13, 17, 18, 31

AFFIRMATION FOR THE MONTH
"My heart is filled with love and joy!"

PRIMARY FOCUS

Buckle down to work now—your efforts can give you the boost you need to achieve success, but watch a tendency to run rough-shod over your best supporters.

HEALTH AND FITNESS

You may feel frustrated by the stress of your work. Although physical activity can help release tension, be sure to allow adequate time for stretching and relaxation, especially midmonth.

ROMANCE AND RELATIONSHIPS

Making contact with a sibling can be a source of support or may offer a chance to mend fences. Philosophical differences can be a source of dispute, and could accelerate if either of you pushes too far. Intimate relationships may suffer from misunderstandings, but these can be addressed during the Full Moon on the 12th when you may realize you agree, but just seem to speak a different language! The New Moon on the 27th emphasizes a need to make contact with family; however, it may be brief.

FINANCE AND CAREER

Disagreements with co-workers or disputes over work conditions can undermine your effectiveness, but may also give you a chance to lead the way through the mire of contracts and legal mumbo-jumbo. Mercury's retrograde through the 17th may provide a good chance to review details, although it's easy to overstep boundaries or to feel taken for granted from the 11th–18th. Search for areas of consensus from the 18th–21st. Then, start anew.

OPPORTUNITY OF THE MONTH

If turmoil reaches a feverish peak mid-month, you can be the catalyst to bring things back into focus. If possible, take charge.

Rewarding Days: 3, 4, 12, 15, 16, 20, 21, 25, 30
Challenging Days: 1, 2, 7, 8, 9, 14, 27

AFFIRMATION FOR THE MONTH
"I am careful to maintain my personal boundaries."

PRIMARY FOCUS

Home and family activities take a stronger priority, but not without conflict between work and your desires to enjoy life. Satisfy your inner needs by remaining creative.

HEALTH AND FITNESS

Worry and mental tension can block your physical vitality, especially from the 9th–16th. Refrain from high-risk activities or circumstances which could lead to physical exhaustion.

ROMANCE AND RELATIONSHIPS

Family obligations you've avoided are best answered, especially near the Full Moon on the 12th when you might enjoy getting back to your roots! Friction with your partner can result from frustrated sexual energy after the 17th, when it's best to bring concerns out in the open. Romance is in the air after the 22nd, when your prowess in love can lead to exceptional intimacy, but curb that "harmless" flirtation from the 21st–29th, when your actions can create more than you bargained for!

FINANCE AND CAREER

A conservative approach in business dealings and professional associations is more successful from the 1st–8th. There's opportunity for more experimental and futuristic thinking mid-month. Speculative ventures fare best after the New Moon on the 27th, when unexpected changes may provide opportunities which did not previously exist. Safeguard against deception from others on the 23rd–25th, when your naivete can be your downfall.

OPPORTUNITY OF THE MONTH

Launch new projects or make contact with individuals who can play a significant role in your future on the 27th and 28th.

Rewarding Days: 1, 9, 10, 13, 14, 17, 18, 22, 23, 27, 28
Challenging Days: 2, 5, 6, 11, 12, 16, 25, 26

AFFIRMATION FOR THE MONTH
"I am safe and secure in times of change."

PRIMARY FOCUS

A highly creative and expressive month, this is an excellent time to take bold steps to satisfy your emotional needs. However, your enthusiasm can be an irritant to others who might prefer subtlety.

HEALTH AND FITNESS

Increase your physical activity level through recreation or sports for entertainment and to improve expertise. Fine-tune your skills from the 10th–29th. Enjoy yourself!

ROMANCE AND RELATIONSHIPS

Love is clearly in the air, and whether you're seeking to improve an existing relationship, begin a new relationship, or just enjoy yourself more, your ability to express your best attributes is enhanced through the 23rd. Powerful interchange during the Full Moon on the 10th can solidify a friendship, but avoid becoming too obsessive on the 21st–22nd or you'll alienate your best allies! Be sure you're not sending mixed signals from the 27th–31st, when you must make your intentions crystal clear to avoid rejection.

FINANCE AND CAREER

Investments or speculative ventures show positive returns from the 1st–21st, although a partner or joint-investor may wobble on the 8th–10th. Generally, finances should improve now, and if you're looking for advancement, make your best efforts from the 5th–14th. Schedule adjustments or changes in working conditions can lead to improvements after the New Moon on the 25th, when attention to detail is crucial to success.

OPPORTUNITY OF THE MONTH

Business meetings, presentations, or conferences lead to new possibilities on the 5th and 6th. Speak out for yourself.

Rewarding Days: 5, 6, 9, 10, 14, 15, 18, 19, 23, 24
Challenging Days: 1, 2, 4, 7, 8, 12, 17, 21, 22, 28, 29

AFFIRMATION FOR THE MONTH
"I am confident in my abilities."

PRIMARY FOCUS

Competition from others can spur you into bringing forth your best abilities. Make a concerted effort to discover the ways you could be your own worst enemy. Take time to improve your skills, too.

HEALTH AND FITNESS

Rash actions can be problematic from the 1st–6th; you may feel best taking some time to yourself during the Full Moon on the 8th. Pace yourself the rest of the month.

ROMANCE AND RELATIONSHIPS

Even though you may know what you want from a relationship, unless you can clarify and express those needs, you may never be satisfied! Open new horizons in your love life by expanding your mind, sharing your views and incorporating new ideas from the 1st–21st. By the New Moon on the 24th you're in an excellent position to determine if you really like your partner (if you have one). If you're tired of feeling alone, look at how you've erected your own shields. Maybe it's time to lower a few.

FINANCE AND CAREER

Friction from authorities can lead to difficulties unless you understand their motivations and circumstances. Before you react, determine the situation. Use Mercury's retrograde cycle, which begins the 22nd, to remedy problems and review, but don't expect more permanent solutions until next month. Make a special effort to listen to others following the New Moon on the 24th, but be sure you understand what they really want before you agree!

OPPORTUNITY OF THE MONTH

Get to the core of any problems, since it's easier to find them now, and you probably can't get too far away from them, anyway!

Rewarding Days: 1, 2, 10, 11, 15, 16, 20, 21, 29, 30
Challenging Days: 3, 4, 5, 17, 18, 24, 25, 26

AFFIRMATION FOR THE MONTH
"I fully embrace each present moment."

PRIMARY FOCUS

Although you may feel bogged down by the demands of others early on, working toward consensus promises greater freedom and expansion on all fronts after the Solar Eclipse on the 23rd.

HEALTH AND FITNESS

Any physical difficulty should be thoroughly explored, since you're in an excellent cycle to determine root causes and treat them, instead of just treating the symptoms.

ROMANCE AND RELATIONSHIPS

Intimate relationships and partnerships take a front seat, and by taking the initiative, you can avoid feeling that you're under attack. The Lunar Eclipse on the 8th emphasizes a need to achieve a real equanimity and balance in your personal relationships. If things have been lopsided, then this is definitely the time to change! Sexual intimacy is both stimulating and solidifying to your relationship from the 8th–19th. However, if you feel there are power-plays, you must address them directly.

FINANCE AND CAREER

Confusing signals from authorities can stymie your best efforts to move ahead until after Mercury leaves its retrograde cycle on the 13th, but you're also dealing with a changing hierarchy, which may be the reason no one is quite sure what to do! Work together with others to find solutions, and you may just place yourself in a position for advancement by the 26th. The wheels of progress are finally turning again and you can feel motion.

OPPORTUNITY OF THE MONTH

Opening a path toward another's advancement or growth on the 7th can be the key to a more effective relationship.

Rewarding Days: 3, 4, 7, 8, 12, 13, 17, 26, 27, 30, 31
Challenging Days: 1, 2, 5, 10, 11, 14, 15, 22, 23, 24, 28, 29

AFFIRMATION FOR THE MONTH
"I am happy to help others who need my assistance."

PRIMARY FOCUS

You're moving into the fast track, and have ample opportunity to broaden your horizons and see the progress you've hoped to achieve. Generously acknowledge others whose help has lead to your success.

HEALTH AND FITNESS

Team activities or group fitness classes can be invigorating now. If you have a chance to coach or teach others, you're likely to enjoy great results. Travel can also benefit your health.

ROMANCE AND RELATIONSHIPS

Share your dreams and your ideals. Consider travel from the 4th–27th as a means to stimulate deeper love (or, if you're looking for a relationship, as a way to meet a fascinating person). If you're hesitant about asking for certain needs, carefully explore your fears, which may be rooted in the past and have little to do with the present situation. Seek out a quiet, intimate environment to explore some exceptional fantasies on the 21st–22nd.

FINANCE AND CAREER

From the 1st through the Full Moon on the 7th, pay special attention to your finances and start thinking more of the future. Certainly take care of your current needs, but also allow time to develop a positive plan for later. Make presentations or attend classes or workshops this month which will improve your professional standing. After the New Moon on the 22nd, you're in a great position to achieve strong recognition for your efforts.

OPPORTUNITY OF THE MONTH

Find ways to get beyond your limitations and reach for new possibilities. It's time to move ahead with hope and confidence.

Rewarding Days: 4, 5, 8, 9, 13, 14, 15, 23, 24, 27
Challenging Days: 2, 7, 11, 12, 18, 1, 20, 24, 25

AFFIRMATION FOR THE MONTH
"I am inspired by Divine Truth and Wisdom."

PRIMARY FOCUS

Travel and/or educational pursuits provide excellent avenues for personal and professional growth. Your ambition may be strong now, and you can move ahead.

HEALTH AND FITNESS

With so much energy invested in getting ahead professionally, you might forget about your physical needs. Allow time to de-stress after the 19th, when relaxation and rejuvenation are necessary.

ROMANCE AND RELATIONSHIPS

Work may be your passion, but can also lead to a romance if you're in the market. Your eagerness can work to your advantage during the Full Moon on the 6th. But regardless of the situation, be sure you know who's on the other end of your advances from the 12th–31st, when you might be more enthralled with a fantasy. Conflict with parents can get in the way of an intimate relationship, but only you can decide if you're willing to take the risks of following your heart.

FINANCE AND CAREER

Favor with superiors can lead to financial advancement, and you're in an excellent position to request a raise or expand your business from the 1st–6th. Be careful in your spending from the 17th–21st, when impulsiveness can be costly. Use your best judgment in investment following the New Moon on the 21st, when you're standing on a firmer foundation for long-term growth. Carefully review details of legal agreements from the 27th–31st.

OPPORTUNITY OF THE MONTH

Act decisively on the 1st, 6th, 28th, and 29th for best results when taking the lead in order to assure long-term stability.

Rewarding Days: 1, 2, 6, 7, 11, 12, 20, 21, 24, 25, 28, 29
Challenging Days: 4, 8, 9, 15, 16, 17, 22, 23

AFFIRMATION FOR THE MONTH
"I am confident, optimistic, and filled with hope!"

TAURUS
The Bull

April 20 to May 21

Element: Earth

Quality: Fixed

Polarity: Feminine/Yin

Planetary Ruler: Venus

Meditation: "I am the steward of my environment"

Gemstone: Emerald

Power Stones: Diamond, rose quartz, topaz, blue lace agate

Key Phrase: "I have"

Glyph: Bull's head

Anatomy: Neck and throat

Color: Green

Animal: Cattle

Myths/Legends: Ceriddwen, Osiris & Isis, Bull of Minos

House Association: 2nd

Opposite Sign: Scorpio

Flower: Violet

Key Word: Conservation

Positive Expression:
Substantial
Conservative
Focused
Loving
Calm
Enduring
Steadfast
Persistent
Prosperous

Misuse of Energy:
Obstinate
Possessive
Unyielding
Greedy
Lethargic
Materialistic
Avaricious
Covetous

♉ TAURUS ♉

Your Ego's Strengths and Weaknesses

Through an unfaltering devotion to the people and things you love, you create stability and security in your life. As "The Maintainer" of the zodiac, your ability to accumulate material and financial stability can be consistently reliable. However, you are driven by the desire to express and experience the deepest possible love.

Ruled by the energy of Venus, you are drawn to the many expressions of love and beauty, and may be especially fond of naturally occurring splendor. Many forms of artistry can attract your interest, and you may be gifted in these areas as a form of creative expression. You search for qualities which will endure through time and appreciate those things which have proven themselves worthy of this test.

While others may lose faith, your steadfastness can provide a welcome haven in the storms of life. Sometimes, however, your stubborn resistance gets in the way of change, since you are determined not to let go of what you possess. Using your ability to create strong emotional safeguards, you can learn to let go by understanding that your integrity and personal strength can allow room for changes.

Through mastering your own sense of values, you are learning ways to recognize those attachments which actually may keep you from experiencing the true nature of love. In fact, by releasing what you no longer need, you make room for even more love to flow into your life.

Your Approach to Romance

Looking for someone "to have and to hold," you express loyalty in love and can be a dedicated and highly affectionate partner. Your tender, yet strong, physical expression of love is enhanced by a natural sensuality and enjoyment of the good things life has to offer. Although you may be seeking love which endures the test of time, you may quickly become attached to anyone who draws your affection or interest. To avoid heartache, watch your tenacity when trying to keep things the way they are instead of allowing for natural evolutionary changes which can occur over time.

As an earth sign, you are most stimulated by a relationship which has substance. You may feel most comfortable with others who share the earthy element—Taurus, Virgo and Capricorn. Capricorn's drive to secure financial stability is highly appealing, and you may truly enjoy the mutual appreciation with another Taurean whose commitment promotes trust and longevity. Virgo understands and supports your need for comfort and will enjoy your quiet solidity.

Aries can be highly attractive, but may push you before you're ready to move. Gemini's versatility challenges you to become more adaptable. Your desire for home and family may be shared by Cancer, with whom you could create an easy contentment. And although you may feel ego conflicts with Leo, their loyalty and drama can be highly appealing. Libra's refined grace is enticing, but their indecision can drive you crazy.

Scorpio, your opposite sign, definitely stimulates powerful passion and may surpass your own possessiveness. Sagittarius' playfulness and generosity is enjoyable, but you may feel you don't see enough of one another. You can be baffled by the detachment of Aquarius, and feel that you are not given enough personal attention. With Pisces, you can share the fantasy of romance, together building a place for your dreams to become reality.

Your Career Development

You can work hard if you know it will lead to reward, and seek a career which presents a stable base and shows a promise of growth. You're likely to have a good head for business and recognize a reliable opportunity when it comes along. With your natural sense of structure and design, you might enjoy working in the building industry, furniture construction, or architectural design. In the arts, you may enjoy floral arranging, sculpting, or pottery, and may also be an accomplished singer. Ranching, farming, gardening, landscape design, and forestry offer positive expressions of your energy.

43

In the world of finance, banking, real estate, and investment are appealing. You can be an encouraging counselor or teacher. Work in a restaurant, bakery, or grocery store appeals to your love for food. Also, the beauty or cosmetic industry, hairdressing or clothing design, sales, and manufacturing can be positive outlets for your desire to remain creative.

Your Use of Power

Your power often comes through building a fortress of strength which no threat can penetrate. By creating this feeling within yourself, you generate personal power. But you may also desire to surround yourself with a loyal company or family and substantial material resources.

Greed or excessive possessiveness can be expressions of an abuse of your power. You may be challenged with the desire "to have" versus the experience "to be," and you can block your own progress when you refuse to yield to necessary changes. Learning to let go is not an easy assignment for you!

Through accepting the value of other people around you and sharing your own resources, you may discover a kinship which knows no boundaries and withstands every imaginable test. You have an innate tie with Mother Earth and can conserve and utilize her resources as part of your quest for true power. Assure a positive future for your children and forthcoming generations by replenishing Earth's riches. This can be your true expression of an endless love which endures beyond time.

Famous Taurus

Scott Carpenter, Emilio Estavez, Betty Ford, Janet Jackson, Jay Leno, Cloris Leachman, Golda Meir, Willie Mays, Al Pacino, Evita Peron, Martha Quinn, Willard Scott, Barbra Streisand, Tchaikovsky, Isaiah Thomas, Tammy Wynette

THE YEAR AHEAD FOR TAURUS

An emphasis on strong spiritual growth, outreach into your community, and achievement of greater satisfaction through your work assures a year of feeling more secure and confident in your place in the world. You are seeking more purposeful expressions of your talents and abilities, and may feel that you're on the brink of a profound breakthrough. Friends can play a powerful role now, and may become your most significant resource for advancement and support.

While Jupiter transits through your Solar 8th House, you may be feeling more curious about the origins of many elements of your life. This cycle can provoke a sense of greater satisfaction from any close partnerships you have formed, but can stimulate jealousy if you're feeling insecure about your own resources or abilities. Take this time to express your gratitude for the love and support of others in your life, instead of taking their help for granted. Use this time to share ventures with other individuals whose resources, coupled with your own, can create greater impact or accumulate more significant rewards. Chiron's transit also enhances this need to join with others in creative pursuits, and may propel you to spend more time expressing your own talents. Using your abilities now can have a healing effect in your life. This may also be a meaningful year concerning your relationship with children.

The Solar Eclipses in Taurus and Scorpio are especially significant for you this year, since they bring emphasis to your need to become more aware of your psychological projections. Many times, the elements of our psyche we have difficulty accepting or incorporating into our own lives are easily projected upon others. Through relationships we can learn about our inner self, and this is the time to determine the elements of your own power as well as uncovering your fears or insecurities so you can develop into a more complete individual. Partnership can flourish under this cycle, but you are challenged to develop a more conscious awareness of the difference between your needs and feelings and those of your partner. Careful attention to physical health is more crucial now, since you are more capable of detecting problems in early stages. As always, the link between emotional, spiritual, and physical needs is important, but this year you are capable of balancing these elements of your life to create greater vitality.

If you were born from April 20–23, you're experiencing a feeling of breaking away from the established order of things while Uranus transits in square to your Sun and Pluto travels in quincunx to your Sun. These cycles influence deep level changes, and may be especially helpful if you're making major alterations in your life. Choices in your career path may be more challenging, since you are likely to feel a need to be more independent. You may be stimulated to seek out directions which are more personally gratifying and which offer a chance for you to express your unique vision and ideas to the world. This is a time of emergence, but you may also feel a bit vulnerable within this period since you might be dealing with people or circumstances which are basically unfamiliar to you. Review your feelings about your relationship with your parents now, since you may find that you are not driven as strongly to satisfy their expectations, and are, instead, feeling a powerful need to create life on your terms. If you know deep within that you need to make changes, but are reluctant to take steps to initiate those changes, you may feel that life is out of control and changing in a confusing way. Sometimes, circumstances change around you, and your only option is to choose the best manner of response! Pluto's cycle can be especially frustrating physically, so it's important to be alert to any changes in your energy and take measures to keep yourself healthy and strong. Chronic problems which have been ignored are likely to surface now so you can deal with them directly. Adjustments to your lifestyle, diet, or attitudes may be necessary to achieve the best level of health during this cycle.

If you were born from April 24–May 17, you'll benefit through creating long-range goals and plans while Saturn transits in sextile to your Sun. One positive effect of this cycle can be the realization that you are actually getting something for your efforts, especially regarding your career. If you are dissatisfied with the rewards your career provides, then it is important for you to reevaluate your reasons for remaining on that path. You may simply need to realign your priorities and set some reasonable goals. But if you do find that you want to make major changes, your previous performance or experience will certainly be one of the primary criteria for your advancement or acceptance in a new position. This is an excellent year to take a leadership role in a group or organization, and would also be a good time to become politically active or express your views through effective and positive outlets. One thing is certain during this period—you will be held accountable for your actions! Any Saturn cycle brings a period of greater accountability, even if the cycle is a supportive one. You might appreciate the fact that you have a wide range of choices regarding this accountability, and that you can make a significant difference is feeling greater happiness about the things for which you have to claim responsibility.

If you were born from May 13–18, Neptune is transiting in trine aspect to your Sun, bringing an energy of increased imagination and creativity. If you are involved in music or the arts, you may find that recognition for your talents soars during this year. You can certainly develop any creative talents more effectively now, and even if you do not feel that you are artistically gifted, your imaginative ideas may offer a wide range of possibilities for improvement in your life. Spiritually, this cycle stimulates a stronger feeling of connection to that realm which is beyond the physical. Psychic abilities can be strengthened, and you may feel that your consciousness is expanding. Since this is also a period of enhanced sensitivity, you may feel drawn to put forth some efforts in charitable causes, or to direct your energy to help others who need assistance. Your sensibilities increase on every level now, including physically, and you may be more sensitive to your environment and the people within it. Avoid the downfall which can result from losing touch with your personal boundaries during this period. Carefully curb alcohol usage, and be aware that you may also be more sensitive to prescription medications than you have been in the past. You might respond quite favorably to natural remedies and changes in your dietary choices. And within the context of relationships, try to remain objective about your actual and realistic role when your partner, lover, parent, or child have problems. They may need your help, but you may also need to allow them to learn some lessons on their own!

Deep and powerful changes are occurring in your life if you were born from May 15–21. You are experiencing two cycles which create the need to break free and eliminate your attachment to things you no longer need. Uranus is transiting in trine aspect to your Sun, stimulating a bit of rebellion and also heightening your intuitive awareness. This cycle is frequently associated with positive changes in personal relationships, and can also be a period in which you seem to be in the right place at the right time! But you are also experiencing some levels of psychological stress from Pluto's transit in opposition to your Sun, and you may not fully trust the opportunities for transformation which are at your doorstep. One thing is sure: what you no longer need will begin to fall away from your life! It's best to cooperate and search for positive ways to utilize these changes instead of bemoaning your fate that you could not stay exactly the same. What is most difficult about such a cycle as this is dealing with your own attachments. Even if you want to make changes, you may still feel a sense of loss. That grief over the loss (even the loss of a detrimental habit) must be acknowledged before you can effectively continue with your life. This is definitely a period in which your spiritual and psychological strength are enhanced. You may not feel like letting new people into your life during these processes of transformational change, but you must acknowledge the new elements of your Self which are emerging. This is a period of profound healing and can be a time of tremendous progress in personal growth and awareness.

Tools to Make a Difference

You can stimulate some positive avenues for growth this year by taking time each day to become aware of your feelings and needs. This year marks a type of reality check, and you'll fare much better if you are in control of these checkpoints instead of feeling that you are constantly having to prove yourself to some outside source of evaluation. In the beginning of the day, spend a few minutes just allowing yourself to connect to the inner core of yourself. Deep breathing, meditation, or physical exercise are all workable techniques. Then, before you close the day and go to sleep, allow yourself to gather your energy once again so you can rest more effectively.

In order to accomplish some of the changes you wish to see in the world around you, you might want to get involved in a special interest group or even take time to become politically active. You don't have to run for office, but you might feel more in control of your destiny if you at least let your legislators know how you feel about issues which are important to you.

To maintain your physical vitality, direct some efforts toward gaining a better understanding of your own particular physical needs. If you have any chronic problems, find out about them, and determine what you can do personally to make a difference. Consider adding more "live" foods to your diet such as sprouts, more fresh fruits and vegetables, and juices to increase your vitality. Use your senses to help you enhance your life by staying in touch with the living, breathing Earth.

During your meditations, concentrate upon creating a feeling of continuity. See yourself walking through an ancient forest which readily welcomes your energy and essence. Stop and listen to the sounds of life. Reach out and touch the soft earth, enjoy the fresh smell of the trees and the fragrant flowers. Imagine the forest changing through the seasons—from the cold solitude of winter, to the new life of spring, the vibrancy of summer, and transformation of autumn. Carry this memory of continual change and growth into every activity, knowing that these processes renew and stabilize your own vitality and creativity.

Affirmation for the Year

"I am revitalized by the knowledge that I am
actively creating my own destiny."

ACTION TABLES FOR TAURUS

These dates reflect the best (but not the only) times for success and ease in these activities according to your Sun Sign.

Change Residence	July 25–Aug. 9
Request a Raise	April 29–30
Begin a Course of Study	Jan. 1–June 28
Visit a Doctor	Apr. 2–16; Aug. 29–Nov. 3
Start a Diet	Jan. 21–22; Feb. 18–19; Mar. 17–18; Apr. 13–14; May 11–12; June 7–8; July 4–6; Aug. 1–2, 28–29; Sep. 24–25; Oct. 22–23; Nov. 18–19; Dec. 15–17
Begin a Romance	Aug. 26–27
Join a Club	March 1–2
Seek Employment	Jan. 7–Mar. 13; Aug. 29–Nov. 4
Take a Vacation	Jan. 28–29; Feb. 24–25; Mar. 23–24; Apr. 20–21; May 17–18; June 13–14; July 11–12; Aug. 7–8; Sep. 4–5; Oct. 1–2, 28–29; Nov. 24–25; Dec. 22–23
Change Your Wardrobe	August 10–28
End a Relationship	May 14
Seek Professional Advice	Jan. 24–25; Feb. 20–21; Mar. 19–20; Apr. 16–17; May 13–14; June 9–10; July 7–8; Aug. 3–4, 30–31; Sep. 27–28; Oct. 24–25; Nov. 20–21; Dec. 18–19
Have a Makeover	April 29–30
Obtain a Loan	Jan. 26–27; Feb. 22–23; Mar. 21–22; Apr. 18–19; May 15–16; June 11–12; July 9–10; Aug. 5–6; Sep. 1–2, 29–30; Oct. 26–27; Nov. 22–23; Dec. 20–21

PRIMARY FOCUS

During this time of powerful creativity, you are challenged to find effective ways to stretch your horizons and move into new territory. Finances need special attention.

HEALTH AND FITNESS

Improving your health now involves reaching into the core of your being and achieving greater self-love and acceptance. Explore enjoyable forms of exercise and activity. Avoid stagnation.

ROMANCE AND RELATIONSHIPS

Blend the spiritual and physical aspects of love. Approach your sexual needs with personal honesty, staying aware of precious moments you share. New love or uplifting an existing relationship arises through developing creativity, enjoying the arts, or improving your spiritual disciplines such as meditation. The New Moon on the 1st emphasizes a period of more flowing communication reaching a peak during the Full Moon on the 16th. Advice from a friend proves helpful after the 22nd.

FINANCE AND CAREER

Although finances may seem stable, details involving jointly-held resources may need special attention after the 8th. Final agreements are best from the 1st–10th, but unresolved issues can deteriorate from the 18th–27th, when power struggles may be highly emotional. Review details after Mercury enters its retrograde on the 26th, and pull back from signing contracts after that time. Satisfy authorities after the New Moon on the 30th.

OPPORTUNITY OF THE MONTH

Get busy on important projects from the 1st–6th, when a successful launch can override future distractions.

Rewarding Days: 1, 5, 6, 10, 11, 15, 16, 20, 28, 29
Challenging Days: 3, 4, 17, 18, 23, 24, 25, 30, 31

AFFIRMATION FOR THE MONTH
"I am certain of my choices."

PRIMARY FOCUS

Although you may be busy at home, you are also enjoying increased exposure through your work. Travel, teaching, or educational pursuits can be highly satisfying.

HEALTH AND FITNESS

Emotionally charged situations can undermine your health unless you find positive ways to express what you really feel. Release anger and build your vitality by staying physically active.

ROMANCE AND RELATIONSHIPS

Although you may experience emotional distress due to poor communication with parents or authorities, there are ways to move beyond the situation and enjoy inner peace. A new level of love emerges as you blend spiritual yearnings and emotional desires. Improved understanding of yourself and your partner helps to override much of the inner turmoil that arises from power struggles or anger. Find common ground instead of concentrating on differences during the Full Moon on the 15th.

FINANCE AND CAREER

Mercury's retrograde through the 15th emphasizes a need to satisfy obligations in your job which you may have postponed. If you feel competitive or angry about your work situation, find things you can do within yourself to change first. Then negotiate agreements. Take action to finalize contracts after the 16th, and pay particular attention to your chance to take a role of leadership. After the 20th you'll see more light than tunnel!

OPPORTUNITY OF THE MONTH

Take advantage of surprising changes on the 24th–25th to take a definitive stance which radically improves your circumstances.

Rewarding Days: 1, 2, 6, 7, 11, 16, 17, 24, 25
Challenging Days: 5, 13, 14, 15, 20, 21, 26, 27

AFFIRMATION FOR THE MONTH
"I have an open mind."

PRIMARY FOCUS

Career and work activities take top priority, although you may be experiencing some conflict regarding the amount of time consumed by work. Set strong short-term goals as a means to focus your energy.

HEALTH AND FITNESS

Activities within your home may be more appealing than getting outside or going to a gym, but it is crucial to remain active to release energy and build stamina.

ROMANCE AND RELATIONSHIPS

Developing friendships is much easier after the 14th, although you may find work relationships growing friendlier throughout the month. Getting romantically involved with someone at work can be ticklish, and may have a negative backlash unless you are clear about your objectives from the beginning. Romance fares best near the time of the Full Moon on the 16th, although social situations look promising from the 14th–31st. Allow time for quiet, intimate conversation from the 28th–30th.

FINANCE AND CAREER

Earn points at work by showing a more forgiving attitude. Special efforts to clarify agreements provides successful results from the New Moon on the 1st through the 4th. Avoid the temptation to spend beyond your means now, since it could lead to financial problems later. Investments fare best on the 16th, 24th, 25th, 29th, and 30th. Getting involved with community activities or special interests after the 19th can enhance your status.

OPPORTUNITY OF THE MONTH

By bringing a project, an idea, or an experience into its completion on the 15th–16th, you guarantee longer term success.

Rewarding Days: 1, 5, 6, 8, 15, 16, 23, 24, 28, 29
Challenging Days: 3, 13, 14, 19, 20, 22, 25, 26

AFFIRMATION FOR THE MONTH
"I gladly release anger and hostility."

♉ TAURUS/APRIL ♉

PRIMARY FOCUS
Complete projects or commitments early in order to open the way for new opportunities by month's end. Allow time for friends, and stay alert to improve your home life.

HEALTH AND FITNESS
Mars continues its square to your Sun, and can stimulate agitation or irritability. Find outlets to release energy, use reasonable caution when taking risks, but stay active!

ROMANCE AND RELATIONSHIPS
Solidifying a relationship through honest commitment can bring a real sense of progress, but you may still feel an internal restless energy that seems difficult to satisfy. This is a period of increasing personal awareness, and, with the Solar Eclipse in Taurus on the 29th, you cannot hide from your real needs. By becoming truly supportive of your friends, and making a special effort to communicate with those who share your life, you can overcome your anxiety. Sensing that you are on the brink of great change can be disconcerting. Trust yourself.

FINANCE AND CAREER
Most of your progress in career is the result of hard work behind the scenes which may not gain you much recognition, but can be highly satisfying. Presentations, conferences, or workshops offer a chance to move ahead from the 17th–30th, although you may run into some strong competition on the 26th. Before you put on your armor, decide if the risk is worthwhile. Patience may be the key to emerging as the clear victor.

OPPORTUNITY OF THE MONTH
Ascertain your connection to your inner self during the Sun's eclipse, when answers from within yourself are most satisfying.

Rewarding Days: 2, 3, 7, 11, 12, 20, 21, 24, 29, 30
Challenging Days: 5, 9, 10, 15, 16, 17, 22, 23

AFFIRMATION FOR THE MONTH
"I lovingly strive to satisfy my inner yearnings."

PRIMARY FOCUS

Put the finishing touches on projects around the house. You might also benefit from a new approach to handling finances, and will want to evaluate your financial stand.

HEALTH AND FITNESS

Although staying active is important, spending time each day clearing your mind and creating a sense of inner peace can improve your ability to concentrate.

ROMANCE AND RELATIONSHIPS

Your imagination can run away with you now, and if you're bored with your love life, you may be spending more time in fantasy than dealing directly with the reality. If you're drawn to someone new, it's possible you're simply seeking a diversion! Bring your needs and concerns to the surface during the Full Moon on the 14th when your sweetheart may help you make your dreams come true! But be careful of new romance from the 10th–17th, since there may be little substance remaining after the fire has diminished.

FINANCE AND CAREER

Before you decide to make any major purchases or investments, carefully review your current and projected financial picture. Impulsive actions can be costly, and you may also be more easily deceived by others who would take advantage of your resources. Delays in contracts after the 21st give you a chance to reconsider. Family members may exert pressure over money matters and you need to be honest about your feelings to avoid guilt.

OPPORTUNITY OF THE MONTH

Eliminate clutter and things that you simply do not need any longer from the 13th–27th. You're making room for something better.

Rewarding Days: 4, 5, 9, 10, 17, 18, 21, 22, 26, 27
Challenging Days: 6, 7, 13, 14, 15, 19, 20, 24

AFFIRMATION FOR THE MONTH
"My heart is filled with compassionate love."

PRIMARY FOCUS

A powerful thrust of creative vitality stimulates improvements in your love life, enhancing professional growth. Present your talents in satisfying and lucrative ways.

HEALTH AND FITNESS

Recreation and sports provide an excellent outlet for fitness. But you may have a tendency to push beyond your limits, leading to injury or excessive fatigue from the 6th–18th. Use caution.

ROMANCE AND RELATIONSHIPS

Venus and Mars transits support considerable improvements in your love life, primarily due to greater confidence in expressing your feelings. You're eager to get beneath the surface from the 1st–11th, and have little patience for playing games. Even though some of your expectations may be too high, you are in a strong position to make long-term commitments. But if a relationship needs to end, you can also walk away, knowing you've done your part to make it work. Hope emerges with the New Moon on the 27th.

FINANCE AND CAREER

While Mercury retrogrades through the 17th you need to stay on top of spending and finances. There's a tendency to spend beyond your limits from the 13th–21st, when risky investments could be especially costly. Research uncovers valuable information from the 1st–23rd, which you can put to good use in persuading others to support your ideas or projects. Conferences, presentations, or meetings bring good results from the 23rd–30th.

OPPORTUNITY OF THE MONTH

Your persuasiveness is difficult to resist from the 22nd–24th, and can lead to an exciting project after the 27th.

Rewarding Days: 5, 6, 13, 14, 18, 22, 23, 24, 27, 28
Challenging Days: , 3, 4, 9, 10, 15, 16, 30

AFFIRMATION FOR THE MONTH
"I am inspired by the beauty of life."

PRIMARY FOCUS
A highly romantic and productive period for career and personal development, this month's cycles support enhanced self-worth and improved circumstances.

HEALTH AND FITNESS
Build stamina and endurance now through activities you find entertaining or pleasurable. Allow plenty of time to play, and consider vacationing after the 10th.

ROMANCE AND RELATIONSHIPS
The Full Moon on the 12th emphasizes a need to express your thoughts and feelings, which can stabilize an existing relationship or offer a good beginning to a new romance. Watch a tendency to be either too self-critical or critical of your lover or children from the 7th–18th. Not only must you show responsibility for your own actions, but also you need to allow others to do the same. Time away with your loved ones is most enjoyable from the 11th–23rd, and can be confusing or hectic from the 24th–30th.

FINANCE AND CAREER
A slow-down in forward progress from the 3rd–10th can be discouraging, but does offer a chance to review the situation and get rid of trouble spots. A more conservative approach works best, although you can try something innovative after the 22nd. But straying too far from the established order of things can alienate important friends. Look for ways to bring out your individuality while still honoring the stability of what has gone before.

OPPORTUNITY OF THE MONTH
Commitments made now can be lasting, but need to incorporate room for change to avoid stifling your personal growth.

Rewarding Days: 2, 3, 11, 12, 15, 16, 19, 20, 21, 25, 30
Challenging Days: 1, 7, 8, 13, 14, 18, 27, 28

AFFIRMATION FOR THE MONTH
"I trust and honor my intuitive thoughts."

PRIMARY FOCUS

Home and family take top priority, and there may be some friction at home as a result of pressures from work. A little creative attention on your part can rectify any problems which arise.

HEALTH AND FITNESS

With Mars transiting your 6th House of health, it is imperative that you take direct action when dealing with any physical concerns. Passivity can be costly.

ROMANCE AND RELATIONSHIPS

Taking time to enjoy family oriented activities can bring increased harmony and understanding, and may even improve your love life! In addition to entertaining more at home, you might also use this time to redecorate or beautify your home. Contact with parents during the Full Moon on the 10th may open a healthy dialogue, or you may experience a breakthrough in unlocking old emotional blocks. New love or revitalization of an existing relationship proves invigorating following the New Moon on the 25th.

FINANCE AND CAREER

Concentrate on building long-term financial security, but be wary of advice from "authorities" who readily appear on the scene. Seek out information from those who have proven their integrity. Difficulties in joint ventures can lead to dissolution of a partnership from the 9th–13th or later, from the 20th–24th unless you can clarify areas of dispute. Be on the alert for deception in the ranks at work from the 27th–31st.

OPPORTUNITY OF THE MONTH

You're in the best position to launch a pet project or introduce a new plan on the 26th–27th. Go for it!

Rewarding Days: 7, 8, 12, 16, 17, 21, 22, 26, 27
Challenging Days: 3, 4, 9, 10, 19, 23, 24, 30, 31

AFFIRMATION FOR THE MONTH
"I express my feelings honestly and clearly."

PRIMARY FOCUS

Relationships, particularly romantic involvements, can be both rewarding and frustrating. Rewards arise from more open expression of your needs; frustrations, from trying to maintain control!

HEALTH AND FITNESS

Competitive sports are an excellent outlet for developing your physical stamina. At the very least, set some goals and get started working toward them!

ROMANCE AND RELATIONSHIPS

Through the time of the Full Moon on the 8th you may feel energy building to a peak in your personal relationships. If you're uncertain, consulting with a close friend can help you clarify your best direction. Turmoil in your partnership can result from holding back (or fooling yourself!) from the 7th–14th. Concern yourself with the reality of a situation, not what it could be. Avoid vague or manipulative forms of communication after the 20th, when hedging works against your best interests.

FINANCE AND CAREER

Carefully examine ventures involving joint resources, since you may need to reevaluate the situation before continuing your commitment. Mercury's retrograde from Sep. 22 to Oct. 13 can bring an especially trying time when dealing with situations at work, although you can get to the bottom of grievances. Beautifying your work environment after the 17th pays off through improved attitudes and increased productivity.

OPPORTUNITY OF THE MONTH

Review your work situation during the New Moon on the 24th, when you may find you've been missing some valuable resources. Use them.

Rewarding Days: 4, 8, 9, 12, 13, 17, 18, 22, 23
Challenging Days: , 6, 7, 11, 20, 21, 27, 28

AFFIRMATION FOR THE MONTH
"I gladly praise the efforts of others."

PRIMARY FOCUS

Conflicts with others may arise from your inability to take responsibility for your own feelings, especially any anger or frustration you may be experiencing. Work on your inner self now.

HEALTH AND FITNESS

A solid program of fitness and nutrition instituted now can bring significant changes in your health. Take a personal inventory or consult with an expert during the Lunar Eclipse on the 8th.

ROMANCE AND RELATIONSHIPS

Friction with your partner can escalate into a stubborn battle of wills unless you step back and seriously consider what all the fighting is about. Power issues, especially those of a sexual nature, can be rooted in circumstances from the distant past. Dig deep into your feelings from the 12th–21st to uncover your real feelings. Now is the time to heal any guilt, shame, or disappointment that has kept you from having the love you deserve. You are the one who can make the difference now!

FINANCE AND CAREER

Before finalizing any contracts or agreements, take time to review the fine print and consult an expert if you have questions. Blindly accepting that everything is perfect can be costly! Emotional volatility in work situations from the 1st–10th can be distracting, so be sure you stay on task. This is a good time for research. Action and leadership are more productive next month.

OPPORTUNITY OF THE MONTH

Deeper insights into yourself during the Solar Eclipse on the 23rd can provide empowering, healing vitality. Focus and absorb it.

Rewarding Days: 1, 2, 5, 6, 10, 11, 15, 20, 28, 29
Challenging Days: 3, 4, 13, 17, 18, 23, 24, 25, 30, 31

AFFIRMATION FOR THE MONTH
"I take responsibility for my own needs and feelings."

PRIMARY FOCUS

Others may demand more time and attention than you feel they deserve. But you can also benefit from shared experiences. Just be sure your expectations are realistic.

HEALTH AND FITNESS

Stress takes its toll now unless you take direct action to decrease its effect. Get a massage on the 12th, 16th, 17th, or 29th. Take a break during the Full Moon on the 7th.

ROMANCE AND RELATIONSHIPS

If you've been reluctant to make commitment to a relationship, consider the reasons for your hesitation and what you fear. Perhaps the gains could outweigh the potential losses if you can honestly address those fears. Your sexual relationship can be much more fulfilling from the 1st–11th, but tensions can arise from the 12th–18th due to your expectations. Show appreciation to your partner and accept love when it is offered to you. This is a time of receiving even if you are single, but you must open the door to your heart.

FINANCE AND CAREER

Watch your spending, especially if you are inclined to borrow money or use your credit in ways you had not anticipated. Impulsive action now can lead to heavy burdens later, so if you are increasing your debt, make sure you can handle it in the long run! After the New Moon on the 22nd, finances are likely to improve and you may be in a better position to take risks. Sign contracts from the 28th–30th for best results.

OPPORTUNITY OF THE MONTH

Get rid of things that are holding you back —whether they are attitudes, material possessions, or people. You're cleaning house.

Rewarding Days: 1, 2, 6, 7, 11, 16, 24, 25, 29, 30
Challenging Days: 5, 13, 14, 15, 20, 21, 22, 26, 27

AFFIRMATION FOR THE MONTH
"I am whole, strong, and powerful."

PRIMARY FOCUS

Open your mind to new ideas or concentrate on further developing your skills, knowledge or ability. Education, travel, and cultural experience are highly rewarding.

HEALTH AND FITNESS

Increased vitality improves your desire to stay active. Build stamina and endurance now, but remember to stay flexible! A vacation could work wonders this month.

ROMANCE AND RELATIONSHIPS

A sense of inner peace and harmony is the result of greater self-acceptance and more confident expression of your needs and feelings. To revitalize a love relationship or begin a new one, consider travel, or at least get involved in enjoyable cultural activities. Friends can also be important allies and may be a good source for romantic inspiration mid-month. Exchange vows or renew your commitment from the 3rd–22nd. Allow plenty of time for romance throughout the month, and especially from the 8th–14th.

FINANCE AND CAREER

You may be feeling unusually generous and can benefit from sharing your expertise, ideas, and talents with others. But be sure you know who you are trusting with your assets or valuable information during the Full Moon on the 6th, when you could be more vulnerable to deception. Business travel fares beautifully all month, but you may gain most from the 1st–6th and after the New Moon on the 21st. Find ways to broaden your horizons.

OPPORTUNITY OF THE MONTH

Incorporating ideas or experience which allow you to further your influence brings advancement and reward on the 3rd and 4th.

Rewarding Days: 3, 4, 8, 13, 14, 22, 23, 26, 27, 30, 31
Challenging Days: 2, 11, 12, 18, 19, 20, 24, 25

AFFIRMATION FOR THE MONTH
"I value my connection to my Higher Self."

GEMINI
The Twins

May 21 to June 22

Element: Air

Quality: Mutable

Polarity: Masculine/Yang

Planetary Ruler: Mercury

Meditation: "My mind is linked to The Source"

Gemstone: Agate

Power Stones: Herkimer diamond, Alexandrite, Celestite, Aquamarine

Glyph: Pillars of Duality

Key Phrase: "I think"

Anatomy: Hands, arms, shoulder, lungs, nervous system

Colors: Orange & yellow

Animal: Monkeys, talking birds, flying insects

Myths/Legends: Castor and Pollux, Peter Pan

House Association: 3rd

Opposite Sign: Sagittarius

Flower: Lily of the Valley

Key Word: Versatility

Positive Expression:
Inquisitive
Rational
Articulate
Perspicacious
Flexible
Incisive
Clever
Sophisticated

Misuse of Energy:
Prankish
Distant
Gossipy
Erratic
Unsettled
Frivolous
Nervous
Skillful

♊ GEMINI ♊

Your Ego's Strengths and Weaknesses

Your role as "The Questioner" often leads you into highly interesting situations which spark your eager mental abilities. Your youthful aura springs from your eagerness to embrace and explore new ideas. With a strong desire to communicate and "link-up" with other people, you have diverse interests and a powerful capability to get along in changeable circumstances. In fact, you may go out of your way to create changes if none are forthcoming!

Rather than become bored by simply doing one thing at a time, you tend to juggle several activities (or relationships!) at once. Others who need definite commitments from you may be frustrated by your life of distractions. Yet your debonair attitude usually helps you find a way out of sticky situations! As the original networker and negotiator, you have the knack for bringing together the right people at the right time. But watch that tendency to try to play both sides at once!

Your love of travel, intelligent ideas, literature, and accumulation of information stem from the powerful influence of Mercury, your planetary ruler. You may also possess strong intuitive abilities, which, when linked to factual understanding, often adds a brilliance to your cosmopolitan air. You are learning the lesson, "What you think, you become," by surrendering your mind to a connection to the Source of All Knowledge.

Your Approach to Romance

Relating is natural for you, and your easy social grace may open the way to explore several relationships before you decide to settle down. Unless you feel a mental link with someone, it is unlikely you will keep your interest, for long intellectual repartee might be your strongest turn-on! You also require a reasonable amount of personal freedom, and can be capable of offering the same to your partner. Although it may seem safer to stay in your head, you do tend to use ideas or abstractions as a diversion or shield when confronted with your deeper feelings.

All the Air signs—Gemini, Libra, and Aquarius—will share your love of conversation and social participation. Libra's allure may be the refinement and artistry which appeal to your romantic side. Aquarius stimulates your higher thoughts and may share your approach to spirituality. Another Gemini can be highly exciting, but you can also drive each other nuts with all the distractions, unless your keep your personal boundaries in tact.

Aries' independence and exuberance are invigorating, and although you may be mesmerized by Taurus' sensuality, you may feel like it takes forever to get things moving! Cancer is comforting, but you may have different ideas about the best ways to use your time or resources. Leo's flare for the dramatic and love of play can be highly appealing.

You can enjoy Virgo's thought-provoking energy for a while, but then you're likely to feel restless. And Scorpio's intense emotionality is engaging, yet difficult to figure out. Your Zodiac opposite, Sagittarius, can be very attractive; however, you can have trouble deciding who is in charge. The problem with Capricorn is control, and if you work it out, you might actually have a deeply engaging connection. The imaginative sensibilities of Pisces are intriguing, but occasionally very confusing.

Your Career Development

To make the most of your career, take time to fully develop your communication skills. By enhancing your natural ability to relate to people, you have a wide variety of options which can hold your interest and lead to a highly satisfying career path. Allow plenty of room for diversification and growth, and make sure the job is mentally challenging.

Public relations, politics, writing, speaking, advertising, or broadcasting can be excellent choices. Your fascination with the mind may lead you to a career in teaching or counseling. Highly technological areas can present the right opportunity to work with your mind and hands together. Or, you can use your manual dex terity in drafting, carving, design, secretarial, or musical pursuits. The performing arts (including clowning, pantomime, and juggling) can be good areas to express your charm and wit.

Your Use of Power

The strength of ideas and knowledge provide real power to you. Circumstances which require knowledge and persuasive communication offer your best opportunities to exercise a positive sense of personal power. You can incorporate an awareness of many facets of human experience, thereby attracting people from a wide array of backgrounds. Your lively wit and enthusiasm can be contagious and often give you a chance to dazzle others with your brilliance. But you must safeguard against appearing too superficial by developing a depth of understanding and maintaining a focus on your priorities.

At this time when technology and communication are at the forefront of social and economic development, you can easily move into positions of influence. You can help to bridge differences between divergent factions or cultures while encouraging experimentation and change. Your identification with the eager spontaneity of youth may lead you to devote time to inspiring young people to manifest their own hopes and dreams. While soaring through life, your perspective can be finely honed by surrendering to Divine Intelligence. Through opening your mind to greater truth and understanding, you are uplifted, and the spirit of humanity flies with you.

Famous Geminis

Emanuel Ax, F. Lee Bailey, Mel Blanc, Christopher Dodd, Michael J. Fox, Steffi Graf, Lisa Hartman, Jackie Mason, Philip Mountbatten, Bill Moyers, Mary Kate and Ashley Olsen, Prince, Isabella Rosellini, Erich Segal, Maurice Sendak, Bonnie Tyler

THE YEAR AHEAD FOR GEMINI

Exciting changes begin for you this year—changes which encourage you to develop new ideas in a world of shifting priorities. You are challenged to strike a balance between your need to maintain expanding social opportunities while taking more responsible steps toward professional growth and development. Although you may feel that things are not moving along as quickly as you would like, you can sense that you are on the brink of important breakthroughs.

The planets Uranus and Pluto begin their ingress into new signs this year. These slow-moving planets spend a long time in one sign, and the year of transition from one sign to another is always significant. This year is particularly significant with Uranus moving into its ruling sign, Aquarius, for a brief period during the spring and summer. Then, from 1996–2003, Uranus transits in this sign, forming a trine to your Sun sometime during this long cycle. (The exact year is determined by your birth date.) It is this energy which stimulates that feeling of anticipation which begins in 1995. Pluto also begins its long transit in Sagittarius, through the year 2008! Sometime during this cycle, Pluto will oppose your Sun. Whether you experience these influences soon or later on, you will feel the energy of change through healing and transformation in your partnerships or relationships, and with a truly significant opportunity to strongly develop your link with the spiritual elements of your life.

Jupiter's transit in Sagittarius during 1995 provides a special avenue for you to reach out to others. Whether through increasing your social participation, developing a new partnership, or renewing commitments to an existing relationship, this cycle gives you a chance to feel more a part of life around you. If you've felt too isolated, the breaking free this energy stimulates can feel like a new lease on life. It's also time to check out your philosophical beliefs, since you may be challenged to incorporate some ideas which broaden your understanding. Generally, confidence and optimism are increased during this phase, but it is difficult to know when to draw the line. Concentrate on maintaining reasonable boundaries, particularly in your commitments of time and money! Otherwise you may leave this cycle feeling completely spent.

The Solar Eclipses bring emphasis to your physical-emotional-spiritual link. If you've been experiencing any physical problems, this can be a time of discovery of core level causes, allowing you to take action to improve your condition. But the most significant side of your physical well-being is likely to be the connection between your mind, soul, and body. Incorporating time for practices which enhance your spiritual awareness is crucial now. Not only can you alter your physical health, but you may also find that by going more deeply into yourself, you uncover important keys to expressing your creative talents and abilities. Find ways to reach out to others who are in need, since just concentrating on yourself alone may feel rather shallow during this time.

If you were born from May 21–24, you are feeling the powerful impact of awakening to deeper elements of yourself while Pluto transits in opposition to your Sun and Uranus trines your Sun. This cycle will continue through 1996 and marks an important transition period. If you've been waiting for a time to break through the barriers to your progress, then these energies can help you take those steps. In many ways, this is a time of spiritual awakening and can help you see the differences between all the things you may have accepted just because they were taught and those things you know to be true. These challenges to your belief systems are more likely to feel like the experience of blossoming. You can remain a "bud" for just so long! Additionally, you may feel challenges from your personal relationships, particularly partnership. It is crucial that you examine your own attitudes and determine what you may need to change. From a psychological viewpoint, this is one period in which you must claim the aspects of your innermost self. If there are elements which you have denied, now is the time to embrace those feelings and memories and work toward healing the past so you can have a more fulfilling present and brighter future. Address any feelings of inadequacy or self-doubt (especially if this is linked to shame or guilt) and work toward eliminating these from your life. Concentrate on opening to the beauty within yourself so you can more easily project that love and beauty to everyone around you. Release those attachments to things, situations, or people which you no longer need, and learn how it feels to fly free!

For Gemini's born from May 25–27, forward progress is more easily attained, now that you have endured the tests of last year. Saturn is moving beyond its long cycle of tension with your Sun, and you may be seeing many of those blocks, which last year seemed insurmountable, finally dissolving or moving away. But watch a tendency to overextend your limitations, which could lead to your becoming involved in too many projects at once. Jupiter's square to your Sun during the summer may also stimulate greater distractions or difficulty concentrating on the present moment. This is definitely a year to expand your mind and become more involved in social concerns, but you will enjoy these things more if they fit into your goals or plans.

If you were born from May 28–June 17, you may feel frustrated by the restraining, focused energy of Saturn transiting in square to your Sun. This cycle marks a year in which personal discipline is extremely important. You are also likely to face increased responsibilities, and may feel that you have to work doubly hard to attain the recognition or respect you deserve. Many times during the year you may feel strongly challenged by your own sense of self-doubt. These feelings are signals about things which may need to be eliminated or released. Elements from your past which are no longer necessary or part of your growth can be readily relinquished. You need to concentrate on your utmost priorities instead of becoming unnecessarily distracted. Are you carrying burdens which belong to someone else? Take a careful look at control issues in both personal and professional relationships. You need to take a stand for yourself instead of backing away from challenges. Physically, pay careful attention to any symptoms which seem excessive or persistent, and avoid indulging in activities or experiences which are draining to your vitality. You may feel limitations now where they failed to exist in the past, but you can also create a new level of freedom by letting go of burdens which are simply no longer yours to carry.

Feelings of confusion or uncertainty can undermine your self-confidence this year if you were born from June 13–19. Neptune is transiting in quincunx to your Sun, prompting an inner experience of probing into new territory. This cycle is much like learning to understand a foreign language. Once you begin to correlate the changes in your consciousness to your previous life experience and personal understanding, you'll get your bearing. Until then, there is a tendency to feel out of touch with these changing realities. What is actually taking place is a difference in your experience of connecting your inner self to the outside world. This cycle often leads to greater gullibility, so be especially careful when signing contracts or making long-term agreements, since you may not have sufficient facts about the new situation to fully appreciate the extent of your commitment!

If you were born from June 17–21 you are likely to experience profound personal growth and change. Uranus and Pluto are both transiting in quincunx to your Sun. This can be a period of powerful personal alchemical transformation—a feeling that you are shifting into a higher level of personal expression. There are a number of adjustments which may need to be accomplished in order to achieve the greatest possible success now. A careful examination of your physical needs is crucial to your well-being, and you can also increase your vitality by uncovering some previously hidden physical problems. At work, look for ways to get rid of things which are not producing, or make changes to allow for an easier flow of activity and utmost productivity. In your personal relationships, be honest about your deeper feelings, and especially aware of your sexual needs. Any repressed emotions can surface now, and may distort your real feelings unless you are honest about their origins. You can make changes now which will lead to a more gratifying existence—on all fronts!

Tools to Make a Difference:

Since most of the long-term cycles to your Sun this year are stimulating changes in your connection to the outside world, determine positive new directions for your creative energy and ideas. Find ways to make a difference in the quality of life around you—charity work, volunteering to help teach or train others, getting information to others about important issues—find time for experiences that help to solidify your link with society.

Clear communication is a high priority, too, and you might enjoy exploring more effective ways to both express your own ideas and feelings and understand those of others. You may have a natural talent for understanding and using neurolinguistic programming, hypnosis, and subliminal suggestion can provide you with better tools to connect with others. But you are also developing a more exceptional way to stay linked to your inner self. Increase the development of mindfulness by paying more careful attention to your experiences of the moment. Listen to your inner thoughts. Watch the effect your actions and words have on the world around you. Learn to recognize the difference between just going about the motions of life and completely participating in your life experience. It is so easy now to feel your attention drawn away from the moment into what "could be." The "now" is your doorway to the future.

During your periods of contemplation or meditation, make sure you are allowing yourself to thoroughly relax. Try some comforting herbal teas—such as chamomile, hops, or passion flower—when you sit down for the evening. Close your eyes and fill your mind with the colors of peace: blues, indigo, violet. Then envision a beautiful golden star. Feel yourself drawn into this light, which permeates every cell of your being. Know that at any time you can link with this force to awaken your mind and connect you to the Source of All Knowledge.

Affirmation for the Year

"My mind is open, my heart is free
and I am filled with joy!"

ACTION TABLES FOR GEMINI

These dates reflect the best (but not the only) times for success and ease in these activities according to your Sun Sign.

Change Residence	Aug. 10–28
Request a Raise	May 29–30
Begin a Course of Study	Jan. 30–31; July 27
Visit a Doctor	Apr. 17–May 4; Nov. 4–21
Start a Diet	Jan. 24–25; Feb. 20–21; Mar. 19–20; Apr. 16–17; May 13–14; June 9–10; July 7–8; Aug. 3–4, 30–31; Sep. 27, 28; Oct. 24–25; Nov. 20–21; Dec. 18–19
Begin a Romance	Sep. 24–25
Join a Club	Mar. 31
Seek Employment	Mar. 15–Apr. 1; Nov. 4–21
Take a Vacation	Jan. 3–4, 30–31; Feb. 26–27; Mar. 26–27; Apr. 22–23; May 19–20; June 15–16; July 13–14; Aug. 9–10; Sep. 6–7; Oct. 3–4, 30–31; Nov. 26–27; Dec. 24–25
Change Your Wardrobe	Aug. 29–Nov. 4
End a Relationship	June 13
Seek Professional Advice	Jan. 26–27; Feb. 22–23; Mar. 21–22; Apr. 18–19; May 15–16; June 11–12; July 9–10; Aug. 5–6; Sep. 1–2, 29–30; Oct. 26–27, Nov. 22–23; Dec. 20–21
Have a Makeover	May 29–30
Obtain a Loan	Jan. 28–29; Feb. 24–25; Mar. 23–24; Apr. 20–21; May 17–18; June 13–14; July 11–12; Aug. 7–8; Sep. 3–4; Oct. 1–2, 28–29; Nov. 24–25; Dec. 22–23

PRIMARY FOCUS

Travel may figure prominently in your schedule, but to avoid conflict on the home front be sure to stay alert to those demands rather than creating too much distance.

HEALTH AND FITNESS

Careful evaluation of your physical needs now helps to provide the best directions for increasing your physical energy level. Use caution or avoid high risk situations from the 12th–23rd.

ROMANCE AND RELATIONSHIPS

Although your intention may be to restore balance and harmony in your relationship, you may find that things seem to spiral out of control more easily. Expectations can be a real problem, and it is crucial that you avoid the temptation to allow others to believe what they want instead of setting them straight. Honest expression of your needs and feelings brings better results. Sexual tension may be high during the Full Moon on the 16th. Seek areas in which you share ideals or beliefs after the New Moon on the 30th.

FINANCE AND CAREER

Jointly held finances can be a headache from the 1st–6th, when it's better to wait for turmoil to die down before you make a final decision. Contracts or legal concerns move forward from the 6th–16th, but can escalate into powerful battles for the remainder of the month. Once Mercury begins its retrograde cycle on the 25th, review career concerns and seek a solution.

OPPORTUNITY OF THE MONTH

Negotiations flow more smoothly on the 12th and 13th, although you may still have to give way to a conservative course of action.

Rewarding Days: 3, 7, 8, 12, 13, 17, 22, 30, 31
Challenging Days: 1, 2, 5, 6, 15, 16, 19, 20, 26, 27

AFFIRMATION FOR THE MONTH
"I am an attentive listener"

PRIMARY FOCUS

Educational pursuits, travel, or teaching offer opportunities for professional advancement. However, you may see more promises than direct results!

HEALTH AND FITNESS

You'll make progress by finding a healthier way to handle stress. Concentrate on increasing flexibility.

ROMANCE AND RELATIONSHIPS

You and your partner may not agree on some major changes in your relationship, but at least you can start talking about your concerns. Repressing your feelings now will only damage the integrity of your relationship, and if expressing your needs causes problems, then you need to reevaluate the relationship! The Full Moon on the 15th marks a powerful time for reaching consensus. You may also discover that some discontent results from circumstances in your distant past which are unresolved. Forgive yourself.

FINANCE AND CAREER

Meetings, conferences, negotiations, and presentations are the order of the day this month, but you may feel that they produce minimal results. Every time you move forward, there may be two steps back. Get to the core of everybody's fear, since that is really what is blocking progress! Once Mercury leaves retrograde on the 15th, you may still be dealing with the same issues, but all the hidden agendas should be more apparent.

OPPORTUNITY OF THE MONTH

Even though it may seem everyone has lost their sense of humor, be sure to maintain your wit as a means to stay objective!

Rewarding Days: 4, 8, 9, 13, 14, 18, 19, 26, 27
Challenging Days: 1, 2, 3, 12, 16, 17, 21, 22, 23, 28

AFFIRMATION FOR THE MONTH
"I am clearly aware of my feelings."

PRIMARY FOCUS

Advancement in your career is most likely through your efforts in enhancing education, writing, teaching, or traveling. Focused attention to your goals is important now.

HEALTH AND FITNESS

Activities which raise your energy level, such as aerobic forms of exercise, cycling, walking, or running improve your stamina and release some of the stress you feel.

ROMANCE AND RELATIONSHIPS

Breathe new life into your relationship by sharing travel from the 3rd–27th. Even if you're away on business, you might still have time for romance, although you're likely to feel stronger stress on all fronts from the 12th through the Full Moon on the 16th. Promises you make will be taken seriously now, so be sure you know what you really want before you take decisive action. Pressures from family may seem unreasonable after the 15th, and you'll have more control over the situation by maintaining a solid position.

FINANCE AND CAREER

Your intellectual prowess shines, and you may have to use your quick wits to get you out of a jam from the New Moon on the 1st to the 6th. Stay alert to solutions to problems, and act quickly to resolve situations which have been dragging on too long. Stubborn resistance from the 10th–17th may slow things down, but doesn't have to cripple your efforts. Long-term investments need careful scrutiny now, and may fare best later on. Be patient.

OPPORTUNITY OF THE MONTH

If everything seems to come to a grinding halt, wait until the New Moon on the 30th to act, when greater momentum overcomes resistance.

Rewarding Days: 3, 8, 9, 13, 17, 18, 26, 30, 31
Challenging Days: 1, 2, 12, 15, 16, 21, 22, 28, 29

AFFIRMATION FOR THE MONTH
"I have faith in myself."

♊ GEMINI/APRIL ♊

PRIMARY FOCUS
Friends, lovers, and children can bring great delight into your life, and may even play an important role in helping advance your career. Enjoy yourself, but stay on track.

HEALTH AND FITNESS
Team sports or group fitness activities are highly enjoyable and may even give you a chance to experience a new level of fitness. Take time to do some "inner fitness" work after the 19th.

ROMANCE AND RELATIONSHIPS
Through the Moon's Eclipse on the 15th, you may feel solid improvement, both giving and receiving love. Concentrate on opening to the experience of love in your life and incorporate this fullness by trusting your creative energy more completely. A confrontation with unresolved issues from your past can be more easily conquered by finding positive support from a counselor, or, at the least, honest communication with your inner self during the Solar Eclipse on the 29th. Develop trust.

FINANCE AND CAREER
Building stronger alliances with others in your professional field or within your local community can bring some much needed excitement into your career. You may still be struggling to please a demanding boss or deal with regulations which seem to limit your options, but these are beginning to be less problematic. Diversity works to your benefit from the 9th–15th, but pull in the reins a bit from the 16th–21st. Spend frugally, since everything is tempting this month!

OPPORTUNITY OF THE MONTH
Others may be more open to trying a different approach, so launch plans on the 4th and 5th and follow through.

Rewarding Days: 4, 5, 9, 10, 14, 22, 23, 26, 27
Challenging Days: 7, 11, 12, 18, 19, 24, 25

AFFIRMATION FOR THE MONTH
"I am alert and prepared when changes occur."

PRIMARY FOCUS

Increase effectiveness in communication by improving your speaking, writing, and listening skills. Reach out and network with others. Take opportunities to connect!

HEALTH AND FITNESS

Stay active, but allow time to pull back and relax. Inner work, such as meditation, or contemplative activities such as yoga or Tai Chi can help balance and vitality.

ROMANCE AND RELATIONSHIPS

Socializing with friends gives you a lift through the 15th, and may provide an opportunity to meet someone new. However, jumping into an untried romance from the 11th–18th may leave you feeling a bit vulnerable. Enjoy the fireworks, but wait a while before you decide on anything long-term. An existing relationship can try your patience, especially if you are each unwilling to pay attention to your real needs. Talk about your concerns, and be ready to take a fresh approach by the time of the Gemini New Moon on the 29th.

FINANCE AND CAREER

Get organized in your work, since allowing too much unfinished business to clutter your desk will only be distracting. If you've been putting off addressing work-related issues, the Full Moon on the 14th is likely to bring the situation to a peak. Meetings or presentations can be successful, and any contacts made after Mercury turns retrograde on the 24th may open the door for further exploration. Final decisions are more likely next month.

OPPORTUNITY OF THE MONTH

Make the most of Mercury's retrograde May 24–June 17 by making your new contacts early this month and following up after the 24th.

Rewarding Days: 1, 2, 3, 6, 7, 11, 12, 19, 20, 29, 30
Challenging Days: 9, 10, 13, 15, 16, 21, 22, 24

AFFIRMATION FOR THE MONTH
"I am alert, incisive and clear."

♊ GEMINI/JUNE ♊

PRIMARY FOCUS
Your creative ideas can save the day, giving you a chance to advance in your career, but you also need to enhance personal fulfillment by developing emotional needs.

HEALTH AND FITNESS
Nervous tension and emotional stress take their toll on your body unless you make a special effort to relieve them. Be sure you're getting plenty of foods high in B-vitamins now—you need them!

ROMANCE AND RELATIONSHIPS
Your desire for some real romance may be frustrated by emotions that simply do not make any sense (they rarely do!). Pay special attention to any feelings of anger which seem to get in the way. Follow your heart instead of just trying to please everyone else, including parents. Partnerships are emphasized during the Full Moon on the 12th, and this is a good time to think about the future. You can easily accept love, but tend to anticipate, which can take away from the joy of the moment.

FINANCE AND CAREER
Carefully examine all documents and follow through on all communication, especially if you will be held responsible! Legal or contractual agreements may be in dispute from the 8th–24th—the more attentive you are to details, the happier you will be with the results. Curb unnecessary spending, and eliminate activities in work which are too costly or wasteful, particularly mid-month. Launch new work projects after the New Moon on the 27th.

OPPORTUNITY OF THE MONTH
Your intuitive insights are working overtime, although you may be frustrated with yourself for not listening to them. Pay attention!

Rewarding Days: 3, 7, 8, 15, 16, 20, 21, 25, 26, 30
Challenging Days: 1, 5, 6, 11, 12, 13, 18, 19

AFFIRMATION FOR THE MONTH
"I respect my intuitive awareness."

PRIMARY FOCUS

Power struggles with those in positions of superiority can escalate, and it may seem the effort is useless. Before you give up, take another look.

HEALTH AND FITNESS

Stress can undermine your vitality now unless you find ways to release tension. Stretch, dance, breathe and bend! Schedule a massage on the 7th, 8th, 12th, 22nd or 23rd.

ROMANCE AND RELATIONSHIPS

Family friction can intensify now, especially if you've been avoiding your feelings or allowing someone else to control your actions. Through the Full Moon on the 12th, Mars and Saturn are building an energy of increasing tension. Deal honestly with any anger which emerges, especially if you feel disappointed. Find ways to bolster your self-esteem. Love flows much easier after the 22nd, when you may be more confident in expressing your needs and more open about your desires. The New Moon stimulates hope on the 27th.

FINANCE AND CAREER

Stay strong in your position and go into presentations or meetings armed with facts and evidence to sway your audience from the 1st–8th. Forward progress may seem to grind to a halt from the 5th–15th, but patience will be rewarding. If your test of a situation fails during this time, regroup and plan to take a new approach after the 27th. Be conservative in spending or investing, and especially so from the 23rd–30th when you can be gullible.

OPPORTUNITY OF THE MONTH

Now's the time to test an idea, project, or even a relationship for its relevance and to determine the best way to make improvements.

Rewarding Days: 1, 5, 13, 14, 17, 18, 22, 23, 27, 28
Challenging Days: 2, 3, 9, 10, 12, 15, 16, 30, 31

AFFIRMATION FOR THE MONTH
"I am strong in the face of adversity."

PRIMARY FOCUS

Bring vast improvement into your love life by taking an active part in pursuing the fulfillment of your desires and expression of your feelings and needs.

HEALTH AND FITNESS

Recreation or sports activities which you truly enjoy not only improve your vitality, but also may increase your zest for life. Pay more attention and avoid taking great risks after the 27th.

ROMANCE AND RELATIONSHIPS

Your confidence in expressing the love you feel allows you to reach out with greater openness. A new relationship beginning now shows great promise, and an existing one can be significantly enhanced by sharing activities which are pleasurable and entertaining. Travel, even for a short period, can be especially memorable from the 1st thru the Full Moon on the 10th. Priorities on the home front increase after the New Moon on the 25th.

FINANCE AND CAREER

Business travel, conferences, or presentations provide an exceptional opportunity to advance your position through the 20th. Differences in opinions or ethics may prompt you to reconsider your loyalties after that time. Your alertness to any undermining or hidden agendas can make the difference between success and failure. Investments show great promise (and even rewards) through the 12th, but discretion in spending is warranted after that time.

OPPORTUNITY OF THE MONTH

The alliances you create from the 1st–10th can become part of a powerful network supporting the development of your career.

Rewarding Days: 1, 2, 9, 10, 14, 18, 19, 20, 28, 29
Challenging Days: 5, 6, 11, 12, 26, 27, 31

AFFIRMATION FOR THE MONTH
"My words are inspired by truth and wisdom."

PRIMARY FOCUS

Creative inspiration stimulates excitement and activity which can further your career and enhance your personal satisfaction. Any writing or communicative activities can be advantageous.

HEALTH AND FITNESS

Adjust your schedule to have plenty of time for physical activity. However, watch a tendency to be easily distracted or to push beyond your limits.

ROMANCE AND RELATIONSHIPS

From the 1st–5th, although you may be highly attracted to someone, you may take inappropriate actions which leave the wrong impression. Think before you speak or act! The Full Moon on the 8th offers an opportunity to mend past misunderstandings by taking full responsibility for your own actions, particularly in relationship with family, including relinquishing responsibilities which belong to someone else. Romance improves after the 17th, and the New Moon on the 24th can open the way for a gratifying flow of loving energy.

FINANCE AND CAREER

This is an excellent time to begin a creative project which will require about ten weeks, especially if you begin before the 7th. Getting started after the 24th is also workable, but you may run into unfinished business which brings delays due to Mercury's retrograde cycle from Sep. 22–Oct. 13. Even in the midst of hard work, there's time to enjoy the rewards. Cooperate with requests for business-related social activities after the 14th.

OPPORTUNITY OF THE MONTH

Presentations on the 2nd, 3rd, 6th, 15th, 16th, or 24th help you establish a new level of respect and expertise.

Rewarding Days: 6, 7, 10, 11, 15, 16, 20, 24, 25
Challenging Days: 1, 2, 8, 9, 18, 22, 23, 29, 30

AFFIRMATION FOR THE MONTH
"I am confident in my creative abilities."

PRIMARY FOCUS

If you're "sick of your job," then it's time to make some changes. If reforms in your attitude or in the situation do not suffice, you may want to consider a new position.

HEALTH AND FITNESS

Physical health problems and emotional upset are powerfully tied to one another now. To improve your well-being, be sure you're in touch with your emotional feelings at the core of the symptoms.

ROMANCE AND RELATIONSHIPS

Open dialogue in your personal relationships can be a creative and rewarding process now. The Lunar Eclipse on the 8th marks a powerful time to share your feelings of love, and may help you clarify your real feelings. Also, situations you've outgrown can come to a point of closure. A new attraction from the 1st–9th may be infatuation—give it time before you jump to a conclusion. In an existing relationship, find inventive ways to achieve deeper levels of intimacy from the 6th–14th and from the 22nd–31st.

FINANCE AND CAREER

Poor communication can lead to power struggles in your work. You can diffuse some time-bombs by attentive observation and listening. If political conflicts arise, determine where you stand before you act, since you may be tempted to switch loyalties! Thoroughly research the facts you present from the 13th–21st, since you can be influential and may be held accountable for this information near the time of the Solar Eclipse on the 23rd.

OPPORTUNITY OF THE MONTH

Keep a cool head in the midst of the chaos and you can rise to the top quite quickly from the 1st–8th.

Rewarding Days: 3, 4, 7, 8, 12, 13, 17, 18, 22, 30, 31
Challenging Days: 2, 5, 6, 11, 19, 20, 21, 26, 27

AFFIRMATION FOR THE MONTH
"I trust my creative insights."

PRIMARY FOCUS

Your patience wears thin this month. Apply your excessive energy toward an important career project, but realize that most people will not be able to keep your pace!

HEALTH AND FITNESS

With a tendency to burn the candle at both ends, it's easy to exhaust yourself before you know it! Be especially aware of your physical needs from the 8th–24th, when stress levels are peaking.

ROMANCE AND RELATIONSHIPS

Partnerships can be steamy with Mars, Venus, and Jupiter transiting your Solar 7th House. A committed relationship needs some fresh energy now. Find exciting ways to improve sexual intimacy. A casual relationship can get serious, but you may resist making a commitment. Look at your fears and honestly talk about them with a trusted advisor near the time of the Full Moon on the 7th. The "heaviness" seems to lift after the 22nd, when you can begin again with more confidence.

FINANCE AND CAREER

Everyone has expectations of you now, and you may feel pressured by their demands. If you've been staying on top of things, and know where you stand professionally, you can meet those demands. But if you've been playing around, then you may have to work double-time to meet all the responsibilities. Concentrate on priorities. Take a serious look at your finances after the New Moon on the 22nd, when reorganizing can give you breathing room.

OPPORTUNITY OF THE MONTH

Social contacts can lead to exceptional occasions for meeting the right people at the right time from the 8th–10th and 18th–27th.

Rewarding Days: 4, 5, 8, 9, 10, 13, 18, 19, 26, 27
Challenging Days: , 2, 16, 17, 20, 21, 22, 23, 29, 30

AFFIRMATION FOR THE MONTH
"I am centered and aware of my personal boundaries."

PRIMARY FOCUS

Joining forces with others provides a chance for sure financial success, and may give you a solid basis from which to launch a creative project. Just read the fine print!

HEALTH AND FITNESS

If you've had questions about a physical complaint, research or testing reveals the root causes of the problem. Speed your way toward healing by eliminating factors which drain your energy.

ROMANCE AND RELATIONSHIPS

Improve your sex life by discovering exceptional ways to achieve pleasure. Share your fantasies, and concentrate on both giving and receiving energy from one another, especially during the Gemini Full Moon on the 6th. A distraction or flirtation from the 15th–20th can be more trouble than it's worth, but if you are really available to explore the possibilities, you may have uncovered something highly unusual. Just be sure you can afford it! Travel can spark romance after the New Moon on the 21st.

FINANCE AND CAREER

Jointly held finances can be both a source of strength and a point of contention. If you are in dispute over financial problems, then the battle escalates from the 1st–6th, and then may become mired by details and the introduction of a red herring after the 15th. Research is highly fruitful this month, helping you to uncover some previously overlooked details. With this knowledge, you can be more convincing and can generate stronger support.

OPPORTUNITY OF THE MONTH

With strong efforts on your part from the 1st–6th, you can generate support that will follow you for years.

Rewarding Days: 1, 2, 6, 7, 11, 12, 16, 24, 25, 28, 29
Challenging Days: 4, 9, 13, 14, 20, 21, 26, 27

AFFIRMATION FOR THE MONTH
"I gladly release my attachments
to things I no longer need."

CANCER
The Crab

June 22 to July 23

Element: Water

Quality: Mutable

Polarity: Feminine/Yin

Planetary Ruler: Moon

Meditation: "I am aware of my inner feelings"

Gemstone: Pearl

Power Stones: Moonstone, chrysocolla

Glyph: Breast or crab claws

Key Phrase: "I feel"

Anatomy: Stomach, breasts

Colors: Silver, pearl, white

Animal: Crustaceans, cows, chickens

Myths/Legends: Hecate, Asherah, Hercules and the Crab

House Association: 4th

Opposite Sign: Capricorn

Flower: Larkspur

Key Word: Receptivity

Positive Expression:

Sensitive
Tenderhearted
Tenacious
Concerned
Sympathetic
Protective
Intuitive
Patriotic
Maternal
Nurturing

Misuse of Energy:

Moody
Smothering
Manipulative
Anxious
Defensive
Brooding
Suspicious
Isolationistic
Crabby
Insecure

♋ CANCER ♋

Your Ego's Strengths and Weaknesses

Growth is the essence of your vitality. As "The Nurturer" of the zodiac, you can provide comfort, support, and understanding to others around you. Your family may seem like an extension of yourself, and you may find that you create a sense of family with others wherever you may be.

You may have a well-defined psychic sensitivity and a strong ability to sense what is happening beneath the surface. Your easy and natural connection to the Moon, which represents the quality of cyclical change, encourages you to accept the processes of evolution which flow with the rhythm of life. Your surroundings need to reflect an atmosphere of ease, and you may enjoy creating a cozy warmth through crafts, cooking, or other related activities.

You have a deep reverence for the past, which you may sometimes use as an excuse to avoid making change. Allow this sensibility to provide part of your inner security instead of insulation against growth. It's also just as easy to forget your boundaries and become smothering when you really intended to be comforting. Remember that what you instill in those you care for goes with them, even when they've moved out of the nest.

Through your concern for maintaining a high quality of life, you can help to sustain your connection to the essence of the Divine Feminine. To keep this energy flowing smoothly, you need only learn the lesson of the cycles—"for everything there is a season."

Your Approach to Romance

As an expert in "hug-therapy," you can be a supportive partner and seek a relationship which will mature through caring for one another and creating a sense of family. Since you tend to feel the emotions of those around you, it might be difficult to keep positive boundaries in a love relationship, but remember that you alone are not responsible for the happiness of the one you love.

And watch your own tendency to withdraw when you're feeling hurt instead of seeking the comfort and closeness you crave.

Getting along with the other water signs—Scorpio, Pisces, and Cancer—may be easier, since you each understand the importance of emotional sensitivity. With Cancer, you can merge your energies to develop a strong family and home life as a foundation for your relationship. Scorpio encourages you to trust your deeper passions and develop your creativity. The mystical imagination of Pisces inspires you to reach beyond your limits.

Although you may be strongly attracted to Aries, you can be easily burned. Taurus provides a safe support, helping you develop your hopes and dreams. Watch your tendency to mother a playful Gemini, who may have different ideas. Leo definitely loves the attentiveness you offer, but might not give back in kind. As an understanding partner, Virgo provides a good base for your free self-expression.

Libra may seem too detached when you want their support, and can throw you off-balance. And, although you enjoy the presence of a Sagittarian, you have to be willing to give them plenty of freedom. You're likely to be strongly attracted to your opposite, Capricorn, whose determination to succeed creates a strong foothold for your own security. Intimate surroundings may not fit with Aquarius, who, for you, is a more reliable confidant than lover.

Your Career Development

Develop your special awareness of the energy around you to assure your career success. With your ability to hold onto your assets and possessions, you may become quite wealthy and influential. Your pride in your nation or community may lead you to pursue a political career. Teaching may feel natural for you, and you might also enjoy history, anthropology, or archaeology. Any position of prominence can be suitable, and your aptitude for influencing others can assist your climb up the ladder.

Working in the restaurant business, hotel industry, home furnishings, antiques, or real estate businesses may be enjoyable and lucrative for you. Or, you may prefer to use your enviable green thumb in landscaping or the floral industry. The medical field can be an excellent outlet for your desire to care for others, and you can also be an effective counselor.

Your Use of Power

You feel most powerful when you know you can take care of not only today, but that you're also prepared for that inevitable "rainy day!" Your own emotional nature can provide a positive environment for your personal growth while encouraging the growth of others, building a powerful foundation for long-term stability. Your energy may provide a haven in the storm, ingratiating others and offering you a wide range of influence.

You might find that your most powerful position is within your family, but in a business, you can also create a feeling of family, forging a network of devoted individuals who share a common goal. You tend to allow the traditions from the past inhibit your power, unless you can find a way to reshape the traditions within the new framework of current trends. Your most profound sense of power emerges when you feel secure and know that you and those you love are sheltered from harm and have an opportunity for future growth. In order to stay strong, you must maintain an open awareness of your own needs and continue to find ways to remain connected to the Source which constantly fills and sustains you.

Famous Cancers

P. T. Barnum, Diahann Carroll, Bill Cosby, Brian Dennehy, Bill Haley, Angelica Huston, Richard Lewis, Gustav Mahler, Amedeo Modigliani, Richard Petty, Rembrandt, Richard Rodgers, Carly Simon, John Tesh, Clarence Thomas

THE YEAR AHEAD FOR CANCER

This is a year to set meaningful goals for your personal and professional growth. You may be concentrating on increasing your knowledge or expertise and can have many opportunities to stabilize your understanding of the wide variety of cultural, social, and educational experiences blanketing the world. Outreach within your community is important, and may take many forms. By making connections now, you assure a more consistent level of growth for your future.

The planets Uranus and Pluto change signs this year, but only briefly; then they retrograde back to their last degrees of Capricorn (Uranus) and Scorpio (Pluto). This brief ingress of Uranus into its ruler, Aquarius, and Pluto into Sagittarius provides a preview of the energy forces which will work at a collective level to bring about significant changes well into the next decade. The impact of these changes for you is likely to be felt most strongly in your attitudes toward physical health and deeply held emotional attachments. Allow time to develop a stronger connection to your inner being, surrendering to the possibilities of personal transformation and healing which will affect your life through the remainder of this century.

Jupiter's transit in Sagittarius throughout the entire year brings opportunities to improve your physical health, but may also provide the temptation to take your physical needs for granted. By working with this energy to increase your stamina and vitality, you can affect positive radical changes in your sense of well-being. But it is crucial that you examine your attitudes toward taking care of yourself, since over-extending now can be quite costly next year! In addition to the physical focus, this cycle also emphasizes a need to create better circumstances in which to work. You may need more independence and room to grow than you've wanted in the past, but it is up to you to find the best avenues to make these alterations. If you work with others, this is an exceptional time to become positively involved in creating a better support system for one another.

The Solar Eclipses during 1995 draw your attention to your experience of giving and receiving love. Increasing your creative output may seem important, and you may also have more emphasis on activities which involve children and family. One critical factor during the April 29 Eclipse connects to your willingness to open and receive the support and love you need from others. Whether friends, family, or lovers, this cycle challenges you to locate any blocks you may have created and release them in the name of love. You also have a chance to give more of yourself in ways which can enhance your growth and self-awareness.

If you were born from June 22–24, you're experiencing a series of adjustments while Uranus and Pluto both transit in quincunx to your Sun. These transiting planets form a planetary aspect pattern with your Sun called a "yod" (which I call the fickle finger of Fate!). This pattern indicates a period during which your awareness of yourself and your needs undergoes major changes. Not only is it important to realign your priorities, but also you may find that many of your life situations take on a different meaning. Of critical importance is your attention to your physical health, since this time can mark a period of powerful healing and it can also bring to the surface situations which may have gone undetected in the past. By taking action now, you may be able to literally turn your life around! Your personal relationships are also changing, since your needs now are likely to be significantly different than they were in the past. Trying to hang onto things that have outgrown their usefulness can now be quite a problem, since this cycle is all about fine-tuning and moving forward with the changing times. This includes your old attitudes toward the way you handle your needs for intimacy. Some of your barriers may be the result of circumstances which occurred long ago, and although they may have been difficult or traumatic, you can move beyond them now. It's time to clear away all those old cobwebs, open the windows and doors, and let your Sun shine!

For Cancerians born from June 25–29, it's time to use your talents and add your special expressive touch while Pluto transits in biquintile to your Sun. Although this period is not filled with a powerful identity crisis, this can be a time of some challenge to your creativity. You're needing to feel that life offers a chance for you to enjoy something exceptional, and if you do not see it around you, then perhaps you can produce it by digging deeply into yourself and trusting that creative power which lies at the center of your Being. This cycle can be like adding icing to the cake!

If you were born from June 29–July 19, the focused energy of Saturn transiting in trine to your Sun encourages you to become more positively aware of your personal responsibilities. This can be a highly productive cycle for your career, and is especially important if you are involved in educational or legal pursuits, teaching, political action, writing, or publishing. If you are working toward establishing a particular level of expertise or enhancing your professional reputation in some way, then this period can be significant in its effects. Also, if you've been uncertain about your abilities, this can be the time to prove to yourself that you can accomplish your aims. However, if you fail to apply yourself during this period, you may feel that you have lost valuable time. By making a realistic assessment of your circumstances and setting your goals accordingly, you may see tremendous gains. Any Saturn cycle implies some type of restraint, although this particular period may involve more choice on your part. This is a time to take control of your life situation and decide for yourself the directions you want to pursue.

However, if you were born from June 28–July 2, you may be tempted to overextend your obligations from June through September of this year, since Jupiter is traveling in an irritating quincunx to your Sun. Even though you may have a certain amount of self-discipline thanks to Saturn's cycle (above), you may still feel that you can push beyond your limits. If you do, you'll probably get a quick lesson in instant karma—finding out right away that you have to stay on track! This is an excellent time to promote yourself, your business, or your talents, and receive excellent feedback and create a better reputation. Just be sure you can deliver what you promise!

Neptune is opposing your Sun this year if you were born from July 14–20. This can be a period of some confusion, since what you think you perceive may not be the reality in all cases. Your imagination can easily work overtime, which is useful if you have a career in the arts, literature, or other highly creative areas, but on the side of everyday activities, reality can seem rather dull compared to the possibilities you're entertaining! You may feel that you're ready for some true romance, and you can be drawn to look for it in situations which are not what they seem to be. This period is designed to help you dissolve some of your attachments, and is quite helpful in your spiritual growth if you maintain an honest connection with yourself, but there is a tendency to view others as saviors and yourself as a martyr. If relationship problems occur, ask yourself if you are being realistic. You may be expecting another person to show their best side, when all you really see is their neediness. You can also experience the healing which arises from forgiveness of yourself and others. Look for ways to strengthen your spiritual life. Honor and respect your deep longings, dreams, and visions. Know that you deserve love and compassion. Then, when you do reach out to others, your compassion and warmth will embrace the situation, bringing real fulfillment instead of just feeling that you've exhausted all your energy on a situation which has only taken from you and given nothing in return.

You're breaking away from some old restraints and expressing more of your uniqueness this year if you were born from July 18–23. Uranus is transiting in opposition to your Sun, and may stimulate a feeling of revolutionary change. This is an excellent time to review your personal relationships and to break out of stagnant circumstances. You can breathe new life into a stale relationship by allowing yourself to be more expressive of your needs. Awaken the passion and power which reside deep within you. If, in the past, you've felt restricted by a situation, then you are ready now to break free. Things which are no longer useful to your growth lose their purpose in your life during this cycle. Opportunities to make changes may seem to arise out of nowhere. Expect the unexpected now—and don't be surprised if other people seem to comment on the changes you've made or are making. In fact, once this period is over, you may not even recognize yourself!

Pluto is transiting in trine aspect to your Sun this year if you were born from July 18–23. Combined with the influence of the Uranus cycle described above, you may be more willing to release the things from your past which are no longer relevant to your life. This does not mean that situations which are still vital and meaningful cease to exist. In fact, you may even be able to restore vitality to situations, relationships, or yourself which had seemed to be lost. This is a time to restore and rejuvenate, but within the context of eliminating elements which inhibit that growth.

Tools to Make a Difference

Consolidate your efforts as much as possible now, since it is tempting to scatter your energy a bit. Find ways to bring the spiritual aspect of your life into your everyday life experience, instead of finding isolated times to experience spirituality. Listen to your own thoughts; find ways to affirm your own value and worth.

Pay special attention to your diet. Try to add high vitality foods and investigate the addition of herbs if you aren't already using them. You might be especially fond of soups and sauces which have an herbal flair. Also, this is an important time to increase your awareness of your physical body. T'ai Chi, yoga, or martial arts might be especially interesting now, since you are likely to be drawn to a system which has a strong philosophical or spiritual basis.

In your meditations, concentrate on finding a quiet, comforting aspect of your inner self. See yourself kneeling beside a clear, pure stream of water. Drink this water, knowing that it flows from the Source of All Life. Feel an ease and flow in your life force as it moves through your body. Be whole. Be well. Be filled.

Affirmation for the Year

"I am filled with joy, love, and strong vitality."

ACTION TABLES FOR CANCER

These dates reflect the best (but not the only) times for success and ease in these activities according to your Sun Sign.

Change Residence	Aug. 29–Sep. 21; Oct. 15–Nov. 3
Request a Raise	June 28–29
Begin a Course of Study	Mar. 11–12; Aug. 26–27
Visit a Doctor	May 2–July 9; Nov. 23–Dec. 10
Start a Diet	Jan. 26–27; Feb. 22–23; Mar. 21–22; Apr. 18–19; May 15–16; June 11–12; July 9–10; Aug. 5–6; Sep. 1–2, 29–30; Oct. 26–27; Nov. 23–24; Dec. 20–21
Begin a Romance	Oct. 24, 25
Join a Club	Apr. 29, 30
Seek Employment	Apr. 2–16; Nov. 23–Dec. 11
Take a Vacation	Jan. 5–6; Feb. 1–2, 28; Mar. 1–2, 28–29; Apr. 24–25; May 21–22; June 18–19; July 15–16; Aug. 11–12; Sep. 8–9; Oct. 5–6; Nov. 1–2; 29–30; Dec. 26–27
Change Your Wardrobe	Nov. 4–21
End a Relationship	July 21–22
Seek Professional Advice	Jan. 28–29; Feb. 24–25; Mar. 24; Apr. 20–21; May 17–18; June 13–14; July 11–12; Aug. 7–8; Sep. 4–5; Oct. 1–2, 28–29; Nov. 24–25; Dec. 22–23
Have a Makeover	June 28–29
Obtain a Loan	Jan. 30–31; Feb. 26–27; Mar. 26–27; Apr. 22–23; May 19–20; June 15–16; July 13–14; Aug. 9–10; Sep. 6–7; Oct. 30–31; Nov. 26–27; Dec. 24–25

PRIMARY FOCUS

Networking with others in your field helps you build confidence and may offer a chance to improve prospects for advancement in your career. Reach out and participate!

HEALTH AND FITNESS

Although you may be sincere about improving your health, it's easy to overindulge in foods or adopt a lazy attitude. Begin a program of solid nutrition.

ROMANCE AND RELATIONSHIPS

Frank discussions about emotional and physical needs in an intimate relationship offer you a chance to explore more effective avenues to true fulfillment. The New Moon on the 1st stimulates an honest look at partnership and social ties. It's time to own up to your real needs, or you may find yourself feeling quite dissatisfied by the 16th, during the Cancer Full Moon. Old resentment can raise its head from the 14th–23rd, when openness is difficult, but you can release a grudge by really communicating.

FINANCE AND CAREER

Your work load and increasing responsibilities may take more of your time. Before you jump at a chance for advancement, investigate the offer. Conditions may require you to repair a badly damaged situation. Jealousy or undermining can be diffused by documenting your actions and creating strong alliances. Watch your spending, especially after the 25th, when Mercury turns retrograde. The New Moon on the 30th marks a good time to review taxes.

OPPORTUNITY OF THE MONTH

Strike a balance in negotiations from the 13th–16th, but watch for power plays, since you can become caught in an old battle.

Rewarding Days: 1, 5, 6, 10, 11, 15, 16, 20, 24
Challenging Days: 3, 7, 8, 21, 22, 26, 28, 29

AFFIRMATION FOR THE MONTH
"I am whole, healthy, and powerful."

PRIMARY FOCUS

Even though you may feel that it's time to be recognized for your expertise or knowledge, you still may have to put forth extra effort to be noticed this month. Maintain your priorities.

HEALTH AND FITNESS

Stress on the job can take its physical toll, especially if you fail to release tension. Do yoga, stretch, dance, or swim. Schedule a massage on the 15th.

ROMANCE AND RELATIONSHIPS

If you're feeling unappreciated, look at the things you do to show appreciation to yourself! Your self-worth is under scrutiny now, and if you feel vulnerable it could be because you have not been taking care of your own needs. You may be tempted to leave a relationship which is not offering the support and understanding you require, but before you do, take time near the Full Moon on the 15th to look into your attachments to the past. It's time to release old baggage and move into a brighter future.

FINANCE AND CAREER

If you've been holding the bag for someone else, reconsider. You may be losing valuable energy or time and damaging your own reputation. Carefully explore financial obligations before you take on any more debts during Mercury's retrograde through the 15th. Business conferences give you a chance for important growth from the 20th–28th. However, there can be confusion over details after the 26th, so get the facts straight.

OPPORTUNITY OF THE MONTH

Achieve greater personal fulfillment by giving more of yourself on the 20th and 21st, but remember to allow yourself to receive, too.

Rewarding Days: 2, 3, 11, 12, 16, 21, 22, 25, 26
Challenging Days: 1, 6, 7, 13, 14, 15, 27, 28

AFFIRMATION FOR THE MONTH
"I am inspired by a higher truth."

PRIMARY FOCUS

Making the best use of your resources, including time,
allows you to accelerate career growth. Take a responsible attitude toward improving your knowledge about
your wo k.

HEALTH AND FITNESS

Build stamina and endurance by remaining active, even
if you have to squeeze it into your schedule. Careful
attention to diet mid-month helps improve energy.

ROMANCE AND RELATIONSHIPS

Disagreements over "yours versus mine" can permeate
everything from your love life and emotional needs, to
possessions and career success. If you've been feeling
unappreciated, turn the tide by honestly appreciating
yourself more. Then, be sure to compliment your partner,
friends, and family from the 1st–4th. Bring greater emphasis to the spiritual elements of your life during the Full
Moon on the 16th. Travel or cultural events may offer new
light in your love life from the 14st–31st.

FINANCE AND CAREER

Take advantage of conferences or presentations as a way
to advance your career this month. When presenting
plans, double-check your evaluations of time and money
required to complete a project. In your personal finances,
keep a close watch on expenditures, especially with a
major purchase planned after the 20th. Your efforts shine
in educational pursuits, despite the challenges. Take
leadership positions after the New Moon on the 30th.

OPPORTUNITY OF THE MONTH

The New Moon on the 1st stimulates a positive period of
reaching beyond your old limitations into new horizons.
Go for it!

Rewarding Days: 1, 5, 6, 10, 11, 15, 16, 20, 28, 29
Challenging Days: 3, 4, 8, 17, 18, 23, 24, 25, 30, 31

AFFIRMATION FOR THE MONTH
"My thoughts are guided by Divine Wisdom."

Everything is likely to revolve around work now, and your ability to deal with those in dominant positions is tested. Ameliorate tensions by encouraging better communication and avoiding innuendo.

HEALTH AND FITNESS

Take some time away from your routine to relax your mind, which may seem to be running nonstop. Meditation can be a powerful healing tool during this busy period.

ROMANCE AND RELATIONSHIPS

Family tension can accelerate, especially if there are power struggles. Vague or misleading information creates problems in any relationship during the Lunar Eclipse on the 15th. Your tendency to sidestep issues can get you into trouble, so make it a point to know where you stand. Develop your friendships and take time to support one another after the 17th. Find better ways to open your heart to those who care for you, and carefully examine any fears which may be blocking love during the Solar Eclipse on the 29th.

FINANCE AND CAREER

Progress on the career front seems assured from the 1st–10th, when your leadership and encouragement draws powerful allies. Undermining or misleading information from the 14th–18th may be the result of jealous envy, and you can perpetuate the situation if you fail to address the issues. By taking a creative approach and focusing on future growth and development, you can use the situations now as a platform for increasing stability.

OPPORTUNITY OF THE MONTH

The adjustments you make from the 1st–10th can result in long-term improvements in your career and life circumstances.

Rewarding Days: 2, 3, 7, 8, 11, 12, 16, 24, 25, 29
Challenging Days: 4, 5, 13, 14, 15, 20, 21, 26, 27

AFFIRMATION FOR THE MONTH
"I honor my intuitive guidance."

PRIMARY FOCUS

Less pressure from your job allows more time for you to become involved with your special interests or in community projects. This is an important period to connect with others of like mind.

HEALTH AND FITNESS

Watch your limits, since it's easy to overindulge and feel yourself frustrated by a grinding halt in energy from the 6th–17th. Find healthy ways to enjoy the pleasures of life.

ROMANCE AND RELATIONSHIPS

Love is in the air, and you may be smitten with a desire to indulge your fantasies. Be cautious in new situations from the 11th–20th, when you may like what you think you see, but may be missing part of the picture! The Full Moon on the 14th is powerful for romance, and can stimulate a need to make a strong commitment, but if you've gotten in too deeply you're likely to withdraw, bringing confusion to your partner and a sense of disappointment to yourself near the New Moon on the 29th.

FINANCE AND CAREER

Your rewards from your career efforts are likely to be more satisfying this month, although you can run into some frustrating delays after the 21st. Social obligations can distract your focus mid-month, but may also be an important part of building your reputation. Power plays among peers can also ruffle your feathers after the 20th. Try to step out of the battle to maintain your objectivity. Also, avoid impulsive spending after the 21st.

OPPORTUNITY OF THE MONTH

Cooperative ventures or partnerships can lighten your load midmonth, but be sure to read the fine print before you sign.

Rewarding Days: 4, 5, 9, 10, 13, 14, 21, 22, 26, 31
Challenging Days: 2, 11, 12, 17, 18, 24, 25

AFFIRMATION FOR THE MONTH
"I am clearly aware of my goals."

PRIMARY FOCUS

Even though you may be traveling and/or are required to communicate more, you may feel that you're moving in circles. Avoid the dizziness by setting your priorities and knowing the facts.

HEALTH AND FITNESS

Spend time in the open air walking, running, or cycling to increase and rejuvenate your energy. Be cautious in sports or risky activities from the 11th–18th.

ROMANCE AND RELATIONSHIPS

Allowing others to reach their own conclusions about you may seem safe emotionally, but can lead to misunderstandings unless you set the record straight. Make an effort to reach out, expressing your feelings about important issues. Competitive attitudes can be channeled into more playful games from the 8th–13th, but be sure to make room for quiet, romantic time with your sweetheart from the 18th–30th, when you can create memorable moments together. The Cancer New Moon on the 27th is an excellent time to initiate love.

FINANCE AND CAREER

During Mercury's retrograde through the 17th, you may feel that you're in foreign territory when it comes to getting correct information to others. Take this time to follow through on situations which reached a stalemate in late May. Watch for more hectic schedules at work, although things seem to be in better control after the 23rd. Keep a cap on your spending, since it can be easy to go way over budget before you've even noticed.

OPPORTUNITY OF THE MONTH

By connecting to friends or others who share your special interests after the 22nd, you can create strong alliances.

Rewarding Days: 1, 5, 6, 10, 18, 19, 22, 23, 27, 28
Challenging Days: 3, 7, 8, 13, 14, 15, 20, 21

AFFIRMATION FOR THE MONTH
"I am an effective communicator."

PRIMARY FOCUS

An easy-going energy permeates your life. This is a strong period for love, sharing with family, exercising your creativity, and enjoying the fruits of your labors.

HEALTH AND FITNESS

Although you may be enjoying life more, there's still a tendency to feel some tension. Concentrate on increasing your flexibility by stretching, dancing, yoga, or T'ai Chi.

ROMANCE AND RELATIONSHIPS

If you've been waiting for the right time to take bold steps in your love life, it has arrived! Bring new life into a relationship during the Full Moon on the 12th by evaluating the nature of your own commitment. Any relationship which ends during this cycle can be more easily released through forgiveness and love, and you may find that a new or existing relationship gains momentum due to your own willingness to let go of the past and establish a firmer foundation. However, watch your own gullibility after the 22nd.

FINANCE AND CAREER

Satisfy the conservative faction at work from the 1st–8th, then you'll have a chance to modify or revise an old situation later in the month. Business travel, conferences, or presentations may play an important role now, but can be demanding through the 16th. You still must pay attention to details from the 20th–28th, when an oversight can be confusing and costly. Safeguard your possessions from loss from the 21st–30th.

OPPORTUNITY OF THE MONTH

Show your most creative and inventive ideas or projects to those who can help you promote them on the 15th and 16th.

Rewarding Days: 2, 3, 7, 8, 15, 16, 20, 21, 25, 26, 30
Challenging Days: 5, 6, 11, 12, 13, 17, 18, 23, 24

AFFIRMATION FOR THE MONTH
"My heart is filled with love and joy!"

PRIMARY FOCUS

Increased activity or turmoil at home may command your energy, but you also need to be more aware of your own feelings of self-worth. Positive self-esteem helps you weather any storm!

HEALTH AND FITNESS

You may feel more irritable and restless than usual, although releasing tension through physical exercise or activity can help. Just be sure to know your limits, since you can easily overdo it.

ROMANCE AND RELATIONSHIPS

Family conflicts can be problematical, and may be the result of financial disputes near the time of the Full Moon on the 10th. Identify your attachments and emotional involvement before you stubbornly cling to something (even an idea), since your objectivity may be limited! Reach out to a sibling for support and understanding after the New Moon on the 25th. Romance can be rocky, especially if you're feeling too controlled or confined after the 20th, but before you stage a revolt, talk about it.

FINANCE AND CAREER

Speculative interests are more risky through the 9th, since you may not see the problems beneath the surface. This is a good period to investigate or perform research. Continue the momentum of a project by building a network of support from the 11th–29th. Take care of communications, schedule conferences or meetings, and sign documents after the 12th, with best success after the 25th.

OPPORTUNITY OF THE MONTH

Take initiative on important emotional or career issues from the 26th–31st, but realize that your past will factor into your progress.

Rewarding Days: 3, 4, 11, 12, 16, 17, 21, 22, 26, 30, 31
Challenging Days: 1, 2, 7, 8, 10, 14, 15, 28, 29

AFFIRMATION FOR THE MONTH
"I clearly communicate my thoughts."

PRIMARY FOCUS

A highly creative and expressive period, this is an excellent time to showcase your talents and abilities. Romance can also flourish during this cycle.

HEALTH AND FITNESS

Center your activities within a framework of enjoyment and recreation. Calm feelings of nervousness by taking plenty of time to relax. A soothing cup of herbal tea might do the trick.

ROMANCE AND RELATIONSHIPS

Improve your love life by finding inventive ways to communicate your feelings. A fascinating person close to home can become a new love interest. However, an existing relationship gains momentum from the 1st through several days beyond the Full Moon on the 8th, when you break out of routine and try a new approach to pleasure. Children may play a prominent role after the 10th, and you'll also find your own inner child more eager to play. A novel approach to family works wonders after the New Moon on the 24th.

FINANCE AND CAREER

Avoid risky financial situations through the 5th, and make adequate provision to safeguard your possessions. You're more confident about expressing your talents after the 7th, and may see exceptional results presenting yourself, a project or an idea during the Full Moon on the 8th. Follow-up on contacts, activities, or responsibilities very carefully this month to avoid having to repeat yourself once Mercury moves into its retrograde on the 22nd.

OPPORTUNITY OF THE MONTH

Participation with and support of others who share your ideals helps progress your career on the 12th and 13th.

Rewarding Days: 8, 9, 12, 13, 17, 18, 22, 23, 27
Challenging Days: 1, 4, 5, 10, 11, 24, 25

AFFIRMATION FOR THE MONTH
"I see joy in every moment."

PRIMARY FOCUS

Despite some frustrations from family, you may still find your productivity and artistry working wonders in both your personal and professional life. Trust your own power, and express your feelings!

HEALTH AND FITNESS

It's easy to burn the candle at both ends, and you may find that you simply cannot shut down and relax. Work in time for a massage midmonth; pamper yourself.

ROMANCE AND RELATIONSHIPS

Passion runs high, and you may spend an inordinate amount of time pursuing the fulfillment of your desires. A new romance beginning from the 1st–8th may be unrealistic, but you'll quickly discover if there is any substance near the Lunar Eclipse on the 8th. Before you give up on an existing commitment, try to reestablish trust and understanding. Any romance works best now in a quiet, more secluded situation. Invite your sweetheart to help you create that perfect circumstance from the Solar Eclipse on the 23rd–24th thru the 25th.

FINANCE AND CAREER

During Mercury's retrograde through the 14th, you may be met with a series of confusing situations which distract you from your primary objectives. Watch your spending during this time, and avoid signing contracts which have a financial basis. You're in a better position to negotiate and reach agreement on the 24th and 25th. Creative and artistic pursuits fare nicely, although they produce the best results from the 14th–25th.

OPPORTUNITY OF THE MONTH

Trust your feelings and find ways to express them to those you love from the 24th–25th.

Rewarding Days: 5, 6, 10, 15, 16, 20, 21, 24, 25
Challenging Days: 1, 2, 7, 8, 13, 22, 23, 28, 29

AFFIRMATION FOR THE MONTH
"I trust my creative abilities."

PRIMARY FOCUS

Emotional power and intensity add significant impact to your creativity and may stimulate higher levels of productivity in your career. You get more by reaching out.

HEALTH AND FITNESS

Even if you've ignored the need to build physical strength in the past, it is crucial to take an active role in improving your health now. Why make excuses?

ROMANCE AND RELATIONSHIPS

Love is an experience which occurs within and grows best when it is shared with others in the world around you. Communicate your loving feelings; take the risk of sharing yourself with those you love during the Full Moon on the 7th. If you have children, give them special attention from the 4th–21st. Watch your own responses to the demands you feel from others, since you can alienate those you want to impress if you appear gruff or unsympathetic. Make a fresh start in your approach with the New Moon on the 22nd.

FINANCE AND CAREER

Evaluate your working conditions and attitudes toward your job. If you've been complaining and doing nothing to rectify the circumstances, then this is the time to invigorate your career. Antagonism from those around you may seem threatening, so be sure you're pulling your own weight. Legal or contractual disputes may stalemate from the 10th–20th, but progress after the 22nd.

OPPORTUNITY OF THE MONTH

Balance your expectations with the reality of your life situation and then take definite action to move ahead on the 2nd or 22nd.

Rewarding Days: 1, 2, 6, 7, 11, 12, 16, 17, 20, 21, 29
Challenging Days: 4, 5, 18, 19, 24, 25

AFFIRMATION FOR THE MONTH
"I am willing to do the work necessary
to make my dreams a reality."

PRIMARY FOCUS

Competitive circumstances can inspire you to move forward, although you may tend to withdraw in the beginning. Create a safe space, do your homework, then make a strong statement through your actions and attitudes.

HEALTH AND FITNESS

It's easy to burn the candle at both ends or to burn out your own enthusiasm. Pace yourself, set aside time to relax, and remain strong by keeping up fitness activities.

ROMANCE AND RELATIONSHIPS

With Venus and Mars both transiting through your house of partnerships, relationships may become a big issue. Even though it may seem that the other person is the focus of your attention, you actually may hold the trump card. Express your appreciation and caring to your partner. Renew or initiate vows or commitments from the 12th–31st. After the New Moon on the 21st, take some time to reflect on your relationship with your inner self and seek ways to release your anxieties about meeting another's expectations.

FINANCE AND CAREER

Gain through partnership or association with others is promising. Near the time of the Full Moon on the 6th you may feel that something is brewing, but it's hard to get the details. Seek counsel, but be sure you know the fine points and the integrity of others with whom you take on joint responsibilities from the 16th–31st, when it's easy to get involved in the dream without setting a firm foundation.

OPPORTUNITY OF THE MONTH

Balance your needs and interest with your partner's on the 8th and 9th—you'll find that life is more harmonious.

Rewarding Days: 3, 4, 8, 9, 13, 14, 26, 27, 31
Challenging Days: 1, 2, 6, 7, 16, 17, 22, 23, 28, 29

AFFIRMATION FOR THE MONTH
"I present myself to others with honesty,
integrity and confidence."

LEO
The Lion

July 23 to August 23

Element: Fire

Quality: Fixed

Polarity: Masculine/Yang

Planetary Ruler: The Sun

Meditation: "Self glows with Light from the Source"

Gemstone: Ruby

Power Stones: Topaz, Sardonyx

Key Phrase: "I will"

Glyph: Lion's tail

Anatomy: Heart, upper back, sides

Colors: Gold

Animal: Lions, large cats

Myths/Legends: Apollo, Isis, Helius

House Association: 5th

Opposite Sign: Aquarius

Flower: Marigold

Key Word: Magnetism

Positive Expression:
Honorable
Bold
Elegant
Loyal
Benevolent
Creative
Dynamic
Regal
Self-confident
Dramatic

Misuse of Energy:
Pompous
Domineering
Arrogant
Selfish
Chauvinistic
Insolent
Dictatorial
Ostentatious
Egocentric

♌ LEO ♌

Your Ego's Strengths and Weaknesses

Your self-expressive energy may often draw you into the center of attention. You can easily stand alone in the spotlight, but can also be a powerful guide to those who need leadership and direction. As "The Loyalist" of the zodiac, you have a strong ability to encourage others to consolidate and focus their efforts, using your own confidence, deep sense of conviction, and legendary creativity as a beacon of hope.

It seems natural for you to be the center of attention, much like the Sun, your ruler, is at the center of our own planetary system. Your loving and benevolent nature magnetically draws others to you, and you are most remembered for your warmth. Although your personal expression can range from regal to garish, your generosity is rarely overlooked. You sparkle when you see evidence of loyalty from those you love, but if you're hurt, you can just as easily lash out and demand attention in negative ways.

Honor ranks high in your priorities, and those individuals and situations to which you're committed can count on your devotion. As a capable champion, you show courage and steadfastness when the going gets tough, but you can become excessively prideful and stubborn, and can be unwavering when you hold a grudge. In order to truly create life on your own terms, you need positive ways to focus your magnetic power and abilities. By placing your ego at the disposal of your higher nature, you can create a true monument to Divine Power.

Your Approach to Romance

Being in love is pure delight for you! Special attention in an intimate atmosphere encourages you to be lavish with your own affections. You're a master in romance, and can also be a steadfast partner. Once you extend your love to another, you can be eternally loyal, and you may find it difficult to end relationships. When you do find the right partner, you can keep your love alive by rekindling warm romance on a regular basis.

Active relationships keep your fiery energy alive, and you may be most excited in alliances with other fire signs. Aries is spontaneously attractive, but you are concerned about real loyalty. Sagittarius' sense of adventure harmonizes with your own desire to have a good time. Although the heat can be intensely exciting with another Leo, be sure you each have your own turn in the limelight.

Taurus is attractive, although possessive. The intelligence and wit of Gemini stimulate your imagination, and you can be excellent traveling companions. Cancer's nurturance is comfortable, but not necessarily exciting. Although Virgo's precision and attention to quality are inspiring, you may be better friends than lovers.

Enticed by Libra's charm and refined beauty, you may feel perfectly at ease, and sensual pleasures with Scorpio may be enjoyable, but you can feel choked by the intensity. Capricorn, although good for business, may not feel romantic. With your opposite, Aquarius, you feel your heart strings dance, but have to deal with lessons in equality and autonomy! You may enjoy the alternative reality into which you are wooed by Pisces, but you may not be comfortable with the sense of losing control which can result if you lose touch with your own center.

Your Career Development

You may feel most excited by the challenges which come with positions of authority and leadership, and seek a career which allows you to receive recognition for your achievements. You can excel when you reach the top, whether you are chairman of the board or line foreman. You can also be an inspiring teacher, stimulating a positive sense of self-importance in others. You can be a great promoter and capable supervisor.

Since you like to be in places where others are enjoying themselves, you might successfully develop businesses such as clubs, restaurants, amusements, or theaters. In the performing arts, you may excel as an actor, musician, model, producer, or director. Politics may also be a choice, although you might prefer to promote and direct a candidate rather than becoming one yourself.

Your Use of Power

Your sense of authority arises when you feel your own natural connection to the force of life. Just as the Sun stimulates and sustains our life force, you are closely connected to the Power of Life. Your vitality is strongest when you tap into this energy and shine as brightly as possible. Fueled by the recognition and acknowledgment you gain from others, you may feel most powerful when you take the lead and can be their inspiration.

Whether at work or at home, you can be a benevolent ruler. Those around you feel safe and comforted by your magnetism and strength of will. But you can be dictatorial, stealing power from others to maintain your own, if you've lost your own sense of personal control. Observe the effect you have upon others as a positive guideline to your ability to wield power. Remember that you can become self-absorbed to the extent that the efforts and needs of others may not be as noticeable to you as they once were.

Your path is not always an easy one, since you may feel that your only ally is often the will of The Creator. Maintain communion with this power, and your own light will radiate a beacon of hope and love.

Famous Leos

Loni Anderson, Delta Burke, Robert DeNiro, Frank Gifford, Alex Haley, Alfred Hitchcock, Dustin Hoffman, Gerald McRaney, Jacqueline Kennedy Onassis, P. D. Ouspensky, Beatrix Potter, Martin Sheen, Willie Shoemaker, Lord Tennyson

THE YEAR AHEAD FOR LEO

Through increasing your focus on developing your creative talents and abilities during 1995, you expand possibilities of new opportunities for growth on all levels. You may feel that you are on the brink of important changes, although the exact circumstances have not yet manifested themselves. You can play an important role in engineering new directions by carefully examining your attachments and releasing elements from your past which impede healing and transformation. Other people, particularly those with whom you have intimate ties, have a powerful influence on your life in the year ahead.

You may feel especially confident now, while Jupiter travels through your Solar 5th House in trine aspect to your Sun. The energy of Jupiter serves to encourage you to reach beyond your current limitations and experience more of the good things life has to offer. This can be especially satisfying if you are involved in artistic or creative pursuits, and you may have better situations in which to develop and express these abilities. If you have been waiting for a good time to develop special hobbies or interests, this period can also provide the right energy to trust and express yourself. The primary downfall of this cycle is laziness or overindulgence, and a combination of the two can be lethal to your personal growth! Also, take care that your ego doesn't grow beyond reasonable proportions, since a snobbish attitude now will only alienate those you wish to impress! Certainly, it's time to enjoy yourself, but you'll gain more from the experience if you actively reach out in productive ways. Additionally, expressing your generosity and love to others can provide tremendous joy. Children may be a special source of inspiration and delight. This is a period of bearing fruit for your efforts while enjoying sharing the harvest with others.

Maintaining a balance between your personal needs and professional development is emphasized through the cycles of the Solar Eclipses during 1995. You may feel that your career has become increasingly demanding, but you are also seeing ways to develop which have not previously existed. Those who have guided and taught you in the past may now rely upon you to lead the way or take on the responsibilities, a challenge which can prove to be highly gratifying. But you are also likely to feel increasing pressures to build a stable base for future security and growth for yourself and your family. Listen to your inner voice; find ways to touch your own soul. Incorporate room in your plans and dreams for true personal evolution.

If you were born from July 23–25, you are feeling the power of exceptional change. You're experiencing energy from two highly potent planetary cycles: Uranus is opposing your Sun while Pluto is trine to your Sun. Many of the avenues for change are likely to open on their own, with little for you to do but respond to them, but you are also in the enviable position of writing your own ticket in some situations. Taking the risk of showing your real individuality allows you to break free. You may feel that you're turning the tables on tradition and exploring virgin territory. In many ways, you may also feel rather rebellious, and will definitely resent others who try to place excessive controls on your freedom or self-expression. Although you may be tempted to stage a dramatic protest of some sort, be sure you are aware of and ready for the risks before you raise your flag! For relationships to survive this cycle, you have to be honest about your individual needs and willing to give your partner the same types of freedoms you demand for yourself. Although you may have thought you understood love, you are now experiencing an opportunity to welcome the flow of the power of love in your creative expression, and feel that energy healing every aspect of your life. The key to your success may very well be your willingness to surrender to that power and become the manifestation of love itself in all that you do.

For Leos born from July 26–30, Pluto's transit is bi-quintile to your Sun. During this cycle, special gifts or talents which may have been underdeveloped, or which have not been given a chance to develop, can emerge. If you feel that you are lacking in creativity, you may discover aspects of yourself which are quite delightful, but this period can also move by with very little effect in your outside world and can elude your personal awareness unless you work with the energy directly. Spend

112

time listening to your inner voice. Find ways to allow your spontaneity to emerge, and trust that if you can envision it, you may very well be able to manifest it in some way!

You may be feeling some frustration with the need for continual adjustments this year if you were born from July 31–August 19. Saturn is transiting in quincunx to your Sun, stimulating a feeling of dissatisfaction with the elements of your life which are not working. You may even be discontent with situations which seemed fine before, but now need some fine-tuning. Now's the time to take personal inventory and adjust your priorities to reflect your responsibilities and needs more effectively. You may also find that redistributing your energy allows more time to do the things which bring greater satisfaction. If you've allowed your personal relationships to grow stale, you may need to revise your attitudes and make a stronger effort to give the kind of energy to the relationship that will bring it back to life. Evaluate your physical needs more carefully now, too, since this cycle has a reputation for undermining your vitality, and stimulating the emergence of physical factors which have been chronically weak. You can probably make a significant difference by simply altering your diet and lifestyle, eliminating the things which sap your energy, and increasing those which give you strength.

If you were born from August 15–20, you are feeling the influence of Neptune transiting quincunx to your Sun. During this year, you are likely to feel more sensitive than usual, and may also feel more inclined to focus on the spiritual elements of your life. Increasing awareness of the more intangible forces can be highly stimulating to your imagination, and may also inspire new areas of personal expression, but you may also feel that your physical form has to struggle to keep up with your expanding consciousness. Make this cycle work for you by allowing time in each day to focus and balance your energy, and by also paying careful attention to the nature of your interactions with others. You may not notice it at first if you're having trouble maintaining your personal boundaries, but the symptoms can be the feeling that somehow your needs got pushed aside for someone or something else. Although you may have some valid situations for extending yourself to others, be sure you're clear about your own motivations. Also, take a careful look at any business or personal relationship before you make commitments, since you may be drawn into a situation which is not at all what it seems to be.

You may feel that it is time to carefully reevaluate your life if you were born from August 18–23. The planets Uranus and Pluto are both transiting in quincunx to your Sun. These two energies set up a pattern with your Sun called a "yod," which marks a period of phenomenal change in consciousness leading to a change in circumstances. You may meet with situations which seem especially "fated," and are likely to feel more inclined to search for the deeper purpose in your personal activities. It will be quite difficult to hang onto things that are no longer contributing to your personal growth (especially, self-defeating attitudes). This is a period of healing and personal transformation, and marks a time of breaking through the barriers. Once you've stepped into the next dimension of yourself, you may find that your old life is simply not as valid or interesting as it once had been. As your consciousness expands during this cycle, you may also feel that some of the situations which were once nurturing or important seem stagnant or repressive. You are being reborn into a more complete expression of yourself, although you may feel that it is happening by degrees rather than occurring suddenly, at once. It's much like blossoming: the changes are quite apparent once they are in full bloom, but while they are taking place, you may not notice the contrasts they are creating. Give this cycle some time, and give yourself plenty of room to renew and rejuvenate.

Tools to Make a Difference

Explore the deeper meanings of love and your ability to allow love to reside within yourself. Although you may be involved in a relationship or career which seems satisfying, your most exceptional tool for growth this year may arise from learning to love yourself honestly and freely. If you've been hungry for love from others, you may discover that you have been blocking the type of energy you really want from a relationship because you have not been growing love within yourself, sharing that love through self-expression, and receiving love. Artistic and creative pursuits can be a primary part of this flow of energy, but you can also develop a level or artistry in your relationships!

To improve your physical health, seek out forms of exercise which are more playful and recreational. You might also enjoy learning one of the martial art forms. Be sure to include foods and supplements in your diet which support your nervous system, such as food high in B-vitamins and minerals such as calcium, magnesium, and phosphorus. To eliminate, or heal, any old or chronic physical problems, get in touch with your own fears of losing control. Surrendering to the process of healing is not always easy, especially if old emotional trauma is connected to the physical distress. To aid in release of the past, you might respond very well to restorative body work in the forms of acupuncture, rolfing, or Trager therapy. Since you are entering a period of spiritual breakthrough, you may sense that there is a realm of consciousness to be explored which you have never tapped. Regression hypnosis work can be highly therapeutic and illuminating. In your personal time of meditation, concentrate on the process of opening to a new dimension. See yourself walking up the steps of a magnificent temple toward a brilliant light. As you enter the threshold, feel the power which washes over you and enjoy the feeling of warmth deep within the center of yourself. On the walls of the temple are inscriptions which tell the story of your life journey, but in ways that you had not understood before. On an altar you find a tool which allows you to inscribe your own message. Pay attention to this message you give yourself, and know that each time you enter this temple, you will learn more about the journey of your soul.

Affirmation for the Year

"I am an instrument of love and joy."

ACTION TABLES FOR LEO

These dates reflect the best (but not the only) times for success and ease in these activities according to your Sun Sign.

Change Residence	Nov. 4–21
Request a Raise	July 27–28
Begin a Course of Study	Mar. 31–Apr. 1, Sep. 24–25
Visit a Doctor	Jan. 1–5; July 10–24; Dec. 12–31
Start a Diet	Jan. 28–29; Feb. 24–25; Mar. 23–24; Apr. 19–20; May 17–18; June 13–14; July 11–12; Aug. 7–8; Sep. 3–5; Oct. 1–2, 28–29; Nov. 24–25; Dec. 22–23
Begin a Romance	Dec. 21–22
Join a Club	May 29–30
Seek Employment	Jan. 1–6, Apr. 17–May 1, Dec. 11–31
Take a Vacation	Jan. 7–8; Feb. 3–4; Mar. 2–4, 30–31; Apr. 26–27; May 23–25; June 20–21; July 17–8; Aug. 13–15; Sep. 10–11; Oct. 7–8; Nov. 3–5; Dec. 1–2, 28–29
Change Your Wardrobe	Nov. 22–Dec. 11
End a Relationship	Aug. 21–22
Seek Professional Advice	Jan. 2–4, 30–31; Feb. 26–27; Mar. 25–27; Apr. 22–23; May 19–20; June 15–16; July 13–14; Aug. 9–10; Sep. 6–7; Oct. 3–4, 30–31; Nov. 26–27; Dec. 24–25
Have a Makeover	July 27–28
Obtain a Loan	Jan. 5–6; Feb. 1–2, 28; Mar. 1–2, 28–29; Apr. 24–25; May 21–22; June 17–19; July 15–16; Aug. 11–12; Sep. 8–9; Oct. 5–6; Nov. 1–2, 28–30; Dec 26–27

PRIMARY FOCUS

Even though you may have a high level of creative energy, your efforts may be frustrated by some financial and/or emotional difficulties tied to the past.

HEALTH AND FITNESS

Tension can be high and may stimulate a flare-up in chronic physical problems. Watch a tendency to over-obligate your time and energy early in the month.

ROMANCE AND RELATIONSHIPS

Your eagerness to move forward in a love relationship may place you in direct confrontation with unfinished emotional issues. Take time during the Full Moon on the 16th to reflect and get in touch with your inner feelings. Obstacles against your progress diminish mid-month, although you may still have a tendency to anticipate more than is possible. Talk about fears, explore mutual needs with your partner and determine if the love in your relationship can be a vehicle for true spiritual healing.

FINANCE AND CAREER

Jointly-held resources, tax liabilities, and financial debt are likely sources of concern. Collect the details and avoid the a tendency to think that ignoring the situation will make it go away. You may have a reprieve after Mercury turns retrograde on the 25th, which will allow you time to determine the best way to get rid of the source of the problem. Advancement in career through using your talents is promising from the 7th–19th and after the New Moon on the 30th.

OPPORTUNITY OF THE MONTH

Calculate the risks before you make an offer on the 17th or 18th, but still take advantage of the chance to move ahead.

Rewarding Days: 7, 8, 12, 13, 17, 18, 22, 26, 27
Challenging Days: 2, 3, 9, 10, 24, 25, 30, 31

AFFIRMATION FOR THE MONTH
"I trust my creative abilities."

PRIMARY FOCUS

While demands from others occupy much of your time and energy, you may also find that you have much to gain. Strive to cooperate by improving your own attitude and putting forth better efforts.

HEALTH AND FITNESS

Build strength and stamina by increasing your activity levels. Winter sports can be both playful and beneficial to your health. Consider the social benefits of taking a class.

ROMANCE AND RELATIONSHIPS

A committed partnership needs extra attention. By giving more of yourself, and increasing consideration of your partner, you may see promising personal growth from the 1st through the Full Moon in Leo, the 15th. Sexual tension arises from unreasonable expectations, and sharing your concerns can bring you closer. Your tendency to send mixed messages can create resentment. Make an effort from the 19th–28th to spend selected time in intimate surroundings expressing what you really feel.

FINANCE AND CAREER

With Mercury retrograding through the 15th you may run into unexpected difficulties reaching agreements or signing contracts. This is a good time to release something, but carefully consider before taking on increased financial responsibilities. Disputes over joint finances can continue, although you're getting closer to the core of the issue mid-month. Seek alternatives and present new plans from the 22nd–28th.

OPPORTUNITY OF THE MONTH

Evaluate your finances and seek ways to eliminate burdensome debt. Make sure your partner is carrying their share of the load.

Rewarding Days: 3, 4, 8, 9, 13, 14, 18, 10, 22, 23
Challenging Days: 1, 6, 7, 12, 20, 21, 26, 27

AFFIRMATION FOR THE MONTH
"I listen carefully before I speak."

PRIMARY FOCUS

Your talents may place you ahead of the competition, but you still may need support or alliance from others to reach your goals.

HEALTH AND FITNESS

Keep your energy level consistent by adjusting your schedule to allow time to be active and to relax. Burning the candle at both ends can be exhausting!

ROMANCE AND RELATIONSHIPS

You can break through the barriers and finally achieve the level of intimacy you desire, while feeling less vulnerable than you had feared. Express supportive energy to your partner by addressing his or her concerns early in the month, but allow time for introspection and self-exploration during the Full Moon on the 16th. A playful approach to your sexual interaction enlivens what may have become a stale relationship. Travel enhances your love life after the 21st, and your self-confidence improves after the 24th.

FINANCE AND CAREER

Improve business partnerships by reevaluating roles and concentrating more on the areas where you each show the best expertise and potential. Contractual agreements signed now are promising; however, investments may show a slow start frustrated by some type of regulatory difficulties which will be resolved later. If you're in a hurry to see results, take action in investments from the 23rd–31st. Business travel after the 21st opens doors.

OPPORTUNITY OF THE MONTH

The more traditional view can dampen your spirits early in the month, but your new ideas are well-received on the 22nd and 31st.

Rewarding Days: 3, 4, 8, 13, 14, 17, 18, 21, 22, 30, 31
Challenging Days: 5, 6, 15, 19, 20, 25, 26, 27

AFFIRMATION FOR THE MONTH
"I believe in myself and honor my dreams."

PRIMARY FOCUS

Expand your horizons now through increasing your knowledge and taking advantage of opportunities to share your expertise. Travel, educational pursuits, writing, and public speaking are highlighted.

HEALTH AND FITNESS

Using mental imagery aids in alleviating physical distress and can also help keep you healthy. Work to deliberately balance the spiritual, emotional, and physical aspects of your life.

ROMANCE AND RELATIONSHIPS

Love relationships deepen in their bonds, and you can do your part to assure a commitment by taking positive risks and releasing elements from your past which are no longer relevant to your needs. The Lunar Eclipse on the 15th emphasizes a need to connect your heart, mind, and spirit with those you love. A vacation, spiritual retreat, or inspiring experience from the 2nd–18th can be highly confirming. Avoid the pitfalls of vague communication from the 14th–20th, and ask for clarification if you need it.

FINANCE AND CAREER

Enlisting a pledge of support from others strengthens your position and may give you what you need to sell a project or an idea from the 1st–20th. Conferences, meetings, and presentations fare well and provide a strong forum to illustrate your talents. From the 15th through the time of the Solar Eclipse on the 29th, strive to satisfy a sense of higher purpose in your career efforts. Be aware of your responsibilities, since they cannot be ignored now.

OPPORTUNITY OF THE MONTH

Use your persuasive abilities to gain the acknowledgment and support of others on the 9th and 10th.

Rewarding Days: 4, 5, 9, 10, 13, 14, 18, 19, 26, 27
Challenging Days: 1, 2, 3, 15, 16, 22, 23, 29, 30

AFFIRMATION FOR THE MONTH
"I am a powerfully creative person."

PRIMARY FOCUS

Career progress may be reliant upon your ideological or political affiliations, with opportunities to lead others who share your ideas. Some power struggles may ensue, but you can tower above them.

HEALTH AND FITNESS

Even though you want to build strength, increasing your flexibility is crucial to avoid injury. Emphasize B-vitamins in your diet, since this is a mentally stressful time.

ROMANCE AND RELATIONSHIPS

Friends play an important role, and this is also an excellent time to get involved in special interest groups which support your creative or artistic pursuits. Strengthen your romantic options through travel, when you can either deepen a current bond or attract a new love. A flirtation from the 12th–18th may lead to unexpected results. Power struggles with family members from the 20th–29th may simply be a difference in priorities. Be honest when determining for yourself the best approach for your growth.

FINANCE AND CAREER

Uniting disagreeable factions may place you in a position of power, but be sure you understand the cost to yourself personally before you go out on a limb. Sign contracts and address legal issues before the 17th; if there is a delay, consider it a chance to learn more about possibilities you had not entertained. Reconsider your long-range plans and goals, and lay the groundwork for change during Mercury's retrograde from May 24–June 17.

OPPORTUNITY OF THE MONTH

Get back in touch with an old friend or an important business connection during the New Moon on the 29th.

Rewarding Days: 1, 6, 7, 11, 12, 15, 16, 23, 24, 25, 28, 29
Challenging Days: 5, 13, 14, 19, 20, 26, 27

AFFIRMATION FOR THE MONTH
"I respect my intuitive insights."

PRIMARY FOCUS

Careful attention to your finances helps you avoid the temptation to spend money you don't have! Provocative situations which require immediate action on your part may be more costly than you realize.

HEALTH AND FITNESS

Increasing muscle strength and endurance improves overall vitality. Consider getting involved in team sports or activities of a more playful and recreational nature.

ROMANCE AND RELATIONSHIPS

You may feel more like taking in as much attention and affection as you can, but try to keep the situation reciprocal to avoid alienating the affections of the one you love. Strong emphasis on love and romance during the Full Moon on the 12th can lead to a lasting commitment or the renewal of vows. And if you're looking for a new love, you may find just the person you need through connection with a good friend. Although highly engaging, your dramatic flair can try another's patience if taken too far.

FINANCE AND CAREER

Wait until after Mercury moves into direct motion on the 17th to sign important documents or contracts. Meanwhile, use your enthusiasm to generate support from others. Just be sure you don't appear to be too self-serving. Safeguard finances by making a careful assessment before you invest or spend, and avoid impulsive expenditures until after the 20th when judgment is more balanced. Attend to business alliances from the 11th–30th.

OPPORTUNITY OF THE MONTH

Channel your impatience toward diversifying or improving your creative or artistic pursuits. Plan a showcase on the 11th and 12th.

Rewarding Days: 2, 3, 4, 7, 8, 11, 12, 20, 21, 25, 30
Challenging Days: 9, 10, 15, 16, 17, 22, 23

AFFIRMATION FOR THE MONTH
"I am inspired by Truth."

PRIMARY FOCUS

Unfinished business from the past can stir up trouble, but may also give you a chance to finally rectify a situation which has undermined your sense of stability.

HEALTH AND FITNESS

Stress and tension can quickly take their toll, stimulating a flare-up of chronic, or weak, physical areas. Increase highly nutritional foods, exercise, and take a few breaks!

ROMANCE AND RELATIONSHIPS

Denying your feelings can cause problems now, so be honest with yourself about inner conflicts or desires. Otherwise, you could undermine the quality of a close relationship. Engineer your schedule to allow time for yourself, especially near the time of the Full Moon on the 12th, when introspective insights give you an emotional boost. Resolving psychological trauma from the past now can give you the room to develop greater intimacy. By the time of the New Moon in Leo on the 27th, you're ready to open up again.

FINANCE AND CAREER

Any struggles over jointly-held resources can seem unending, but are reaching their conclusion. Take a positive stand for yourself, and watch your tendency to become overbearing if you're feeling threatened. Finish projects which are ready for completion, and prepare to launch into some new directions after the 27th, when your ideas and approach are likely to receive accolades for their insightfulness.

OPPORTUNITY OF THE MONTH

Get all your work, preparation, and research in order and plan to launch into a new, positive direction on the 27th and 28th.

Rewarding Days: 1, 5, 6, 9, 17, 18, 22, 27, 28
Challenging Days: 2, 3, 7, 8, 13, 14, 15, 19, 20

AFFIRMATION FOR THE MONTH
"I am honest with myself and others."

PRIMARY FOCUS

Not only is this a powerful time for self-expression, but you can also join forces with others in creative pursuits to generate an impact that will be long remembered.

HEALTH AND FITNESS

Improvements in physical health are accelerated by time in the open air and finding ample outlets for play and recreation. Mental stress increases from the 10th–28th.

ROMANCE AND RELATIONSHIPS

If you've been waiting for the right time to make your move, then this is it! Find a unique way to communicate your feelings from the 1st–10th. Take some time during the Full Moon on the 10th to explore your partner's desires. Consider taking some short trips or changing your daily schedule in such a way to allow breaks for play and romance through the 25th. Immediate attention to family demands from the 18th–31st helps to keep things in perspective. Avoid disappointment by clarifying misunderstandings on the 28th or 29th.

FINANCE AND CAREER

Networking with other professionals in your field creates long-term alliances. Taking a position of leadership now may open the way for immediate advancement and increased recognition. Review the details of your finances from the 10th–30th. Be alert to the possibility of confusing or undermining actions on the part of co-workers or another who could be jealous of your success after the 27th. Openness on your part can make a difference in the outcome.

OPPORTUNITY OF THE MONTH

Expedite progress in a relationship or a business transaction from the 1st–10th. Waiting will prove frustrating.

Rewarding Days: 1, 2, 5, 6, 14, 19, 23, 24, 28
Challenging Days: 3, 4, 9, 10, 16, 17, 30, 31

AFFIRMATION FOR THE MONTH
"My heart is filled with love and harmony."

PRIMARY FOCUS

Home and family require greater energy this month. If moving, remodeling, or renovating your home, be certain of financial details before you finalize contracts.

HEALTH AND FITNESS

Your tendency to worry can drain vitality, especially if you're trying to maintain controls when others are not cooperating. Concentrate on letting go.

ROMANCE AND RELATIONSHIPS

Even though you may be trying to work things out, it's easy to feel overburdened by expectations from your family. Tension is likely to arise in your love life, too, and may be related to issues about money, taxes, or other pressures. Quiet time with your partner during the Full Moon on the 8th may give you a chance to explore the deeper bonds of your relationship and extract those things which are getting in the way. Consider going back to a place which holds fond memories after the 24th.

FINANCE AND CAREER

Your career progress may be thwarted by regulations or red tape from the 1st–12th. Before you present your plans, develop an adequate budget, since you will be asked to present detailed descriptions of expenditures! With Mercury's retrograde on the 22nd you may be given a chance to review or revise materials, but try to get things clear prior to this cycle. Networking shows great promise after the New Moon on the 24th.

OPPORTUNITY OF THE MONTH

If progress stalls from the 20th–26th, take time to complete unfinished business and review the details of transactions.

Rewarding Days: 2, 10, 11, 15, 20, 21, 24, 25, 29
Challenging Days: 4, 5, 6, 7, 12, 13, 26, 27

AFFIRMATION FOR THE MONTH
"I gladly release those elements of my past
which I no longer need."

PRIMARY FOCUS

Communication over everyday circumstances may seem inordinately difficult, and it's easy to feel pressured in senseless ways. Keep centered, stay alert, and breathe!

HEALTH AND FITNESS

Emotional tension continues to take its toll on your physical energy. A conscious effort on your part to release is helpful. Schedule a massage (or two).

ROMANCE AND RELATIONSHIPS

Instead of keeping your feelings inside, use the energy near the time of the Lunar Eclipse on the 8th to talk about your needs and express your emotions. You may feel confused by a situation or misunderstanding that has no basis in reality, but if there is deception going on, you also want to know for sure. Power struggles with family can be especially trying from the 14th–25th, and may intensify during the Solar Eclipse the 23rd–24th. Look at your own attachments and determine what you can give up to ease the tension.

FINANCE AND CAREER

Rather than trusting that things will be your way, take the time to follow through on important communication, documentation or personal contact until after Mercury turns direction the 14th. Contracts involving financial expenditure should be avoided, since there is a strong indicator of missing information or possible deception through the 5th. New creative projects fare beautifully after the 21st, also a good period of self-promotion.

OPPORTUNITY OF THE MONTH

Any unfinished business (whether personal or professional) which stands in the way of your progress needs review and, possibly, release.

Rewarding Days: 7, 8, 12, 13, 17, 18, 22, 26, 27
Challenging Days: 3, 4, 10, 11, 16, 24, 25, 30, 31

AFFIRMATION FOR THE MONTH
"I am an excellent communicator."

PRIMARY FOCUS

You're gaining momentum, especially in the realm of creative self-expression, and can effectively use this period to increase your productivity, artistic expertise, and professional reputation.

HEALTH AND FITNESS

Increase your activity level by finding recreational outlets for exercise and fitness. Team sports, winter sports, and dancing are excellent choices. You might also enjoy some healthy competition!

ROMANCE AND RELATIONSHIPS

That dry spell you've been experiencing is finally over. It's time to take the initiative and go after what you want and need in your love life. If you're single, you're likely to find a new love interest by participating in artistic or recreational pursuits which bring you personal pleasure. Any relationship will gain significant benefit from sharing favorite pastimes or amusements. Children may play a strong role, and their needs and interests can be quite fulfilling. Take care of family business during the Full Moon on the 7th, so you'll have more time to play.

FINANCE AND CAREER

Put your talents to work, and find ways to share your gifts. Opportunities to lead or direct others can be highly significant, offering a chance to launch a plan you've long envisioned. Clear away liabilities early in the month to make way for speculative investments after the New Moon on the 22nd. However, it is tempting to spend impulsively from the 1st–17th, so watch your budget.

OPPORTUNITY OF THE MONTH

It is definitely time to produce. Forget talking—take action and let the world know what you have to offer!

Rewarding Days: 4, 5, 8, 9, 13, 14, 18, 22, 23
Challenging Days: 1, 2, 6, 7, 20, 21, 26, 27

AFFIRMATION FOR THE MONTH
"I am confident in my creative abilities."

PRIMARY FOCUS

Even though you can still enjoy yourself, many of your activities seem to be oriented toward work or duty. Solicit assistance from others who are competent and reliable.

HEALTH AND FITNESS

Instead of complaining about your limitations or aches and pains, find the best way to handle them. Make a difference in healing yourself by becoming more fully responsible for your well-being.

ROMANCE AND RELATIONSHIPS

Love grows, although some of the time you may feel that your relationship takes a lot of effort. If things seem difficult, look to yourself to determine your level of inner satisfaction. Begin a program of positive self-improvement, finding ways to consistently affirm your own strengths and support yourself in areas which you feel vulnerable. The Full Moon on the 6th stresses your need to fill yourself with love and by the New Moon on the 21st, you're ready to share that love with others. See this energy as a circuit which you control by opening your heart.

FINANCE AND CAREER

Coordinate your efforts at work with others, but watch a tendency to become overbearing if you feel they're not doing their job effectively! Clear things away from your schedule that clutter your calendar and concentrate on activities which produce the best results. You may finally see some results from investments, but are likely to take a conservative approach to your use of the proceeds.

OPPORTUNITY OF THE MONTH

Schedule important meetings or conferences from the 5th–7th, when cooperation and support from others can advance your own efforts.

Rewarding Days: 1, 2, 6, 7, 11, 12, 16, 20, 21, 28, 29
Challenging Days: 3, 4, 10, 18, 19, 24, 25, 30, 31

AFFIRMATION FOR THE MONTH
"I enjoy my work."

♍ VIRGO ♍
The Virgin

August 23 to September 23

Element: Earth

Quality: Mutable

Polarity: Feminine/Yin

Planetary Ruler: Mercury

Meditation: "I experience love through service"

Gemstone: Sapphire

Power Stones: Rhodochrosite, peridot, amazonite

Colors: Taupe, blue-gray

Key Phrase: "I analyze"

Glyph: Greek symbol for "virgin"

Anatomy: Abdomen, intestines, gall bladder, duodenum, pancreas

Animal: Domesticated animals

Myths/Legends: Demeter, Astraea, Hygeia

House Association: 6th

Opposite Sign: Pisces

Flower: Pansy

Key Word: Perfection

Positive Expression:

Discriminating
Helpful
Meticulous
Efficient
Conscientious
Practical
Methodical
Humble
Precise

Misuse of Energy:

Hypercritical
Intolerant
Nervous
Tedious
Skeptical
Hydrochondriacal
Superficial
Self-deprecating

129

♍ VIRGO ♍

Your Ego's Strengths and Weaknesses

With your keen analytical abilities always functioning, you're the efficiency expert of the zodiac, forever seeking a high level of personal perfection. While others may be distracted by the obvious, your observational skills keep you ahead of the game and aware of the finer details. Learning may be one of your passions, and you truly appreciate quality in everything. You love to share what you know, and have an easy ability to teach and guide others.

Your basic nature as "The Modifier" stems from your studious approach to every life situation, and you may feel that almost anything or anyone can stand a bit of improvement! You may be driven to such extremes that you rarely give yourself, or others, much leeway in your scale of perfection, and even though others may think Virgos are neatness freaks, they might be surprised to find your special hide-away which serves to catch all the surplus. You can avoid a reputation of nitpicking by learning to apply your critical powers to include those things you appreciate about yourself, another person, or a situation. In fact, you can be an easy companion, as long as others allow you to do things your way.

In your quest for expertise or excellence you may follow intellectual pursuits which can isolate you from the world-at-large, but your spiritual lesson beckons you to find ways to develop your own proficiency within the world while allowing others to follow their own paths.

Your Approach to Romance

Your sensuality may be one of your best-kept secrets, since you don't let just anyone get close enough to find out about your tender side. There's no doubt that you have an ideal mate, and may have a long list of qualifications before a relationship can become romantic. Once you've opened the door to intimacy, your loving touch can be magical and soothing. Your commitment is inspired by a relationship that offers ample room for positive personal growth, and you'll blossom in an atmosphere of trust and acceptance.

Contact with other earth signs (Taurus, Capricorn, and Virgo) may be most comfortable, since you prefer to take your time to develop a worthwhile relationship. Taurus feels stabilizing and you will enjoy that earthy sensuality. Capricorn's dry wit is a delight for you, and you may enjoy a special playfulness once you've developed mutual trust. With another Virgo, you may find it easy to be yourself, and will have a mutual understanding about keeping all that grumbling to yourselves.

You're excited by Aries' playful creativity, but may not like being distracted from your focus. Although you enjoy Gemini's intellectual curiosity and levity, you can be confounded by their changeability. With Cancer, you may feel both a strong friendship and powerful physical bond. Leo's dramatic warmth can be the stuff of your most romantic dreams, but you may feel most comfortable as friends. With Libra, you can be objective and open, but have to continually clarify where you stand with one another.

The passion and depth of love with Scorpio can be thoroughly satisfying. And you may find that you can easily share your most private pleasure and favorite pastimes with Sagittarius, even if you don't see much of each other. With Aquarius, there can be fireworks and spiritual strength, but you may feel alone when you're ready to settle into a sweet caress, and even though you may be magnetically attracted to your opposite, Pisces, you may have difficulty relating on the same plane of awareness.

Your Career Development

Strongly influenced by Mercury's energy of mentality and communication, you'll flourish best in a career which challenges your mind and provides opportunities for self-improvement. You need a job which allows you to feel you've produced or accomplished something, and may enjoy running your own business. Service-oriented fields such as medicine, social work, counseling, or related areas may draw your interest. Writing, speaking, or teaching can provide outlets for your desire to share knowledge. Or, you may want to use your natural planning abilities in accounting, administration, office management, secretarial service, systems analysis, or research.

Occupations which require adept manual dexterity can be rewarding. Most crafts-oriented fields, detail work in the building industry, drafting, design, or graphic arts can be good choices. You may actually develop more than one career throughout your lifetime, and can probably juggle more than one job at a time. Whatever your choices, you will do your reliable best.

Your Use of Power

You are drawn to the idea of influencing others and changing the course of events, even though you may not seek power for its own sake. You see the power of the mind as primary, and strive to make honest use of information and wisdom. Since you tend to make things appear effortless, others may not recognize the breadth of power you possess (until you're gone!). It is crucial that you learn to appreciate your own worth and that you find ways to give yourself praise for a job well done.

You can help others help themselves more effectively by finding healthy ways to give and receive. But be cautious of your motivations if you're drawn into fields of ministry or service, since you can become caught in the quagmire of codependency. You may discover that you're compelled to call attention to mankind's inhumanity to other life forms or to humankind, and may have the power to speak or act in their stead. Learn to use the power of service to help improve the quality of life and to bring a higher quality to your own existence.

Famous Virgos

Elizabeth Ashley, Ben Bradlee, Peter Cetera, Maurice Chevalier, James Coburn, Jose Feliciano, Jesse James, Swoosie Kurtz, Ricki Lake, Tom Lasorda, D. H. Lawrence, Arnold Palmer, Charlie Sheen, Tom Skerritt, David Souter, Al Stewart

THE YEAR AHEAD FOR VIRGO

With a powerful desire to enlarge your base of operations and some inventive creative ideas, you can use the energies of 1995 to help you move in directions which enhance your stability and help you to further define your personal and professional image. The primary challenges involve establishing a balance between the various elements of your life without alienating yourself from those circumstances which provide your basic needs. You may be tempted to blame the demands you feel from others for the stress in your life, but you have more choices than you realize!

One of your outstanding quests this year arises from a need to reach beyond your old limits into areas of increased influence, and possibly affluence. Jupiter's transit in Sagittarius certainly stimulates a feeling of desire to get out of those old ruts, especially some of the traditions you may view as outworn or useless. But before you gallop away from the family picnic, you may discover that your ride has been cut short by some obligations you had forgotten. Saturn's energy brings the light of reality back into the picture, reminding you of your promises and possibly curtailing some of the fun you had planned. One of the best ways to work with this cycle is to make sure that you have allowed sufficient time, energy, and money to take care of your promises—and that some of those promises are to yourself. Otherwise, you may feel frustrated, since your deeper desire is to prove that you do indeed have something valuable to offer.

The Solar Eclipses in Taurus and Scorpio emphasize the development of your mind and stimulate even greater curiosity than you might normally employ. This is a fantastic time to get involved in educational or cultural pursuits, and you might also enjoy more travel. You may have a greater investment in writing, speaking, or publishing than you have experienced in the past, and can benefit by using your communication skills to build a positive career support network. Additionally, you may find that others are more likely to seek out your expertise and advice.

If you were born from August 23–24, you may feel that your life is on the brink of overwhelming changes. The planets Uranus and Pluto are both beginning a two-year cycle in aspect to your Sun. Uranus is transiting in quincunx to your Sun, stimulating the mixed feelings of excitement and uncertainty in the face of surprising changes. This cycle requires that you use every bit of your personal flexibility to learn to adapt to situations changing around you, and can be a period of interesting experimentation in areas which you had previously ignored. Pluto transits in square aspect to your Sun, drawing you into a deeper connection to the inner aspects of your self, and helping you uncover some of the old mysteries which have driven you from the dark recesses of your unconscious mind. Through working with this energy, you can free yourself of the burdens of shame, guilt, or disappointment which have undermined your self-worth and inhibited your personal expression, but you will need courage to face your own dragons, and support from the center of your spiritual self to overcome many of the fears which have haunted you. This is a period of rebirth and transformation, and brings phenomenal changes in every aspect of your life. The most challenging elements may come from confronting your past, sometimes uncovering things that are buried deep in your soul-pattern. This is your time to let go of those aspects of your life which have been holding you back, to remove your mask, and to emerge as a fully functioning and complete individual.

If you were born from August 25–29, you may be feeling more open to expressing your talents and gifts than you have in the past. Uranus is transiting in biquintile aspect to your Sun. Although this cycle may not seem to shake the foundations of your life, if you are willing to apply yourself, you may be able to bring forward some of the best elements of your creativity. This is also a period during which your intuitive faculties can be more finely honed and utilized.

Saturn is transiting in opposition to your Sun if you were born from August 30–September 18. During this year, you may feel more pressured by responsibilities and need to take a careful look at the way you have chosen to order your life. The issue of control may arise more than once, especially in the realm of relationships. But you may also feel pressured by controls in your career or restraints from outside forces which seem to be thwarting your opportunities to get ahead. It's easy to focus only on the things that are going wrong, and you can undermine some significant options to stabilize your life if you become too short-sighted. Before you leap off the nearest cliff, stop to evaluate. Look at your life for the areas in which you need to relinquish control. Find ways to return to others any responsibilities you have been carrying for them. Evaluate circumstances which are not producing and determine if you still want to use your energy to support them. Set your priorities to deal with the things that are truly important to your growth, but primarily, make an effort to release those things from your past which are no longer part of your life. Once you've taken these steps, you may discover that not only are you feeling more stable and secure, but that you can handle your obligations more easily.

For Virgos born from September 3–7, Uranus is transiting in sesquiquadrate to your Sun. Watch your impulses, because you can get yourself into trouble by responding in knee-jerk-like fashion to the pressures of your life. This is definitely a time to break free, and you may find new interests which are exceptionally tempting. As long as you find outlets which are appropriate for your personal evolution, this energy works to your benefit. The problem resides in moving along too quickly and failing to see the complete picture. Before you make commitments, evaluate the situation, then make the appropriate choices.

It's time to take a leap of faith, if your birth occurred from September 6–15. Pluto's transit in quintile to your Sun marks a period of self-expression which allows you to display your unique aptitudes and enhances your mental creativity. This can be a remarkable time of spiritual evolution, and you may feel more inclined to view life from the perspective of universality. By making an effort to connect with your own inner strength, you are also experiencing a deep level of healing. This energy can also permeate your self-expression in ways which can have a profound effect upon others around you.

You may be feeling more powerfully in touch with your sense of purpose this year if you were born from September 14–23. Chiron's cycle in conjunction to your Sun provides a penetrating look into your needs to make a difference in the world. Perhaps one of the more challenging aspects of this cycle is honesty with yourself, since you cannot dispute your needs to do the things which open a pathway to your true spiritual and psychological growth. You may experience some levels of physical discomfort related to chronically weak areas in your body, but you can also connect with the core-level causes of these problems. It is crucial that you adopt a holistic attitude, recognizing the interconnection between your physical, emotional, and spiritual needs and experiences.

If you were born from September 15–20, your sensitivities and imagination may be increased while Neptune transits in trine aspect to your Sun. Artistic expression is enhanced during this cycle, and you may begin to see life around you through different filters. Your awareness is likely to expand in ways which are subtle, yet profound. From an emotional level, this cycle marks a time of forgiveness and releasing. It is time to let go and surrender your life to the force of Divine Love. In your desire to grow close to the Source, you may be more inclined to spend time meditating or in spiritual practice, but you can also find ways to make life your meditation instead of having to isolate yourself from the vital experiences which inspire growth and vitality.

Exciting changes and tremendous insights can be the results of the transiting cycles this year if you were born from September 18–23. Uranus is transiting in trine aspect to your Sun while Pluto's transit sextiles your Sun. This is a period of breakthrough, but can also challenge you to draw on your inner courage and take the steps what will bring you back to life. If you've been feeling too pressured or downtrodden, then it's time now to drop any feelings of self-limitation and take the risk of going for your dream. Your special attributes and creativity are more likely to put you ahead of the pack, and can give you the boost you need to establish yourself in your chosen field. In personal relationships these energies can help you reach out more effectively and allow you to develop more meaningful ways to express your love and affection.

Tools to Make a Difference

Because you may feel somewhat overwhelmed by some of the situations life offers this year, it is crucial that you find ways to pull back and make contact with your inner self. Set aside time for physical exercise, relaxation, and play in the midst of your demanding schedule. Hatha yoga and T'ai Chi are excellent choices for helping you to maintain a positive contact between the physical and spiritual aspects of yourself, but you might also enjoy more demanding forms of exercise.

Incorporate highly nutritious foods into your diet, and begin to reshape your tastes for those foods which will strengthen your vitality. Get back to basics, and remember to use herbs and natural products as healing and nutritional supports. You may also respond well to homeopathic remedies and flower remedies.

In your periods of meditation and contemplation, seek ways to release the inner pressures you may be feeling and open to greater self-love and self-acceptance. See yourself entering a corridor heading toward a soft blue-pink light. As you enter the field of light, you are given a basket of flowers, and are beckoned to enter another hallway. This corridor is lined with mirrors. As you stop to catch your reflection in the mirrors, you see yourself at different ages and in different situations over the course of your life. View these images with compassion and understanding. Lovingly offer some of the flowers from your basket to the images you see in the mirror. Feel warmth spreading throughout your body. Know that you are healing your past and present, and opening the way for a more fulfilling future.

Affirmation for the Year
"I lovingly accept myself."

ACTION TABLES FOR VIRGO

These dates reflect the best (but not the only) times for success and ease in these activities according to your Sun Sign.

Change Residence	Nov. 23–Dec. 11
Request a Raise	Aug. 26–27
Begin a Course of Study	Apr. 29–30; Oct. 24–25
Visit a Doctor	Jan. 7–Mar. 13; July 26–Aug. 9
Start a Diet	Jan. 2–4, 30–31; Feb. 26–27; Mar. 25–27; Apr. 22–23; May 19–20; June 15–16; July 13–14; Aug. 9–10; Sep. 6–7; Oct. 3–4, 30–31; Nov. 26–27; Dec. 24–25
Begin a Romance	Jan. 1–2
Join a Club	June 28–29
Seek Employment	Jan. 7–Mar. 14; May 2–July 9
Take a Vacation	Jan. 9–10; Feb. 6–7; Mar. 5–6; Apr. 1–2, 29–30; May 26–27; June 22–23; July 19–21; Aug. 16–17; Sep. 12–13; Oct. 10–11; Nov. 6–7; Dec. 3–4, 30–31
Change Your Wardrobe	Jan. 1–5; Dec. 12–31
End a Relationship	Sep. 9
Seek Professional Advice	Jan. 5–6; Feb. 1–2, 28, Mar. 1, 28–29; Apr. 24–25; May 21–22; June 17–19; July 15–16; Aug. 11–12; Sep. 8–9; Oct. 5–6; Nov. 1–2, 29–30; Dec. 26–27
Have a Makeover	Aug. 26–27
Obtain a Loan	Jan. 7–8; Feb. 3–4; Mar. 3–4, 30–31; Apr. 26–27; May 24–25; June 20–21; July 17–18; Aug. 13–15; Sep. 10–11; Oct. 7–8; Nov. 4–5; Dec. 1–2, 28–29

PRIMARY FOCUS

Initiate creative projects early. Even though your goals may be defined, you also have to contend with demands and expectations from others, especially at home.

HEALTH AND FITNESS

It's easy to get caught up in the stress of the moment and forget about your physical needs until you're already exhausted. Avoid burn-out by allowing time to rejuvenate. Try a massage midmonth.

ROMANCE AND RELATIONSHIPS

Make time for romance from the New Moon on the 1st through the 7th. You may also enjoy sharing some social activities from your home, although it's a good idea to keep it simple. Tension from your partner may arise unless you're paying adequate attention to the needs of your relationship, and it can be easy to get caught up in everyday demands and forget about expressions of intimacy. Sort through issues over a friendly lunch during the Full Moon on the 16th, and consider taking time away from it all on the 28th–29th.

FINANCE AND CAREER

Get the ball rolling on your pet projects from the 1st–15th. You may be spending more time fulfilling the social obligations associated with your job than you like this month, but you can use this time to break through barriers which are difficult to scale through purely business channels. Before you agree to additional responsibilities, clarify the details to avoid getting swamped. Use Mercury's retrograde beginning the 26th to review.

OPPORTUNITY OF THE MONTH

Schedule important presentations, conferences or meetings from the 1st–6th, when your unique ideas are more likely to be accepted.

Rewarding Days: 1, 5, 10, 15, 16, 19, 20, 24, 25, 28, 29
Challenging Days: 3, 6, 12, 13, 26, 27, 30, 31

AFFIRMATION FOR THE MONTH
"I am confident in my abilities."

PRIMARY FOCUS
Your work obligations may spread your energy a bit thin and can lead to disappointment from your family or partner unless you solicit their support and understanding. Keep communication open.

HEALTH AND FITNESS
Worry and job stress can take their toll unless you are actively working to diffuse the tension. Concentrate on "inner fitness" through the next four months, using affirmations, meditation, and inspiring visualization.

ROMANCE AND RELATIONSHIPS
Share your feelings and express yourself more openly to those you love after the 4th, while Venus travels through your Solar 5th House. Children, creative activities, and favorite pastimes offer a positive balance to your busy life if you allow yourself to enjoy them. To invigorate a partnership after the 20th, spend some time sharing your hopes and fantasies, and create a situation in which you can both make some dreams come true on the 25th.

FINANCE AND CAREER
Mercury's retrograde cycle continues through the 15th and may stimulate confusing and frustrating communications. To avoid feeling out of control, allow extra time to complete background work, and gather the facts before you take action. You may be able to use some of the information gained by waiting when making a presentation or reaching an agreement on the 16th. Take note: Offers for advancement may entail intense responsibilities.

OPPORTUNITY OF THE MONTH
Reaffirm a commitment of love or support by sharing special time together on the 24th or 25th. You'll be pleased with the results.

Rewarding Days: 6, 7, 11, 12, 16, 17, 20, 24, 25
Challenging Days: 1, 2, 8, 9, 13, 22, 23, 28

AFFIRMATION FOR THE MONTH
"I trust my inner feelings."

PRIMARY FOCUS

Agreements, partnerships, and social obligations play a large part in structuring your time. Clearly define your role, since you could end up with all the responsibility and little glory!

HEALTH AND FITNESS

Take a more nurturing and kind attitude toward yourself now, since the positive energy and love with which you fill yourself has a great effect on your sense of well-being.

ROMANCE AND RELATIONSHIPS

An existing relationship can be excessively demanding, but you can also restore a sense of stability and confidence by becoming more openly supportive of your partner. It is also critical to be aware of any projections within the relationship, since it's easy to be the scapegoat for another's discontent with themselves. (Be sure you're not the one throwing darts, either!) You'll definitely know where you stand by the Virgo Full Moon on the 16th, and need to tell others what you need from them, too.

FINANCE AND CAREER

Details of financial agreements and contracts may seem ominous, but if you really want to proceed, you have to allow your confidence and courage to emerge and help see you through. Examine the facts, weigh the options, then make your own offer by the 16th. If the other side doesn't budge and you cannot agree, then seek a new alternative on the 30th. Others look to you for confirmation when dealing with family resources or joint agreements mid-month.

OPPORTUNITY OF THE MONTH

Polarization in a situation can limit objectivity, but you must determine your position and confidently maintain it.

Rewarding Days: 5, 6, 10, 11, 15, 16, 19, 23, 24
Challenging Days: 1, 8, 9, 21, 22, 28, 29

AFFIRMATION FOR THE MONTH
"I am one with my Higher Self."

PRIMARY FOCUS

You benefit through the resources and support of others, particularly a partner. However, you may also feel restricted by their actions and attitudes.

HEALTH AND FITNESS

Once the smoke clears, plan to take time away from the stress of career after the 18th. Adjust your schedule, allowing time to build stamina and endurance through exercise.

ROMANCE AND RELATIONSHIPS

Develop an intimate relationship by creating more effective means of communication regarding your mutual needs. A new relationship can take flight early in the month, but if you are currently involved, you may also see the validity in confirming your feelings for one another. The Lunar Eclipse on the 15th may stimulate the release of an old attachment, making room for new emotional growth. By the time of the Solar Eclipse on the 29th, you're ready for a change of scenery, and might enjoy traveling with your sweetie.

FINANCE AND CAREER

Gathering support from others provides a more stable platform for your career this month. You can also benefit by showing your own loyalty to a partner or colleague. Business conferences, presentations, or meetings provide an excellent forum to showcase your talents after the 17th, and may give you a chance to break into a new level of recognition or respect in your profession. Your own financial position may stabilize due to your partner's success.

OPPORTUNITY OF THE MONTH

Take advantage of a chance to shine from the 16th–29th, and be confident when expressing your viewpoints.

Rewarding Days: 2, 7, 8, 11, 12, 16, 20, 21, 29, 30
Challenging Days: 4, 5, 10, 18, 19, 24, 25

AFFIRMATION FOR THE MONTH
"I am inspired by Truth and Guided by Wisdom."

PRIMARY FOCUS

Your professional development is enhanced through writing, speaking, teaching, or publishing. Academic or educational pursuits and travel may also figure prominently in your career growth now.

HEALTH AND FITNESS

You may need more rest than usual, and be protective of personal time. Mental stress is more marked, and you can benefit from increasing B-vitamins to help stay alert.

ROMANCE AND RELATIONSHIPS

The magic and alchemy of your love relationship can be enhanced now through a greater sharing of energy. If you've not experienced a tantric approach to sexuality, this cycle marks an excellent period to explore this possibility, especially near the time of the Full Moon on the 14th. Blending the spiritual, physical, and emotional elements of a love relationship can lead to the level of ecstasy you desire, but you must begin by exploring your own inner needs more thoroughly.

FINANCE AND CAREER

Business travel can be highly profitable, and you may also be connecting more effectively to influential individuals. You may be tempted to overextend your budget from the 10th–20th, when impulsive spending can be quite costly. Be wary of agreements which involve another's promise of financial support during this period. Action on a pending agreement may be forthcoming during Mercury's retrograde from May 24–June 17.

OPPORTUNITY OF THE MONTH

Take the initiative in a situation which has been at a standstill during the New Moon on the 29th. Your nudging gets things moving.

Rewarding Days: 4, 5, 9, 10, 13, 26, 27, 31
Challenging Days: 1, 2, 15, 16, 21, 22, 28

AFFIRMATION FOR THE MONTH
"I am an effective communicator."

PRIMARY FOCUS

Even though Mercury is retrograding until the 17th, you are raring to go! Get everything in order and plan to see exceptional results in your career efforts after the 22nd.

HEALTH AND FITNESS

You may feel more energetic now that Mars is transiting in Virgo for seven weeks, but be aware that you can reach burnout more quickly unless you pace yourself.

ROMANCE AND RELATIONSHIPS

Taking time away from it all from the 1st–10th can give you a chance to get a better look at your love life. Travel may have romantic overtures, and may stimulate a new relationship or lead to improvement in an existing relationship, but only if you surrender your need to keep everything planned and under control! A private party may be more palatable during the Full Moon on the 12th. Plan a gathering of friends on the 23rd–24th or after the New Moon on the 27th (and don't forget some of your colleagues or co-workers!)

FINANCE AND CAREER

Avoid the tendency to scatter your energy at work or to become distracted by the changes in your work environment. Use this time to clear away unfinished business and make way for new, significant opportunities as the summer progresses. Travel or meetings from the 1st–16th may require follow-up. However, you can also lay the groundwork for long-range programs. Your mental ingenuity can lead to career advancement after the 20th.

OPPORTUNITY OF THE MONTH

Schedule presentations, conferences or meetings on the 23rd, 27th, or 28th, when your ideals for the future are more readily received.

Rewarding Days: 1, 5, 6, 9, 10, 13, 14, 22, 23, 27, 28
Challenging Days: 11, 12, 17, 18, 19, 25, 26

AFFIRMATION FOR THE MONTH
"I can clearly define my hopes for the future."

PRIMARY FOCUS

Increased involvement in community activity or special interests gives you a chance to use your talents and build friendships. Gratifying rewards from your career efforts confirm your worth.

HEALTH AND FITNESS

You may feel that your schedule is too cramped to allow time for fitness, but you'll benefit tremendously by making the time. Consider team sports or shared activities.

ROMANCE AND RELATIONSHIPS

Enjoy the company of your friends, making a special effort to get in touch with your closest allies. A romantic involvement improves as the result of a friendly connection; in fact, you may even feel a strong sexual attraction to a friend. The Full Moon on the 12th emphasizes a romantically exciting period which can lead to fireworks if you're willing to open your heart. You're more willing to develop an attitude of unconditional love, and can benefit by allowing your own uniqueness to bring you closer to those you love.

FINANCE AND CAREER

Professional associations may provide the support network you've needed to bolster your career. You may also become more personally involved in political action with positive results from the 1st–25th. To avoid feeling that you're carrying all the burden while someone else gets the credit, carefully redefine your role in partnership or cooperative activities. You're in no mood to carry another person along on your coat tails!

OPPORTUNITY OF THE MONTH

Bring important projects into full realization on the 11th and 12th. Reach out into new areas on the 30th and 31st.

Rewarding Days: 2, 3, 7, 8, 11, 12, 20, 21, 25, 30, 31
Challenging Days: 1, 9, 10, 15, 16, 22, 23

AFFIRMATION FOR THE MONTH
"I am loving, gentle and kind."

PRIMARY FOCUS

Financial dealings may be more pressing and time-consuming than anticipated. Attempt to stay within your budget, since there is a tendency to waste your resources.

HEALTH AND FITNESS

Increasing your endurance, building lean muscle mass, and developing your strength adds vitality and confidence. You might enjoy bicycling, walking, or running as part of your routine.

ROMANCE AND RELATIONSHIPS

You may feel that your secret yearning will never be realized, especially if you are uncertain if your attraction to another is shared. Search within yourself to determine how you really feel. If you're feeling pressured, you might prefer some time to yourself during the Full Moon on the 10th. However, your desire to make contact gets you out of the house and into the flow following the New Moon in Virgo on the 25th, when love blossoms and you feel alive again.

FINANCE AND CAREER

Your patience runs thin, especially with limiting attitudes which allow little room for change or growth. Power struggles arise in the workplace due to individuals pressing their own agenda, and you will benefit by refusing to be drawn into the foray. Watch your spending, whether in personal areas or for investment, since you may not know all the facts. Finances improve after the 24th, but you still need to be conservative.

OPPORTUNITY OF THE MONTH

Gather all the facts and do your work behind the scenes, then plan to launch your ideas on the 26th and 27th.

Rewarding Days: 3, 4, 7, 8, 16, 21, 22, 26, 27, 30, 31
Challenging Days: 5, 6, 11, 12, 18, 19, 25

AFFIRMATION FOR THE MONTH
"I respect my personal boundaries
and honor the boundaries of others."

PRIMARY FOCUS

You move ahead by applying mental ingenuity and may see financial improvement through writing, speaking or teaching. Launch public relations campaigns now.

HEALTH AND FITNESS

It's easier to stay active. Outside activities may even afford a chance to get to know your neighbors better. An improvement in your attitude about yourself now has positive effects on your health.

ROMANCE AND RELATIONSHIPS

Instead of wondering how others are feeling, take the time to find out! This is an important time to express yourself, and encourage personal expression from others who share your life. Partnerships and commitments gain strength during the Full Moon on the 8th. Any hesitation on your part may result from unexplored fears. Search your heart and ask questions to alleviate (or confirm) suspicions. It's time to know what's going on. You aren't happy with half-way: you want the complete experience.

FINANCE AND CAREER

Personal contact with clients or co-workers improves your career situation. Schedule meetings or presentations from the 4th–19th for best results. Old agreements may frustrate a pending situation once Mercury moves into its retrograde cycle on the 22nd. However, you can clarify the particulars and explore fresh options following the New Moon on the 24th. After a few adjustments, progress should be forthcoming.

OPPORTUNITY OF THE MONTH

Find ways to become more involved with life, avoiding your natural tendency to isolate yourself. Socialize from the 8th–20th.

Rewarding Days: 4, 5, 12, 13, 17, 18, 22, 23, 26, 27
Challenging Days: 1, 2, 8, 9, 15, 16, 29, 30

AFFIRMATION FOR THE MONTH
"I am open to receiving love."

PRIMARY FOCUS

Substantial increases in your worth are likely to occur, and it can be easier to get your foot into the right doors. Research, study, and accuracy give you the advantage

HEALTH AND FITNESS

You can enjoy feeling more physically powerful by continuing to build strength and vitality. However, you also need to stabilize your mental energy through extra nourishment or supplementation.

ROMANCE AND RELATIONSHIPS

Mixed messages can complicate your personal life early in the month unless you make a special effort to clarify your thoughts and f eelings. Watch your own tendency to jump to conclusions! Plan a romantic get-away with your sweetheart on the 15th, 16th, 24th, 28th, or 29th. The Solar Eclipse on the 23rd–24th may stimulate more intensive communication, and offers an excellent period during which you can make meaningful contact. Reach out to siblings to heal old wounds, or at least to satisfy your own need to share.

FINANCE AND CAREER

Efforts to reestablish contact, or follow-through on previous connections, during Mercury's retrograde until the 14th can bring positive results. Be wary of financial negotiations, and be sure there is substance to back up the claims from the 3rd–9th. Watch your own spending, and safeguard your possessions from loss. Your thorough research of details works to your benefit midmonth, and can stabilize your professional network of support later.

OPPORTUNITY OF THE MONTH

Attend conferences, meetings or make presentations on the 24th, 25th, 28th, or 29th.

Rewarding Days: 1, 2, 10, 15, 19, 20, 21, 24, 25, 28, 29
Challenging Days: 3, 5, 6, 12, 13, 26, 27

AFFIRMATION FOR THE MONTH
"I am an effective and clear communicator."

PRIMARY FOCUS

Improve your skills or abilities by taking classes or workshops. You may also be concentrating more energy on home and family, and can make significant breakthroughs in developing personal security.

HEALTH AND FITNESS

Pressure and stress take their toll, and may drain your vitality. Find effective ways to stay active, but be sure to allow plenty of time to relax and release tension.

ROMANCE AND RELATIONSHIPS

Friction in the family seems more marked, but may be the results of everyone's reactions to changes. You may be making improvements in your home environment, or may just see an increase in family activities. If you're feeling pressured by others, find ways to ameliorate the situation. Your needs to feel both emotionally and spiritually connected during the Full Moon on the 7th may prompt you to seek out inspirational experiences. Sharing these with those you love can raise the level of your relationship. Travel may offer a chance to stabilize a relationship near the New Moon on the 22nd.

FINANCE AND CAREER

Business travel, meetings, or presentations have the most significant impact on your professional advancement this month. You may feel more challenged by competitors midmonth, but have choices about the way you handle their confrontations. Maintain your sense of humor, and enjoy situations which challenge your knowledge and understanding. You may even learn something!

OPPORTUNITY OF THE MONTH

Your sharpness and clarity on the 17th, 20th, and 21st can surprise those who underestimate your abilities.

Rewarding Days: 6, 7, 11, 12, 16, 17, 20, 21, 24, 25
Challenging Days: 1, 2, 8, 9, 19, 22, 23, 28, 29

AFFIRMATION FOR THE MONTH
"My mind is linked to the Source of All Wisdom."

PRIMARY FOCUS

During this creatively expressive period you have ample opportunities to share your special talents. Children may play a significant role in stimulating your productivity.

HEALTH AND FITNESS

Recreational activities can be both enjoyable and physically invigorating. Improvements in your sense of vitality increase your sense of confidence and allow you to be more productive.

ROMANCE AND RELATIONSHIPS

This is a playful period, and can be especially satisfying. Romantic relationships flourish, and if you've been waiting for the right time to express your feelings, this is it! A new love can be quite delicious, but if you are already committed, then you may experience greater contentment by addressing your concerns and discovering a real support from your partner. You're leaving the past behind and moving into a fresh future. Use the energy of the New Moon on the 21st to open to pure joy.

FINANCE AND CAREER

Speculative interests show promising results. However, you need to be especially cautious when investing or spending from the 15th–21st, since you may be jumping into a situation which is not what it seems to be. If you are involved in artistic or creative areas, you may feel greater inspiration and creativity this month than you've experienced for a long time. Take advantage of the energy and express yourself! Make positive improvements in your working conditions after the 22nd.

OPPORTUNITY OF THE MONTH

Your individual talents are your best resource, and you can further your career and enhance your personal satisfaction by using and developing them this month.

Rewarding Days: 3, 4, 8, 9, 13, 14, 18, 19, 22, 23, 30, 31
Challenging Days: 1, 6, 7, 20, 21, 26, 27

AFFIRMATION FOR THE MONTH
"My heart is filled with joy!"

LIBRA
The Scales

September 23 to October 23

Element: Air

Quality: Cardinal

Polarity: Masculine/Yang

Planetary Ruler: Venus

Meditation: "Creating beauty and harmony"

Gemstone: Opal

Power Stones: Tourmaline, kunzite, blue lace agate

Glyph: Scales, Setting Sun

Key Phrase: "I balance"

Anatomy: Kidneys, adrenals, lower back, appendix

Colors: Blue, pastels

Animal: Brightly plumed birds

Myths/Legends: Hera, Venus, Cinderella

House Association: 7th

Opposite Sign: Aries

Flower: Rose

Key Word: Harmony

Positive Expression:
Impartial
Considerate
Refined
Sociable
Agreeable
Artistic
Gracious
Logical
Diplomatic

Misuse of Energy:
Indecisive
Placating
Conceited
Distant
Inconsiderate
Critical
Unreliable
Argumentative

♎ LIBRA ♎

Your Ego's Strengths and Weaknesses

When diplomacy, refinement, and courtesy are necessary, you're the right person for the job. Your easy grace and agreeable manner make you a welcome addition and draw many people to you. Your objectivity arises from your ability to see both sides of an issue and serves you well in situations which require a mediator and advisor. Others may view you as highly artistic, since your finesse and elegance are apparent in your words and actions.

As "The Judge" of the zodiac, you continually seek logical alternatives, symmetry, and harmony in relationships, life situations, and self-expression. However, you need to safeguard against requiring impossible ideals for yourself and others. Everything is relative for you, and you need to keep a perspective on the whole picture to avoid getting thrown out of balance. Use your natural attunement to the energy of Venus to help you maintain a clear sense of your own personal values, since measuring your values and worth according to the wishes of others will never bring the satisfaction you desire.

You may exhibit a level of indecisiveness which can drive other people crazy, especially if you've been thrown off balance! By learning to set goals involving your personal needs, you can avoid the conflict arising from placing another person or their situation at odds with your own desires. By learning to harmonize with your inner partner you can more easily preserve a sense of harmony within your self and radiate that energy to others around you.

Your Approach to Romance

You clearly love to be around other people and may yearn for that perfect fairy-tale relationship, only to be frustrated by the discovery that those ideas rarely occur in real life! As a result, you may have a list of stories to share about your conquests and losses. You can become the quintessential partner, but can also vacillate between absolute involvement and cool detachment. You may fear you'll lose part of yourself if you lose the relationship.

Your lovemaking mood is heightened by a beautiful and safe atmosphere which allows you to open to your innermost desires. You are likely to feel magnetically attracted to Aries, your opposite, but can be frustrated by the lack of egalitarianism in the relationship! With the other air signs—Gemini, Aquarius, or Libra—you may enjoy a comfortable meeting of the minds. The mental acrobatics of Gemini can lead to a delightful companionship. Aquarius' uniqueness feeds your creativity and sparks romance. And, although you may feel a powerful understanding with another Libran, you may not feel very stable with one another. With Taurus you share a love of the aesthetic, but may not be comfortable with the underlying agenda of control issues, and you may feel smothered or trapped by Cancer's nurturance. Leo's passion for life inflames your own ardor, but Virgo's grounding practicality may not feel especially romantic to you. It's easy to become inexplicably intertwined after being overtaken by Scorpio's intense tidal wave of energy.

You may enjoy traveling with Sagittarius and can relish sharing life's grand adventure. Capricorn's attraction can be powerful, but may lead to tense, open conflict. The high emotionality of Pisces, which may at first seem uncomfortable, can be just what you're looking for when you're in the mood for a romantic interlude.

Your Career Development

You add a touch of class to any career, and may feel most at home with a career in the arts. You may choose to develop your own artistry, or represent and maintain the arts and literature of others through boutiques, museums, conservatories or galleries. A career in the fashion, beauty industry, or interior design might also be profitable.

With your knack for public relationship, you might enjoy personnel management, advertising, or retail sales; or you might use your ability to see and enhance the strengths of others in areas such as image consulting, counseling, or in more dramatic arenas such as costume or set design. You can be an effective attorney or judge, and might also enjoy relationship counseling.

Your Use of Power

You may prefer to ignore the idea that you want power, but once you reach an understanding of the nature of power, you may discover you have more than you realized! Your power results from your ability to use a logical, impartial approach to any circumstance, rather than allowing your emotions to get in your way. This approach can give you the appearance of aloofness, and you can also deliberately project an icy exterior when you're hurt.

You can undermine your own power by continually comparing yourself and your life situation with others. Allow yourself to feel positively about your own personal desires and needs, but also recognize that you will always seek high ideals for yourself and your world. Establish strong personal boundaries and begin to use your power to create life on your own terms, sharing yourself as a whole person.

With your awareness of your environment and the people within it, you can inspire improvement and change where it's needed most. You can offer hope that a peaceful solution is possible by demonstrating the other side of an option. When you allow the energy which flows through you from the Source to empower you, you will discover that your outer life reflects a more stable, balanced reality. You can then blend the perfect colors and textures which become a beautiful portrait of your life experience.

Famous Librans

Brian Boitano, Truman Capote, John le Carre, Cervantes, Joan Cusack, Dizzy Gillespie, Christopher Lloyd, Yo-Yo Ma, Wynton Marsalis, Johnny Mathis, Meat Loaf, Pope John Paul I, Dmitri Shostakovich, Chris Wallace, Sigourney Weaver

THE YEAR AHEAD FOR LIBRA

Your sense of confidence and optimism are a bright spot throughout 1995, and you may feel that you can finally see the light at the end of the tunnel. Even though this cycle does require a certain application of energy and productivity, you have more choices about the way you're using your time. You may feel that you are on the brink of a new level of personal expression, and can sense that you are moving in the right direction with your decisions and actions.

Throughout the entire year, the planet Jupiter is traveling through your Solar 3rd House, stimulating a desire to open your mind to new ideas and open your life to new opportunities. Now's the time to network—connecting with people, circumstances, and concepts which expand your outreach and influence. If you're involved in a field of communication, travel, or writing, the energy throughout this cycle provides ample stimulus to express your ideas in ways which are more readily accepted. You're in a good position to learn, but may also be strongly involved in teaching others or sharing your knowledge. The sense of restlessness which accompanies this period may result in your spending more time traveling or away from your everyday environment, but you may also discover better ways to utilize technology to link with others. The primary downfall of this cycle involves a tendency to spread yourself too thin, mainly because there are so many options that look attractive, and you just don't want to miss out on any of them! Carefully consider before you agree to an obligation of your time or energy, since you are more likely to feel that you can do just about anything.

The Solar Eclipses draw your attention to your finances, including those you share with others. However, you cannot afford to lay blame on others for your financial situation, since this is also a time to be more clearly aware of the way you feel about your own worth as a person, and the way you utilize your personal energy and resources. The most critical aspect of this cycle focuses upon your self-esteem and your attitudes and value systems. You may determine that you have been unfair to yourself with some of your life choices. By embracing your deeper values and needs, you're likely to discover that some of the forces which had driven you in the past are not longer viable.

If you were born from September 23–27, you're entering a two-year cycle of exciting new directions. Two major transits are playing a role in your life, with Uranus transiting in trine to your Sun, and Pluto traveling in sextile aspect to your Sun. The influence of these cycles will remain through the end of 1996, allowing you ample time to accommodate for the changes. In many respects, this can be a period of exceptional creative self-expression, since both of these energies stimulate the development of a positive sense of personal power. If you've been waiting for the best time to experiment with your creative talents and abilities, you may feel more inspired now than you've felt for years. These cycles also support the elimination of things you no longer need in your life, especially any self-defeating attitudes or insecurities. You may feel more willing to share the experience of love, and are in the perfect position to allow yourself to be loved for who you are, and to seek out a relationship which encourages greater unconditionality in loving. Most significantly, this is your time to appreciate yourself, and allow time and energy to develop the types of life situations which support your unique individuality.

If you were born from September 28–October 2, you'll need to concentrate on completing projects and building your database or improving your professional skills. During January and February you may still be dealing with some left-over projects from 1994, but you can still make progress by staying in touch with the right people and situations. You are experiencing a strong influence from Jupiter's transit in sextile to your Sun from January through October, and may be feeling more confident about your future than you've felt for a long time. Travel can figure prominently, whether related to business, or simply for personal pleasure. This can be an exciting period for any communicative form of expression. You might also feel more inclined to improve your relationships with the people in your everyday activities by becoming more involved and showing more concern than you have expressed in the past.

You're clearing away unnecessary factors from your life and making a strong leap of faith this year if your birth occurred from October 3–11. Pluto is transiting in semi-square aspect to your Sun, drawing your attention to your deeper feelings of self-worth (or lack thereof!), and intensifying your desire to connect with your inner self. You may feel that you're ready to move into the next level of your growth, although there may seem to be a gap in the path. Consider your life situation and determine which elements you no longer need, and discard or release them. This is especially true of habits or attitudes which are detrimental to your physical and emotional health. Then you may feel more willing to jump over that small ravine in your path of life onto a more rewarding platform of life experience.

If you were born from October 6–19, you're feeling some tension from Saturn's transit in quincunx to your Sun. This can be a frustrating cycle, especially if you're unhappy with your work and can see no way to change things. But you may also be experiencing physical distress, particularly if you suffer from any chronic weaknesses or condition. If you honestly pay attention to these areas of difficulty, you can, with persistence, get to the core of the problem and find ways to alleviate the tension. But if you ignore the fact that you're unhappy or not feeling well, then the energy of this cycle seems to intensify your distress in an unrelenting manner. You'll discover quickly enough the things which are too burdensome, but whether or not you'll be willing to release those burdens is another story! Be particularly aware of your resentments or feelings of guilt, since these are your primary trigger points now. If you really feel that you are being forced into a situation for which you are not responsible, or into a circumstance which you know is not good for you, this is the time during which you must stand up for yourself and say, "No," once and for all!

You're likely to feel a strong desire to escape from the ordinary into a more idealistic existence this year if you were born from October 15–20. Neptune's transit squaring your Sun can bring a profoundly increased artistic sensibility, and may also draw you in a more spiritual direction. However, you can also be the victim of deception (including self-deception) more easily than you have been in the past. It is crucial that you determine healthy outlets through which to express these urges to touch the beautiful and divine. If you are artistic, allow your dreams and imagination to reach into areas which you've not explored. Regardless of your special talents, music can play a significant role in helping you maintain a positive balance of energy. You can also use creative imagery more effectively. Pay special attention to your dreams, since you may be able to tap into levels of consciousness which had been previously closed to you. However, be aware that your dreams are not literal! This is a period of transcendence from the ordinary, but can be a dangerous time when dealing with the mundane reality of the world, since you're likely to see what you want to see instead of what is actually there. You may feel more physically sensitive than you have been in the past, especially to your environment, but you can also show greater sensitivity to medications or alcohol. Be aware that you are in a period of transition, and that your boundaries are changing. Relationships and life situations are also part of this transitional phase, and in your desire to create a more idealistic life situation, you can be highly suggestible. You may still be in the same circumstances once this cycle has ended, but you are likely to have an entirely different perspective on them! Carefully navigated, this can be a period of spiritual awakening, forgiveness, and release.

You're feeling a desire to break away from the past and move into an exciting new future if you were born from October 19–23. The urge to revolutionize your life results from Uranus' transit in square to your Sun, but you are also influenced by deep inner changes while Pluto transits in semi-sextile to your Sun. The temptation to try to wipe the slate clean and begin your life anew can result in alterations which leave you feeling empty if carried too far. However, it is necessary to look carefully at your life circumstances and determine whether or not you can continue with some of them. If you're trapped by situations which are stifling your growth, this is the time to free yourself. You may also need to take some risks now which would have been unthinkable in the past. Many times, situations change unexpectedly during these cycles, leaving you feeling out of control. Your manner of response is your best way to stay in charge, so keep that connection to your inner self while trying to make the right decisions.

Tools to Make a Difference

Basically, this is a year during which you will be drawn to many forms of self-improvement. Learn to apply and use creative visualization, meditation and affirmations while effectively changing your life situation—things move along more quickly and in the directions you most prefer! Listen to your inner voice (including all those things you say to yourself under your breath) and trust your intuitive guidance. Find ways to improve your health by connecting mind and body more positively.

Keep your personal environment in harmony with your needs by using color, light, and sound to create the energy you desire. Wear your favorite colors when you're feeling the need for a boost of energy and confidence. Use aromatherapy to restore your sense of balance.

During your meditations, concentrate on your need to free your mind. See yourself entering a spaceship ready to launch. Once you've centered yourself and calmed your mind, give the signal for ignition. Feel yourself rising from earth's atmosphere into the heavens. Then, feel the quiet release of energy which occurs as you soar effortlessly in your craft through the galaxy. Take in the view. Look back upon the earth, floating peacefully in space. If you decide to visit another planet or fly into another galaxy, be aware of the differences and changes you experience. Bring your new perspective with you as you return to the bounds of earth, and keep in your mind the understanding that time and space do not limit your awareness.

Affirmation for the Year

"I am loving, gentle, and kind."

ACTION TABLES FOR LIBRA

These dates reflect the best (but not the only) times for success and ease in these activities according to your Sun Sign.

Change Residence	Jan. 1–5; Dec. 12–31
Request a Raise	Sep. 24–25
Begin a Course of Study	May 29–30; Dec. 22
Visit a Doctor	Mar. 15–Apr. 1; Aug. 10– 28
Start a Diet	Jan. 5–6; Feb. 1–2, 28;
	Mar. 28–29; Apr. 24–25;
	May 21–22; June 17–19;
	July 15–16; Aug. 11–12;
	Sep. 8–9; Oct. 5–6;
	Nov. 1–2, 28–30;
	Dec. 26–27
Begin a Romance	Jan. 30–31
Join a Club	July 27–28
Seek Employment	Mar. 15–Apr. 1; July 10–24
Take a Vacation	Jan. 12–13; Feb. 8–9;
	Mar. 8–9; Apr. 4–5;
	May 1–2, 28–29;
	June 25–26; July 22–23;
	Aug. 18–19; Sep. 15–16;
	Oct. 12–13; Nov. 8–9;
	Dec. 6–7
Change Your Wardrobe	Jan. 7–Mar. 13
End a Relationship	Oct. 8–9
Seek Professional Advice	Jan. 7–8; Feb. 3–4; Mar. 3–4,
	30–31; Apr. 26–27;
	May 23–25; June 20–21;
	July 17–18; Aug. 13–15;
	Sep. 10–11; Oct. 7–8;
	Nov. 3–4; Dec. 1–2, 28–29
Have a Makeover	Sep. 24–25
Obtain a Loan	Jan. 9–10; Feb. 6–7;
	Mar. 5–6; Apr. 1–3, 29–30;
	May 26–27; June 22–23;
	July 19–21; Aug. 16–17;
	Sep. 12–13; Oct. 10–11;
	Nov. 6–7; Dec. 3–5, 30–31

PRIMARY FOCUS

Strive to keep a balance between the time you spend with others in social or family activities and the time you need for yourself. Effort expended behind the scenes now gives yo . a leading edge later.

HEALTH AND FITNESS

If you're not feeling up to par, then break away from situations which waste your energy. Holding in your frustrations or stress can quickly undermine your vitality. Schedule a massage midmonth.

ROMANCE AND RELATIONSHIPS

Even though you may have the best of intentions, you may still find that others are not in agreement with your ideas or decisions. Family tension or stress from your job can distract you from romantic desires, especially near the Full Moon on the 16th. However, you're in a more lovable frame of mind from the 21st–31st, when some of the tension lifts and you might enjoy a romantic getaway. Even if you're alone, a short trip to recover your energy and heal your soul could feel great the 26th–28th.

FINANCE AND CAREER

Business conferences or meetings from the 1st–20th may be filled with political back-stabbing and manipulation which you find distasteful and non-productive. If you are called to mediate, focus on future possibilities instead of staying stuck on problems from the past which may be a lost cause. Your persuasiveness can be highly effective after the 21st, when a chance to review a situation can bring it back to life.

OPPORTUNITY OF THE MONTH

Use Mercury's retrograde cycle, which begins on the 25th, to bring the positive side of a conflict to light, resulting in a turning point.

Rewarding Days: 3, 12, 13, 21, 22, 26, 27, 30, 31
Challenging Days: 1, 5, 7, 8, 14, 15, 16, 28, 29

AFFIRMATION FOR THE MONTH
"I am an impartial advisor."

PRIMARY FOCUS
Increased productivity in your career may be the result of the influx of creative ideas, but you can also feel greater support from others, adding buoyancy to your advancement and recognition.

HEALTH AND FITNESS
Getting involved in team sports or group fitness activities may be the best way to keep your physical energy strong, and can also be great fun. Anything boring is not recommended!

ROMANCE AND RELATIONSHIPS
You're feeling frisky and ready for love, but may still be restrained by the demands of your work or schedule. However, your inventive approach can make up for the lack of time which seems to plague your life these days. Romance can be especially satisfying near the time of the Full Moon on the 15th, when a combination of entertainment and quiet time alone together is your best bet, but watch a tendency to send the wrong message from the 24th–28th by appearing to be detached when you may want real closeness.

FINANCE AND CAREER
Investigate carefully before signing contracts or making major purchases, since Mercury is retrograding until the 15th. You may also need to rethink a political stance from the 1st–7th to be sure your position is in harmony with your ethical standards. Demands from others at work late in the month can seem unfair, but may be satisfied if you eliminate activities or situations which are non-productive. Avoid making empty promises.

OPPORTUNITY OF THE MONTH
Solidify your friendships by spending time or making contact with those you consider to be supportive allies.

Rewarding Days: 8, 9, 13, 14, 18, 19, 22, 23, 26, 27
Challenging Days: 1, 3, 4, 5, 11, 12, 24, 25

AFFIRMATION FOR THE MONTH
"I am a loyal and supportive friend."

PRIMARY FOCUS

Answer demands from others by determining the relevance of their requests to your needs and responsibilities. Commitments made now are best if they are short-term.

HEALTH AND FITNESS

Even though you may not be looking for "fitness" as the goal, staying active by enjoying dance, recreation, or sports can improve your health. Be kind to yourself and honor your physical limits.

ROMANCE AND RELATIONSHIPS

You're definitely in a romantic frame of mind and can feel more comfortable expressing love if you have a demonstration of trust from your partner. An existing relationship may need a boost, which can result from finding more opportunities to play instead of just concentrating on problems all the time. A friend can be the catalyst for a new romance from the 1st–18th, but you may not feel like making a socially obligatory stance about your commitment until after the New Moon on the 30th.

FINANCE AND CAREER

Work can be highly demanding, especially if you've fallen behind in your responsibilities. Use the energy of the New Moon on the 1st to reorganize your schedule and priorities in such a way that you see better productivity. Difficulties with co-workers can escalate during the Full Moon on the 16th, especially if there are undercurrents of jealousy or deception. Instead of backing away, take a direct approach to resolve the conflicts.

OPPORTUNITY OF THE MONTH

To avoid being pigeon-holed into a position determined by someone else, make your feelings and ideas known on the 8th–9th.

Rewarding Days: 8, 9, 13, 14, 17, 18, 21, 22, 26, 27
Challenging Days: 1, 2, 3, 4, 10, 11, 23, 24, 28, 29

AFFIRMATION FOR THE MONTH
"I am confident in myself and my abilities."

PRIMARY FOCUS

Social activities flourish and can be the key to creating more personable interactions with your peers or co-workers. Boost your career through political involvement or community activities.

HEALTH AND FITNESS

If you're feeling emotionally balanced now, your health will improve; but emotional pressure can just as easily drain your vitality. Nourish your sense of humor.

ROMANCE AND RELATIONSHIPS

Expressive communication improves your love life, but watch a tendency to manipulate the conversation so that you seem to be the nice guy and the other person, the villain. Get what you want through honest interaction and expression of your feelings and needs during the Lunar Eclipse in Libra on the 15th. A situation which has outlived its usefulness can wither away near the Solar Eclipse on the 29th, but one which still serves a vital purpose can be reborn. Reach out with love.

FINANCE AND CAREER

Turn the tide in your work situation by showing an honest concern for the welfare of others and real effort toward self-improvement. A selfish attitude will only alienate your support system, and can damage your reputation. Deceptive or incomplete communication confuses negotiations from the 14th–19th, so be sure you have all the facts before you set out to bargain. Know your competition and you'll stay ahead of the game. Turn away and you'll lose ground.

OPPORTUNITY OF THE MONTH

Schedule presentations or meetings on the 4th, 18th, 19th, 22nd or 23rd to showcase your most outstanding abilities and ideas.

Rewarding Days: 4, 5, 9, 14, 15, 18, 19, 22, 23
Challenging Days: 1, 6, 7, 8, 20, 21, 26, 27

AFFIRMATION FOR THE MONTH
"I clearly project my true self to others."

PRIMARY FOCUS

Travel or educational pursuits improve your career and may offer a chance to enhance a relationship. You may also benefit from the support or financial success of others.

HEALTH AND FITNESS

Your mind may be working overtime, adding an increased level of fatigue at the end of your busy days. Elevate your intake of foods or supplements high in B-vitamins to stay alert and clear.

ROMANCE AND RELATIONSHIPS

Demonstrate your appreciation for and gratitude toward others to solidify your relationships. Your partner may surprise you by a change of heart on an important issue, which could lead to a crisis in your relationship if you fail to notice. Consider a romantic vacation to invigorate an existing relationship or discover a new love. A "harmless" flirtation from the 12th–18th can lead to a power struggle, but if you're clear about your intentions, it may open the door for an exceptional experience near the New Moon on the 29th.

FINANCE AND CAREER

Negotiate contracts prior to the 10th, unless you're reaching a closure of a long-standing negotiation or agreement. Loss of support from a partner or investor can jeopardize a situation from the 10th–14th, but can be clarified after the Full Moon on the 14th. Business travel, conferences, or presentations bring recognition your way after the 15th. However, you're in the best position to influence others after the 24th.

OPPORTUNITY OF THE MONTH

Use Mercury's retrograde cycle after the 24th to follow through on important negotiations, contracts or discussions.

Rewarding Days: 2, 3, 11, 12, 17, 21, 22, 25, 26, 29, 30
Challenging Days: 4, 5, 14, 17, 18, 23, 24, 25, 31

AFFIRMATION FOR THE MONTH
"I trust my intuitive guidance."

PRIMARY FOCUS

Your outreach into the world continues to expand, and this is an exceptional time to concentrate on writing, travel, or educational pursuits.

HEALTH AND FITNESS

You may need extra time for rest and relaxation to balance your otherwise high level of activity. Use relaxing herbs in a soothing bath to help take the edge off your busy days.

ROMANCE AND RELATIONSHIPS

The sexual chemistry of your relationship can be quite strong from the 1st–11th, but you may be reluctant to explore your desires. Create the right environment which will give you the room and safety to express your needs. Travel may fare better after the 15th, especially if you're wanting to bring some vitality back into an existing love. Share your philosophical ideals with your sweetheart and make plans for your future during the Full Moon on the 12th. Be sure to allow time for family from the 27th–29th.

FINANCE AND CAREER

Jointly held finances or properties need reevaluation from the 1st–10th, and may be the source of useable capital for a new venture. During Mercury's retrograde through the 17th you may feel caught between the expectations of what could be and the reality of a situation. Keep faith, but allow a realistic approach when making final decisions. Try not to push someone else into action if they show reluctance from the 11th–17th.

OPPORTUNITY OF THE MONTH

Work out details behind the scenes, then put forth your proposal on the 30th to launch a new project.

Rewarding Days: 3, 7, 8, 12, 15, 16, 25, 26, 30
Challenging Days: 1, 10, 13, 14, 20, 21, 27, 28

AFFIRMATION FOR THE MONTH
"My mind is guided by Divine Wisdom."

PRIMARY FOCUS

Career growth and recognition keep you on your toes this month, and you may have difficulty safeguarding your private time. Leave your work when you leave the office or work place.

HEALTH AND FITNESS

Job stress weighs more heavily than usual, requiring you to be more diligent in your efforts to stay healthy. Release tension, stretch, and increase physical flexibility.

ROMANCE AND RELATIONSHIPS

A more understanding connection to your partner arises from your shared beliefs, and you'll appreciate the comfort you experience from developing your spiritual bond. Cultural, educational, or religious activities provide a good outlet to make new contacts. Get in touch with your parents near the time of the Full Moon on the 12th, even though you may prefer only a short visit. You're likely to see more differences than similarities in the way you think these days, but you can still remain supportive.

FINANCE AND CAREER

Conferences or business meetings provide a fantastic outlet for your career growth, particularly from the 1st–7th, and then after the 16th. Delays from the 9th–15th can be discouraging, but you can overcome them through sheer persistence and attention to detail. Some confusion over finances can be disturbing from the 23rd–28th, and you need to proceed with care before making large investments or signing contracts.

OPPORTUNITY OF THE MONTH

Seek counsel with others who share your views and show your mutual support to one another on the 27th–28th.

Rewarding Days: 5, 6, 9, 13, 14, 22, 23, 27, 28
Challenging Days: 3, 11, 12, 17, 18, 24, 25, 26

AFFIRMATION FOR THE MONTH
"I am confident about my career choice."

PRIMARY FOCUS

Your participation in community activities, with friends or special interest groups, can be highly satisfying and provide confirming support. Create exciting long-range goals.

HEALTH AND FITNESS

With Mars transiting in Libra you may feel more restless and have a tendency to push beyond your limits before you realize you've reached them. Set a reasonable pace and allow time to wind down.

ROMANCE AND RELATIONSHIPS

This can be an exceptional period of opening to love, and you can either begin a new relationship or strengthen an existing tie with greater ease and confidence. Your friends play a significant role, providing the impetus for positive change. You're eager to create a memorable experience of love during the Full Moon on the 10th. Be wary of new attractions from the 20th–31st, when taking your time to get to know one another allows you to savor the experience. You may be onto something, but need to slow down and make sure.

FINANCE AND CAREER

Your career activities are more rewarding and you may see new opportunities for advancement from the 1st–10th. To gain greater cooperation, be sure everyone understands their roles and possible results, especially from the 17th–21st, when financial disputes can arise due to power struggles. Network from the 1st–23rd, but allow extra time to apply yourself to tasks behind the scenes after the New Moon on the 25th.

OPPORTUNITY OF THE MONTH

Make an investment in your future on the 9th–10th by giving of yourself and showing others how you feel.

Rewarding Days: 1, 2, 5, 6, 9, 10, 18, 24, 28, 29
Challenging Days: 7, 8, 12, 13, 14, 15, 21, 22

AFFIRMATION FOR THE MONTH
"My heart is filled with love."

PRIMARY FOCUS

Your ability to say the right things at the right time has tremendous influence on the outcome of events this month. Strive to maintain impartiality when mediating the conflicts of others.

HEALTH AND FITNESS

Concentrate on building stamina and endurance, particularly after the 10th, when you may need extra energy to handle a demanding schedule. Schedule a massage on the 8th, 12th, or 22nd.

ROMANCE AND RELATIONSHIPS

Your patience with others wears thin early in the month, and taking some time to yourself can be the best solution from the 1st–4th. It may be easier to reach an understanding over important issues, even though you may have to repeat or clarify the situation once Mercury turns retrograde on the 22nd. Your tolerance for poor taste is minimal from the 1st–16th, when you can lose your interest in someone who doesn't meet your standards. Try again after the New Moon on the 24th, when you're more open.

FINANCE AND CAREER

Whether you're making presentations, negotiating, or acting as an advisor, your ideas carry more weight and your ability to communicate your position is enhanced. Mercury will be transiting in Libra through early November, providing excellent outlets to network and communicate with others. You may feel especially confident about your prospects from the 17th–30th, but need to take a conservative approach to be most successful.

OPPORTUNITY OF THE MONTH

Contact the old line on the 20th–21st to determine a solid position before launching forward on the 24th.

Rewarding Days: 2, 6, 15, 16, 20, 24, 25, 29, 30
Challenging Days: 3, 4, 10, 11, 17, 18, 22, 23

AFFIRMATION FOR THE MONTH
"I am an effective communicator."

PRIMARY FOCUS
Carefully attend to the details of your finances. Stabilize your position, and consider the needs of others along with your own when using your influence in any situation.

HEALTH AND FITNESS
An increase in mental stress can quickly deplete your B-vitamins, so be sure to increase these nutrients in your diet. Concentrate on building muscle tone and endurance.

ROMANCE AND RELATIONSHIPS
You may feel strongly attracted to someone new and are in a flirtatious mood from the 1st–11th. It's easy to become involved in a situation which may be inappropriate to your needs, since you may be unconsciously seeking a diversion. By staying aware of your real needs, this can be a rewarding period of self-discovery. Your true feelings about a partnership surface during the Lunar Eclipse on the 8th. Plan a romantic getaway from the 22nd–27th, and allow time to share your favorite pleasures on the 30th and 31st.

FINANCE AND CAREER
Impulsive spending has negative repercussions now, so make a careful assessment of your needs before you go shopping or make investments. You're in a better position to stabilize your finances after the Solar Eclipse on the 23rd. Take extra care when traveling during Mercury's retrograde through the 13th, since you're likely to be less tolerant of delays or inconvenience. Write letters or make important calls after the 24th.

OPPORTUNITY OF THE MONTH
This is a time to keep an open mind and try a different approach, realizing that you are not making a definite commitment.

Rewarding Days: 3, 4, 12, 13, 22, 23, 26, 27, 30
Challenging Days: 1, 2, 7, 8, 15, 16, 28, 29

AFFIRMATION FOR THE MONTH
"My mind is open to new ideas."

PRIMARY FOCUS

Business or personal travel are profitable. You can also benefit by attending classes or workshops or applying yourself to improving your professional skills or abilities.

HEALTH AND FITNESS

You're likely to prefer to stay more active now, and can enjoy time spent enjoying the beauty of nature. This can be a positive period of strong vitality and good health.

ROMANCE AND RELATIONSHIPS

Try not to put your foot in your mouth from the 1st–4th, when jumping to conclusions or speaking too soon can be embarrassing. An existing love relationship grows through consistent effort toward improving communication, and you might prefer to spend time talking about your needs, feelings, and dreams instead of just watching television or other diversions. Plan a party this month, and make an effort to get to know your neighbors (you never know who you'll meet!). Vacation travel looks great from the 19th–28th.

FINANCE AND CAREER

Isolation at this time would be counterproductive to your career growth, so get out there and do some networking! If you work in a communicative field, you'll see tremendous progress. To stabilize your finances, consider spending time with a knowledgeable advisor near the Full Moon on the 7th, but try to stay objective. Launch a plan to make better use of your resources after the New Moon on the 22nd.

OPPORTUNITY OF THE MONTH

Take advantage of situations which give you a chance to reach more people or increase your reputation from the 19th–30th.

Rewarding Days: 8, 9, 13, 18, 19, 22, 23, 26, 27
Challenging Days: 1, 3, 4, 5, 11, 12, 24, 25

AFFIRMATION FOR THE MONTH
"I enjoy my independence."

PRIMARY FOCUS

Home and family play a powerful role, and you may be making improvements in your home or even considering a move. You can draw to yourself a situation which is more suitable for your needs.

HEALTH AND FITNESS

Emotional stress or worry over family pressures can take its toll on your body unless you find healthy ways to relax and release tension. Work off your frustrations through exercise.

ROMANCE AND RELATIONSHIPS

Your family needs more of your time and energy, and you are likely to be more involved than usual for this time of year. Make contact with siblings from the 1st–11th, with a special effort to mend fences during the Full Moon on the 6th. Keep the fires of passion burning by staying emotionally available to your partner, since you may need support to help deal with some family conflicts. Try to stay out of battles that have little to do with you. Learning objectivity is crucial from the 21st–31st.

FINANCE AND CAREER

Progress in your career path is strongest from the 1st–12th, and can be accentuated by staying involved in outreach activities. Good news about future opportunities is likely during the Full Moon on the 6th, but you may not see the manifestation until after the New Moon on the 21st. Avoid the temptation to distract yourself from your priorities at work from the 14th–22nd. It will be easier to keep your concentration after the 24th.

OPPORTUNITY OF THE MONTH

An especially creative period gives you a boost on the 24th and 25th. Use this time to show your love to others.

Rewarding Days: 6, 7, 11, 16, 17, 20, 24, 25
Challenging Days: 1, 2, 8, 9, 22, 23, 28, 29

AFFIRMATION FOR THE MONTH
"I see joy all around me."

♏ SCORPIO ♏
The Scorpion

October 23 to November 23

Element: Water

Quality: Fixed

Polarity: Feminine/Yin

Planetary Ruler: Pluto

Meditation: "Mastery through Transformation"

Gemstone: Topaz

Power Stones: Obsidian, citrine, garnet

Glyph: Scorpion's tail

Key Phrase: "I desire"

Anatomy: Reproductive organs, genitals, rectum

Colors: Burgundy, black

Animal: Reptiles, scorpions, birds of prey

Myths/Legends: Hades and Persephone, Shiva, Ereshkigal

House Association: 8th

Opposite Sign: Taurus

Flower: Chrysanthemum

Key Word: Intensity

Positive Expression:

Healing
Transforming
Incisive
Erotic
Passionate
Regenerating
Incisive
Investigative
Sensual
Transforming

Misuse of Energy:

Destructive
Overbearing
Obsessive
Lascivious
Jealous
Violent
Vengeful
Extreme

♏ SCORPIO ♏

Your Ego's Strengths and Weaknesses

As "The Catalyst" of the zodiac, your energy provides the impetus for transformational healing. You are drawn to what lies beneath the surface, preferring to explore the depths as an exercise in creativity. Your charisma can be fascinating, and you are a master of intrigue. With piercing insight into human nature, you are keenly aware of the inner conflicts which are part of life experience.

With a tendency to keep the volcano of emotion under control, you may project an energy which is in contrast to what you really are feeling deep within yourself. Those who have something to hide are often uncomfortable in your presence, since you have a natural sensibility which alerts to you their hidden agendas. You are not likely to expose the details of your life or your feelings, except in circumstances which are safe and secure, or with people who have proven themselves to be worthy of your trust.

You are ruled by Pluto, the energy of regeneration and restoration, and are walking the path of the healer. Through your ability to experience the heights of joy or the depths of despair, you understand the essence of the shamanic journey. By directing your energy toward higher principles, you can rise to heroic action, but if you've been deeply wounded, you can become compulsively vengeful. Your lesson involves learning to forgive yourself and others by releasing pent-up emotions of guilt and shame, and experiencing true spiritual rebirth.

Your Approach to Romance

You spin a mesmerizing romantic web when you're ready for love, drawing your partner into a fascinating experience of sensuality. With you, the art of lovemaking can be a continually intriguing experience, opening the gates to ecstasy. Even though you may long for a person who can share the depths of your soul, you may be unwilling to unlock your doors once you've sent out the invitation! You're more likely to keep your feelings hidden until you've established trust. Once hurt, you can lock the door to love forever, which protects your vulnerability, but also leaves you longing for a special tender touch.

You may require patience in your search for the right partner, and need to allow time to develop the level of intimacy you desire. You may be most comfortable with the water signs —Cancer, Scorpio, and Pisces. Cancer may share your ideals and you'll enjoy the nurturance. Pisces stimulates your creative, romantic side while providing plenty of imaginative sensitivity, and another Scorpio may feel like your soul-mate, with the relationship ranging from extreme passion to volatility.

Because you don't appreciate being teased, you may not feel at ease with Aries. Taurus, your zodiac opposite, demonstrates a sensuality and steadfastness which can be highly attractive. But watch out for disagreements, since it's difficult to say who's the most stubborn. Gemini's entertaining wit is fun, but can become distracting when you seek continuity and support. Although Leo's magnetism shivers your timbers, you can be frustrated by their self-absorbed attitude.

With Virgo, friendship and support can grow into lasting passion. You may feel at ease with Libra until it's time to make a decision about something. Lusty, adventurous Sagittarius is inviting, but you may have difficulty accepting their carefree independence. Capricorn understands you and supports your success. Although Aquarius may intrigue you, there's likely to be too much distance to achieve the far reaches of passion you require.

Your Career Development

You're well-suited for a career which allows you to be involved in bringing about changes. Healing arts, including counseling, can offer an opportunity to help others restore their lives. Work involving research, scientific probing, or renovation can be gratifying. Or, you might find creative expressions such as music, painting, or writing strong outlets which have a positive transformational effect.

You're well-suited to positions of influence and power, and have a knack for making the most of the resources of others. You can become an exceptional director, producer, or performer in the entertainment field. Or, in business, you might prefer the options of financial counseling, investment banking, career management, insurance, or corporate law. History and archeology may be appealing as a hobby or career. Whatever your choices, you can transform what appears to be useless into something of value. Ultimately, you might even turn a tidy profit!

Your Use of Power

If anyone understands power, it's you. Even as a child you may have been drawn to powerful people or omnipotent heroes. Through your innate understanding of the natural transformational rhythms of life, the process of birth, life, and death, you know that changes are merely a part of existing, yet your desire to hold onto life's richest experience may be driven by a feeling that you want to control these natural processes in some way.

Reach deep within your own soul for your true needs and healing, otherwise you may undermine your power by hiding behind a massive shield against emotional pain. Once you've touched that inner realm, you'll find a strong warrior spirit residing at the core of your being, which constantly guards you from harm. Once you've allowed yourself to feel that you deserve to have your inner needs fulfilled, you can embrace this strength and power instead of feeling it as a threat. Your compassion for yourself will give you the strength to reach out toward the world and bring about the changes which impart growth and hope, now and for the future.

Famous Scorpios

Howard Baker, Lisa Bonet, John Cleese, Hillary Rodham Clinton, Nadia Comaneci, Keith Emerson, Sally Field, Larry Holmes, Telma Hopkins, Bob Hoskins, Calvin Klein, k. d. lang, Claude Monet, Kevin Nealon, Dan Rather, Julia Roberts, Fernando Valenzuela

THE YEAR AHEAD FOR SCORPIO

Throughout 1995, you may feel more confident about your abilities to express your most creative energies. You are finding ways to improve your life situation by allowing continued growth in the areas which you expanded through last year's opportunities. You may feel a bit restless, as though you are primed for some significant alterations in your life, although you may not be entirely clear about the end result of the changes you're sensing.

The Solar Eclipses complete their cycle in the Taurus-Scorpio axis for the last time this century, and have a significant impact on your personal awareness and growth. If you've been developing an enhanced sensibility to your inner self and integrating your spiritual and emotional needs with your life experience, this period should be one of positive self-expression. Relationships can also improve now by becoming more balanced and supportive. If you've been ignoring the deeper levels of awareness and growth, you may find it more difficult to get what you need from your life situation or from personal relationships. Even if things have been going well, you may discover some old resentment or pain which has stood in the way of experiencing the love and acceptance you deserve. You are learning to become whole and embrace your life in ways that allow continued evolution and personal growth. Additionally, increasing your alertness to physical needs can help you feel healthier and more vital. If you've had any chronic physical challenges, this cycle affords you the chance to discover some of the underlying emotional and spiritual aspects at the core of your physical distress. You are ready to release past trauma and move into a period of real healing.

Jupiter's transit in Sagittarius blazes a path through the 2nd House of your Solar Chart, increasing your focus on self-worth and material wealth. You may indeed have more money to spend, but you can also be tempted to spend more than you have! The energy of this cycle is directed toward unlocking a more positive outlook and opening to a greater appreciation of yourself and your resources. Be wary of the temptation to give in to accumulating status symbols. By making the most of what you have now, you can assure your long-term financial and material stability in ways that will be effective for years to come. But if you take for granted the things you have or misuse the energy you possess, you may find that you've wasted a chance to bring more substantial prosperity into every aspect of your life.

If you were born from October 23–26, you're challenged to become more uniquely expressive. Uranus is transiting in square to your Sun, while Pluto's transit is semi-sextile to your Sun. Primarily, this is a period of intensive and unexpected changes, especially involving your connection to your roots. The thrust of the Uranus cycle is self-expression and acceptance of those aspects of yourself which mark your individuality. During this time of personal revolution, you may feel that you are ready to walk away from your old life and begin anew. You are likely to experience changes in your family as well, and may feel that it's time to break out of the nest and establish your own security. Pluto's influence underscores the need to make changes, and stimulates an examination of your personal values. Yes, you are moving on, but you cannot effectively release restrictive elements from your life by simply taking the next stagecoach out of Dodge City. The true revolution occurs within, through changing your attitudes toward yourself, your talents, and your life situation. You may not have to go anywhere or make a move to make these changes, since looking in the mirror should tell you what you need to know, but you are likely to discover through this self-examination why you've been hanging onto situations, relationships, or ideals that are not really in harmony with your needs. The difficult part is incorporating the internal changes with your external life in such a way as to promote real progress instead of just burning all the bridges out of vengeance, hurt, or resentment.

If your birth occurred from October 27–November 1, you need to be particularly careful about dealing with your responsibilities from April through December of this year. Although you may have made some commitments during 1994 which seemed to be perfectly acceptable, you may be discovering that there are demands you had not considered. Saturn is transiting in sesquiquadrate to your Sun during this cycle, and you need to be alert to the ways you can trap yourself by taking actions which place you at unnecessary risk. Be especially aware of enticing physical attractions to others, and do a bit of research before you put your feet to the fire. It is possible that you've finally met your match, or that you are ready to make or renew a commitment. But if there are elements which cause you to hesitate, it's a good idea to explore them to avoid future regrets.

If you were born from October 30–November 11, you're feeling increased stability while Saturn transits in trine to your Sun from the months of January through early April. This is the time to make long-term commitments, take on greater responsibilities at work and share your expertise with others. Although this cycle does not last through the year, its effect can last for many years to come if you have prepared yourself and if you perform at your best.

You're experiencing enhanced sensitivity and opportunities to increase your creative expression if you were born from November 2–8. The energy of Neptune traveling in quintile to your Sun does not arrive with a marching band, and can be quite subtle in its influence, but if you are involved in any form of creative or artistic expression, you can refine your skills and augment your creativity in ways that add mastery and intrigue. In your personal life this can be a time of greater acceptance, forgiveness, and understanding of others. You might also make some unusual discoveries through study or travel.

If you were born from November 5–19, you're experiencing real growth and greater security while Saturn transits in trine aspect to your Sun from April through December. Because this cycle lasts through the greater part of the year and into early next year, you may be thinking more about long-range goals and long term stability. Also you're likely to have the opportunity to manifest greater success in your career efforts and can benefit by your willingness to be accountable for your own actions and efforts. Your discipline and focus increase now, and you may be interested in advancing your education or improving your professional skills in some way. Relationships evolve into deeper bonds and greater fulfillment due to your own self-confidence and integrity. This is your time to clarify your life direction and place yourself on the track to long-term success.

Your imagination and sensitivity are strengthened this year if you were born from November 14–19, while Neptune travels in sextile to your Sun. You may also be feeling more inclined toward the spiritual aspects of your life than you have been in the past, and can experience some truly rapturous moments if you surrender to this energy. Relationships improve through your application of this sensitive, intuitive cycle, and you can feel a more compassionate understanding of others during this time. Any form of artistic expression gains momentum, since you're rather enticed by the Muses now. Your willingness to release the past, to forgive yourself and others, also brings greater internal peace and harmony.

If you were born from November 17–23 you're experiencing a period of power, passion, and intensity for life which can reshape your existence. Not only are you feeling the energy of Pluto conjuncting your Sun, but also Uranus is transiting in sextile to your Sun. If you've been looking for the right time to make modifications, it has arrived (actually, you have arrived at the right levels of self-acceptance to make those changes!). Anything in your life which no longer serves to fulfill your true needs or encourage your growth can be eliminated or released, and may seem to disappear on its own in some circumstances. Be especially aware of your personal relationships, since this period requires honesty about your real feelings and needs. Any situation which still has enough energy, vitality, and material to support your higher needs can be improved, revitalized, or restored, but circumstances which are out of harmony with your needs are now ending. Physically, this is a period of healing, and you may find solutions to problems which have been plaguing you for quite some time. You may also become more involved in actions which have a healing effect upon the environment or society, and can be highly influential in making certain that these types of programs are carried out in the best possible manner.

Tools to Make a Difference

Seek out experiences which will build your self-esteem and promote self-improvement. Find ways to show your gratitude to others and to the Universal Spirit for sustaining your life. Get involved in making your dreams happen, instead of just wishing they would come true, by developing your mind, talents, and body. Investigate physical exercise programs which have a positive philosophical basis, such as martial arts, Tai Chi or yoga.

You may not feel that simply voicing a few affirmations will make much difference in your life, but using affirmative statements along with changing your actions and thoughts only adds emphasis to the growth you are directing. Avoid the tendency to isolate yourself from the world. Get involved with special interest groups which are making a difference.

You are likely to respond quite positively to natural healing methods, and can benefit from learning more about herbal therapies, homeopathy, and flower essences. Seek out herbal remedies designed to help you cleanse or purify your body, and remember to drink plenty of clear, pure water.

During your meditation, see yourself traveling in a canoe down a river which flows deep within the earth through a cavern. Feel the coolness of the air and the quiet calmness. Your journey takes you into an opening, and you see before you a waterfall which seems to shimmer in the moonlit darkness. Step out of the canoe onto the soft, yet firm, earth, and walk toward the waterfall. Stand under this stream and feel yourself filled with energy and power. Know that you can return to this place to revitalize and renew yourself anytime you feel low levels of energy.

Affirmation for the Year

"My life is filled with abundance in all things."

ACTION TABLES FOR SCORPIO

These dates reflect the best (but not the only) times for success and ease in these activities according to your Sun Sign.

Change Residence	Jan. 7–Mar. 13
Request a Raise	Oct. 23–24
Begin a Course of Study	Jan. 1–2; June 27–28
Visit a Doctor	Apr. 2–16; Aug. 29–Nov. 4
Start a Diet	Jan. 7–8; Feb. 3–4; Mar. 2–3, 30–31; Apr. 26–27; May 23–24, 25; June 20–21; July 17–18; Aug. 13–15; Sep. 10–11; Oct. 7–8; Nov. 3–4; Dec. 1–2, 28–29
Begin a Romance	Mar. 1–2
Join a Club	Aug. 26–27
Seek Employment	Apr. 2–16; July 26–Aug. 9
Take a Vacation	Jan. 14–15; Feb. 11–12; Mar. 10–11; Apr. 6–8; May 4–5, 31–June 1, 27–29; July 24–26; Aug. 21–22; Sep. 17–18; Oct. 14–16; Nov. 11–12; Dec. 8–9
Change Your Wardrobe	Mar. 15–Apr. 2
End a Relationship	Nov. 7–8
Seek Professional Advice	Jan. 9–10, 11; Feb. 6–7; Mar. 5–6; Apr. 1–3, 29–30; May 26–27; June 22–23; July 19–20; Aug. 16–17; Sep. 12–14; Oct. 10–11; Nov. 6–7; Dec. 3–4, 30–31
Have a Makeover	Nov. 22
Obtain a Loan	Jan. 12–13; Feb. 8–9; Mar. 8–9; Apr. 4–5; May 1–2, 28–30; June 25–26; July 22–23; Aug. 18–19; Sep. 15–16; Oct. 12–13; Nov. 8–9; Dec. 6–7

PRIMARY FOCUS

Professional and community activities keep you on your toes and may extend to travel, educational opportunities, or increased interaction with others. Keep a close watch on your finances.

HEALTH AND FITNESS

Team sports or group fitness activities are most enjoyable through the 22nd, although you may feel pressured by your own sense of competitiveness. Relax your attitudes.

ROMANCE AND RELATIONSHIPS

Even though you may desire more time with loved ones, especially in pleasurable or romantic activities, you may feel that duties and daily responsibilities diminish your opportunities. Friends or close relatives provide understanding support from the 1st–7th. Keep personal needs in perspective, and make plans for a long weekend away from everyday pressures near the Full Moon on the 16th. You'll feel more like staying close to home after the 20th, enjoying a break from the tests of the world.

FINANCE AND CAREER

Schedule important meetings or conferences from the 1st–6th, when your presentation of a new idea or project is well-received. Careful research or probing exposes the information or support you need to proceed. Watch your budget from the 8th–15th, when it's easy to miss steadily increasing costs until you've gone too far. Keep a firm stance on your position from the 15th–24th, when pressures from others can undermine your self-esteem.

OPPORTUNITY OF THE MONTH

Take advantage of the New Moon energy on the 1st to clarify or formulate important communications, meetings or concepts.

Rewarding Days: 1, 5, 6, 15, 16, 20, 24, 25, 28, 29
Challenging Days: 3, 4, 9, 10, 17, 18, 30, 31

AFFIRMATION FOR THE MONTH
"My mind is clear and open to truth."

PRIMARY FOCUS

Your drive to build your professional reputation and influence can lead to great success, but may also alienate others if you ignore their feelings or needs.

HEALTH AND FITNESS

You may feel restless, emotionally tense, and physically stressed throughout the month, and need to find time to rejuvenate. Take breaks instead of driving yourself at full throttle all the time.

ROMANCE AND RELATIONSHIPS

Part of your internal drive now may arise from trying to prove yourself, and if you're feeling conflict about your life choices, then you might benefit from reaching deep within yourself to determine why you're pushing so intensely. You may be feeling more on edge or more easily angered, and need healthy ways to deal with these feelings. Instead of stuffing your real feelings, deal directly with any family conflict arising near the Full Moon on the 15th. Romance is most promising from the 20th–28th.

FINANCE AND CAREER

Watch your expectations while Mercury retrogrades through the 15th, and be particularly careful when signing any contracts or making investments. Review your financial position now, and strive to eliminate situations which are draining your resources, or at least bring them down to a manageable level. Children, pet projects or hobbies can drain your budget now, so keep a little extra set aside for these expenditures.

OPPORTUNITY OF THE MONTH

Reach out, make contact and let your feelings or ideas be known on the 20th, 21st, 24th, or 25th.

Rewarding Days: 1, 2, 11, 12, 16, 20, 21, 24, 25, 28
Challenging Days: 4, 6, 7, 13, 14, 26, 27

AFFIRMATION FOR THE MONTH
"I trust my intuitive instincts."

PRIMARY FOCUS

The pressures of your job may be at odds with demands from your family and your own desire to move at an easier pace. Avoid wasting your efforts or your resources and concentrate on your obligations.

HEALTH AND FITNESS

Mental and emotional stress begin to diminish after the 18th, but until then, you may find it difficult to unwind. Frequent, active workouts might help balance the tension; just remember to stretch!

ROMANCE AND RELATIONSHIPS

Clear up family tensions as they arise, but watch your own tendency to jump to conclusions. You may also hold high expectations of your sweetheart or your children which are met with disappointment. Support those you love with unconditional love, and find it in your heart to forgive yourself while you're at it! A long-term commitment seems possible from the 13th–31st, and frank discussion about your needs during the Full Moon on the 16th can be quite illuminating.

FINANCE AND CAREER

Creative projects launched during the New Moon on the 1st show tremendous promise, but may take extra time to get off the ground. Build a foundation with your peers from the 1st–6th by listening to their concerns, and form a creative alliance with others from the 15th–31st. Continue to take a conservative approach to your spending or investing, particularly from the 19th–26th. Speculative interests fare best on the 24th and 25th.

OPPORTUNITY OF THE MONTH

Take actions designed to stabilize your position from the 10th–19th, and avoid compromising circumstances on the 8th and 9th.

Rewarding Days: 1, 2, 10, 11, 15, 19, 20, 23, 24, 28, 29
Challenging Days: 5, 6, 13, 14, 22, 25, 26, 27

AFFIRMATION FOR THE MONTH
"I am safe and secure."

PRIMARY FOCUS

Disciplined efforts to strengthen your talents lead to gratifying recognition. Avoid hostility from your superiors or professional peers by channeling your eagerness to succeed in ways that will not create defensiveness.

HEALTH AND FITNESS

Overexerting yourself physically can lead to exhaustion or injury near the time of the Lunar Eclipse on the 15th. Stay active, but honor your limitations!

ROMANCE AND RELATIONSHIPS

Maintaining honesty with yourself about your feelings and needs helps you stay out of trouble in romantic situations. But if you're ready to go for the long haul, you may have to take the risk and make the first move to make your dreams a reality. To determine whether or not to proceed ask yourself, "Is it really worth the cost or effort?" You may decide that the price is too high. Reexamine your feelings near the Solar Eclipse on the 29th, when you should have a clear sense of what you want from your partner.

FINANCE AND CAREER

Empty promises about career advancement or opportunity are not worth your efforts, so look for ways to gain real advancement. By applying yourself to getting the job done from the 3rd–18th, you can make the type of progress that leads to long-term success, but watch for deception or unexpected interruptions from the 14th–20th, and be prepared to take action. Use your imagination in solving problems from the 17th–23rd and you'll be ahead of the game.

OPPORTUNITY OF THE MONTH

Your wit and ingenuity work to your advantage on the 16th. Use them!

Rewarding Days: 7, 11, 12, 13, 16, 17, 20, 21, 24, 25
Challenging Days: 1, 2, 3, 9, 10, 22, 23, 29, 30

AFFIRMATION FOR THE MONTH
"I strive for mastery in my self-expression."

PRIMARY FOCUS

Your drive to accomplish your aims may be frustrated by external demands on your time and conflict between your own values and the values of others. Cooperative efforts require finesse and patience.

HEALTH AND FITNESS

Even though you may still be experiencing high stress levels from your work, you may find that balancing your energy is best accomplished through spending more time in playful activities.

ROMANCE AND RELATIONSHIPS

From the 1st through the Full Moon in Scorpio on the 14th you may feel increasing tension with your partner. Secretive or deceptive actions from the 10th–16th can lead to mistrust and rebellion from the 17th–20th. To improve your love life, consider the importance of your own attachments before you ask your partner to give up theirs. Better communication enhances sexual sharing on the 21st and 22nd, but you can slip into vague misunderstandings about personal needs or family ties after the 24th.

FINANCE AND CAREER

Even though you feel frustrated by the actions of authorities, you may still have to consider their influence in your career advancement or success. One thing is certain—you will not enjoy being pushed around! However, you may also tend to run rough-shod over the path of others in your climb to the top now. Stay positive and confident and be sure to clarify your plans before Mercury moves into its retrograde cycle on the 24th.

OPPORTUNITY OF THE MONTH

Investigate financial opportunities presented near the New Moon on the 29th, but avoid taking a risk unless you can afford it.

Rewarding Days: 4, 5, 9, 13, 14, 17, 18, 21, 22, 31
Challenging Days: 6, 7, 8, 19, 20, 26, 27, 28

AFFIRMATION FOR THE MONTH
"I am confident in myself and my abilities."

PRIMARY FOCUS

Seek professional advice regarding your finances, investments, or long-range business plans and use this time to reorganize your budget before launching into expanded professional development.

HEALTH AND FITNESS

Stay active by getting involved in team sports or fitness classes. Increasing mental activity can stress your body's need for B-vitamins and minerals, so watch your diet, too.

ROMANCE AND RELATIONSHIPS

If your feelings about your partner are undergoing change, it may be a normal part of the development of a love relationship. A strong love grows deeper now, but if you feel that there is nothing more to be gained from the connection, you owe it to yourself and to your partner to be honest without creating emotional damage. You may feel more open to romance on the 18th and 19th, and can definitely bring more energy to your love life through sharing your spiritual ideals or traveling following the New Moon on the 27th.

FINANCE AND CAREER

During Mercury's retrograde through the 16th you may find it difficult to obtain commitments from others, particularly in regard to joint finances, loans or taxes. Try to remain objective during the Full Moon on the 12th, and avoid the temptation to close your mind or reach a conclusion before all the evidence is presented. Your expectations are more reasonable after the 18th, and you're ready to move into new territory after the 27th.

OPPORTUNITY OF THE MONTH

Listen to the concerns of other on the 22nd and 23rd, and then present your own plans or ideas on the 28th.

Rewarding Days: 1, 5, 9, 10, 14, 18, 19, 27, 28
Challenging Days: 2, 3, 4, 15, 16, 22, 23, 30

AFFIRMATION FOR THE MONTH
"I respect the wishes of others."

PRIMARY FOCUS

Political action, business travel, or educational pursuits highlight this period. You can stabilize your professional reputation by taking a stand for your ideals and values.

HEALTH AND FITNESS

Be sure to keep a healthy attitude during any form of competitive activity from the 8th–15th, since you can undermine your own goals by forcing a situation, or by pushing yourself beyond your limits.

ROMANCE AND RELATIONSHIPS

Your love life gains momentum, with an existing relationship moving into higher levels of satisfaction, or a new love manifesting in unexpected circumstances with exciting results. If you can get away, traveling from the 14th–27th to a place which is out of the ordinary can create just the right atmosphere for intimacy and passion. The Full Moon on the 12th encourages you to connect with your spiritual needs and may also inspire you to take the risk of reaching out to experience greater love.

FINANCE AND CAREER

Professional associations provide the right support for your career goals, and you can also benefit from business travel, attending conferences, or taking advantage of educational opportunities during this time. Take a conservative approach in your attempts to influence others from the 9th–15th, and save your more innovative ideas until the 16th–27th. Career recognition on the 27th–28th may be the result of persistent efforts on your part.

OPPORTUNITY OF THE MONTH

Allow your creative energy to lead you and follow your instincts on the 15th and 16th.

Rewarding Days: 2, 3, 7, 8, 11, 12, 15, 16, 25, 26, 30
Challenging Days: 1, 6, 13, 14, 19, 20, 21, 27, 28

AFFIRMATION FOR THE MONTH
"I am guided by Truth and Wisdom."

PRIMARY FOCUS

Even though you may be in the spotlight as a result of your career, you may long for the solitude of your personal space. Spend as much time as you can working behind the scenes.

HEALTH AND FITNESS

Mental health activities such as releasing the past and clearing out the cobwebs in your emotional attic can actually increase your physical vitality this month.

ROMANCE AND RELATIONSHIPS

Friends provide exceptional emotional support, but may differ with you on some fundamental issues. If these differences create conflicts, determine for yourself where the conflict rests within your own psyche. The Full Moon on the 10th brings your attention to your parental relationship, which may be the source of some of your own issues with self-esteem. Get involved in your community after the New Moon on the 25th, when your leadership and creative energy can be the impetus for positive new directions.

FINANCE AND CAREER

Opportunities for career advancement can improve finances early in the month, but be aware of a tendency to focus too much on the future instead of concentrating on enjoying the now. Differences with authorities over your financial ideas or proposed budget can sting from the 16th–24th, but you should be able to reach agreement after the 26th. Schedule important meetings or presentations on the 8th, 21st, 22nd, 26th, 27th, 30th, or 31st.

OPPORTUNITY OF THE MONTH

Take time to thoroughly research you suspicions about a situation before you take action, since responding too quickly can be costly.

Rewarding Days: 3, 4, 7, 8, 11, 12, 21, 22, 26, 27, 30, 31
Challenging Days: 2, 9, 10, 16, 17, 18, 23, 24

AFFIRMATION FOR THE MONTH
"I appreciate and honor myself."

PRIMARY FOCUS

You're entering a period of greater courage and more powerful influence, but need to carefully distinguish between your personal agenda and what is important for the situation as a whole.

HEALTH AND FITNESS

Your physical energy is on the increase with Mars transiting in Scorpio from Sep. 7–Oct. 20, but watch a tendency toward burn-out—it's easy to overdo everything!

ROMANCE AND RELATIONSHIPS

A strong friendship can lead to romantic involvement, if you're emotionally available, from the 10th-22nd. This is definitely the time to open to the experience of enjoying love and receiving the support and affection from others you desire. If you've been waiting for the right time to share romantic love and affection, the energy during the Full Moon on the 8th is supportive, but only if you're willing to commit to your true feelings. Take time to clear your energy and retreat from the chaos after the 24th.

FINANCE AND CAREER

Continue to network with professional associates through the 16th, and make new business contacts during this time. But don't be surprised if you're dealing with trouble-shooting from the 1st–7th due to a breakdown in communication. Mercury's retrograde period from Sep. 22–Oct. 14 may be the best time to reorganize your efforts before trying again with a situation which has reached a stalemate. Investments may show disappointing results from the 18th–30th.

OPPORTUNITY OF THE MONTH

By tapping into your creative storehouse, you can turn a difficult situation into a positive alliance on the 8th or 9th.

Rewarding Days: 4, 8, 9, 17, 18, 22, 23, 27, 28
Challenging Days: 1, 6, 7, 12, 13, 20, 21

AFFIRMATION FOR THE MONTH
"I have positive goals for my future."

PRIMARY FOCUS

Clear away the things from your past which are no longer relevant to your life experience or needs, but avoid the temptation to burn all the bridges; crossing them will be sufficient progress!

HEALTH AND FITNESS

You may feel compulsively driven to accomplish your aims and can exhaust yourself in the process. Find creative ways to release and relax. Schedule a massage during the Lunar Eclipse on the 8th.

ROMANCE AND RELATIONSHIPS

You may be distracted by a tempting infatuation from the 1st–10th, although it may not lead anywhere. However, your attempts to revitalize an existing relationship can be successful if your partner is willing to exert similar effort. If you're uncertain, give yourself some time to do a little soul-searching during the Lunar Eclipse on the 8th. More substantial romantic opportunities await you following the Solar Eclipse in Scorpio on the 23rd. Instead of hoping for love from outside yourself, create a healthy mechanism to fill yourself with true love and appreciation.

FINANCE AND CAREER

Deceptive or undermining communication may not be intentional from the 1st–13th, but can still have devastating results if you fail to take responsibility by following up with correct information or action. Finances show significant improvement after the 20th, with particular support for investments or long-term contracts on the 24th, 25th, 28th, or 29th.

OPPORTUNITY OF THE MONTH

Contact those you wish to include in your personal or professional support system on the 28th or 29th.

Rewarding Days: 1, 2, 5, 6, 15, 20, 24, 25, 28, 29
Challenging Days: 3, 4, 10, 11, 17, 18, 30

AFFIRMATION FOR THE MONTH
"I deserve to experience the love I need."

PRIMARY FOCUS

This is the time to network and build your reserves—of material worth, professional support, and emotional stability—but avoid a tendency to be purely self-serving.

HEALTH AND FITNESS

Concentrate on building stamina and endurance. You may feel uncertain about your limitations, so take it at a reasonable, measured pace.

ROMANCE AND RELATIONSHIPS

Even though you might enjoy the praise and support of others, you will not feel satisfied unless you are in situations which honestly enhance your self-esteem. Talk with your partner about your needs during the Full Moon on the 7th. If you're single, you may feel awkward pursuing a new love midmonth, but can alleviate the tension by sharing an activity or interest which is mutually enjoyable. Although romance can be highly enjoyable from the 11th–22nd, it can be financially draining, so set some positive limits.

FINANCE AND CAREER

You may be tempted to spend impulsively on items which you do not need, but only because you're feeling a bit low. Keep your credit cards on ice from the 7th–20th unless you have the expenditure allowed in your budget. You can be highly persuasive from the 4th–23rd and may have opportunities to make presentations or solicit support. Strike out into new territory following the New Moon in Scorpio on the 22nd.

OPPORTUNITY OF THE MONTH

Get involved in activities which have a significant impact on your standing in the community on the 16th, 25th, or 26th.

Rewarding Days: 1, 2, 11, 12, 16, 17, 20, 21, 24, 25, 29, 30
Challenging Days: 6, 7, 13, 14, 26, 27

AFFIRMATION FOR THE MONTH
"I use my resources wisely."

PRIMARY FOCUS

Efforts to improve your professional skills or increase your connection to others involved in your line of work stabilize your career and can lead to long-term success.

HEALTH AND FITNESS

You'll feel more driven to increasing activity levels, but may be spending much of your time on the road or in mental pursuits. Stay balanced by allowing ample time to keep your body strong.

ROMANCE AND RELATIONSHIPS

An honest, open exchange with family members or romantic partners can lead to the understanding you've hoped to achieve. It's crucial that you drop any judgmental attitudes in favor of greater acceptance and tolerance if you are to accomplish your goals. Unexpected news or contact from the 17th–21st may lead to a breakthrough in a personal relationship, but can also be the key to success in your creative endeavors. Travel can be enjoyable and fulfilling, especially from the 22nd–31st.

FINANCE AND CAREER

Careful evaluation of your financial situation during the Full Moon on the 6th can be illuminating. If you've been attentive, you may even feel satisfied that you can take a few speculative risks. These appear promising from the 13th–20th, and again on the 26th and 27th. Schedule conferences or presentations for the 8th, 9th, 18th, or 19th, but strike out into virgin territory after the New Moon on the 21st.

OPPORTUNITY OF THE MONTH

Communication is crucial to your success, so break away from isolation into a more positive sense of connecting to the world.

Rewarding Days: 8, 9, 13, 14, 18, 19, 22, 23, 26, 27
Challenging Days: 2, 3, 4, 11, 12, 24, 25

AFFIRMATION FOR THE MONTH
"My mind is open to new ideas."

✗ SAGITTARIUS ✗
The Archer

November 23 to December 22

Element: Fire

Quality: Mutable

Polarity: Masculine/Yang

Planetary Ruler: Jupiter

Meditation: "All things in harmony with Higher Law are possible"

Gemstone: Turquoise

Power Stones: Lapis lazuli, sodalite, azurite

Glyph: Archer's arrow

Key Phrase: "I understand"

Anatomy: Hips, thighs, sciatic nerve

Colors: Royal blue and purple

Animal: Fleet-footed animals

Myths/Legends: Athena, Chiron

House Association: 9th

Opposite Sign: Gemini

Flower: Narcissus

Key Word: Expansion

Positive Expression:
Philosophical
Understanding
Athletic
Generous
Optimistic
Jovial
Wise
Tolerant
Adventurous
Philanthropic

Misuse of Energy:
Bigoted
Inconsiderate
Gluttonous
Opinionated
Self-righteous
Condescending
Foolish
Blunt
Extravagant

♐ SAGITTARIUS ♐

Your Ego's Strengths and Weaknesses

Your quest for truth and wisdom stimulates you to reach out with enthusiasm into the world around you. As "The Adventurer" of the zodiac, you may cross many frontiers as you strive to achieve knowledge and understanding. Your straightforward approach is refreshing amidst stale situations, and you can be sincere, direct, and optimistic in almost any circumstance.

Your desire to experience as much of life as possible may lead to travel, educational pursuits, or a voracious appetite for reading. Your fascination with cultures other than your own may lead to your mastery of at least one foreign language, but your most heartfelt search is for a connection to spiritual understanding and higher consciousness, which may be partly responsible for your discontent with the status of being "merely human."

You can be generous and witty, and stimulate trust from others, but since you're always looking forward, you can easily grow impatient when the pace of life fails to keep up with your ideals of the way things should be. You must watch your tendency to allow your expectations of yourself or others to get in the way of your personal growth.

Through your zeal, you can blaze a pathway to wisdom, but you can just as easily fall into a rut of self-righteousness and judgmental fanaticism. The greater truth may be that you may not know everything, and furthermore, that you don't have to! You carry the torch of hope, and through your expressive words can illustrate the wisdom of higher spiritual law to the world.

Your Approach to Romance

For you, love can be the most grand of all adventures and the game of romance an absolute delight. Your needs for freedom are primary in relationship, and you prefer to be the one calling the shots. While you're experimenting with different relationship models, you may leave your former loves behind in the confusing wake of a sudden disappearance, but once you're ready to make a commitment, you can be a steadfast and sensual partner. You're inspired by love, and may feel most excited by a relationship with other fire signs—Aries, Leo, and Sagittarius—who share your appreciation of passionate interchange.

With Aries, an invigorating excitement can keep your love strong. However, Taurus' slow pace may feel cumbersome to you. Your magnetic attraction to Gemini, your zodiac opposite, can lead to exceptional intellectual exchange and may spark an exciting partnership, and although you may enjoy the cooking while Cancer takes care of you, you may feel claustrophobic if they carry things too far. Leo's dramatic flair stimulates your passion.

Although you may appreciate Virgo's ideas, your differing viewpoints can spark disagreements. You are fascinated by Libra's refined grace and good taste, but you'll have to stay on your toes to avoid falling victim to the allure of Scorpio. With another Sagittarian you can enjoy sharing your beliefs and ideals, and may be perfect traveling companions (just have two sets of traveler's checks!). You may not feel completely open with Capricorn, despite their offer of steadfast security. Companionable Aquarius shows a level of independence which supports your own needs for individual expression. However, you may feel occasionally confused by the enticing imagination of Pisces, since their approach is often difficult for you to follow.

Your Career Development

Your interest in career is most stimulated by a situation which offers you a feeling of unlimited potential with plenty of room for independent action. With an ability to relate to people from varied backgrounds, you're a natural in sales situations and can be quite adept in public relations, advertising, or acting as an agent representing the talents of others. You may also find foreign service or diplomatic duties interesting.

Writing, journalism, or publishing may offer excellent opportunities to express your ideas, and with your abilities to sway others through speech, you may be drawn to law, politics, or the ministry. Your constant desire to learn and teach may stimulate you to seek a profession in education where you can stimulate incentive in your students and reach higher levels of personal mastery yourself. Speculative investments can be lucrative for you, whether in sports, racing, stocks, real estate, or other markets. No matter what your career choice, you think big!

Your Use of Power

Wisdom is power for you, and you are readily aware of the foolishness of power which lacks understanding. Your sense of power arises when you have plenty of room to express your own ideas and actualize your potential; otherwise, you feel stifled if you are confined. You can feel frustrated by the time required to develop wisdom, but you are willing to put forth the effort to get through all the useless double-talk in order to achieve true enlightenment.

You may also feel that abundance is equivalent to power, but may not truly experience the abundant life you desire until you learn to harmonize your actions with your Higher Needs. The truth does, indeed, set you free. And although you may seek truth, you have to be careful to avoid shutting your mind and looking for truth only as you see it. Otherwise, you can fall into a trap of dogmatic beliefs which become, in themselves, your own prison.

Your gifts and personal energy can help to unlock the minds of humanity to higher truth and wisdom, a power which may come in many forms. Through study, writing, traveling, teaching, or guiding others, you learn to recognize that your real power is connected to shaping the future through improving understanding among humankind.

Famous Sagittarians

William F. Buckley, Dick Clark, Tim Conway, Crazy Horse, Bob Guccione, Gary Hart, Tom Hulce, Chet Huntley, John Larroquette, Bruce Lee, Margaret Meade, Bette Midler, Lesley Stahl, James Thurber, Janine Turner, Mark Twain, Flip Wilson

THE YEAR AHEAD FOR SAGITTARIUS

During 1995, Jupiter makes its return to your sign, Sagittarius, marking a period of increased optimism, confidence, and hope for the future. This period is closely linked to the year 1983, when Jupiter was last transiting in your sign and you may have experienced some exciting new changes or breakthroughs. The contrast during this year involves the difference between the feeling of revolution you were experiencing in 1983, and the need for stability you are feeling now. By balancing your responsibilities with your needs to reach toward broader horizons, you may achieve more than you ever dreamed possible!

Another feature of the Jupiter cycle conjuncting your Sun is the stimulus to explore more of the world and its inhabitants. Consequently, you may become involved in travel or educational pursuits which help you understand and experience the different cultures, beliefs, and histories of humankind. If you are involved in writing, publishing, or other communicative activities, this year can be the time for significant opportunities to expand your influence and advance your career. Any professional activities which are linked to advertising or promotion should fare nicely. From a spiritual viewpoint, you may also feel more compelled to find the answers to deeper questions about your connection to something beyond mere humanity. This is a period of outreach and exploration and can be a time of high adventure. However, because Saturn's transit is in conflicting square to the Jupiter transit, you may not be able to reach out as far as you would like unless you are well-prepared. By making wise choices, you can begin a period of positive change and enhanced prosperity, but you cannot afford the experience of pure self-indulgence now, and must incorporate the concept of prosperity at every level of your existence.

The Solar Eclipses of 1995 emphasize your need to apply the knowledge and expertise you have gained in ways that will bring improvement to your personal life and to your everyday experiences. You may find that you are more willing to release the past and concentrate on the present and its implications for your long-range plans. Get in touch with your feelings about the rewards you're receiving for your work. If you are dissatisfied, determine what you can do to make a change for the better. The Lunar Eclipses underscore your need to be more creative and expressive, particularly in your love relationships. You also need to be aware of the balance between giving and receiving, by allowing the process to be a continual flow instead of just going one way.

If you were born from November 23 to 26, you are experiencing a particularly powerful year of innovative change. Pluto is making a once-in-a-lifetime conjunction to your Sun (in fact, you'd have to live a couple of lifetimes to experience this cycle again!). Also, the planet Uranus is transiting in supportive sextile to your Sun. These two cycles together are much like the ingredients necessary to split the atom—and you may feel like that atom! Now, this can be a highly positive period, so don't panic, but recognize that you are making drastic changes in your own perceptions about yourself and your ideas about the world. The difference between your sense of success or failure is largely dependent upon your willingness to fully embrace yourself as a whole, powerful being or your tendency to reject yourself. This is definitely the time to release your attachment to things you've outgrown, including self-defeating attitudes or dead-end relationships, and you may be capable of assimilating more information than you've ever taken into your consciousness, so take advantage of the new horizons at your portal and open your mind. The influence of this cycle lasts through the next two years, giving you plenty of time to assimilate the changes and make the alterations necessary to your life experience as a being emerging into the full Light of Truth.

If your birth occurred from November 27 to December 2, you are feeling the influence of the completion of Saturn's transit in square to your Sun during the first quarter of the year. However, you are also experiencing the strongest influence of Jupiter's conjunction to your Sun from January through September, allowing you to take advantage of your new understanding of your responsibilities in context with your opportunities to advance your reputation and recognition. You may feel that things are moving rather slowly at the beginning of the year, but you should start to see progress by the late spring and through the summer. Take advantage of educational opportunities which allow you to advance your career or improve your skills. By patiently attending to your duties, eliminating your entanglement with situations which are nonproductive, and taking charge of your life, you'll find that this is a year of definite rewards for your efforts.

You may feel frustrated by the restraint and discipline required this year, if you were born from December 3 to 18. Even though Saturn is transiting in square aspect to your Sun, you can still make good use of this cycle and even see progress, but you cannot afford to waste your energy, since the responsibilities you are carrying can take their toll if encumbered by unnecessary burdens. Look at your life for situations which seem to be out of control, and your response to those circumstances. If you have been ignoring your own responsibilities, then you may feel rather shocked to discover them on your doorstep demanding immediate attention, but if you've been making an honest, accountable effort in your career, relationships, and personal growth, then this will be a time of questioning which should confirm your choices and life direction. This is a good time to explore educational options which will provide you with the skills or knowledge necessary to support your needs. You may also feel more demands from your family, and may even see an increase in your family obligations. However, it is important that you determine where your duties begin and end, and that you relinquish control of situations which belong to someone else. Pay careful attention to any physical problems which arise now, since ignoring distress or difficulties could lead to chronic conditions.

If you were born from December 14 to 19, you are taking steps to expand your spiritual awareness while Neptune transits semi-sextile to your Sun. This cycle involves subtle changes in many aspects of your life, but may be especially noticeable in your attitudes toward your values and material needs. This is a good time to incorporate more imaginative ideas and take a more creative approach to your career. Since you are somewhat vulnerable to deception during this time, move carefully when making financial plans, especially if they involve long-term agreements.

You're experiencing a breakthrough in consciousness and a need to release the past if you were born from December 18 to 22. You are feeling the energy of Uranus and Pluto both transiting in semi-sextile to your Sun. Many elements from your past are dissolving, including some situations which may have been a strong part of your life for some time. This is an excellent period for introspective work or psychoanalysis, since you can delve more deeply into your psyche during this cycle. You may also feel more capable of handling psychological wounds which have blocked your self-realization. Additionally, you are motivated to move into new directions which allow you to utilize your unique abilities and express your individuality. In some circumstances, you may feel that things are happening outside your control which create a definite change in your plans. But even in those situations, you still have choices in your response. You can restore your life to a true feeling of prosperity at every level, but only if you are willing to move forward while cooperating with a time of change.

Tools to Make a Difference

One of your greatest opportunities throughout this year involves finding ways to increase your sense of abundance and personal prosperity. Not only can you explore your financial or material conditions for possibilities of improvement and change, but also you must determine aspects of your physical, emotional, and spiritual life which need to be restored or revitalized. Prosperity is, as much as a physical state, a state of consciousness. To develop this consciousness, listen carefully to your own inner voice. If you hear doubt, sadness, anger, or depression in your inner dialog, then this is the time to change it.

You can derive tremendous benefit by applying the principles of neurolinguistic programming (NLP), and through determining your own internal drive for creating your life as it is. If you wish to make changes, you will be most successful by determining your real needs and eliminating the blocks in your path which impair realizing those needs. Learn effective ways to communicate, not only with others, but with yourself. Keep a journal of your thoughts. Write affirmations to help you in your quest for change. One of the best tools you can apply now involves writing a letter to yourself. Imagine your life as you want it to be in five years. Then, write a long letter, dated five years in the future, to a close friend or relative as though you are living that life you have visualized for your future. Describe your activities, your successes, your feelings and your life experiences. Envision everything as clearly as you can. File this letter away in a safe place. You may be surprised to discover that many of the things you describe in your letter begin to happen rather quickly!

To keep yourself physically strong, set aside plenty of time to stay active throughout the year. You are the perfect candidate for martial arts, yoga, or Tai Chi, since the philosophical approach to physical health will make a great deal of sense to you. You might also enjoy applying new principles to your eating habits, and need to determine your own philosophy about diet and wellness.

During your meditations, see yourself walking through a valley surrounded by mountains on one side and open space on the other. Call to Pegasus to come and carry you up onto the mountain top. As you soar above the valley, feel the warmth of the Sun on your back and see the beauty of the land beneath you. Once you are set upon the mountaintop, breathe in the cool, clean air and allow your mind to rest. Feel the peace and harmony. Take that feeling into your life as you go about your daily tasks, knowing you can always rise above any problem.

Affirmation for the Year

"My life is filled with abundance in all things."

ACTION TABLES FOR SAGITTARIUS

These dates reflect the best (but not the only) times for success and ease in these activities according to your Sun Sign.

Change Residence	Mar. 15–Apr. 1
Request a Raise	Dec. 22
Begin a Course of Study	Jan. 31, July 27–28
Visit a Doctor	Apr. 17–May 1; Nov. 4–21
Start a Diet	Jan. 9–10; Feb. 6–7;
	Mar. 5–6; Apr. 1–3, 29–30;
	May 26–27; June 22–23;
	July 19–20; Aug. 16–17;
	Sep. 12–13; Oct. 10–11;
	Nov. 6–7; Dec. 3–4, 30–31
Begin a Romance	Mar. 31
Join a Club	Sep. 24–25
Seek Employment	Apr. 17–May 1; Aug. 10–28
Take a Vacation	Jan. 17–18; Feb. 13–14;
	Mar. 13–14; Apr. 9–10;
	May 6–7; June 2–4, 30,
	July 1, 27–28; Aug. 23–24;
	Sep. 20–21; Oct. 17–18;
	Nov. 13–15; Dec. 11–12
Change Your Wardrobe	Apr. 2–16
End a Relationship	Dec. 7–8
Seek Professional Advice	Jan. 12–13; Feb. 8–10;
	Mar. 8–9; Apr. 4–5;
	May 1–3, 28–29, 30–June 26;
	July 22–23; Aug. 18–19;
	Sep. 15–16; Oct. 12–13;
	Nov. 8–9; Dec. 6–7
Have a Makeover	Dec. 22
Obtain a Loan	Jan. 14–15; Feb. 11–12;
	Mar. 10–11; Apr. 6–7;
	May 4–5, 31–June 1, 27–29;
	July 25–26; Aug. 21–22;
	Sep. 17–18; Oct. 15–16;
	Nov. 11–12; Dec. 8–10

PRIMARY FOCUS

Your drive and ambition are strong, but may be frustrated by resistance from traditional or conservative forces. Satisfy the misgivings of others by making certain you're adequately prepared.

HEALTH AND FITNESS

Emotional stress can easily drain your physical vitality now, so increase your nutritional support and allow plenty of time to release tension through regular exercise and positive relaxation.

ROMANCE AND RELATIONSHIPS

Pressures from your family may get in the way of your feelings of independence. Watch your expectations, since you can be easily disappointed if you anticipated that someone would be there to bail you out in an emergency. Keep the lines of communication open and strive to use your natural optimism to keep things moving smoothly during the Full Moon on the 16th. You're in a better position to have things your own way after the 21st, and may even have time for a romantic getaway. Explore new surroundings on the 30th–31st.

FINANCE AND CAREER

A change in plans from the 1st–6th may not be clear until you're left scrambling to make up for lost time, so keep your antennae tuned-in. Budgetary problems stifle progress through midmonth, but the stalled time gives you a chance to review your figures. Make revisions and present a modified plan of action after the 22nd. Be alert to power plays in your career from the 1st–23rd, and make sure you're showing your best efforts.

OPPORTUNITY OF THE MONTH

Apprise yourself of the competition, and use networking skills to forge a path to success from the 21st–31st.

Rewarding Days: 3, 7, 8, 17, 18, 22, 26, 27, 30, 31
Challenging Days: 5, 6, 12, 13, 19, 20

AFFIRMATION FOR THE MONTH
"I am a messenger of love and hope."

PRIMARY FOCUS

Educational pursuits and travel play an important role in helping you further your career aims and establish your professional reputation.

HEALTH AND FITNESS

Take time to enjoy your favorite winter sports, or, if you prefer indoor exercise, make a promise to yourself to increase your activity level. A vacation offers positive benefits to your health.

ROMANCE AND RELATIONSHIPS

Get back in touch with a sibling to clarify misunderstandings or seek the support you need on important issues from the 1st–17th. You may also be spending more time getting to know your neighbors, and may find an interesting new friend in your immediate vicinity. The Full Moon on the 15th marks a positive time to plan a romantic interlude apart from your daily routine. Watch your tendency to underestimate your own worth, and strive to establish a stronger sense of self-esteem as part of your personal growth this month.

FINANCE AND CAREER

Even though Mercury is in retrograde through the 16th you can still make progress in your career. Be sure to complete any projects you've left hanging, and make a special effort to follow through on lagging communication. Your direct action keeps things moving. Schedule presentations, conferences, or meetings this month to showcase an idea or pet project and generate support from others. But take a conservative stance financially.

OPPORTUNITY OF THE MONTH

Maintain your concentration and avoid distractions if you want to assure a successful outcome in business endeavors this month.

Rewarding Days: 3, 4, 13, 14, 18, 19, 22, 23, 26, 27
Challenging Days: 1, 2, 8, 9, 10, 14, 15, 17, 28

AFFIRMATION FOR THE MONTH
"I am an effective communicator."

PRIMARY FOCUS

Sharing your ideas with others creates a network of personal or professional support which can further your career success. Writing, attending conferences, or travel are excellent options.

HEALTH AND FITNESS

Your physical vitality continues to be robust, and by increasing your activity level now, you can improve your overall endurance. Team sports offer a good option.

ROMANCE AND RELATIONSHIPS

Overall improvement in personal relationships is likely to be the result of your attempts to create better communication, and you can finally let others know your real feelings. Expectations from your family can continue to be emotionally demanding, but you can take an honest approach during the Full Moon on the 16th and clarify any misunderstandings. Romance improves dramatically from the 21st–31st; however, you may have disagreements about financial choices on the 24th and 25th. Share your favorite pleasures on the 30th and 31st.

FINANCE AND CAREER

Business travel, presentations, or conferences provide an opportunity for you to shine from the 1st–27th. Your enthusiasm sparks support from others, and may draw positive acknowledgment of your talents and abilities from the 3rd–9th and again on the 13th, 14th, 17th, 18th, and 22nd. Attention to the details of your career responsibilities is crucial from the 12th–18th, when you can fall out of favor by overspending your time or your budget.

OPPORTUNITY OF THE MONTH

Initiate communication or a significant project from the 3rd–14th, when you can be magnetically persuasive.

Rewarding Days: 3, 4, 13, 14, 17, 18, 21, 22, 26, 30, 31
Challenging Days: 1, 2, 8, 9, 15, 16, 28, 29

AFFIRMATION FOR THE MONTH
"My thoughts are clear. My mind is guided
by Divine Intelligence."

PRIMARY FOCUS

Powerful, creative energy boosts your imagination and can have a positive influence on your career. However, you might also be inspired to more adventurous and romantic experiences.

HEALTH AND FITNESS

Take time away from your daily routine to participate in activities which are rejuvenating, challenging, and, most of all, fun. Laughter is your best medicine this month.

ROMANCE AND RELATIONSHIPS

Sharing love and making room for the full expression of your most passionate desires is emphasized, and becomes intensified during the Lunar Eclipse on the 15th. Travel can provide the right ingredients for romance, but you might also enjoy quiet time in your most personal surroundings. Whether you're initiating a new romance or strengthening an existing relationship, your charm and panache may be difficult to resist. Just be sure the circumstances are appropriate if you're taking an emotional risk.

FINANCE AND CAREER

Your inventive and creative approach can stir the mix sufficiently to get things moving in the direction you desire. Be alert to the possibility of deception or poor judgment from the 13th–16th, when you may be tempted to jump into a situation before you know enough about it. Focus on making improvements in your work conditions, or strengthening relationships with your peers from the 21st through the Solar Eclipse on the 29th.

OPPORTUNITY OF THE MONTH

Trust your creative instincts, incorporating your intuitive sensibilities with your knowledge of your work to boost your career.

Rewarding Days: 9, 10, 13, 14, 18, 19, 22, 23, 26, 27
Challenging Days: 2, 4, 5, 11, 12, 24, 25

AFFIRMATION FOR THE MONTH
"My life is filled with love."

PRIMARY FOCUS

Other people can have a strong influence on your reputation and may play an important role in your future success. Choose your friends and associates wisely, and honor your ethical standards.

HEALTH AND FITNESS

Take time to reevaluate your nutritional support and examine any physical limitations for their root causes. Armed with knowledge, you can strengthen your vitality and enjoy better health.

ROMANCE AND RELATIONSHIPS

You may feel most at ease expressing your feelings of love to others from the 1st–17th, but watch your fantasies near the time of the Full Moon on the 14th, when you may be drawn into a situation which is inappropriate to your needs. Your partner may require extra attention from you after the 22nd, and a more open approach to your relationship breathes life back into it during the New Moon on the 29th. Get away from your routine on the 6th, 7th, 15th, 24th, or 25th, allowing room for spontaneity to light your fire.

FINANCE AND CAREER

Investments show positive rewards from the 1st–13th, although you might do better to allow a situation to ripen more fully before you cash in on the harvest. Communication can be problematic due to delays or regulatory red tape from the 21st–31st—a situation which is amplified by Mercury's retrograde from May 24–June 17. Initiate new contacts before the 14th, and plan to follow through on existing situations after the 24th.

OPPORTUNITY OF THE MONTH

Conservative factions can slow you down from the 5th–18th unless you are prepared for them. Get the facts.

Rewarding Days: 6, 7, 11, 12, 15, 16, 19, 20, 24, 25
Challenging Days: 1, 2, 9, 10, 21, 22, 28, 29, 30

AFFIRMATION FOR THE MONTH
"I am an effective listener."

PRIMARY FOCUS

Cooperative ventures, partnerships, and social activities figure prominently. Your drive to achieve your ambitions for your career is also powerful, and can enhance your social standing.

HEALTH AND FITNESS

The stress you feel from your job now can take its toll on your physical energy. Use exercise and physical activity as a means to release tension and increase your vitality at the same time.

ROMANCE AND RELATIONSHIPS

Your social life will be more fulfilling if you participate in activities which you truly enjoy instead of just going because you're expected to attend. However, if you simply cannot be released from an obligation, you'll find more pleasure in the experience if you share it with someone you admire. Tension in an existing relationship can be the result of family pressure, but sharing your concerns with your partner during the Full Moon on the 12th can turn things around.

FINANCE AND CAREER

A competitive spirit arises this month and can spur you to achieve more than you thought possible, but you need to watch a tendency to take on more than you can carry from the 11th–18th, since the extra burden can undermine your effectiveness later. Tense communication from the 10th–21st may spark arguments. Proceed carefully when dealing with joint finances, and prepare an alternative approach to be launched after the New Moon on the 27th.

OPPORTUNITY OF THE MONTH

Leave nothing to assumption, since vague or incomplete information can get you into trouble from the 8th–17th.

Rewarding Days: 3, 4, 7, 8, 11, 12, 16, 20, 21, 30
Challenging Days: 1, 5, 6, 17, 18, 19, 25, 26

AFFIRMATION FOR THE MONTH
"I am in harmony with my inner self."

PRIMARY FOCUS

The energy and attention required to keep your career moving toward advancement can strain your personal relationships unless you make a special effort to maintain balance and harmony at home.

HEALTH AND FITNESS

Emotional distress has a strong effect on your sense of well-being. Discontent with your love life or your job is likely to be felt somewhere in your body during the Full Moon on the 12th.

ROMANCE AND RELATIONSHIPS

Instead of waiting until there's a "convenient" time to address emotional issues in your love relationship, make an effort to dig into the core of your feelings. You may crave more closeness now to help confirm your commitment, and if you resist those needs, you can actually weaken the bonds you've forged. New romance can blossom after the 24th, or an existing relationship can be stimulated by making room for passionate and playful experiences during the New Moon on the 27th.

FINANCE AND CAREER

Legal disputes may take some time to resolve, particularly if either party is taking a stubborn stance and refusing to consider the possibility of change. Pay careful attention to finances from the 17th–28th, when you can lose control of a situation by failing to read the fine print or to keep up with the current facts on an issue. Supporters or investors can be more easily convinced to join with your plans on the 13th, 14th, 27th, or 28th.

OPPORTUNITY OF THE MONTH

Find ways to expand your horizons, making room for future growth in your career on the 27th and 28th.

Rewarding Days: 1, 5, 9, 10, 13, 14, 17, 18, 27, 28
Challenging Days: 2, 3, 12, 15, 16, 22, 23, 30, 31-

AFFIRMATION FOR THE MONTH
"I value the efforts and support of others."

PRIMARY FOCUS

Your accomplishments elevate your professional reputation, and may result in career advancement and recognition. Travel, writing, or education are emphasized.

HEALTH AND FITNESS

Team sports or fitness classes give your vitality a boost and can also keep you connected to your community, but watch a tendency to exhaust your energy reserves from the 27th–31st.

ROMANCE AND RELATIONSHIPS

Bring a spiritual focus into your intimate relationship. Sharing your ideals and hopes for the future can strengthen your commitment to one another. Your fascination with a new relationship can lead to something spectacular near the Full Moon on the 10th, or you can use this energy to revitalize an existing relationship which has grown routine. A personally inspiring period from the 1st–23rd lifts your spirits and helps boost your confidence about expressing your most treasured secrets or fantasies to the one you adore.

FINANCE AND CAREER

Conferences, meetings, presentations, and business travel show promise, and may lead to contracts or agreements which have a long-term effect on your career. Your enthusiasm is contagious from the 1st–19th, and if you're thinking about looking for a better position, you can showcase your talents and skills very effectively during this time. Take direct action to avoid undermining of your position by others from the 18th–22nd.

OPPORTUNITY OF THE MONTH

You intelligent approach to situations can draw the praise and support of others, so don't be afraid to let your light shine!

Rewarding Days: 1, 2, 5, 6, 9, 10, 13, 14, 15, 23, 24, 28
Challenging Days: 4, 11, 12, 18, 19, 26, 27

AFFIRMATION FOR THE MONTH
"I am inspired by Truth and Wisdom."

PRIMARY FOCUS

Your involvement with special interest groups or political action strengthens your professional reputation. Just be certain that you really share mutual values and ethical standards.

HEALTH AND FITNESS

Even though you may be more active, there's a tendency toward inattentiveness from the 1st–7th. Avoid high-risk ventures and be sure to remain aware of your limits in physical exertion.

ROMANCE AND RELATIONSHIPS

Familial ties, particularly relationships with your parents, require extra attention, with significantly greater involvement near the Full Moon on the 8th. You may see a real contrast in your experience of each of your parents, and may feel that you are finally releasing pent-up emotions from the past. Extend yourself to your friends after the 17th, where you may discover an emerging support system which enhances your personal growth. Romance fares best after the New Moon on the 24th.

FINANCE AND CAREER

Your favor with superiors at work is enhanced and can lead to rewards or promotion before month's end. Your attitudes have a strong influence upon your reputation, and if you show appreciation for your situation and for the value of your own work, others are likely to follow suit. Make an extra effort to join in activities which support your special interests, or which have positive political ramifications from the 24th to 30th.

OPPORTUNITY OF THE MONTH

Be prepared for Mercury's retrograde on the 22nd by renewing your commitments to situations which help you realize your goals.

Rewarding Days: 1, 2, 6, 10, 11, 20, 25, 29, 30
Challenging Days: 4, 8, 9, 15, 16, 22, 23

AFFIRMATION FOR THE MONTH

"I have clearly defined goals for my future."

PRIMARY FOCUS

Political alliances or special interest groups provide an excellent outlet for your leadership and influence. Association with others allows you to accomplish larger aims.

HEALTH AND FITNESS

Take extra time to relax and rejuvenate from the 1st–20th, concentrating on "inner fitness" as much as physical strengthening. Your energy level is likely to increase after the 21st.

ROMANCE AND RELATIONSHIPS

You may hear from friends who've been long absent from your life from the 1st–14th; this is also a good time for you to take the initiative and get back in touch with someone special. Differences in values can spark a misunderstanding with someone you love from the 5th–12th, when you need to avoid jumping to conclusions before you have all the facts. Romance can accelerate during the Lunar Eclipse on the 8th, when you're feeling highly expressive, but by the time of the Solar Eclipse on the 23rd you may want some time alone.

FINANCE AND CAREER

Before you make significant changes or agree to long-term commitments in career or investments, be sure you read the fine print, since you could get tangled in loopholes which escape your attention from the 1st–10th. Use Mercury's retrograde thru the 13th to investigate. Then, plan to launch your plans on the 17th, 26th, 27th, or 30th. Charitable activities allow you to use your influence within your community after the Eclipse on the 23rd.

OPPORTUNITY OF THE MONTH

By renewing connections with others who acknowledge your worth and efforts from the 1st–13th, you may uncover a gold mine.

Rewarding Days: 3, 4, 7, 8, 17, 22, 23, 26, 27, 30
Challenging Days: 2, 5, 6, 12, 13, 19, 20, 21

AFFIRMATION FOR THE MONTH
"I am open to receive love."

PRIMARY FOCUS

Your confidence and optimism show significant improvement, stimulating you to forge ahead into the directions which assure your long-term personal and professional fulfillment.

HEALTH AND FITNESS

You may feel driven to work especially hard and can accomplish a great deal. However, it's easy to reach burn-out, so try to maintain a consistent activity level.

ROMANCE AND RELATIONSHIPS

Romance can flourish, whether you're seeking a new love or deeply involved in an existing commitment. You'll prefer quiet, private, and beautiful surroundings from the 4th–21st, and might enjoy escaping to a romantic hide-away during the Full Moon on the 7th. Showing your generosity and expressing your feelings from the 3rd–26th can bring the results you desire, but you need to be certain you can emotionally support any commitment you're making, since you'll probably have to stay with it for a while.

FINANCE AND CAREER

Before you impulsively spend or invest from the 1st–10th, research the situation to be sure you're getting the best deal. Your efforts may be thwarted by familial obligations or old debts which impede your progress from the 7th–20th. After the New Moon on the 22nd, you are likely to see fewer blockades and may even reach a better agreement than the one you previously negotiated. So delays can actually work in your favor this month!

OPPORTUNITY OF THE MONTH

You're in an exceptional position to initiate a new project or begin a new direction on the 22nd and 23rd. Go for it!

Rewarding Days: 4, 13, 14, 18, 19, 22, 23, 26, 27
Challenging Days: 1, 2, 8, 9, 16, 17, 28, 29, 30

AFFIRMATION FOR THE MONTH
"I am filled with joy and happiness!"

PRIMARY FOCUS

It's time to build on the foundation you've been creating for the last few months and expand the horizons of your opportunities for professional and personal growth. Just watch your budget!

HEALTH AND FITNESS

Concentrate on increasing your stamina and endurance now along with building strength. Staying active actually increases your available energy.

ROMANCE AND RELATIONSHIPS

During the period from the 1st–11th you may have more time to develop your intimate ties with those you love. But obligations from family take priority from the 12th–22nd. Watch your tendency to resent feeling "forced" into situations which are not your preference and strive for a more honest approach during the Full Moon on the 6th. If you lay the proper groundwork then, you can be in the situation you most desire by the New Moon on the 21st! Travel for pleasure after the 22nd.

FINANCE AND CAREER

You can stabilize your financial picture by making shrewd moves and using your best judgement in investment situations from the 1st–16th. Presentations, written communications, or networking on the 5th and 6th give you an advantage. However, be especially alert to the possibility of deception or financial loss from the 17th–21st, when impulsiveness or a lack of thorough investigation can have negative repercussions.

OPPORTUNITY OF THE MONTH

By taking the initiative on the 5th, 6th, or 21st you can make significant breakthroughs in establishing a strong position.

Rewarding Days: 1, 2, 6, 11, 12, 16, 20, 21, 24, 25, 28
Challenging Days: 7, 13, 14, 26, 27

AFFIRMATION FOR THE MONTH
"My mind is open to Truth and Wisdom."

♑ CAPRICORN ♑
The Goat

December 22 to January 21

Element: Earth

Quality: Cardinal

Polarity: Feminine/Yin

Planetary Ruler: Saturn

Meditation: "Mastering the Challenge of the Physical Plane"

Power Stones: Diamond, quartz, onyx, black obsidian

Glyph: Head of goat, knees

Key Phrase: "I use"

Gemstone: Garnet

Anatomy: Knees, skin, skeleton

Colors: Black

Animal: Goats, thick-shelled animals

Myths/Legends: Cronus, Pan, Vesta

House Association: 10th

Opposite Sign: Cancer

Flower: Carnation

Key Word: Structure

Positive Expression:
  Cautious
  Prudent
  Sensible
  Responsible
  Frugal
  Patient
  Disciplined
  Ambitious
  Conscientious

Misuse of Energy:
  Melancholy
  Fearful
  Repressed
  Inhibited
  Miserly
  Rigid
  Machiavellian
  Controlling

♑ CAPRICORN ♑

Your Ego's Strengths and Weaknesses

You operate most effectively when you're the one in charge, and apply your natural sense of structure to keep things working smoothly. Your aspiration to achieve your ambitions, along with your persistent determination, helps you to accomplish the success you desire. Other people may remember your dry wit, but your desire to achieve mastery may be the trait which ultimately sets you apart from the crowd.

Even if everything around you has come to a grinding halt, your desire to reach your goal can keep you moving forward. You thrive on challenges, and easily rise to the occasion when there's pressure to meet a deadline or beat the clock. As "The Pragmatist" of the zodiac, you are always looking for ways to make things work out the way you think they should. Your affinity with the energy of Saturn has taught you the importance of building a strong foundation if you're going to manifest your dreams, but you can allow your fears or inhibitions to block your path. By getting back to basics you can always get back on track.

Since you prefer to maintain control, others may complain that you're taking advantage of them. And even though you may grumble about being required to follow the rules, you're more than happy to devise a few of your own (or change them as it suits your needs). In order to create a structure which will survive the test of time, base it upon realistic needs. Your quest to achieve mastery over the physical plane will be more easily accomplished if you maintain a connection to your Higher Self. By uniting your sense of the spiritual with the tangible physical plane, you can create a pattern for success which serves you well, and which may be eagerly followed by others.

Your Approach to Romance

Stability is an important factor in relationships, and you'll be most comfortable with a love which gradually takes shape and matures over time. Your sensitivity may be masked by your matter-of-fact manner, although those who know you well probably suspect that there's a soft spot beneath your reserved veneer. You may feel restrained in matters of the heart until you've established a foundation in your career. Once you do open and allow yourself to share love, you may discover that the sensual pleasures can be your forte.

The Earth signs—Taurus, Virgo, and Capricorn—may be most patient with your "long-term" approach to love. Taurus' earthiness gets your motor running and can be a perfect longtime partner and lover. With Virgo's companionship, your future feels assured. Even though another Capricorn may have your dedication, you both need time for recreation to keep the relationship from becoming stale.

Aries' playful teasing is fun and compelling, but can get on your nerves when you're not in the mood to play. You may be frustrated by Gemini's fickle nature, but nurturing Cancer, your opposite, can become your quintessential partner. In order to decide if it can last with Leo, define who's in charge and get your territories established before you become embroiled in a battle.

You may be strongly drawn to Libra's refined taste and gentility, but feel put off by their detachment. Scorpio's enticing sensuality appeals to your understanding of the alchemy of love. You have to give Sagittarius plenty of freedom, although you're inspired by their search for the best life has to offer. Friendship with Aquarius can be satisfying, but Pisces' imaginative approach provides your perfect escape from the ordinary.

Your Career Development

You're a natural in the world of business and can apply your sense of responsibility in ways that will enhance any career. You prefer positions of authority or management which give you a chance to be in charge, and you're adept at delegating responsibility to others. When working for others, your executive and administrative abilities can shine, but you might prefer to be self-employed.

You may be drawn into the practice or teaching of life sciences, healing arts, geology, or physics. Education

219

or administration are also good choices for your instructional abilities. Your ambition may lead you into positions ranging from politics to the ministry, and as a natural metaphysician, you may also be drawn into healing work through naturopathy, herbology, or chiropractic medicine. In the construction industry, you might excel at contracting, design, or development. Managing a forest, ranch, or farm can answer your need to stay in touch with nature. Whatever your choices, you'll be determined to make them successful.

Your Use of Power

Power may be more a means than an end, since you can have a strong influence upon others once you gain the position you desire. In your quest to maintain control, you may have to learn that real command is more easily achieved when you allow certain levels of flexibility. The struggle to keep the structure you've established intact can lead to conflict if someone else suggests changes, but by incorporating periodic evaluation and review, you can assess and initiate revisions on your own. You can easily undermine your own power by holding rigidly to traditions or concepts which have outlived their usefulness.

Other people may look up to you, and you can easily influence those who see you as their mentor, but you may find that a hidden agenda of control issues lurks behind the mask of guiding others. Remember that you cannot be in charge of anyone's life other than your own. Only through support and direction which serves more than your ego can you have the power to help others positively shape their own destiny.

Famous Capricorns

Alvin Ailey, Isaac Asimov, Mary Higgins Clark, Robert Duvall, A. J. Foyt, Naomi Judd, Robert F. Kennedy, Jr., Martin Luther King, Jr., Ben Kingsley, Midori, Dolly Parton, Maury Povich, Gwen Verdon, Denzel Washington, Paramahansa Yogananda

THE YEAR AHEAD FOR CAPRICORN

There are signs of stability and order in your life for the year ahead, which may be a welcome change from some of the disruptions you've been experiencing over the last few years! Even though you may still be in the midst of shifting some of your priorities, you may feel more confident about your own choices and more assured of life direction and long-range plans.

Jupiter's cycle during 1995 emphasizes the spiritual aspect of your life, and brings a period of deepseated confidence and stronger connection to your inner self. In many ways, this transit provides a feeling of acceptance of the natural order of things, which, in itself, can create a sense of peace, but you are also likely to feel that you can take a breather from the struggles and enjoy the results of your hard work instead of keeping your nose to the grindstone all the time. Concentrate on developing an attitude of gratitude for the things you truly appreciate, and demonstrate those feelings to others more frequently. Allow time in your life for contemplation, and shift your consciousness to listen more carefully to your intuitive voice. This is your time to discover new dreams or awaken dreams which have lain slumbering for decades. It's also a cycle of releasing the past with love and opening to the possibility of letting go in order to make room for what is yet to come.

The Solar Eclipse cycles accentuate your need to give and receive love, and may also provide the stimulus for new creative endeavors. If you are involved with children, this can be a period of increasing participation in their lives or in activities which provide opportunities for children to show their own talents. Even more important is your acceptance of yourself as a person who was once a child, and to allow that aspect of your consciousness to feel more safe and secure. You can accomplish this by staying connected to your real values instead of selling out your deeper needs in exchange for a quick profit. With the transiting nodes of the Moon moving into the 4th/10th House axis of your Solar Chart, you may also feel that you want to devote more time to your family, home life, and security needs, instead of always making

221

work your first priority. This doesn't mean that your job is unimportant, but only that you are striving to achieve a greater sense of harmony and balance between your work and your emotional needs.

If you were born from December 22 to 24, you're experiencing a significant change in your perception of yourself, and may develop new interests which reflect these changes. You are influenced by the transits of Uranus and Pluto, both semi-sextile your Sun, a cycle which will continue through the end of 1996! You may feel that you are caught in the middle of a time-warp, although the effect is not necessarily a negative one. You can be ahead of the game by listening more carefully to your inward guidance and surrendering some of your needs for control to the processes of time and change, and you can also gain greater influence now, since many of your assets are likely to be more easily accessible or recognizable. It is important that you step into the present and move onto a path that will keep you in line with future trends and developments instead of staying stuck in archaic conditions or feeling impaired by useless attitudes.

You're feeling stronger support and stability this year if you were born from December 25 to 28. Saturn is transiting in quintile to your Sun from January through March, stimulating a feeling of trust in your own abilities to create the life you most desire. Even after this cycle ends, you may still feel its effects in subtle ways, particularly in your ability to make connections with other people more readily. This is a great time to build a network of support, either in personal or professional relationships, by sharing ideas and getting to know one another better. Additionally, this is an exceptional time to fine-tune skills or abilities, particularly your special talents.

If you were born from December 29 to January 7, you're feeling the supportive energy of Saturn transiting in sextile to your Sun from January through March of 1995. This cycle is continuing in its influence from last year, allowing you to further develop your sense of stability and sense of self, but you are also feeling the effects of Jupiter transiting in semi-sextile to your Sun from January through November of this year, and can make greater progress than you might have anticipated! This is the perfect time to expand your professional influence and can be an excellent period to become more deeply involved in activities which keep you connected to your community. Additionally, if you are doing your best quality work, you can make significant progress in your career, which leads to advancement and recognition.

You are feeling a need to clear away the blocks from your path to success if you were born from December 31 to January 6. You are feeling the influence of Pluto transiting semi-square to your Sun, and may be more determined than ever to achieve your goals, but there is a potential problem if you are trying to hang onto situations that are no longer supporting your growth. You may also run into trouble if you are trying to direct all the traffic instead of just getting into your vehicle and moving along. By relinquishing unnecessary controls, you may actually gain more freedom and greater power. Additionally, you may discover that others do better if you leave them to their own devices. But where you do have responsibilities, you may need to make some changes. Even if you are only responding to changes in a situation beyond your control, you have a wide range of choices.

Saturn is transiting in sextile to your Sun throughout the year if you were born from January 8 to 16. This period marks a time of positive focus and clarification. You may also be ready to take on increased professional or personal responsibilities, and can show significant maturity in every aspect of your life. If you have educational opportunities this year, take them. Whether you're teaching or learning, you're ready to strengthen your knowledge and understanding. Your willingness to discipline yourself, embrace your obligations, and do your best can even have a positive effect upon your reputation. Even if you feel you've already accomplished much of what you set out to do, your efforts now can leave a lasting impression, but you have to apply some elbow grease, since sitting by while others do the work may not be nearly as rewarding.

223

You may feel less motivated toward external achievements and more directed toward inner accomplishments if you were born from January 12 to 16. Neptune is conjuncting your Sun, bringing an increased sensitivity to the more subtle elements of life. You may feel more drawn toward spiritual, creative, or artistic pursuits. The temptation to withdraw can be overwhelming, and it is crucial that you find healthy outlets to achieve the need to connect more effectively to your "inner plane." Even though this period does mark a spiritual initiation, it can also bring situations which can be ultimately disappointing, but those disappointments can be kept to a minimum by your willingness to deal with yourself, your choices and your needs in a realistic manner. Personal relationships can be especially critical now, and you owe it to yourself to take the time to allow for the changes you are experiencing. Physically, be more alert to susceptibility to environmental pollution, toxic materials in food or water, and greater sensitivity to medication or to alcohol. This is a period of rising above the ordinary, but you still have to keep one foot on the ground!

You're feeling the influence of several cycles if you were born from January 16 to 21. Uranus is transiting in conjunction to your Sun, Pluto is sextile your Sun, and Saturn semi-square your Sun. Any of these cycles alone can bring about a period of significant personal transformation, but together they mark a year of major importance. It's time for the breakthroughs you've been hoping to achieve, and the most interesting element may be the yardstick by which you are measuring your progress. Your personal awareness is intensified, allowing you to make determinations about choices which are more suitable to fulfilling your needs and desires. Relationships may undergo positive alterations, and you can restore a relationship which may have been faltering into one of greater fulfillment. If you've been hanging onto situations which are no longer valid or which have outgrown their usefulness, then this is the time to let go of your attachments. And if you've been waiting to move into a new direction which will allow you to demonstrate your true worth and abilities, then this is your shining hour!

Tools to Make a Difference

One of the most significant things you can do for yourself during 1995 involves your commitment to your spiritual growth. This does not mean that you have to leave your life behind and hide away in a cave in Tibet. You need to find ways to integrate the spiritual elements of your life into every other part of your life experience. Instead of just giving to charitable causes during the holidays, be generous with your energy and support throughout the year. Instead of dedicating only part of your time to your spiritual needs, infuse every aspect of your life with inspiration! Instead of just finding time to meditate, make life your meditation.

You can carve meaning into your relationships this year by sharing your dreams and hopes with those you love. Their support and interest may actually help you achieve your aims more quickly or effectively. Target opportunities to receive and give love, instead of always judging yourself so harshly before you allow yourself to experience love. Concentrate on developing greater love and self-acceptance. Try to mirror technique. Each morning after you brush your teeth, look into the mirror. Gaze into your own eyes and look for the light which is your spirit shining. Say these words to yourself: "I love you!" This may seem silly, embarrassing, or too easy, but you will be amazed at the remarkable results.

Physical fitness needs a multilevel approach this year. On the activity side, take more time to build stamina and strength through exercise. Yoga, Tai Chi, or martial arts may offer more for you than other activities, but you can also be successful in your aims in sports (especially winter sports). Inner fitness now also has a strong effect. During your meditation periods, reflect on your connection to the natural order of things. See yourself walking through a forest during each of the seasons. Observe all the changes. Feel them deep within yourself, and carry that knowledge into all your decisions and actions in your everyday life.

Affirmation for the Year

"I believe in myself!"

ACTION TABLES FOR CAPRICORN

These dates reflect the best (but not the only) times for success and ease in these activities according to your Sun Sign.

Change Residence	Apr. 2–16
Request a Raise	Jan. 1–2
Begin a Course of Study	Mar. 1–2; Aug. 26–27
Visit a Doctor	May 2–July 9; Nov. 23–Dec. 11
Start a Diet	Jan. 12–13; Feb. 8–9; Mar. 8–9; Apr. 4–5; May 1–2, 28–30; June 25–26; July 22–23; Aug. 18–19; Sep. 15–16; Oct. 12–13; Nov. 8–9; Dec. 6–7
Begin a Romance	Apr. 29–30
Join a Club	Oct. 24–25
Seek Employment	May 3–July 9; Aug. 29–Nov. 4
Take a Vacation	Jan. 19–20; Feb. 15–16; Mar. 15–16; Apr. 11–12; May 9–10; June 5–6; July 2–3, 29–31; Aug. 26–27; Sep. 22–23; Oct. 19–21; Nov. 16–17; Dec. 13–14
Change Your Wardrobe	Apr. 17–May 2
End a Relationship	Jan. 16–17
Seek Professional Advice	Jan. 14–15, 16; Feb. 11–12; Mar. 10–11; Apr. 6–8; May 4–5, 31–June 1, 27–29; July 24–26; Aug. 21–22; Sep. 17–18; Oct. 14–15; Nov. 11–12; Dec. 8–10
Have a Makeover	Jan. 1–2
Obtain a Loan	Jan. 17–18; Feb. 15–16; Mar. 13–14; Apr. 9–10; May 6–8; June 2–4, 30; July 27–28; Aug. 23–24; Sep. 20–21; Oct. 17–18; Nov. 13–15; Dec. 11–12

PRIMARY FOCUS

Your thrust toward expansion or new goals helps get things started right this year. Business travel, conferences, or educational pursuits are especially noteworthy.

HEALTH AND FITNESS

Higher activity levels from the 1st–7th can be exhilarating, but be sure to follow safety procedures to avoid unpleasant surprises. Developing a more positive attitude improves health after the 6th.

ROMANCE AND RELATIONSHIPS

You may be fascinated by the prospects of a romantic nature early in the month, and may even meet an intriguing person. However, before you take the leap, make a reality check, since it's easy to see only what you wish to see about a person. You might also be tempted to project an unrealistic picture of yourself! Partnerships are highlighted during the Full Moon on the 16th, and you may resent any strong controls in your relationship during this time. Find ways to support your individual interests and love will bloom beautifully.

FINANCE AND CAREER

Significant business negotiations or professional meetings can launch you into an exceptional position from the New Moon on the 1st through the 20th. Assess financial plans from the 6th–24th, and attempt to reach agreements before Mercury enters its retrograde cycle on the 25th. Financial agreements may reach a stalemate from the 15th–20th, or you may discover that something is not as valuable as you once thought it to be.

OPPORTUNITY OF THE MONTH

Use your influence to move into new territory from the 1st–6th, and take advantage of a mutually supportive situation with friends.

Rewarding Days: 1, 5, 6, 9, 10, 11, 19, 20, 24, 28, 29
Challenging Days: 3, 7, 8, 12, 14, 15, 16, 22, 23

AFFIRMATION FOR THE MONTH
"I honor my moral standards."

PRIMARY FOCUS

Finances take top priority, and you may find ways to stabilize your financial picture through the resources of others. Just be sure you read the fine print before you make commitments.

HEALTH AND FITNESS

You may feel on edge early in the month as a result of nervous tension. Make an effort to let go of stress before you sleep. Try a cup of relaxing herbal tea in the evening.

ROMANCE AND RELATIONSHIPS

Emotional anxiety may be the result of underlying problems within an intimate relationship. Determine how you really feel, since you may be caught up in a situation which makes it easy to confuse your needs with those of others. Your love life shows strong improvement after the Full Moon on the 15th, and you may even feel inclined to experiment by sharing your creativity or exploring your favorite entertainment after the 21st. Indulge your fantasies from the 25th–28th, but be sure you're not just infatuated with an impossible dream.

FINANCE AND CAREER

Clarify details of financial dealings during Mercury's retrograde through the 15th, and wait to make a final decision if you feel mistrustful of a situation. Your plan of action or presentation of an idea meets with favorable evaluation on the 16th and 17th as the result of your hard work. Put the finishing touches on a pet project from the 22nd–28th, when your intuitive and imaginative ideas can blend beautifully with the facts at hand.

OPPORTUNITY OF THE MONTH

Schedule business meetings or important conferences on the 16th, 17th, or 21st to stabilize your career situation.

Rewarding Days: 1, 2, 6, 16, 17, 20, 21, 24, 25
Challenging Days: 3, 4, 8, 11, 12, 18, 19

AFFIRMATION FOR THE MONTH
"I make the best use of my resources."

♑ CAPRICORN/MARCH ♑

PRIMARY FOCUS

This is the time to get the facts straight, make contact with significant individuals, and develop positive support for your personal and professional growth. Get into the mainstream.

HEALTH AND FITNESS

Although you may feel that you're constantly pushing beyond your limits, you can ease the stress on your physical body by seeking ways to build your stamina while maintaining your flexibility.

ROMANCE AND RELATIONSHIPS

Avoid fighting over "yours versus mine" by examining your own feelings of self-worth. If you're hooked into defending yourself, perhaps you need to reconsider why you're so vulnerable. Reclaim your power by setting new priorities which allow for mutual fulfillment in your relationships. Honest communication can banish doubts about your best choice of action. Pay attention to family demands from the 24th through the New Moon on the 30th, when you need to be aware of your feelings.

FINANCE AND CAREER

From the New Moon on the 1st through the Full Moon on the 16th, your concentration on networking, communication, and data gathering leads to clarification of the facts. This allows you to make informed decisions, although you may not feel that you're moving forward with your plans until sometime next month. Use the stall in energy to research facts or fine-tune your skills. Review details of joint ventures.

OPPORTUNITY OF THE MONTH

Show your appreciation to those who have extended their time or resources to create a strong alliance now and for the future.

Rewarding Days: 5, 6, 15, 16, 20, 23, 24, 28, 29
Challenging Days: 3, 4, 10, 11, 17, 18, 21, 30, 31

AFFIRMATION FOR THE MONTH
"I am aware of the power of my words."

PRIMARY FOCUS

Even though your everyday activities may seem to flow more easily, you're likely to feel some underlying frustration regarding your career decisions. Who are you trying to please?

HEALTH AND FITNESS

Stress factors remain high, and some situations may seem to escalate midmonth to a more frenetic pace. Keep your cool by taking breaks to clear your energy and calm your mind.

ROMANCE AND RELATIONSHIPS

Your feelings of rebellion against the controls others place on your life may stem from unresolved frustrations with your parents. The Lunar Eclipse on the 15th stimulates an opportunity for introspective awareness of your deeper needs for stability and security. Take action after the Solar Eclipse on the 29th to create a platform for your growth. Clear up misunderstandings with a sibling from the 9th–15th. And be ready for romance after the 21st, when you're ready to open your heart to love.

FINANCE AND CAREER

If you run into blockades from behind the scenes, seek out information which will allow you to break the stalemate from the 1st–16th. It's crucial to be aware of the hidden agenda operating in the workplace (including your own) midmonth, since these pressures can undermine your success. Watch your spending, avoiding impulsive decisions from the 2nd–20th, since they can be more costly than you realize at the time.

OPPORTUNITY OF THE MONTH

Launch important plans or projects on the 29th–30th, but only if you're prepared to take full responsibility for the outcome.

Rewarding Days: 2, 3, 11, 12, 16, 20, 21, 24, 29, 30
Challenging Days: 1, 4, 6, 7, 13, 14, 15, 26, 27

AFFIRMATION FOR THE MONTH
"I am aware of my deepest needs."

PRIMARY FOCUS

By applying your creative energy to any situation you can make improvements and gain favor with others. Find ways to give more of yourself, and you'll be satisfied with the results.

HEALTH AND FITNESS

Get to the core of any physical problems through careful exploration and analysis. Your attention now can alleviate difficulties later.

ROMANCE AND RELATIONSHIPS

An existing relationship may suffer from the pressures which arise from repressed or unresolved issues from the past. Dig into your deeper feelings to uncover the source of your own discontent. Explore your sexual needs with candid honesty to allow a deeper bonding with your partner. If you're involved in a relationship which is deteriorating and you are unable to revitalize it, you may find the strength to reach closure and end it. However, if you are free to explore a new love or to strengthen an existing one, you can experience significant progress.

FINANCE AND CAREER

Taking unnecessary financial risks can damage your stability. However, you must address any issues which involve taxes, jointly-held resources, or indebtedness. Try to reach some resolution before the Full Moon on the 14th. Otherwise, you might do better to deal with these issues from the 26th–31st. Work relationships can be rocky after the 12th due to unfulfilled expectations. Make careful evaluations before you make promises.

OPPORTUNITY OF THE MONTH

Your efforts to probe beneath the surface and clear away outworn situations through the 25th allows room for new growth.

Rewarding Days: 9, 13, 14, 17, 18, 26, 27
Challenging Days: 2, 4, 5, 11, 12, 23, 24, 25, 31

AFFIRMATION FOR THE MONTH
"I can easily release the past."

PRIMARY FOCUS

Educational pursuits, workshops which help you improve your professional skills, and networking with others who share your interests all offer positive avenues to advance your career.

HEALTH AND FITNESS

Restore or enhance your health by learning more about your individual physical needs. Evaluate your health status near the time of the Full Moon on the 12th.

ROMANCE AND RELATIONSHIPS

New relationships are more likely to develop through work connections, and you may experience a transformation in a friendship from the 1st–10th. Your desire to reach beyond the ordinary into a more stimulating experience can be more easily fulfilled than in the past, but you may experience a breakdown in communication unless you make a special effort to bridge misunderstandings. Get out and socialize more if you're feeling isolated. Partnership draws your focus after the New Moon on the 27th.

FINANCE AND CAREER

Even though you may have some great ideas, you may feel that they fall on deaf ears until after the 18th. Part of the problem can result from trying to push something when you really need to stand still and explore the situation more carefully. Use Mercury's retrograde through the 17th to restore alliances and stir enthusiastic support of those you know. Then launch your plan into successful action on the 28th.

OPPORTUNITY OF THE MONTH

Instead of rushing around to get there first from the 11th–17th, ignite support of others whose influence can help your reputation.

Rewarding Days: 5, 6, 10, 13, 14, 18, 19, 22, 23, 28
Challenging Days: 1, 7, 8, 12, 20, 21, 27

AFFIRMATION FOR THE MONTH
"I gladly cooperate with others."

PRIMARY FOCUS

Interactions with others can be more rewarding and may seem to offer reciprocal support. However, a confrontation concerning ethical or moral issues can stimulate an end to an association.

HEALTH AND FITNESS

Competitive sports offer a chance for you to show your skill or improve your abilities. Balance strength with flexibility now, and honor your personal limitations.

ROMANCE AND RELATIONSHIPS

Partnerships are a strong focal point, although you may not feel entirely cooperative if you sense that your partner is gaining more recognition. Find healthy ways to channel your ego's need to compete (games, sports), instead of playing psychological games which undermine the integrity of your bond. The Full Moon in Capricorn on the 12th marks a sensitive period when you may feel more vulnerable, but you can also make your feelings known. Apply your imagination to improve your love life from the 13th–21st.

FINANCE AND CAREER

Business travel brings excellent results from the 1st–9th, but watch for resistance from excessive conservatism from the 10th–14th (including your own). Address concerns by uncovering facts instead of giving into emotional responses. Your drive to succeed in reaching your goals is powerful after the 21st, but be careful to avoid stimulating jealousy from others and make sure you're not stepping on the wrong toes on your climb to the top.

OPPORTUNITY OF THE MONTH

By weighing the evidence in a situation and determining where you stand, you can establish an influential position on the 11th and 12th.

Rewarding Days: 2, 7, 8, 11, 12, 15, 20, 30, 31
Challenging Days: 1, 4, 5, 6, 17, 18, 24, 25, 26

AFFIRMATION FOR THE MONTH
"I am guided by Divine Wisdom."

PRIMARY FOCUS

Careful evaluation of your finances helps you determine the best actions for expansion of your career. You are definitely driven to succeed in reaching your goals.

HEALTH AND FITNESS

It's easy to exhaust your energy by pushing beyond your limits, so stay aware of the way you feel and allow ample time to build strength and to rest.

ROMANCE AND RELATIONSHIPS

Work, work, work! Even though you may have a particular aim in mind, you can alienate your emotional support system if you fail to give energy back to others who care about you. You may think you're doing this "for them," but stop to be sure of your motivations. Plan time to travel or get away from your routine after the New Moon on the 25th, sharing your appreciation of nature with someone you love. Spend time in inspirational activities or developing your spiritual path from the 10th–31st.

FINANCE AND CAREER

Before you take financial risks, make sure you have a clear understanding of your budget. And before you take on investors or partners in a business venture, be sure you each understand your areas of influence or control. Unforeseen expenses can stall progress from the 18th–22nd, but you should be back on track by the 26th. However, you can lose ground by ignoring trouble spots at work after the 27th, so deal with them immediately.

OPPORTUNITY OF THE MONTH

Your intuitive faculties blend beautifully with your rationale through processes on the 25th and 26th, so tune in and move forward.

Rewarding Days: 3, 4, 7, 8, 11, 16, 17, 26, 27, 30
Challenging Days: 1, 2, 13, 14, 15, 21, 22, 28, 29

AFFIRMATION FOR THE MONTH
"I deserve the love I need."

PRIMARY FOCUS

Travel and increased activities which allow you to further your career help you develop strong alliances with those who share your aims. Take positive steps to reach the goals you set last month.

HEALTH AND FITNESS

After a frustrating period of restlessness from the 1st–9th, you are likely to feel more balanced and physically strong, but avoid high-risk activities early in the month, and watch your driving!

ROMANCE AND RELATIONSHIPS

You may lose your temper with your family, especially if you feel your parents or their priorities are taking control over a situation you want to manage, from the 1st–7th. Efforts on your part to communicate your honest feelings and needs during the Full Moon on the 8th can lead to a resolution, but you may decide to pursue your own aims, anyway. Your love life gains momentum from the 9th–15th, when romantic play may lead to long-term commitment. It's time to increase your capacity for love.

FINANCE AND CAREER

Keep a flexible attitude early in the month, but be ready to take a stand if necessary. You can make significant progress professionally by presenting a plan which brings traditional values in line with innovative ideas. Following the New Moon on the 24th, your desire to move forward may be frustrated by the pressure of unfinished business. Don't let it get you down: deal with it during Mercury's retrograde from Sep. 22–Oct. 13.

OPPORTUNITY OF THE MONTH

Attend meetings or schedule presentations from the 12th–15th which allow you to influence others or generate support.

Rewarding Days: 4, 8, 9, 12, 13, 22, 27
Challenging Days: 10, 11, 15, 17, 18, 24, 25

AFFIRMATION FOR THE MONTH
"I am an effective communicator."

PRIMARY FOCUS
Your ambition to succeed is powerful, and you can be highly effective in promoting yourself or your ideas. Make sure you're willing to pay the price for your decisions and actions.

HEALTH AND FITNESS
Team sports or group fitness classes can help you improve your health and may be the source of great enjoyment, too. You're finally starting to see some results for your hard work.

ROMANCE AND RELATIONSHIPS
If you're suddenly drawn into an intense attraction from the 1st–10th, don't be surprised. Just give it some time before you make a commitment, since what you see at first is likely to change. Listen to your heart during the Lunar Eclipse on the 8th. An existing relationship can improve dramatically after the 9th, and may be revitalized during the Solar Eclipse on the 23rd. To discover your deeper feelings you have to open the doors, and you are the one who has to allow the love to flow.

FINANCE AND CAREER
Watch your spending from the 1st–7th, since you can easily miss details or commit yourself in ways you had not realized. After Mercury moves into direct motion on the 13th, several factors begin to change which give you a different viewpoint. Get involved with your community, connect with your allies and friends, and take on leadership roles after the 23rd. You are the right person for the job (but you may have to convince yourself first!).

OPPORTUNITY OF THE MONTH
Change in the line of command may leave an opening for your career advancement. Before you leap, make sure you want the job.

Rewarding Days: 1, 2, 5, 6, 10, 19, 20, 24, 25, 28, 29
Challenging Days: 7, 8, 14, 15, 16, 22, 23

AFFIRMATION FOR THE MONTH
"I joyfully embrace my hopes for the future!"

PRIMARY FOCUS

Even though your friends play a powerful role this month, you may still feel like spending some time alone to rejuvenate. By listening to your limitations, you may actually gain strength.

HEALTH AND FITNESS

Make time for contemplation and relaxation, and expend a special effort observing your own attitudes. Healing now is largely dependent upon working from within yourself to release and forgive.

ROMANCE AND RELATIONSHIPS

Make time for your friends from the 5th–23rd, but especially near the Full Moon on the 7th, when renewing your connection brings you closer. You may become more bonded in intimate relationships, but you're also likely to feel a bit distant if you're pushed into situations which stimulate vulnerability after the 19th. Before you withdraw from a relationship completely, take a look at your needs and your attitudes toward it. You may just need some time alone to regroup. A change of scenery from the 28th–30th offers a new perspective.

FINANCE AND CAREER

Your participation with those who share your special interests helps to advance your reputation, and may lead to career growth from the 4th–22nd. Business travel, meetings, or presentations give your career a boost from the 6th–8th, and may lead to future contacts. Investments may show slow growth, so seek out safe alternatives if you wish to increase your capital. Attend to details of communications from the 12th–23rd to avoid confusion.

OPPORTUNITY OF THE MONTH

Influences behind the scenes can be more powerful than overt actions from the New Moon on the 22nd–30th.

Rewarding Days: 1, 2, 6, 16, 17, 20, 21, 24, 25, 29, 30
Challenging Days: 3, 4, 5, 11, 12, 18, 19, 23

AFFIRMATION FOR THE MONTH
"I am a loyal friend."

PRIMARY FOCUS

Now's the time to manifest your dreams by taking meaningful steps to build them. Your efforts now will have effects which reach far into the future.

HEALTH AND FITNESS

In your drive to keep your life moving at the pace you desire, you can reach burnout before you know it. Set a reasonable pace for yourself—and avoid overindulging from the 16th–21st!

ROMANCE AND RELATIONSHIPS

With Venus and Mars both transiting in your sign, your success in romantic endeavors shows great promise. If you've been waiting for the right time to reach out to a special someone, you may find the courage (and the right reception) from the 15th–31st. Test the water by setting up a positive line of communication. If you get the right response, then you'll be confident about your approach. Bring the magic back to an existing relationship by giving more of yourself. It will be worthwhile!

FINANCE AND CAREER

Alliance with those who share your ideals and politics gives you the right foothold for progress through the Full Moon on the 6th, but don't be deceived by smooth words and the right wardrobe. Know the person before you sign on the line. Contracts and agreements fare best after the 11th, and are especially promising after the New Moon on the 21st. Your high ethical standards can make a significant difference in the outcome of a situation the 17th–20th.

OPPORTUNITY OF THE MONTH

You can have things the way you want them after the 24th, but only if you are operating in harmony with your real needs.

Rewarding Days: 3, 4, 13, 14, 18, 19, 22, 23, 26, 27, 30, 31
Challenging Days: 1, 2, 8, 9, 16, 17, 28, 29

AFFIRMATION FOR THE MONTH
"I am loving, gentle, and kind."

≈≈ AQUARIUS ≈≈
The Water Bearer

January 21 to February 19

Element: Air

Quality: Fixed

Polarity: Masculine/Yang

Planetary Ruler: Uranus

Meditation: "Creating new paths by focusing the mind"

Power Stones: Aquamarine, chrysocolla, black pearl

Anatomy: Ankles, circulatory system

Key Phrase: "I know"

Gemstone: Amethyst

Glyph: Waves of energy

Color: Violet

Animal: Birds

Myths/Legends: Deucalion, Ninkhursag, John the Baptist

House Association: 11th

Opposite Sign: Leo

Flower: Orchid

Key Word: Unconventional

Positive Expression:
Progressive
Unconditional
Futuristic
Ingenious
Friendly
Altruistic
Unselfish
Liberal
Humane
Autonomous

Misuse of Energy:
Fanatical
Aloof
Deviant
Intransigent
Detached
Anarchistic
Rebellious
Undirected
Thoughtless

≈ AQUARIUS ≈

Your Ego's Strengths and Weaknesses

You're willing to step outside the boundaries of the mainstream and risk being different. In your quest to be a genuine friend, you can develop a capacity for unconditional acceptance and love. Uniqueness is your trademark, and you appreciate that which is unusual and rare.

As "The Reformer" of the zodiac, you're always searching for ways to create innovative change, and are drawn to the most up-to-date technological developments. Your artistic and musical tastes lean toward the unconventional, and even though some of your own ideas or creative efforts may seem nonconformist, you may set a precedent for what later becomes classical style. However, you may feel frustrated by many of the traditions which have been used by others as an excuse for lack of progress. By synchronizing your energy with that of your planetary ruler, Uranus, you can develop a powerful connection to your intuitive guidance. Through listening to and trusting this inner voice, you can enhance your creativity and find the path which will lead to your greatest fulfillment.

Others may feel alienated by your aloofness, even though your intention may be to maintain objectivity. To become truly unconditional, you are challenged to build a connection to Universal Love. Through this link, you can illuminate a path toward understanding and self-acceptance for all humanity.

Your Approach to Romance

Even though you enjoy time to yourself, you may yearn for a companion who can be both your best friend and lover. Through your overall friendliness and independent attitude, you are likely to draw a wide variety of people into your life, but seek a special person to be your loyal (and equal) partner. Your intuition gives you the signal if it's love, but beware: your mind may try to talk you out of getting involved! You'll be most comfortable with a commitment which allows opportunities for both partners to express their true individuality.

As an Air sign, communication is important to you, and you may feel most at ease with others who share your element—Gemini, Libra, and Aquarius. Another Aquarian may be difficult to reach at an intimate level, but if you do connect, you may be able to create a remarkable life together. Gemini's wit and intelligence are alluring and difficult to resist, and Libra's charming refinement can lead you to a new world of cultural understanding.

Aries keeps you on your toes and provides stimulating, passionate energy. But Taurus' need to hold onto everything (including you) may feel too heavy. Cancer's need for contact can dampen your feeling of independence, and you may be most magnetically drawn to your opposite sign, Leo, whose fiery playfulness can be completely engaging, albeit demanding!

Although Virgo may inspire you to search your soul, it may be difficult to truly appreciate one another. With Scorpio, you may reach an uncomfortable feeling that you're never quite at the same level. Sagittarius' adventurous attitude and good humor entice you, and you can both enjoy free self-expression with one another. Friendship with Capricorn may be easier than romance, since control issues can thwart your attempts toward intimacy. Similar ideals may connect you with Pisces, although you can easily get lost in the vapors of a different reality with one another.

Your Career Development

A career path which allows plenty of room for your originality, and which challenges your mind will be most fulfilling. Owning your own business offers an opportunity to market your own or other uncommon creations. You may have special talents in writing and communicating, and may be drawn to fields such as public relations, broadcasting, news media, advertising or sales. An interest in politics may lead you to work in public service, especially in the area of civil rights.

Scientific fields may fascinate and reward you well; areas such as electronics, computer science, theoretical mathematics, astrology, meteorology, aviation, or the space industry may be appealing. In fine arts, your talents may range from visionary art to original music, using the ultimate in technology. Whatever your career choice, your unique energy is unlikely to be overlooked.

Your Use of Power

You understand the power of the human mind and spirit, and may desire to merge your consciousness with a higher source to experience pure power. Because you find a misuse of power distressing, you may resist moving into a position of influence until you feel you're ready. You may be more comfortable in a situation which allows you to represent a common cause or universal ideal instead of seeking power for the sake of pure personal recognition. However, once your abilities are acknowledged, others may boost you into a position of prominence.

Through winning trust you can generate clear new directions for a group, company, or nation. Your altruistic spirit may stimulate you to champion causes for those who are repressed. However, you may also find yourself in positions of notoriety which can damage your efforts if your personal actions have offended the sensibilities of society.

You may sometimes feel lonely when stepping into directions that are risky, but your vision may lead you into the unknown without the support of others. The future is quite real for you, and you can create a passage which will make tomorrow brighter for the generations to follow.

Famous Aquarians

Marian Anderson, Justine Bateman, Christie Brinkley, Natalie Cole, Richard Gephardt, John Grisham, Rutger Hauer, Ann Jillian, Robert MacNeil, Norman Mailer, Toni Morrison, Roger Mudd, Graham Nash, Louis Rukeyser, Jane Seymour, Boris Yeltsin

THE YEAR AHEAD FOR AQUARIUS

This year marks the beginning of a long cycle of personal realization and fulfillment, with Uranus, your planetary ruler, moving into Aquarius. Your willingness to release the vestiges of the past which are no longer relevant to your life, and move into a freer form of self-expression, can launch you into a long cycle of positive revolutionary change. To prepare for these changes this year, create a network of friends and professional allies who are truly in synch with your energy and ideas.

Uranus' transit in Aquarius will last until the year 2003, and, depending upon your actual date of birth, can be more strongly influential during different periods of this long cycle. However, the ingress (entrance) of Uranus into your sign is particularly significant since you are an Aquarian. Sometime during the next eight years Uranus will conjunct your Sun, a period of extremely powerful significance, but its influence will be felt in your life for the entire cycle.

Jupiter's transit in Sagittarius influences your desire to reach further into the future, and may stimulate a greater need to set larger goals for yourself. Your feeling of satisfaction with your career grows, although you may be frustrated by a sense of insufficient resources to accomplish your aims, especially if you are wasteful or generally ill-prepared for the "real" world. By carefully balancing your aims with your current circumstances and needs, you can gradually increase your sense of worth. This is an excellent time to increase your association with others who share your ideals or aims, and may mark a year of political involvement.

The Solar Eclipses draw your attention to the need to achieve harmony between your deepest inner needs for stability and security and your desire for recognition and achievement. Family may play an especially significant role throughout the year, and your function in the family is likely to undergo a change. If you've been confused or uncertain about your life path, serious consideration of your motivations and desires in this area now can help you determine the best alternatives and most significant directions for your growth.

Chiron's transit in your Solar 8th and 9th Houses indicates a period of physical and emotional healing, and may mark a time in which you gain greater awareness of your deeper psychological make-up. Your attitudes toward intimacy may need evaluation, and this is an excellent time to heal wounds which are related to abuse, abandonment, or loss.

If you were born from January 21 to 23, you're feeling the impact of Uranus conjuncting your Sun while Pluto sextiles your Sun. These cycles represent a period of significant alterations, some of which may seem to be beyond your control. Every aspect of your life may seem to be affected in some way. The primary influence of this period is one of release, restoration, and revolution. You may feel extremely restless, and need positive directions to funnel these energies of change. Even in those situations which are not under your control, you may have a wide range of choices, and circumstances which you decide to transform or situations you desire to remove from your life can be more easily released. The influence of this cycle will last through the end of 1996, so you have some time to influence change and move into new territory. Physically and emotionally, this can be a period of remarkable healing, especially in areas which link mind and body. You may be feeling a strong preference for independent action, and are likely to resent others who attempt to control your life or get in the way of your progress.

You are experiencing a period of smoother sailing this year, if you were born from January 24 to 30. Even though Saturn is transiting semi-square to your Sun, you may feel that the obstacles you face are less challenging and more easily under your own control. Also, you may still have some house-cleaning to do as a result of the challenges you experienced during 1994. By staying stuck in a situation just because it seems to offer security when you are unhappy or unfulfilled, you can actually start to slide backward in your growth, but if you clear away attitudes or other obstacles and take the leap into a more freely-expressive or opportunistic circumstance, you may actually feel like you can breathe again! Take the time now to prepare for significant changes which will begin next year. Be especially aware of the shifts you hope to make in your career, and get in touch with your feelings about your current situation. Start networking, and establish the credentials you will need to move into a more rewarding future.

You're feeling a strong surge of creative energy this year if you were born from January 28 to February 3. Pluto's transit in quintile to your Sun stirs a deep sense of passion and creativity, and may stimulate a period of restoration of some long-ignored talents you've been saving for "when you have time" to develop them. By applying your unique ideas and talents, you may also gain greater recognition and accelerate your professional growth. It is also possible that you will have an opportunity to act as a mentor for others who can benefit from your guidance and inspiration.

If you were born from February 4 to 14, this is the time to take steps which will provide you with the knowledge, skills, and experience to develop your resources, talents, and abilities. Saturn is transiting in semi-sextile aspect to your Sun, and energizes your awareness of your strengths and liabilities. Not only can you make significant headway in achieving your aims, but it may be easier to eliminate many of the obstacles which have stood in your way. Your attitudes toward your self-worth are critical, and you may have to safeguard against under-evaluating your professional time or energy. On the physical level, it is important that you investigate any problems which may arise, since ignoring symptoms or discomforts now can lead to long-term difficulties later. By making adjustments in your schedule, dietary regimen, or attitudes toward your body, you can actually divert some difficulties and begin to feel more physically well. Chronic problems or weaknesses are likely to flare-up during this cycle, giving you a chance to treat them at their core level, instead of just alleviating symptoms without curing the cause.

You're feeling the influence of Neptune transiting in semi-sextile to your Sun, if you were born from February 11 to 15. Your dreams and visions may carry you into periods of ecstasy, or can alternatively create confusion and illusion. It is important to take time for contemplation, meditation, or creative expression to stay more closely in touch with your real inner self. You may lose faith in a belief or ideal which has guided you for some time, especially if you determine that you have misplaced your loyalty or been deceived, but you can also experience a period of initiation into a more profound awareness and understanding. Be wary of financial situations which leave gaps in contracts, or which obligate you in ways which are difficult to understand, since this is a time during which you can be more easily deceived by others who would take advantage of your good graces.

You may feel that your life is undergoing huge transformational changes if you were born from February 14 to 19. You are experiencing the transits of Uranus semi-sextile to your Sun and Pluto square your Sun. Anything in your life which has outlived its usefulness is likely to disappear or be changed in a significant way, and attachments which are dragging you down need careful evaluation. The thrust of this cycle is transformational healing, elevating you toward a higher form of self-expression. However, the temptation of these cycles tangle a desire for greater power or influence with a need to bring about revolutionary change. These changes actually need to occur within your own life, but may also be played out in political situations or on another large-scale arena. If your ego becomes trapped in the power plays of your life, this can be a period of painful change, but if you learn to surrender some of your own desires to the will of a Higher Power, you may discover that your life is transformed in an unimaginable and magical new direction. Relationships with family, particularly your parents, may undergo massive changes. Your awareness of the differences between yourself and your parents can lead to a greater understanding of yourself, but may create a gap with your parents. To avoid unnecessary alienation, be aware of your own stubborn attitudes or ideas and allow your parents (or others) to have the same freedoms you would demand of them.

Tools to Make a Difference

To take advantage of this period of emotional and physical healing, you may need more effective ways to get in touch with your body and soul. Healing touch, through massage or other body work, can have a powerful effect. You might even want to learn some of the techniques yourself to share with others.

To enhance your awareness of the different ways in which energy flows, investigate as many forms of resonate energy as you can. Toning, tuning, chanting, or singing can help you balance your physical and emotional energy. You can also experience these resonating fields through magnetic fields, crystals, or even ley lines.

Through your involvement with community activities, special interest groups, or political action, you can begin to give back to the world in significant ways. Find activities which are meaningful to you, and take on leadership roles whenever possible, but be wary of any situations which would sap your time or resources and fail to provide positive solutions. You may also find cultural exchanges with others whose backgrounds are different from your own highly rewarding.

During the times you feel the need to keep your energy under greater control, wear your color, violet. The energy of this color is self-contained, and can act as a buffer when you feel vulnerable to the changes in the world around you. Amethyst jewelry can have a similar effect.

During your meditations, concentrate on a feeling of rising above the ordinary. See yourself boarding a beautiful hot air balloon. The brilliant colors of the balloon seem to radiate life. As the balloon rises above the surface of the earth, see the problems, issues, or difficulties you face getting smaller and smaller. Feel the clarity of the air, and experience the freedom of floating above the ordinary. Envision a situation as you want it to be, and when you land in your balloon, step out into a new world of promise and harmony. Take this sensation into your everyday life, knowing you are the creator of your present and future.

Affirmation for the Year

"I have faith in myself."

ACTION TABLES FOR AQUARIUS

These dates reflect the best (but not the only) times for success
and ease in these activities according to your Sun Sign.

Change Residence	Apr. 17–May 1
Request a Raise	Jan. 30–31
Begin a Course of Study	Mar. 31, Sep. 24–25
Visit a Doctor	Jan. 1–5; July 10–24; Dec. 12–1
Start a Diet	Jan. 14–15; Feb. 11–12; Mar. 10–11; Apr. 6–7; May 4–5, 31–June 1, 27–28; July 24–26; Aug. 21–22; Sep. 17–18; Oct. 14–15; Nov. 11–12; Dec. 8–10
Begin a Romance	May 29–30
Join a Club	Dec. 22
Seek Employment	July 10–25; Nov. 4–22
Take a Vacation	Jan. 21–22; Feb. 18–19; Mar. 17–18; Apr. 13–15; May 11–12; June 7–8; July 5–6; Aug. 1–2, 28–29; Sep. 24–25; Oct. 22–23; Nov. 18–19; Dec. 15–17
Change Your Wardrobe	May 2–July 9
End a Relationship	Feb. 15–16
Seek Professional Advice	Jan. 17–18; Feb. 13–14; Mar. 13–14; Apr. 9–10; May 6–7; June 2–4, 30–July 1, 27–28; Aug. 23–25; Sep. 20–21; Oct. 17–18; Nov. 13–15; Dec. 11–12
Have a Makeover	Jan. 30–31
Obtain a Loan	Jan. 19–20; Feb. 15–17; Mar. 15–16; Apr. 11–12; May 9–10; June 5–6; July 2–3, 29–31; Aug. 26–27; Sep. 22–23; Oct. 19–21; Nov. 16–17; Dec. 13–14

PRIMARY FOCUS

Involvement with special interest groups can enhance your standing within the community, although you need to budget your time and expenditures with care. You're movin' and shakin'!

HEALTH AND FITNESS

It's easy to overextend physically, and if you have any problems, taking direct action helps you resolve them. This is not a time to sit back and worry. Do something.

ROMANCE AND RELATIONSHIPS

Financial squabbles can dampen a relationship, especially if your expectations are not met. Before you argue over money, determine the real issue. You may discover some old wounds, and may be reacting to situations which occurred in the past. Get back in the present moment. Do something special together after the 15th. A difficult relationship may end, but one that has substance matures and strengthens. New love is most promising after the 26th. Get together with friends if you feel lonely or need inspiration.

FINANCE AND CAREER

Work behind the scenes from the New Moon on the 1st through the 6th puts you in an excellent position to launch an exciting project from the 7th–13th. Review your budget to be sure you have ample resources, and be ready for unexpected expenditures or blockades from conservative factions from the 9th–16th. Even though Mercury is retrograding from Jan. 26–Feb. 15, you may still be able to make progress. Try a different approach during the New Moon on the 30th.

OPPORTUNITY OF THE MONTH

Travel, presentations, or advertising open doors from the 22nd through 31st.

Rewarding Days: 2, 3, 7, 13, 21, 22, 26, 27, 30, 31
Challenging Days: 1, 9, 10, 17, 18, 24, 25

AFFIRMATION FOR THE MONTH
"My mind is open to new ideas."

PRIMARY FOCUS

You may feel highly competitive, and can use this drive to accomplish your aims. Just be aware of a tendency toward abrasiveness and allow time for those inevitable delays.

HEALTH AND FITNESS

From now through the end of May, you're feeling the strong stimulus of Mars in opposition to your Sun. Pace yourself, since it's easy to burn out before you know it.

ROMANCE AND RELATIONSHIPS

Tumultuous or rocky times in a partnership may be the result of long-standing issues which have never been brought to the surface. Honest communication and compassion for one another can bring about significant healing, but you may also be embroiled in such intensive battles that you see no resolution. If you need to create an ending, this is the time, but if you have substantial reason to hope, hang in there! A new love may exist only in your fantasies after the 20th, so get the facts before you bare your soul.

FINANCE AND CAREER

Safeguard your professional reputation by carefully choosing your associations or alliances. Your impatience from the 12th–19th can cause problems, so keep yourself busy in case you have to wait for progress to get things moving again. The Full Moon on the 15th emphasizes a period of increased social obligations, and a graceful attitude on your part can ward off a disastrous situation. Stay within your budget after the 20th to avoid a financial crunch.

OPPORTUNITY OF THE MONTH

Cooperative assertiveness on the 18th–19th helps to diffuse a stalemate and get things moving on the right track.

Rewarding Days: 3, 4, 9, 18, 19, 22, 23, 26, 27
Challenging Days: 1, 6, 7, 13, 14, 20, 21, 28

AFFIRMATION FOR THE MONTH
"I am aware of my needs and the needs of others."

PRIMARY FOCUS

Life flows more smoothly, and this is an excellent time to mend fences and concentrate on building your self-esteem. Creative or artistic pursuits show promise.

HEALTH AND FITNESS

Your attitudes toward your health have significant impact on the way you feel physically now. Concentrate on balancing strength with flexibility—physically, mentally, and emotionally.

ROMANCE AND RELATIONSHIPS

With Venus transiting in your sign from the 2nd–27th, you may feel more romantically inclined and are likely to crave more attention from your sweetheart. Sometimes, you receive more if you give more, so try reaching out, particularly near the time of the Full Moon on the 16th. A weekend getaway can satisfy your need for adventurous romance from the 17th–19th, but you might have more time to fulfill those fantasies from the 25th–31st! Reaching out to a special someone brings positive results on the 30th and 31st.

FINANCE AND CAREER

Even though you may still be battling a stubborn or conservative attitude on the part of others, there's hope for progressive change from the 1st–15th. However, you may have to link an innovative plan with an existing situation, so avoid a tendency to want ultimate progress in everything. Breakthroughs from the 12th–18th give you hope, and networking, travel, or presentations from the 22nd–31st give you the opening you've been seeking.

OPPORTUNITY OF THE MONTH

Be ready for action on the 21st to 31st, and use this time to make your point, gather your supporters and make progress.

Rewarding Days: 3, 8, 17, 18, 21, 22, 25, 26, 27, 30, 31
Challenging Days: 1, 5, 6, 12, 13, 14, 19, 20

AFFIRMATION FOR THE MONTH
"I am loving, patient, and kind."

PRIMARY FOCUS

To keep up with business, you may be spending more time traveling or in close communication with associates. Exciting changes may allow you to progress quickly.

HEALTH AND FITNESS

Get outdoors and enjoy nature from the 3rd–15th, when you're ready to give yourself a physical and psychological boost. Keep your craving for indulgences in check later in the month.

ROMANCE AND RELATIONSHIPS

Relationships can be rather enjoyable now, although you may not be in the mood for anything deep or heavy. Contact with a sibling during the Lunar Eclipse on the 15th can clear the air and may open a better line of communication. But you can also use this time to clarify any misunderstandings with your sweetie. Family issues may dampen your spirits near the Solar Eclipse on the 29th, although this is a good time to get back in touch with your roots and reclaim the elements of your past which promote self-acceptance.

FINANCE AND CAREER

Business meetings, conferences, or contacts can be quite rewarding from the 2nd–13th, but there may be deception in the ranks from the 12th–16th, so stay alert. A sudden change in direction or attitude can alter your plans from the 17th–21st, but if you're ready for change, it may open the door to progress on the 22nd and 23rd. Watch your finances midmonth, and be cautious in speculative investments after the 7th. Prospects are better on the 23rd and 26th.

OPPORTUNITY OF THE MONTH

Innovative ideas have a good reception midmonth, but you may have to wait a while before they become reality.

Rewarding Days: 4, 5, 14, 15, 18, 19, 22, 23, 26, 27
Challenging Days: 1, 2, 3, 9, 10, 16, 17, 29, 30

AFFIRMATION FOR THE MONTH

"I am an effective communicator."

PRIMARY FOCUS
Power struggles with partners or family can escalate, but you are in an excellent position to break away from unrealistic constraints by using your inventive imagination.

HEALTH AND FITNESS
Emotional stress can weaken your physical vitality unless you regularly release tension. Increasing your activity level can help, but avoid high risk situations or unfamiliar territory.

ROMANCE AND RELATIONSHIPS
Dissatisfaction in a relationship can result in a blow-up, releasing pent-up tension and anger. With positive ways to channel this energy, you can actually breathe life back into a relationship that is worthwhile. Or, if you're beginning a new relationship, you may have to break away from your fears based on past experiences and take the risk of emotional vulnerability. Listen to your own inner voice for guidance. Romance can be highly rewarding after the 24th, and love blossoms during the New Moon on the 29th.

FINANCE AND CAREER
Continual communication with significant others in your professional field leads to advancement in your career. However, you may have strong competition on important issues, or from your areas of creative pursuit. Forego comparing your efforts to those of others, and allow your best to shine through. Avoid taking risks in unknown situations from the 7th–18th, since you could be easily deceived. If you're uncertain, investigate and wait.

OPPORTUNITY OF THE MONTH
Even though you may be strongly challenged, this is a period of breakthrough allowing you to release what you no longer need.

Rewarding Days: 1, 2, 11, 12, 15, 19, 20, 24, 29
Challenging Days: 5, 6, 7, 13, 14, 26, 27

AFFIRMATION FOR THE MONTH
"I trust my intuitive insights."

PRIMARY FOCUS

Love relationships, creative pursuits, and enjoyable ventures have your attention and can be physically and emotionally revitalizing. Greater satisfaction arises if you're willing to release the past.

HEALTH AND FITNESS

A flare-up of a chronic physical complaint can be irritating, but you're in a good cycle to try a different approach which could lead to healing a problem at its deepest level.

ROMANCE AND RELATIONSHIPS

The memory of or contact from an old love can be haunting early in the month, but only if you've failed to resolve your attachments. Get in touch with your deeper feelings during the Full Moon on the 12th, and use this time to strengthen your bond of love in your current relationship. Sexual energy is powerful after the 11th, and intimate interaction with your partner can lead to ecstatic joy. Tantric approaches to love-making can be highly rewarding from the 12th–30th.

FINANCE AND CAREER

Although you may have difficulty or turmoil in situations involving joint finances or investments, you may be able to reach a workable compromise. Just be sure you're not the one left holding all the liabilities while your partner benefits from the assets! Also, before you share your creative or inventive works, take steps to legally protect them. Concentrate on resolving issues in the work place following the New Moon on the 27th.

OPPORTUNITY OF THE MONTH

Improvement in collaborative efforts from the 1st–4th and 21st–28th streamlines efficiency and stimulates fruitful results.

Rewarding Days: 7, 8, 12, 15, 16, 20, 21, 25, 26
Challenging Days: 2, 3, 9, 10, 18, 27, 30

AFFIRMATION FOR THE MONTH
"My creativity is inspired by Divine Love."

PRIMARY FOCUS

Your work definitely keeps you busy, and the demands you feel from others escalate steadily this month. Align yourself with productive individuals and situations which show stability.

HEALTH AND FITNESS

Special attention to your health may be necessary, and if you've been ignoring any problems, they can become quite irritating. Stress continues to play a powerful role in your well-being.

ROMANCE AND RELATIONSHIPS

A love relationship can grow stale and predictable (definitely not to your liking!) and may become more burdensome than joyful. It's possible that you will experience some separation from your loved ones. In either case, you have time to reflect upon your real feelings, and need to determine what you can do, or what you want to do, to make improvements. If you're alone, you might prefer to stay that way for a while, since getting caught in other's problems will not seem at all appealing.

FINANCE AND CAREER

A delay in returns from speculative interests from the 1st–7th can be disheartening, but may not be permanent. This is a good time to eliminate indebtedness and clarify any issues regarding taxes or financial liability. You may end up with responsibilities which you had not agreed to accept midmonth, but can win support from others by completing the tasks at hand. New negotiations after the 22nd place you in a better situation for career growth.

OPPORTUNITY OF THE MONTH

Cooperative efforts with others are most promising from the 22nd–31st. Take a fresh approach after the New Moon on the 27th.

Rewarding Days: 5, 6, 9, 10, 13, 14, 17, 22, 23
Challenging Days: 1, 2, 3, 7, 8, 20, 21, 27, 28

AFFIRMATION FOR THE MONTH
"My life is getting better day by day."

PRIMARY FOCUS

Expanding your options and reaching into new directions can advance your career and may also improve your social position. Cooperative associations with others are crucial to your success.

HEALTH AND FITNESS

Taking time away from your normal routine gives you a fresh perspective. Consider vacationing or taking a long weekend to break the stress of predictability.

ROMANCE AND RELATIONSHIPS

More companionable interaction with your partner arises from showing your appreciation to one another. Since you're likely to feel a bit more emotionally vulnerable during the Aquarius Full Moon on the 10th, you may prefer to keep things simple, but if there are issues you need to discuss, attempt to get to the core and reach for deeper levels of intimacy and understanding. A more honest approach to your sexual relationship strengthens your emotional bonds following the New Moon on the 25th.

FINANCE AND CAREER

Beneficial results from joint ventures confirm your previous decisions about partnerships. However, you may need to renegotiate your roles or positions from the 6th–11th in order to get the most out of your association. Delve into money matters with a professional advisor from the 10th–29th, when you may discover positive ways to eliminate some of your burdens. However, its best to avoid risky speculation after the 24th.

OPPORTUNITY OF THE MONTH

Make plans for future business travel or expansion by opening lines of communication and making new contacts.

Rewarding Days: 1, 5, 6, 9, 10, 14, 15, 19, 28
Challenging Days: 3, 4, 8, 16, 17, 23, 24, 30, 31

AFFIRMATION FOR THE MONTH
"I honor my ethical standards."

PRIMARY FOCUS

Even though financial matters dominate, you are also in a powerful position to take advantage of travel, educational opportunities, teaching, writing, or publishing.

HEALTH AND FITNESS

You may feel that you have little "extra" time to exercise or take care of your health, but the efforts expended to strengthen your body will add energy and help you better utilize your time.

ROMANCE AND RELATIONSHIPS

The alchemy of a love relationship becomes more profound, but whether you are connected to another or single, your link to the inner and higher aspects of yourself can be powerfully developed. If you are not currently involved with someone, you're in a better position to begin a romance after the New Moon on the 24th. Get involved with pursuits which stimulate your mind and enhance your cultural awareness. Those activities which inspire you may also draw you to the person you've been seeking to share your life.

FINANCE AND CAREER

From the 1st through the Full Moon on the 8th you may find it difficult to separate the facts of a financial situation from your feelings about it. Sudden changes can disrupt your plans and may make it more difficult to stay on track. Maintain your drive to achieve your goals, but try not to alienate the wrong people in the process. Educational pursuits which help you fine-tune your skills or attain new knowledge open new career pathways now.

OPPORTUNITY OF THE MONTH

If you've considered getting back into school, doing some serious writing, or attending conferences—NOW is the time!

Rewarding Days: 1, 2, 6, 7, 10, 15, 16, 24, 25, 29, 30
Challenging Days: 4, 9, 12, 13, 20, 21, 27

AFFIRMATION FOR THE MONTH
"My mind is linked to the Source of All Wisdom."

PRIMARY FOCUS

Travel, educational, or cultural pursuits continue to be emphasized. You are also likely to feel more easily agitated and less patient. Learn to effectively direct your energy.

HEALTH AND FITNESS

Stress from the job or family pressures can undermine your sense of vitality. Let go of tension and try to release the temptation of trying to control every situation.

ROMANCE AND RELATIONSHIPS

Getting away from routine can improve a love relationship. However, you may have a tendency toward aloof detachment through the time of the Lunar Eclipse on the 8th unless you remain aware of the needs of your partner. It's easy to become enamored by an idea or even the illusion you project on a lover early this month, so give yourself some time before you jump into something new or trust a situation which feels intuitively wrong. Emotional circumstances with parents can escalate during the Solar Eclipse on the 23rd.

FINANCE AND CAREER

Legal battles or contract disputes may be frustrating. Instead of pushing for a final decision during Mercury's retrograde through the 13th, use the time to uncover the real facts of the situation. Avoid signing contracts through the 10th. You may be glad you waited, since unique opportunities arise late in the month. Concentrate on unfinished business through the 15th, and begin to make new contacts after the 23rd.

OPPORTUNITY OF THE MONTH

Your attunement to that which is out of the ordinary works to your advantage in business and pleasure this month.

Rewarding Days: 3, 4, 7, 12, 13, 22, 23, 26, 27, 30, 31
Challenging Days: 2, 6, 10, 11, 17, 18, 24, 25

AFFIRMATION FOR THE MONTH
"I am guided by Truth."

PRIMARY FOCUS

Your involvement in community ventures or special interests leads to advancement in your career and can bring greater respect. However, it's easy to overextend your time and resources.

HEALTH AND FITNESS

Team sports and group fitness activities can be great fun while improving your health. Just try to slow down, since you're likely to go too fast in everything you're doing right now.

ROMANCE AND RELATIONSHIPS

Support from friends makes all the difference, particularly if you have concerns with family or a partner and need some objectivity. This is a great time to seek out others who share your beliefs and concerns, and to work together to create change. A friendship may transform into a deeper relationship later in the month, but you may have to be the one to take the initiative and get things moving in a different direction. However, this is not a good time to loan money to friends, since you might have regrets.

FINANCE AND CAREER

Clarify expectations and objectives with your employer before the Full Moon on the 7th to avoid feeling pressured by unexpected responsibilities. You're likely to see greater rewards from your work now, including improving finances and advancement, but you may also feel that you're asked to put forth efforts in areas which waste your energy or resources. Know the situation and determine where you stand before you make a commitment.

OPPORTUNITY OF THE MONTH

After the New Moon on the 22nd you're in an exceptional position to strike out into virgin territory and make great progress.

Rewarding Days: 4, 5, 8, 9, 18, 19, 22, 23, 26, 27
Challenging Days: 2, 6, 7, 13, 14, 20, 21

AFFIRMATION FOR THE MONTH
"I am confident about my future."

PRIMARY FOCUS

Utilize your professional allies and network with others who share your convictions. Charitable or volunteer efforts can be highly rewarding this month.

HEALTH AND FITNESS

Inner fitness greatly effects your physical energy level. Make an effort to improve your attitudes about yourself and find ways to experience the healing power of love and compassion.

ROMANCE AND RELATIONSHIPS

Even though you may spend much of your time out of the public eye, a romantic relationship can blossom into a significant commitment. A long-time relationship can also be revitalized now by giving yourselves ample time to share your fantasies, hopes, and wishes with one another. Indulge in your favorite pleasures during the Full Moon on the 6th. Strengthen feelings of love and appreciation for one another by opening some of those "forbidden" doors and risking vulnerability.

FINANCE AND CAREER

Finances show improvement, and you may even enjoy the benefits of reward from investments. Obligations do not demand as many of your resources now, giving you a chance to relax a bit. Consider taking a break after the 17th and just enjoying yourself. You may be vulnerable to deception or undermining in business ventures from the 14th–31st, so be sure you know who to trust, and investigate any areas which are suspect.

OPPORTUNITY OF THE MONTH

Behind-the-scenes efforts now prepare you for experiences which will be more publicly visible in the future.

Rewarding Days: 1, 2, 6, 7, 16, 17, 24, 25, 28
Challenging Days: 3, 4, 10, 11, 12, 18, 19, 30, 31

AFFIRMATION FOR THE MONTH
"I have abundance enough to share."

PISSCES
The Fish

February 19 to March 21

Element: Water

Quality: Mutable

Polarity: Feminine/Yin

Planetary Ruler: Neptune

Meditation: "Surrender to the heart of Divine Compassion"

Gemstone: Aquamarine

Power Stones: Amethyst, bloodstone, tourmaline, sugilite

Anatomy: Feet, lymphatic system

Key Phrase: "I believe"

Glyph: Two fish joined, swimming in opposite directions

Colors: Violet, sea green

Animal: Dolphin, whale, fish

Myths/Legends: Aphrodite, Buddha, Jesus of Nazareth

House Association: 12th

Opposite Sign: Virgo

Flower: Water lily

Key Word: Transcendence

Positive Expression:

Visionary
Imaginative
Quiet
Poetic
Idealistic
Empathetic
Tenderhearted
Impressionable
Compassionate

Misuse of Energy:

Escapist
Susceptible
Unconscious
Victimized
Confused
Co-dependent
Self-deceptive
Addictive

♓ PISCES ♓

Your Ego's Strengths and Weaknesses

Your visionary, imaginative sensibilities draw you to experiences which exist in the sensual, mystical, and creative realms. As "The Illusionist" of the zodiac, you have the capacity to connect with the subtle plane of vibration which may manifest as a keen talent in music or the arts. You have a strong compassion for life which includes an awareness of suffering and despair, and you may feel compelled to reach out to those in less fortunate circumstances.

Your unassuming nature may lead you to choose a quiet life; but even if you are strongly involved with the public, you still need time and room for personal reflection or seclusion. Despite occasional feelings of vulnerability, you can always envision different possibilities. However, the fine line between various levels of reality can be unclear, and you can become victimized by illusion or deception. Learning to safeguard against unscrupulous individuals who would misuse your sympathetic understanding may be one of your most difficult lessons.

Because your awareness of the more subtle planes is strong, you may feel drawn to escape from the heaviness of the physical plane through creative expression or meditation, but you can also fall prey to addictive behaviors, whether in the form or substances, situations, or relationships. By staying in touch with your inner self, you can help maintain the boundaries which balance your relationship with life. You are inspired by the real magic of life: the tender touch of love, the light in the eyes of a child and the beauty of nature. By developing your sensibilities, you can become a vehicle for transcendent inspiration, and easily connect with the haven within yourself which radiates true compassion for yourself and for others.

Your Approach to Romance

Since life without love would be meaningless for you, it should be no surprise that you are the master of romance. You have the capacity to relate to people from all walks of life. Even though your search for your soulmate may lead you into many possibilities, your trust may not always be met by another who understands your depth. You seek the enchantment of love, and can create a magical space into which you and your true love retreat from the harshness of the outside world.

You're most emotionally at ease with the Water signs—Cancer, Scorpio, and Pisces. With another Piscean, you can feel a true understanding of your desires, hopes and dreams. Cancer's nurturant caring helps you open your heart and share the joy of healing through love. Scorpio's magnetic sensuality carries you into another dimension.

Aries can stimulate spontaneous pleasures, but you may wish they would last a bit longer. Taurus' taste for the good things blends beautifully with your imaginative ideas, and, even though Gemini's changeability can throw you off balance, you may enjoy the feeling—temporarily. Love with Leo can be too much work, since their demands can take much of your energy.

Virgo, your zodiac opposite, can be highly attractive and may offer a direction for you hopes and dreams. And although Libra's elegance is intriguing, you may feel you're not quite perfect enough. You're inspired by Sagittarius' spiritual yearnings, but you'll have to stay alert to figure out where they are. Although Capricorn's stability feels safe, you need to carefully maintain your boundaries to experience the most from the relationship. As a friend, Aquarius may be unequaled, but as a lover, they can seem difficult to reach, even when you use your imagination!

Your Career Development

You may prefer to think of your career as a vehicle for expressing your vision of life, and need plenty of room to exercise your imaginative talents. Although ambition may not be your incentive, your desire to reach beyond the mundane may drive you to achieve strong success. Counseling, social work, medicine, or the ministry can be outlets for your desire to uplift the human spirit. Your desire to beautify life may inspire you to work in fashion design, hairdressing, interior design, makeup artistry, the floral industry or landscape design.

The businesses of advertising, television, or movie-making are good outlets for your ability to utilize your awareness of the collective unconscious. Or you may have a taste for the restaurant business. A special sensitivity to animals may draw you into work focusing on their needs. But whatever your choice, your happiness is assured when you're in the flow.

Your Use of Power

The energy of life which pulsates through your soul stimulates your desire to surrender to the ultimate Source of All Life. Your life can become the instrument for the expression of the power of divine love, which conceives and nourishes life itself. Your vitality is charged through the currents of creative power, helping you become a radiant vision of faith and hope. You understand the strength of unity.

As part of your link with Divine Love, you may choose a devotion to a spiritual path or practices. Even when you lose yourself or your direction in this release you're hungry to stay connected. By focusing your mind and your energy, you can find the true teacher which resides deep within yourself. Once you touch The Source, you can become empowered to return that energy to the physical plane through your creative endeavors. Glowing with the light of love, you can become the true healer, radiating joy and hope to those whose lives you touch and uniting them in the spirit of harmony.

Famous Pisceans

Desi Arnaz, Marion S. Barry, Jr., Erma Bombeck, Cindy Crawford, W. E. B. DuBois, Charles Durning, John McLaughlin, Maurice Ravel, Rob Reiner, Knute Rockne, Sharon Stone, Darryl Strawberry, Ivana Trump, Amerigo Vespucci, Bruce Willis, Paula Zahn

THE YEAR AHEAD FOR PISCES

The inspiration to reach into broader horizons, to attain greater recognition for your efforts, and to achieve your career aims helps drive you toward your goals this year. Others may be more aware of your contributions, which can increase your opportunities to influence change and promote greater unity, but you will have to stay in touch with the realities of life to be effective in accomplishing your dreams.

You may feel the stimulus to break through the barriers which have prevented you from realizing your dreams in your career, relationships, and spiritual quest. You are also becoming more aware of the inner elements of your own psyche which have been the greatest blocks to the experience of true joy. With Jupiter transiting through your Solar 10th House, you can experience greater opportunities through your career, and you may also receive more recognition from others for your abilities. To make the most of this cycle, it's important that you put forth your best efforts, since you can also receive greater recognition for your mistakes, or greater notoriety for your faux pas! Rather than allowing others to have unrealistic expectations, you can actually improve your professional and personal relationships by clarifying expectations and defining your obligations.

The Solar Eclipses during 1995 emphasize your need to improve your knowledge, skills, and abilities. Educational opportunities, travel, or networking with others within your field of interest help you expand your proficiency. You may also be exposed to a wide variety of cultural experiences and can benefit from an understanding of both the differences and similarities of beliefs, practices, and ideologies among the world's people. Your own spiritual path can be strengthened. However, with the Lunar Nodes emphasizing both the 8th and 9th Houses of your Solar Chart, you may also be dealing directly with some of your deeper emotional attachments. Certainly, it's important to be connected to the things and people you love, but you may also need to release an attachment to some situations in order to experience the healing you need.

If you were born from February 19 to 22, you're feeling a stimulus to make sweeping changes. The planets Uranus and Pluto are both in aspect to your Sun throughout this year and well into 1996. Uranus is transiting semi-sextile to your Sun, allowing you to feel more confident about breaking into new situations or moving forward within an existing circumstance. Pluto's transit is squaring your Sun, stimulating a period of deep emotional healing and transformational change. Anything in your life which has become stagnant or useless needs to be eliminated now, and you can take the steps to extract yourself from circumstances which inhibit your growth. Some life changes may occur whether you initiate them or not, but you always have choices about your responses to these changes! Your life work or career path may seem unsatisfactory, and this is your chance to make the alterations necessary which will allow you to experience what you sense as "right livelihood." You may also encounter aspects of your inner psyche which allow you to more clearly differentiate between the motivations you have for yourself and the motivations you experience from others. Additionally, you may feel some estrangement from your parents, although you can also make profound changes in the way you relate to them and heal old wounds. Pay particularly careful attention to your health this year, since emotional or spiritual changes are often accompanied by physical transformation. Any problems which surface may seem to be highly challenging, but may also lead to an ultimate improvement in the quality of your life. Self-destructive attitudes or habits can be revolutionized or redirected in ways which allow for the restoration of your power—physically, emotionally, or within the outside world. But continuation with the old way of operating could result in a downfall. You have the power to make a difference. Seize it.

If you were born from February 23 to 25, you may still feel some reluctance to make big changes due to the lessons you learned last year. However, this is an excellent time to strengthen the foundations in your life, complete tasks which will give you the credibility or stability you desire and prepare for changes next year. Even though you may feel some adaptations due to cycles which influence other aspects of your psyche, your sense of ego identity is strong and stable this year.

You're feeling a need to develop greater compassion and forgiveness if you were born from February 26 to March 2. Neptune's transit in semi-square to your Sun can be highly inspiring, but may also bring periods of confusion or self-doubt. It is critical to allow time to stay in touch with your inner feelings, which may be enhanced by spending more time alone or in contemplative activities. Once you are clear about how you feel, you can then consider the feelings, needs, or demands of others, without losing touch with your own boundaries. You may also be more sensitive to environmental influences, and can feel physically below par unless you maintain a fairly clear and clean diet and lifestyle. Your physical energy should start to stabilize somewhat once Saturn moves away from the conjunction to your Sun in March.

Uranus is transiting in semi-square to your Sun if you were born from March 2 to 7. During this time, you may feel exceedingly restless and ready to break out of situations which are inhibiting to free expression of your individuality. The hard work and focus you exhibited last year may have helped you lay the foundations for the changes you make now. And although you may decide to diversify, you can still maintain the stability you've created by avoiding the temptation to throw out everything and begin anew. This is a period of sorting, releasing, and reshaping, but it can also be a time of vacillation and unreliability if you decide to give into every whim. By making reasonable choices which will allow you to move away from the restraints of the past, you can have the freedom you desire and still keep your feet on the ground.

Saturn's transit in conjunction to your Sun is a primary influence all year if you were born from March 6 to 17. This is a period of maturation, clarification, and prioritization, requiring you to determine what you really need and how you honestly feel about yourself and your life. Your commitment to your true needs will influence your health, your relationships, and your career. In fact, you may see powerful improvements in all areas if you're working on them, but if you're ignoring your responsibilities or relying too much on the support or efforts of others, then this can be a difficult time. This cycle is clearly related to your past, and unfinished business from the past is likely to emerge. Fortunately, you can use this energy to finally close the door on the things you no longer need in your life. If you've been wanting to eliminate habits, attitudes, or situations which keep you imprisoned, this is the time. If you are finally ready to develop your talents or skills, you can make greater progress because it is easier to create the structure and discipline necessary to accomplish your aims.

If you were born from March 16 to 20, you are feeling the influence of two major cycles during 1995. Uranus is transiting in sextile to your Sun, stimulating a period of innovation and experimentation. You are also feeling the power of Pluto transiting in trine to your Sun, adding influence to your ability to finally realize many of your dreams. This is a time of healing, hope, and inspiration, and may mark a highly significant period of change in your life. Additionally, you may find that you cannot keep everything the same and still have what you want and need. Some alterations will actually improve your life now, and you need to allow time to celebrate those improvements. You may also feel some grief over these changes, even though you want to make them and welcome them in your life. Allow time and space to release and grieve, then your experience of the transformation and revolution will truly restore your life to its fullest potential. Your attitudes toward your relationships and career choice can be altered to allow more room for love, understanding, accomplishment and acceptance. Enjoy this time. Make it a period of true grace, healing, and enlightenment.

Tools to Make a Difference

One of the primary factors in determining whether or not you enjoy this year may rest in your ability to communicate effectively with others. Not only is it imperative to become more competent in expressing your own thoughts, but also you may need better ways to elicit response or information from others. Neurolinguistic programming can be an exceptional tool in your quest. You might also enjoy learning more about utilizing creative visualization, affirmations, and self-empowered thinking.

To improve your physical health, determine the target areas and make an effort to get to the root causes of your physical discontent. Spend time regularly getting in touch with your physical body through dancing, yoga, tai chi, swimming, or other enjoyable activities. Check your environmental situation for offending agents which you may not even be able to detect with your immediate senses. After all, your intuition about such things should be fairly clear. If you perceive that there's something amiss, investigate it! You may also need to clear the energy in your environment on a regular basis, using techniques such as smudging. Be alert to your work situation, as well, since some of the energy you're experiencing on the job could undermine your physical health or emotional strength.

Daily meditation can help you maintain a balance in your energy, and it might be helpful to begin your day by revitalizing yourself on an inner level. Simple relaxation techniques can be quite helpful, such as getting comfortable, clearing your mind, closing your eyes and slowly counting backward from 10 to 1. Once you reach "1," take three deep breaths. Then, see an image of a beautiful seashore before you. Walk along the shore, listening to the sound of the waves, feeling the sea spray against your skin. Feel the vastness of the ocean and your connection to it. Drink in that sensation and know that you are part of the eternal ebb and flow of life. When you are ready, slowly count forward from 1 to 10, open your eyes, center your energy, and begin your day.

Affirmation for the Year

"I am fully aware of my feelings and needs."

ACTION TABLES FOR PISCES

These dates reflect the best (but not the only) times for success and ease in these activities according to your Sun Sign.

Change Residence	May 2–23; June 17–July 9
Request a Raise	Mar. 1–2
Begin a Course of Study	Apr. 29–30; Oct. 24–25
Visit a Doctor	Jan. 7–Mar. 13; July 26 –Aug. 9
Start a Diet	Jan. 17–18; Feb. 13–14; Mar. 13–14; Apr. 9–10; May 6–7; June 2–3, 30, July 1, 27–28; Aug. 23–25; Sep. 20–21; Oct. 17–18; Nov. 13–14; Dec. 11–12
Begin a Romance	June 28–29
Join a Club	Jan. 1–2
Seek Employment	July 26–Aug. 9; Nov. 23–Dec. 11
Take a Vacation	Jan. 24–25; Feb. 20–21; Mar. 19–20; Apr. 16–17; May 13–14; June 9–10; July 7–8; Aug. 3–4, 30–31; Sep. 26–27; Oct. 24–25; Nov. 20–21; Dec. 18–19
Change Your Wardrobe	July 10–25
End a Relationship	Mar. 16–17
Seek Professional Advice	Jan. 19–20; Feb. 15–17; Mar. 15–16; Apr. 11–12; May 9–10; June 5–6; July 2–3, 29–31; Aug. 26–27; Sep. 22–23; Oct. 19–21; Nov. 16–17; Dec. 13–14
Have a Makeover	Mar. 1–2
Obtain a Loan	Jan. 21–22–23; Feb. 18–19; Mar. 17–18; Apr. 11–12; May 9–10; June 5–6; July 4–6; Aug. 1–2, 28–29; Sep. 24–25; Oct. 22–23; Nov. 18–19; Dec. 15–17

PRIMARY FOCUS

To achieve your goals, find ways to work cooperatively with others. Competitive situations are likely to arise, but you can still accomplish your aims.

HEALTH AND FITNESS

It's easy to push beyond your limits, especially if you fail to assess the requirements of a situation before you jump into it. Avoid exhaustion by pacing yourself and staying flexible.

ROMANCE AND RELATIONSHIPS

A partnership can be tested to the limit this month, with turmoil escalating out of control if either of you fails to be realistic with your needs or demands. Seek counsel from a friend from the New Moon on the 1st through the 6th. Plan to spend time away from everyday hassles with your sweetheart. Romantic pleasures can be delightful during the Full Moon on the 16th, but watch your spending before you head out for a special evening. Instead of trying to avoid conflict, deal with arguments directly this month.

FINANCE AND CAREER

You may feel caught between the demands of different factions at work, so determine where your loyalties reside before you are coaxed into the foray. You may be frustrated by a slow-down in progress, and might even worry that you're caught in a dead-end. Determine your best course of action, but also be sure you know what's expected by superiors or you may run into trouble. Finish projects, since new plans move slowly this month.

OPPORTUNITY OF THE MONTH

Stay in the moment, and avoid a tendency to worry about what you cannot control. Meeting your obligations makes the best impression.

Rewarding Days: 1, 5, 9, 10, 15, 16, 25, 28, 29
Challenging Days: 4, 12, 13, 19, 20, 26, 27

AFFIRMATION FOR THE MONTH
"I am focused on the now."

PRIMARY FOCUS

Demands from your work can wear you down unless you develop a good support system. However, you should start to see more satisfying rewards and fewer power struggles. Keep the faith.

HEALTH AND FITNESS

By allowing time to release tension and maintaining good nutritional support, you can keep the negative effects of stress at a minimum. Stay active, and try relaxing herbal tea in the evening.

ROMANCE AND RELATIONSHIPS

Your friends can be a positive light in your life, and you'll also enjoy the camaraderie of community activities or special interest groups. If you're looking for love, you're more likely to find it while sharing your favorite interests or through an introduction from a friend. But if you're already in a relationship, use the energy this month to strengthen your shared visions and plan for your future together. Indulge in your favorite fantasies after the 20th, and make time for a romantic interlude.

FINANCE AND CAREER

While Mercury retrogrades through the 15th you may feel that you're operating in limbo so far as complete information is concerned. If progress stalls, use the time to clarify details, finish projects, and follow-up on correspondence or communication. Tension in the work place may be uncomfortable unless you take a stand or make a direct effort to alleviate problems in your own area. Waiting for the other guy will only complicate the matter.

OPPORTUNITY OF THE MONTH

If you're pulled in several directions, reestablish your priorities, then try again. Smoother sailing arises on the 20th.

Rewarding Days: 1, 2, 6, 7, 11, 20, 21, 24, 25, 28
Challenging Days: 5, 8, 9, 15, 16, 17, 22, 23

AFFIRMATION FOR THE MONTH
"I easily maintain my concentration."

PRIMARY FOCUS

Determine the best course of action in your work and your relationships by first pinpointing your personal needs. Trust your intuitive guidance, and be aware of the influence of your emotional attachments when making important decisions.

HEALTH AND FITNESS

Whenever possible, take time to relax and soften the edges. Schedule a massage, enjoy a hot tub or sauna, and pamper yourself.

ROMANCE AND RELATIONSHIPS

You're most comfortable when romance is uninterrupted by the pressure of the "real" world, and this is an excellent month to create a special get-away which allows you to satisfy your appetite for sensual pleasure. The New Moon on the 1st spawns the possibility of an exciting love interest, and your commitment can grow during the Full Moon on the 16th. Any competitive or disagreeable aspects of a relationship escalate from the 12th–18th, but you may reach an understanding after the 17th.

FINANCE AND CAREER

Disputes over job responsibilities may result in confusing circumstances from the 3rd–18th. Review your role in a partnership to be sure you're in a balanced situation, and make the necessary changes before the 15th. Communication improves after the 14th, and you may be busy juggling increasing time commitments after that time. Set up a reasonable budget and review your finances after the New Moon on the 30th.

OPPORTUNITY OF THE MONTH

Launch important projects during the Pisces New Moon on the 1st and make alterations early to avoid losing momentum.

Rewarding Days: 1, 2, 5, 6, 10, 11, 19, 20, 24, 28, 29
Challenging Days: 4, 8, 9, 15, 16, 21, 22

AFFIRMATION FOR THE MONTH
"I pay attention to my dreams."

PRIMARY FOCUS

Even though you may have more money to spend, your attention to your finances along with some careful planning can assure a more secure future and greater long-term prosperity.

HEALTH AND FITNESS

You may feel a bit lazy and tend to overindulge in sweets early in month, but your self-discipline improves after the 14th. Get an exercise program going which will build your stamina.

ROMANCE AND RELATIONSHIPS

Love's in bloom, but you may be excessively sensitive and can dampen romantic passion by reverting to your fears from the past. Before you diminish the joys of today by crying about what you lost yesterday, release your attachment to old wounds. Love grows as your own sense of worth evolves and as you release the pain which can only stand in the way of your progress. The Solar Eclipse on the 29th brings energy which allows you to express your feelings, ideas, and needs with greater poignancy.

FINANCE AND CAREER

From the 1st through the Lunar Eclipse on the 15th, you may have greater concerns about your financial obligations. Attention to the details of a budget, whether personal or work-related, may expose funds which can be diverted or used more effectively. Watch a tendency to overreach your time or resources. Meetings or conferences fare well this month, especially after the 17th. You're in your best form on the 20th, 21st, 24th, and 29th.

OPPORTUNITY OF THE MONTH

Your past experience can positively augment your professional standing from the 15th–26th.

Rewarding Days: 2, 3, 7, 8, 16, 24, 25, 29, 30
Challenging Days: 4, 5, 11, 12, 18, 19

AFFIRMATION FOR THE MONTH
"My heart is filled with love."

PRIMARY FOCUS

With a strong drive to finish a long-term project you can meet your deadline and accomplish your aims. Honor priorities, but try not to ignore demands close to home.

HEALTH AND FITNESS

You may find it more difficult to relax and can easily push beyond your limits unless pace yourself. Worry may be your worst enemy, so stay realistic and don't sweat the small stuff.

ROMANCE AND RELATIONSHIPS

Staying in touch with family members can diffuse misunderstandings before they have a chance to escalate into a brawl. Selfish attitudes have a detrimental effect on any relationship now, and you may decide to walk away from a situation which serves only selfish desires. Love grows through sharing inspirational or spiritual experiences during the Full Moon on the 14th. You may also make a special connection to an unusual person. Be sure it's not just infatuation before you take the leap.

FINANCE AND CAREER

Your eagerness to move ahead can be blocked by more conservative concerns or legal details. Avoid protracted battles by determining the hierarchy in advance. Legal or contractual disputes may finally be settled during Mercury's retrograde from May 24 to June 16, but if you cannot work out the details, perhaps it's best to remove your interest from the situation. Get in touch with your best advisors, who have your security in mind, before you make a final decision.

OPPORTUNITY OF THE MONTH

Stay out of situations which do not concern you, since getting involved where you don't belong can be costly on all levels.

Rewarding Days: 4, 13, 14, 17, 18, 21, 22, 26, 31
Challenging Days: 1, 2, 7, 9, 10, 15, 16, 28, 29

AFFIRMATION FOR THE MONTH
"I am guided by Truth."

PRIMARY FOCUS

Competitive situations test your strength of commitment in professional and personal concerns. Avoid becoming distracted by circumstances which undermine your strength.

HEALTH AND FITNESS

You may have very little "free" time, but still need to allow a period each day to clear your mind and focus your energy. The inner work you do now helps you weather the storm.

ROMANCE AND RELATIONSHIPS

Although you may have specific aims for your life, others may try to influence you differently. To remain committed to your real feelings and needs, you may have to work harder to stay in touch with yourself, instead of being swayed by the needs or opinions of others. Reflect on your relationship with your parents during the Full Moon on the 12th. Allow extra time for family matters, and create a space at home which gives you a real sense of comfort and security. Make time for pleasure after the New Moon on the 27th.

FINANCE AND CAREER

Social obligations can be irritating, particularly if you have to be involved in something which is uninteresting to you, but necessary to satisfy an obligation. Be careful of the persons you take into your trust from the 1st–9th, since a confidence can be breached. Watch your motivations for spending after the 11th, since you may be stimulated to spend just to take the edge off an emotionally stressful circumstance.

OPPORTUNITY OF THE MONTH

Your imaginative or creative efforts help divert attention from a difficult situation after the 22nd.

Rewarding Days: 1, 10, 14, 18, 19, 22, 23, 27, 28
Challenging Days: 5, 6, 7, 11, 12, 25, 26

AFFIRMATION FOR THE MONTH
"I am safe and secure."

PRIMARY FOCUS

Favorable circumstances for utilizing your talents and artistry help you advance in your career. Love, pleasure, and enchantment fill the air.

HEALTH AND FITNESS

It's tempting to show off or push beyond your limits, so try to learn something about new sports or activities before you launch into them.

ROMANCE AND RELATIONSHIPS

Tension gives way to romance after the 5th, and you may feel like initiating a new relationship or taking steps to revitalize an existing one. Imaginative and dramatic situations can enhance your desire to share your feelings during the Full Moon on the 12th. Children may also be a special delight. You can become the essence of love, and need ample opportunities to express your feelings. This is a great month to get away to an exotic or fanciful vacation spot and play out your wildest fantasies.

FINANCE AND CAREER

Only if it's enjoyable are you willing to exert yourself in your career. However, you may find this attitude profitable, especially if others can have as much pleasure or experience as much enthusiasm as you feel about a situation. Speculative interests are strongly emphasized from the 5th–12th and again from the 23rd–29th. Just get the details before you invest in something which is entirely new. Creative pursuits make big profits this month.

OPPORTUNITY OF THE MONTH

Cooperative ventures can be both enjoyable and profitable. Just stay aware of the rules and regulations mid-month.

Rewarding Days: 7, 8, 11, 12, 14, 15, 20, 21, 25, 26
Challenging Days: 2, 3, 4, 9, 10, 22, 23, 30, 31

AFFIRMATION FOR THE MONTH
"I have vast creative resources."

PRIMARY FOCUS

Work circumstances may be more enjoyable, but some turmoil over joint finances may distract from your creative focus. Set up a dialogue and maintain communication to keep everyone satisfied.

HEALTH AND FITNESS

Get to the core of physical discomforts or chronic problems. An innovative approach or alternative healing methods may offer additional support or relief.

ROMANCE AND RELATIONSHIPS

Sexual intimacy may seem to be a point of contention in a love relationship, especially if old wounds have surfaced or if either of you has lost trust in the relationship. During the Full Moon on the 10th, go within yourself to discover your own vulnerabilities or hidden fears. You may be responding from previous experience instead of dealing with the current situation. You have much to gain from determining the type of partner you want to be following the New Moon on the 25th. You can only change yourself!

FINANCE AND CAREER

Taxes, insurance, or debt issues can be a thorn in your side. Avoid any temptation to ignore these areas, since they are likely to be even more problematical if you try to sweep them under the carpet. At work, hidden agendas get in the way of progress early in the month, but things are more open after the 16th. Set up a dialogue to air your concerns after the 24th. And make an attempt to win over those who would compete and undermine your position.

OPPORTUNITY OF THE MONTH

Special attention to the link between your emotions and body may allow your to alleviate longstanding problems.

Rewarding Days: 3, 4, 7, 11, 12, 16, 21, 22, 30
Challenging Days: 2, 5, 6, 18, 19, 26, 27

AFFIRMATION FOR THE MONTH
"I show gratitude for all I have."

PRIMARY FOCUS

Pursuits which broaden your understanding of human experience—such as travel, education, cultural activities, or professional conclaves—have a strong influence on your life and career.

HEALTH AND FITNESS

You may be thinking more about your own mortality, and can surprise yourself with some of your attitudes. This can be a period of healing body and spirit.

ROMANCE AND RELATIONSHIPS

Profound interactions with others can create a deeper bond, especially within intimate relationships. Partnerships are emphasized through the time of the Full Moon in Pisces on the 8th, when it's important to bring forward your deeper concerns and needs in order to stabilize and strengthen your relationship. Explore your feelings about your sexual needs, and find positive expressions to satisfy these needs. The New Moon on the 24th stimulates the need to be more honest about your emotional attachments.

FINANCE AND CAREER

Negotiations in regard to long-term contracts, seeking financial support from banks or investors, and clarifying tax and legal issues fare well. However, you may run into competition or power plays from the 1st–4th which are discouraging. Alleviate your anxieties by designing agreements which protect your best interests. If you cannot reach an accord before Mercury turns retrograde on the 22nd, then you might do better to wait a few weeks.

OPPORTUNITY OF THE MONTH

Trust your astute judgment and intuitive insights instead of getting caught up in details which distract from your aims.

Rewarding Days: 4, 8, 9, 12, 13, 17, 18, 27
Challenging Days: 1, 2, 11, 15, 16, 22, 23, 29, 30

AFFIRMATION FOR THE MONTH
"I accept the hidden aspects of myself."

PRIMARY FOCUS

An excellent time for psychological probing, scientific research, or dealing with financial matters, this month's cycles draw your attention to the broader canvas and long-term effects.

HEALTH AND FITNESS

To relieve any physical distress, make an effort to get to the core of the problem instead of just treating symptoms. Emotional healing has a profound effect.

ROMANCE AND RELATIONSHIPS

Unfinished business in relationships inhibits forward progress, unless you're willing to release and get on with life in the present (the same is true of a partner). Even if you feel that some of your dreams or fantasies have taken on a bizarre twist, they may represent a battle within yourself to break away from old wounds and experience true joy. The energy of the Solar Eclipse on the 23rd stimulates a need to reach beyond into what can be. Follow the radiant light of love which leads your way.

FINANCE AND CAREER

While Mercury continues its retrograde though the 13th you may be able to reach conclusions about ongoing negotiations or make breakthroughs in other endeavors. Your creative energy is powerful now, but you can be mislead by a "friend" or associate who would take advantage of your position or resources for their own selfish aims. The whole story may not surface until after the Lunar Eclipse on the 8th. Take action after the 23rd to launch your plans.

OPPORTUNITY OF THE MONTH

By probing as deeply as possible into your feelings, or staying focused and on-track at work, you will reach the truth of a situation.

Rewarding Days: 1, 5, 6, 10, 15, 24, 25, 28, 29
Challenging Days: 4, 12, 13, 19, 20, 21, 26, 27

AFFIRMATION FOR THE MONTH
"I am whole, strong, and powerful."

PRIMARY FOCUS

You may feel more driven to succeed, and may experience a bit of performance anxiety in your career unless you are prepared. Travel, educational pursuits, and cultural events bring opportunities.

HEALTH AND FITNESS

The tendency to do everything a bit too fast can get you into trouble. Try to slow down and pay attention to warning signs instead of wearing yourself to a nub.

ROMANCE AND RELATIONSHIPS

Love intensifies, and feelings of passion can be restored in a situation which you feared lost. Before you make that commitment, make sure you know your own limitations. It's easy to take on responsibilities which are not yours just because you feel emotionally involved, but co-dependency comes with a high price. Instead, find ways to be supportive while still maintaining your boundaries. Honest communication makes all the difference, and may open a clear direction after the Full Moon on the 7th.

FINANCE AND CAREER

Advancement and recognition may come your way quite suddenly (or so it would appear), and your manner of handling your new-found influence makes the difference between success and failure. Use your sensitivity, even if you're in a competitive situation. Business travel, conferences, writing, publishing, or advertising bring positive results. Contacts made following the New Moon on the 22nd may have surprising impact.

OPPORTUNITY OF THE MONTH

Your enthusiasm can be contagious from the 1st–14th. Just be sure to promise only what you can deliver!

Rewarding Days: 1, 2, 6, 11, 12, 20, 21, 24, 25, 29, 30
Challenging Days: 8, 9, 10, 16, 17, 22, 23

AFFIRMATION FOR THE MONTH
"My life is filled with joy!"

PRIMARY FOCUS

Improvements in work conditions and supportive recognition for your career efforts strengthen your self-esteem and may also bring a significant improvement to your financial picture.

HEALTH AND FITNESS

Take advantage of sports or fitness activities which help you reach your fitness goals. Team sports may be rewarding. Relieve stress by staying active.

ROMANCE AND RELATIONSHIPS

Friends play a powerful role and may be the source of your best support. This is the time for you to find ways to open more to allowing love and support into your life, instead of feeling that you always have to give and never can receive. It might be easier to think of love as a circuit of energy—from having to giving to receiving. A new experience of love is promised after the 14th, when you may finally have a chance to have some of your dreams fulfilled. Enjoy it.

FINANCE AND CAREER

By taking a positive action in community or political affairs you may be able to inspire changes which have far-reaching effects. This is a period of high-favor for you, and you can use your connections to open doors which might otherwise be closed. Be alert to your responsibilities during the Full Moon on the 6th, when satisfying superiors or regulations works to your benefit. Take advantage of investment opportunities after the 21st.

OPPORTUNITY OF THE MONTH

Surprising changes offer the chance you've needed to step in and make yourself and your abilities known.

Rewarding Days: 3, 4, 8, 9, 18, 19, 22, 23, 26, 27, 31
Challenging Days: 2, 6, 7, 13, 14, 20, 21

AFFIRMATION FOR THE MONTH
"I am clear about my goals."

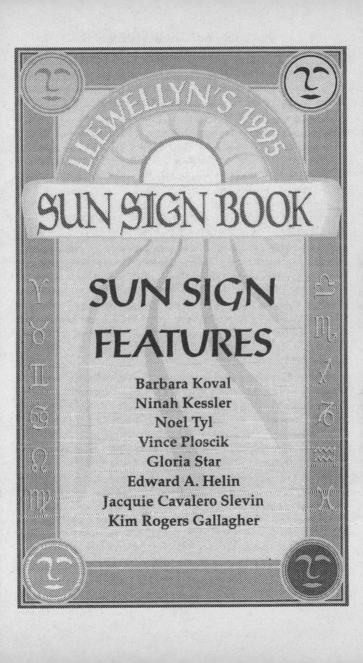

LLEWELLYN'S 1995

SUN SIGN BOOK

SUN SIGN FEATURES

Barbara Koval
Ninah Kessler
Noel Tyl
Vince Ploscik
Gloria Star
Edward A. Helin
Jacquie Cavalero Slevin
Kim Rogers Gallagher

About our Features Writers

Edward A. Helin is a full-time professional astrologer, currently teaching astrology classes at UC-Northridge and other schools. He has appeared on many television and radio programs, lectures and does seminars.

Ninah Kessler is a Florida social worker as well as an astrologer. A regular contributor to the *Llewellyn Sun Sign Books*, and *Astrological Calendar*, she also writes about astrology for local publications, and does consultations.

Barbara A. Koval is a professional astrologer, writing for the major astrological publications, lecturing on astrology, and she frequently appears on radio and TV programs. Her book, *Time and Money: The Astrology of Wealth* (Llewellyn Publications) was published in 1993.

Vince Ploscik, a full-time astrologer in northeastern Ohio, studied under Sophie Mason. He teaches classes, lectures, and does consultations, and has written eclipse articles for the *Sun Sign Book* for a number of years.

Kim Rogers-Gallagher is the author of *User-Friendly Astrology* (ACS Publications), and edits *Kosmos Magazine* (ISAR Publising). Her columns have appeared in *Welcome to Planet Earth Magazine, Dell Horoscope,* and *Mountain Astrologer.*

Jackie Cavalero Slevin taught theater arts for seven years, now is a free-lance writer while caring for her family. She writes a column for *Horoscope Guide,* also has been published in a South African astrology journal.

Gloria Star has written the Introduction and Forecast sections of *Llewellyn's Sun Sign Books* since 1989. A complete biography appears on page 5 of this edition.

Noel Tyl lectures extensively throughout the United States, Europe, and South Africa. His most recent book is *Synthesis and Counseling in Astrology* (Llewellyn Publications, 1994). Tyl is a frequent contributor to Llewellyn's *Moon Sign* and *Sun Sign Books,* and currently edits Llewellyn's New Worlds Astrology anthology series.

Joyce C. Wehrman was a California writer who contributed articles for various Llewellyn books during the 1980s. She died Oct. 8, 1989.

The Way It Will Be

Barbara Koval

A wave of confidence, rising interest rates, and expectations of increasing inflation prompt people to spend, charge, and take out mortgages while rates are still reasonable and prices relatively low.

In times to come, 1995 will appear like an island of prosperity in a decade of high unemployment, ever higher taxes, and the decreasing value of the dollar. 1995 will go down in the history books as a year in which one of the great economies in history finally came face to face with the huge bubble created by its never-ending creation of debt.

As Pluto moves into Sagittarius, we can expect interest rates to continue their slow upward drift, just as Pluto in Scorpio carried them close to pre-World War II lows. Because the tax burden will become more and more onerous, people must seek ways to shelter income, find tax loopholes and deductions, and just plain hide income. The underground economy will grow. People become more and more defensive about their assets and ever more anxious about their physical and financial well-being.

SATURN IN PISCES

Saturn is the planet of rules, restrictions, regulation, discipline and order. Pisces is the sign of dissolution, unrestrained growth, obliviousness, hospitals and institutions, and the bureaucracy. Saturn is one of the major market/price, supply/demand indicators. In Mutable signs it creates conditions for major market disruptions: uncontrolled growth followed by a severe crash. By itself it cannot create a market crash, but it is one of the conditions that promotes severe corrections. Natural forces do not exert any discipline in either direction upon markets or the people involved in them.

Implications for the United States

Saturn will transit the 4th House of the United States chart, the house of land and the products of the land. When Saturn first touched Pisces in the summer of 1993, the Midwest experienced severe floods, and the Los Angeles area severe fires and rain. The Saturn passage of Pisces in the 1930s brought us the dust bowl and massive migrations to the West Coast in search of land and work. Because Saturn stays in Pisces for two and a half years, we can expect severe climatic conditions to impact our crops and our land use. Commodity prices are likely to rise, as will real estate. Real estate prices rise, either because of demand, or because of inflationary pressures. In either case, homes become unaffordable. The family home, maintenance, and taxes put a severe strain on the homeowner's purse. Multiple dwellings, rentals, and condos revive; whatever lowers the price and the cost of owning.

Should there be a worsening recession and subsequent mortgage defaults, we can expect leniency from the powers that be. Many people could lose their homes either to mother nature or to the bank.

As Saturn is the ruler of the U.S. 2nd House, we can see a continuing expansion of the money supply and the consequent dilution of our assets. Though the numbers may rise—more and more of us will become millionaires—the fundamental assets may actually fall in value because of an inability to find buyers. We all look good on paper.

As co-ruler of the 3rd House of domestic trade and exports, we can see an increasing lack of control and restriction as to what circulates in our domestic markets, partially the result of the NAFTA and GATT agreements. Consumers continue to buy cheap foreign products to avoid the marketplace costs of our increasing domestic inflation.

California continues to lose jobs as aliens and foreigners continue to flow into the workplace.

The native population begins to shrink and more and more people look elsewhere for the promised land.

Global

In Japan, export markets continue to shrink and profits slump because of treaties and negotiations with trading partners. "Just say no" seems the response to Japanese exports, but Japan may make major cuts in prices to overcome the resistance and capture purchasers looking for a deal. The U.K. continues to have problems with exports and domestic inflation. Germany is still struggling to keep domestic inflation under control, but not with a great deal of success. In Switzerland we see much the same, all of which suggests that the dollar may not be in all that bad shape this year.

Investment Opportunities

Businesses that do business with the government will expand. Overly large multinationals will continue to downsize, and may move their operations overseas. The international element in investment will continue to be important and financially rewarding. Bureaucratically run schools will find decreasing enrollment as private schools begin to attract a larger segment of the school-age population. There will not be enough nursing and retirement homes to care for the aging population. The latter could be a particularly good investment or business opportunity.

Fashion

Pisces is a sign of glamour and glitz. Saturn is a sign of skin. Pisces is not noted for classical good taste, so we may continue the fashions of beaded and studded leather, and provocative selective nakedness. Slim is still in, but Pisces may be slowly expanding the dimensions.

JUPITER IN SAGITTARIUS

Jupiter is the planet of expansion and growth, religious convictions and belief systems, optimism, and higher education. Sagittarius is the sign of expansion, growth, ethics, travel, and advertising. Since Jupiter is also one of the major market indicators, in its own sign, it can create a heady and steady growth in all markets. Expect the market averages to rise to new heights. Mutable signs are also signs of correction and reversal. The combination of

Jupiter and Saturn mutability with a Jupiter/Saturn square forebodes the possibility of a major market correction late in the year. Expect the growth of religious movements and school reform on all levels.

Implications for the United States

Jupiter brings with it a great confidence and optimism among the people of the U.S., since it will be transiting the U.S. 1st House. It also brings universal denial, enhanced and reinforced by the deteriorating ability to see things as they really are. Saturn usually brings us to our senses, but in Pisces, even Saturn is beleaguered and besieged. Expect hysteria and overreaction in the media that perpetually agitates the population as a whole. Poor judgment is the order of the day. Not only will we see ever-increasing litigation, but important court decisions will impact schools, religion, and freedom of speech. The excesses of Jupiter and Neptune (the long transit of the 70s and early 80s) are about to be transformed by relentless incoming Pluto, but not before we have one last fling with license.

Global

In Japan, we see an expanding workforce and protectionist measures to assure the well-being of labor. Health companies and police also grow. There is also some possibility of sanction for a national army. In the United Kingdom we see a growth in the bureaucracy, retirement homes, hospitals, and institutions. Germany has very active and profitable markets. Corporate profits are up. The German Stock Exchange has a wonderful year. In Zurich, corporations and businesses prosper, but the stock exchange is not strongly affected.

Investment opportunities

If you are thinking of starting your own church, do it. If you would like to start your own cult, ditto. People are eager for education and enlightenment. However, Jupiter in Sagittarius tends to be somewhat conservative. We may see a brief comeback for traditional religion. Televangelism also makes a comeback.

Sagittarius is bullish for all delivery systems from roads to trucking to wholesalers and distributors. It is also great for advertising agencies, publishing, and catalogue sales. Toss in the telecommunications revolution, and put your money on home shopping and interactive TV.

Fashion

The religious look may be popular in some sectors. Ethnic is definitely in, as are large sweeping garments without any linear definition. Droopy suits and wild ties continue to be the thing.

PLUTO ENTERS SAGITTARIUS

Pluto is the planet of sex, death, debt, and taxes. Sagittarius is a sign of expansion, growth, ethics, and correction. The tendency in economic terms of any of the mutable signs (Gemini, Sagittarius, Virgo, and Pisces) is to expand wildly during the first half, and crash during the second half. Although Pluto will only touch Sagittarius early and late in the year, it may give us a preview of things to watch for and guard against in 1996. We can expect increasing sex and violence in the media, which will spur standard setting and controls. Insurance companies, because of health care and natural calamities, will struggle to survive. Between government regulation and massive payouts insurance company profit margins will narrow, despite the massive influx of money from universal health care. Because Sagittarius represents advertising, we will see the beginning of a shakeout in the advertising industry, as cable and pay TV provide opportunities for commercial-free entertainment.

Implications for the United States

The population begins to stagger under increasing debt and tax burdens. Pluto takes things to their logical or illogical extreme. People get fed up, stressed to the max, insanely driven to escape or to take matters into their own hands. Pluto on the Ascendant of a person can lead to a diet, plastic surgery, physical and mental housecleaning, even suicide. The only suicide we can expect of the American people is voting themselves ever more taxes. Surgery will increase. Violence will rise. Expect growth in the vigilante movement. On the plus side, we see people taking responsibility for themselves. The latter can be a double-edged sword when it comes to guns and self-defense. Pluto is the planet of inheritance. Estate taxes will rise. Massive repairs and restructuring of our travel and delivery systems is bullish for the construction, trucking, and rail industries. Breakdowns everywhere in our infrastructure will force major expenditures. Health care will be the big money pit.

Global

In Japan and in the Tokyo Stock Exchange we see a move away from speculation and reforms to control gambling. Pornography and sex dominate the entertainment industry. In the U.K. the National Health Care System undergoes an overhaul, though it still gobbles up a high percentage of tax. German corporations downsize and restructure. Money going into the stock exchange is still inhibited by high interest rates. Pluto on the North Node of the Zurich Exchange suggests a major overhaul or scandal that rocks Swiss credibility. In Switzerland heavy taxation on corporations or retail prices could result in declining profits and sales.

Investment Opportunities

Open your own pawn shop or invest in one. Borrowing will be the theme of the day. Reconstruction, whether of the infrastructure or one's face is a major play. Pluto may not take its full grip until 1996, but the winds are blowing. Everything and everyone is aging; get in on the transformation and repair mania. Health care, surgery, research, construction companies (rather reconstruction companies), and funeral parlors are the major growth industries. Invest early and cheap. On the less positive side, self-defense will be the most pressing concern of the population. Guns, mace, anti-theft devices of all kinds will go big time in a population increasingly worried about survival. Consider a bodyguard business or a private police service if you are looking for a long-term, productive enterprise. The beauty business will thrive. Pluto makes everybody feel ugly.

Fashion

Pluto is sexy and grungy. Sagittarius is outdoorsy and ethnic. Those who don't look like priests and nuns will look like hookers on a hike. Could we repeat the 60s and 70s? Twenty years of super tight fitting jeans under a bra-less poncho? Don't forget Sagittarius rules the hips. We survived 20 years of bosom mania with the pinups of the 40s and 50s. Buns remain the body part of choice.

URANUS ENTERS AQUARIUS

Although Uranus will touch down only briefly in its own sign, we already see the seeds of a new electronic age. Expect major shakeups in the telecommunications and cable systems. Astrology, New Age, and Occult movements will gain renewed popularity. The buying public becomes very fickle, inclined to fads, ever in search of the new and unusual. Electronics of every kind will find a welcome market, from games to computers to home shopping. If it can be done over the wires or on fiber optics, it will be hot. If it can be done in a computer or over a modem or fax, it will be done better and faster, but, don't buy the products just yet. Buy the company. What you get now could be primitive or obsolete.

Implications for the United States

Uranus will touch the 3rd House cusp of the United States Chart. More foreign goods and more electronics flood our domestic trading sector. Uranus also indicates disruptions in our communications systems and revolutionary movements in our public schools. Since Uranus forms a sextile to the Pluto in Sagittarius, the movement to school choice is a very strong possibility by 1996.

Global

Uranus, close to IJupiter in the 7th of the Tokyo Stock Exchange, presages a great influx of foreign money. The mutation for Japan shows the beginning of a strong influx of foreign money and goods. In mid-year, Uranus on the North Node suggests a turnaround or a break in existing financial or trade relationships. We could also see some not quite legal activity developing in their bond market.

The London Stock Exchange is jolted by heavy speculation. Uranus moving into the 2nd House of the mutation chart suggests chaos in their banks or their financial assets. This does not bode well for the pound.

Investment opportunities

Anything that eliminates the wires or travels through the air may be a viable investment. Travel is definitely on the upswing. The combination of Uranus and Pluto in moving signs may indicate the first time in recent memory that Americans start to leave the country. Best bets: international placement and home-finding services, and all cutting-edge electronics. Let's face it, invest in anything that gives you a shock if you touch it the wrong way. Although too early to turn a profit, multiple dwellings, hotels, and guest houses are excellent long-term business or investment opportunities. Foreign language training is hot. If you are bilingual start your own school.

Fashion

Anything goes. Individuality is the keyword. Outrageous is preferable to sheepish. The increasing dichotomy in the population and the growing tendency to separate into groups will create a group identification by clothing. Custom designing for special-interest groups could become a major industry. Groups have always identified themselves by how they dress, but this time there will be an even greater dispersion and differentiation to the point of alienation. We had the military uniform and the gray flannel suit; we had the three-piece suit and the punk look, we may reach a point over the next seven years where we will even more narrowly define our beliefs, our politics, and our preferences by what we wear.

JUPITER SQUARE SATURN

Jupiter is growth. Saturn is restriction. Either planet in Mutable signs sets us up for a major stock market correction. Combined, they signal a major global economic adjustment. The world turns the corner in the Mutation correction decade, picks up the pieces and moves on.

The final square occurs in mid-November at 18 Pisces/Sagittarius, close to the midpoint of Mutation Mars Uranus conjunction. It is also square and opposite the United States' Mars, and incidentally on the Mutation Ascendants of many Middle East oil countries. The collapse of old structures seems assured.

We will also witness the demise of oil as a major factor in world economies. This is extremely bearish for the stock market, because by November's end we will see the Sun, Moon, Venus, Mercury, Mars, Jupiter, Saturn, and Pluto in Mutable signs. Both Jupiter and Neptune will be in mutual reception with Saturn, which leaves only Uranus to mind the store—not very comforting for strength and stability. The good news is that the Mutual receptions will enable us to forestall the worst and postpone the real reckoning to a later date.

URANUS AND NEPTUNE IN CAPRICORN

Our old friends are running out of steam. Although they have been undermining the social, political, and material structure of our economy, they have not, because of their presence in a restrictive sign, been able to destroy them totally. Uranus is disruptive and electronic. Capricorn is the structure, the old guard, existing equipment. Central authority figures in world governments continue to hold shaky positions at best. New discoveries and collusions in the telecommunications industries will make old forms of communication obsolete. Old, long-established companies will not be able to compete unless they restructure, change their culture, and compete on the new and changing models.

Implications for the United States

Our infrastructure, roads, bridges, rails, etc. are deteriorating. The presidency is being transformed and undermined, as are all central ruling bodies. Uranus and Neptune in Capricorn in the 2nd House of the United States chart mean continued inflation of our assets, foreign money entering our economy, and a shaky banking system. Every time you hear of a merger, remember you are hearing about a bank that failed.

Global

Uranus and Neptune dance back and forth over the Moon, Venus, and Node degrees of the Great Mutation chart. Classic trading relationships are broken or undermined. Silver, copper, and food prices receive the brunt of all inflationary activity. Volatility is the key in any and all of these areas. The last time we had a similar confluence of Uranus and Neptune in these and similar degrees we saw the great runup in the gold, silver, and oil. Don't forget that Pluto in late Scorpio adds to the emphasis.

Investment opportunities

Perhaps this should be called divestment opportunities. The fact that all the outer and economic planets are in the mature signs of the Zodiac—from Sagittarius through Pisces—suggests that the old standbys are breaking down, spreading themselves over the globe, or undergoing major reconstruction.

We have seen erosion of the power and profitability of the DJIA companies, deteriorating dividends, and rampant abuse of corporate power in the increasing tendency of CEOs and corporate boards to reward themselves at the expense of their stockholders, customers, and employees. What we will gradually see is a movement toward stable and profitable companies, well-established, but of manageable size. The giant American corporation is a thing of the past. The new giants will be multinational. Our profitable industry will be of medium size. Either invest in multinationals, foreign industry, or medium American companies. With the exception of companies that fit the planets in the signs, new companies and outdated companies will not fare well in 1995.

MUTUAL RECEPTIONS

A mutual reception occurs when two planets find themselves in each other's sign of rulership.

Neptune in Capricorn and Saturn in Pisces are an example of a mutual reception. Saturn is the natural ruler of Capricorn. Neptune is the natural ruler of Pisces. The effect of a mutual reception is to put the planets back in their own signs. Thus, this mutual reception will have the effect of Saturn in Capricorn and Neptune in Pisces. Governments will take more power with pie-in-the-sky promises of a wonderful, compassionate future, and help for the impoverished and the victimized. Victimization will continue to be glamorized, even as victimization and poverty increase. Government structures, regulation, and control become more restrictive in response to the perennial problems of unemployment and entitlements. Since Neptune and Pisces rule oil, we can expect one massive oil spill all over the world, with prices finally reaching their appropriate levels from $5.00 to $12.00 a barrel (barring the early appearance of hyperinflation). The drop in oil prices will mask rising consumer inflation and enable government to enact new rules and regulations, and add new taxes without the citizenry's feeling the initial bite. Since Pisces is also the sign of bureaucracies, expect the bureaucracies of all governments to swell in response to the ever-increasing regulatory power that Saturn in Capricorn foretells. Nursing homes, hospitals, and educational institutions will expand, and with them increasing regulation and government control.

Implications for the United States

Because the mutual reception puts Neptune back into the 4th House, we can expect more water damage to land and property. Saturn put back into the 2nd House puts great financial burdens on people, a shrinking of assets, and a possible contraction in the money supply. Because the mutual reception can move both ways (see above) we may find combinations of drought and flood.

Global

The whole world will be making deals to control the inflation that is beginning to get out of control.

Japan will try barriers to imports to send them back to the United States. Britain will be faced with deflation or inflation, unpleasant no matter which they choose. Germany will keep the pressure on its citizens to not spend. Switzerland is likely to do the same.

Investment Opportunities

If you are in business and experiencing severe problems, the mutual reception affords you an opportunity to work around problems or make deals to minimize the pain. Bankruptcy in its myriad forms is always a possibility. The best of this Saturn/Neptune mutual reception is utilized by staring reality square in the face and using somewhat dubious means to circumvent the worst. Perhaps there is an investment or enterprise opportunity in counseling people how to protect their assets in case of a business failure. Also bullish for film, photography, and the chemical and drug industries.

Fashion

Excessive, status-conscious bad taste.

MARS RETROGRADE

Mars retrograde occurs every two years and can raise havoc in the departments of life it affects.

Mars will retrograde January 3 in 2 degrees and 40 minutes of Virgo and turn direct at 13 degrees 10 minutes of Leo on March 24th. It will complete its double dip in these critical degrees that began on October 29, 1994 when it reaches 2°40 'degrees of Virgo on May 31. That represents seven months of Mars in approximately 15 degrees of the same general area of a chart. If any of these are operating on your individual chart expect arguments, accidents, irritations, burns, and breakdowns.

Implications for the United States

The major activity is in the 9th House of the United States chart and the 10th House Square to the Ascendant. Expect controversy and disagreement in the Supreme Court, disagreements over imports, activism on behalf of churches and religions, and rising protest movements in colleges and universities. This could eventually reach the proportions of the 60s, but the movement in the 90s will find its major voice in the population at large. More likely, many of the reforms and values of the 60s will be overthrown. Students protest the abrogation of their freedom of speech.

Since the station occurs on the 10th Equal House it is likely that the President will provoke some of the controversy, possibly in his State of the Union message. He will certainly be put on the defensive and be subject to attack, probably in the media, with regard to the student loan/exchange program, and from policies that create problems in international trade. Although there could be saber rattling, it may come to nothing, at least during this period. However, the United States always goes to war with Pluto on the angles. It has always added territory under the same conditions. We could see treaty and trade disputes under this transit, as well as debate over the admission of Puerto Rico or the Virgin Islands as states.

Global

The Tokyo Stock Exchange sees a lot of speculative money in its coffers and problems keeping track. Japan has persistent problems with interest rates and the yen. The 12th House of the London Stock Exchange could reveal some scandals or simply trouble with customer service. Debt troubles are high on the list for the United Kingdom, Germany, and Switzerland are also beset by troublesome debt. As Switzerland is a repository for other people's money, we could see some world-class difficulties with numbered accounts.

Investment opportunities

Puerto Rico and the Virgin Islands, Canada, and Mexico.

ECLIPSES

Eclipses in Taurus and Scorpio are bearish for the markets and the economy. Taurus rules banks and financial institutions. Scorpio rules debt and shared resources.

April 15 Lunar Eclipse 25.04 Aries Libra

Although there is no planet in this degree on the United States national or mutation chart, the eclipse itself is disruptive for relationships and disputes—it could start or finish one. Plus, the numerical degree could involve the president, allies and enemies, trade, debt, and Congress. The United States is more likely to be passively affected by this. In other words, decisions elsewhere could come to light or begin to build toward the Taurus Eclipse that quickly follows.

This eclipse falls across the 4th/10th House axis of the Tokyo Stock Exchange. It could give us a big jolt in the Nikkei. Frankfurt gets it right across the Ascendant. Byebye Dax. The worldwide implication, conjunct the mutation Pluto, is for scandal, interest rates, and debt. We get some real world facts.

April 29 8:56 Taurus.

This eclipse, in the degree of the Saturn/Jupiter conjunction on the Great Mutation Chart and on the 7th cusp of the Mutation erected for Washington D.C., could indicate a rift with a trading partner or a change in a trading relationship that enables a freer flow of goods in the domestic economy, or an increase in exports. It may also indicate a critical decision about the balance of trade. Since Mars is still in its "dispute" area, the eclipse could promote military action of some kind.

This eclipse is also in the degree of the United States Uranus in semi-sextile aspect. The American worker is likely to be negatively affected by the export (ruler of 3rd) of American corporations (Uranus) to Canada and Mexico, our neighbors (Gemini) and the subsequent loss or adjustment in wages (in the 2nd of the 6th.). Expect major protest from organized labor.

Several major stock exchanges are affected: Mars in Tokyo, the Nodes in Germany, and Saturn in Switzerland. In Taurus of banks and money, and in a 5th House Trine to the Mutation degree, we can expect a major change in interest rates, currency exchange rates, and the economic system to change the direction of heavy speculation.

October 24 0:14 Scorpio

Scorpio Eclipses are not good for the financial markets, especially in the United States. This could portend the implementation of a major tax policy, or a hike in interest rates with bearish implications for the stock market. On the cusp of the United States 12th, expect news about hospitals, jails, and similar institutions.

Although zero Scorpio does not operate heavily in the selected mundane charts, it is close to a square of the Mutation Moon and Nodes. Watch food and consumer activity. It is also square the Midheaven of the Frankfurt Stock Exchange from the 1st House. Traders and investors may demand changes in the business rules and regulations.

Conclusions

Despite a deteriorating economic and social system, the United States economy appears to prosper. People remain sufficiently confident and optimistic to take on debt or start new enterprises. Continued high unemployment will force people into their own businesses or into seeking employment abroad. In 1995 they do it from confidence and choice—in the coming years they may do it from necessity.

Despite an underlying weakness in our economic system, the surface numbers will look good. The travel, media, and advertising industries should thrive. Although there is some threat of war, the more likely prospect is the continuing domestic violence of gangs and criminals.

Financial Self-Defense

Interest rates continue to rise and move at a much faster rate than the previous year, but it is still a good idea to make your major purchases now before they go much higher. Get in early before the combination of high interest and high prices make purchases too costly. Because we can expect increasing inflation in the consumer sector, leverage will work in your favor, but remember, you could be contributing to a potential hyper-inflationary bubble. Though unlikely for 1995, should we start to experience double digit inflation, pay off as fast as you can. The stock market will hit new highs this year. Mutual funds remain a good investment for average people. If the stock market did not experience a major correction last fall, ride the crest, but be prepared to cash out when the Venus Bear Market starts at the Venus Sun conjunction in late August.

Keep your eye on the federal debt. Monitor your congressmen to cut the deficits, and don't let them get away with off-budget expenditures.

Because Pluto hangs on the United States Ascendant, we can expect increasing crime, tax evasion, an oppressive tax and debt burden on the people of the country. Tax revolts and tax reform movements will flower. Despite the underlying difficulties, 1995 will be a prosperous year, but problems will grow behind the scenes. Make your profits and invest them in hard assets for the coming years.

Fitness from the Stars

Ninah Kessler

I work out in order to do something for
myself—my body and soul.

Nike Advertisement

If without the physical aspects of our being the
purpose of life could be accomplished, the soul
would not have taken a physical body and the
spirit would not have produced the physical
world.

The Sufi Message of Hazrat Inyat Khan,
Book IV

It's another new year. We'll make our resolutions—lose
weight, tone up, get fit. Will we frustrate ourselves by
setting unattainable goals, or can we make productive
changes in our lifestyles? Astrology can help.

There are many reasons to become fit. You might be
a young mother seeking to regain your figure. Perhaps
you're a busy executive whose waistline has been
expanding commensurately with your income level. You
could be a golden-ager who wants to regain stamina.
Some turn to exercise to relieve stress, whether it comes
from deadlines or from sexual frustration. You could be
tired of feeling that you're fat, or just want more muscle
tone. Maybe you're a kid who's looking for a break from
Nintendo.

Whatever motivates you to take better care of your
body, there is a physical, mental, spiritual, and emotional satisfaction that comes from getting in shape.
Regular exercise increases endorphins, decreases stress,
and lifts moods.

Fitness comes one step at a time. First you need to
decide that your physical well being is important. Then

set aside the time and energy to make it a reality. It's okay to start slowly, and if you're a Taurus, that's probably the only way to begin. Maybe you'll walk a mile in twenty minutes. A few months later, you're walking two miles in thirty minutes. Then instead of walking that extra block, you're running an extra mile. Remember that a journey of 1,000 miles starts with a single step.

The most inspiring story I came across was in a book about ordinary women achieving extraordinary goals. It described a skier who was almost paralyzed in an accident on the slopes. Gradually she worked herself back to become a triathlete. It made me realize that no matter how out of shape a person is, success is possible.

A hidden bonus to getting in shape comes with changes in the body. We are talking about a dense material realm that you can see, touch, and feel. When you reach your goals, you know that you've done something. You become self-empowered, and more able to achieve in other areas.

To show how astrology relates to getting in shape, first I'll review how the transits of the outer planets have

influenced fitness trends. Then I'll explore how the signs of the zodiac approach shaping up, assisting you in creating an exercise program that's likely to succeed.

ASTROLOGICAL TRENDS IN FITNESS

Kenneth Cooper coined the term "aerobics" in 1968 and began our national obsession with fitness. Jupiter, Uranus, and Pluto were all in Virgo then, reflecting our focus on diet and exercise.

While Uranus and Neptune were in Sagittarius (Neptune 1970–1984, Uranus 1981–1988) we overdid everything, including the physical. Marathons, triathlons, and mountain climbing were in vogue. Pluto in Scorpio (1984–1994) intensified everything, including our fascination with the transformative powers of physical experience.

With Neptune in Capricorn since 1984, we have become more realistic about our dreams for the ideal fitness level. We're coming to terms with the paradoxes of fitting two hour workouts into the nano-second nineties. Our earlier preoccupation with physical achievements is dissolving. Instead, we're learning that gardening or going for a walk with the kids can enhance our physical well-being.

The combination of Neptune in Capricorn in mutual reception with Saturn in Pisces (1994–1995) facilitates blending the physical with the spiritual. Yoga, tai chi, guided visualization, stretching classes, and relaxation are on the workout schedule. We are no longer interested in just building bulk—we want inner strength and outer flexibility.

Uranus has been in Capricorn since 1989, bringing technological advances to the fitness industry. This was heightened when Saturn was in Aquarius (1991–1993) in mutual reception to Uranus. We've got weight-training machines to scientifically tone our muscles, stair-climbing apparatus that measure the calories we're burning, and treadmills and rowing machines that simulate the changing terrain of the real world. We're likely to continue creating and using these high-tech tools throughout 1995.

Chiron entered Virgo in 1993, heralding an increased interest in fitness and healing, particularly in nontraditional modalities. This event coincided with the Clinton administration's funding of alternative health care. Since Virgo is an earth sign (the body) ruled by Mercury (the mind), we'll continue to see a proliferation of mind/body explorations through October 1995, when Chiron goes into Libra.

Fitness takes on an exotic and expansive flavor in 1995, with both Jupiter and Pluto entering Sagittarius. In addition to working out at the gym, you're likely to find yourself trekking to Nepal or whitewater rafting. Make sure your camping gear is operational and your passport is current. While Sagittarius represents outdoor activities in general, the Centaur is half-horse, so equine activities are likely to be in the news. Look for renewed interest in fox hunting, polo, horse racing, steeplechases and horseback riding.

Ordinarily with this much Sagittarian energy, we'd go overboard with physical activity. However, in the chart for New Year's Day in 1995, Mars, the planet that regulates how we use our energy, has slowed down and is about to turn retrograde. This signals a time for rethinking our fitness agendas, re-evaluating what didn't work before, and formulating a better plan. One way to attain our fitness goals is to use astrology.

FITNESS THROUGH THE ZODIAC

While you're more likely to find Aries as power lifters, Pisces as dancers, and Leos as aerobics instructors, signs are not restricted to certain activities. However, each sign gravitates toward certain styles of physical expression, and they do best when they participate in their own zodiacally appropriate ways.

Aries

Energetic Aries rules iron, including pumping iron, and rams are in their element in the gym. Ruled by Mars, you can be overly aggressive, and a physical outlet can help channel your energies more productively. The martial arts, like aikido and tai chi, are very effective, and can moderate your tendency to be headstrong.

The biggest challenge is transforming your intial enthusiam to commitment. Look for trainers who are aware of the newest trends in fitness. Experiment with new sports and vary your workout routines. If you keep your interest up, you'll keep on exercising.

You're attracted to racing, whether on the slopes or on the track. As the first sign of the zodiac you want to retain the lead. Be careful not to burn yourself out. Activities that increase your endurance can provide the necessary complement to your speed and agility.

The sports world is full of famous Arians. They include Walt Frazier, Sonja Henie, John Havelicek, Pete Rose, Gil Hodges, Kareem Abdul-Jabbar, and former actor and race car driver Steve McQueen.

FITNESS FORECAST: Avoid expensive medical bills by paying attention to your body and getting things moving. It's a good year for an adventure in a foreign land, so consider going on safari or running in Australia. You'll be most energetic in November.

Taurus

Taurus would rather sit in the garden and smell the flowers than exercise. However, your appreciation of good cooking can thicken your middle and send you to the gym. You have too much respect for the physical body to remain out of shape for long. Luckily, your muscles respond well to exercise and can be readily toned.

Like the other fixed signs (Leo, Scorpio, and Aquarius), once you decide to get in shape, there is little that can deter you, which is why so many Taureans suceed in the sports world. Since you can sometimes get stuck , look for a compassionate coach who can vary your workout routines. You'll be happiest at a gym that has a jacuzzi, steam room, and masseuse, to release the stress that you store in your body.

There are basically two types of bulls. One loves red, likes sports cars, and prefers fast paced, competitive activities. These are exemplified by jockey Stevie Cauthen, and runner James Fixx. The other type is slower and more artistic, like dancers Martha Graham, Dame Margot Fonteyn, and Fred Astaire. Because of their tenacity, bulls are famous in all sports. Other athletic Tauruses include Sugar Ray Robinson, Willie Mays, Pancho Gonzales, Yogi Berra, and Joe Louis.

FITNESS FORECAST: Find a recreation program that you enjoy. You may have been focusing too hard on achievements in the world. Now it's time to pursue fun activities with your family. If you've lost your ability to play, your kids can be your greatest teachers. Cultivate spontaneity and have a good time. Yoga can loosen up those stiff joints and transform your consciousness.

Gemini

Mercurial Geminis are agile, graceful, get around quickly, and usually enjoy exercise. You even like reading about it. At the gym, you're likely to go from one machine to the next, rarely embarking on the treadmill without a newspaper or a Walkman. You'll be most attracted to a health club with fitness magazines, a variety of equipment, and others to share ideas.

Easily distracted from your fitness program, you're more likely to stay on a schedule that's flexible and heterogeneous. Team sports or marathons can help by providing opportunities for socialization. Triathalons tempt you (three sports for the price of one), but you need to build up your endurance. Pranayama, the yoga of breath, is very helpful, as it calms your nerves while strenthening your respiratory system.

Gemini rules the arms, and your manual dexterity enhances your performance in all the "ball" sports—basketball, football, tennis, and golf. Well known Gemini jocks include Joe Namath, Lou Gehrig, Jim Thorpe, Bjorn Borg, Marvin Hagler, Mike Tyson, Sam Snead, and Richard Petty. Don't forget Isadora Duncan, the Geminian founder of modern dance.

FITNESS FORECAST: You could be paying a heavy price for succeeding on the professional level. In addition, at the beginning of the year there could be irritations at home. A physical outlet can go a long way to balancing stress and helping you keep things in perspective. Put a treadmill or cross-country ski machine in your home and use it.

Cancer

Cancers often don't feel like exercising. You have to be in the right mood. You're likely to have more success with boating, sailing, or walking on the beach. You enjoy being near the water, not necessarily in it. Since you're so involved with your family, try incorporating them into your fitness program. Family softball games can be relaxing and entertaining. One Cancer I know has a croquet set on the lawn. It's always available for family fun and exercise. Because of the stomach difficulties that can plague you, long walks after dinner can be therapeutic, as well as romantic.

While Cancers join health clubs, you have difficulty going regularly. You're more apt to use the spa on a cruise ship or the mommies and tots class at the YMCA.

If by chance you're the rare Cancer who doesn't like the sea, or if there is no water nearby, you might want an exercise video or a treadmill that you can use in your home. And don't forget a nice bath at the end for your reward!

Even though exercise may not come naturally, it's likely to be quite beneficial. It alleviates the stress that you pick up because of your emotional sensitivity. Unlike food, a major comforter for Cancer, exercise does not tax your digestive system. Also, if you've overdeveloped your nurturing abilities at the expense of your assertiveness skills, exercise can get you more into balance.

Once you get past your blocks, you're apt to find that fitness has become your friend. There are many Cancers who earn their living from sports, including Leon Spinks, O. J. Simpson, Arthur Ashe, Margaret Court, Ilie Nastase, and Saitchel Paige. Notice that few famous Crabs play on teams, and that in tennis, horseracing, and boxing, sideways movement is emphasized.

FITNESS FORECAST: You'll do best with an exercise program that's readily accessible, like walking, jogging, or biking around the neighborhood. Exercise classes that are part of a community education center are another possibility. Pick up the tempo of your workouts in September and October.

Leo

You Leos are sociable beasts and want fitness to be fun. Find a team sport that interests you, particularly if you can be the star player or the team captain. You gravitate toward activities where you can be in the limelight. Many professional athletes are Leos, especially in personality sports where they can be superstars. Examples include Arnold Schwarzenegger, Wilt Chamberlain, Yvonne Goolagong, Ben Hogan, Frank Gifford, Willie Shoemaker, Leo Durocher, Vida Blue, Casey Stengel, and Magic Johnson.

There's usually no problem in getting a Leo interested in exercising. You find sports that you like and stick with them. Ruled by the Sun, you prefer outdoor activities, from swimming to skiing.

Although Leos are robust, you need regular cardiovascular activities to keep your heart healthy. A tendency to be a weekend exerciser can lead to circulatory problems. You may be better off joining a health spa. Look for a large facility with all the amenities, or an outdoor gym on the beach. Check out the clientele and make sure that they meet your standards.

FITNESS FORECAST: Although you're usually quite energetic, health problems or worries may have kept you quiet recently. The first half of the year offers opportunities for changing things around. Re-evaluate your fitness program and consider returning to activities that you enjoyed in the past.

Virgo

Worries about your health can lead to an interest in fitness, and once you're involved, you want to learn all the details. Perhaps this is why many Virgos are so proficient in sports. Famous Virgo athletes include Jesse Owens, Jean Claude Killy, Rocky Marciano, Arnold

Palmer, Roger Maris, Rosemary Casals, and Jimmy Conners.

If you go to a gym, make sure that the trainers are knowledgeable, as you will want to know which exercises provide a workout for which muscles. Additionally, look for a club that has an organic juice bar and immaculate showers. When you go, make sure you have the right clothes and the appropriate equipment. Virgos like to be prepared.

If you want to make a walking program stick, get a small dog. Since you'll be devoted to your pet, you'll take your constitutional regularly.

Don't overlook relaxation or breathing exercises. They can keep you centered and keep your thoughts uplifted. Virgos also benefit from guided visualizations, yoga, and other disciplines that unify the mind and the body.

FITNESS FORECAST: Interest in your health is likely to be high this year, and you could reconnect with some ancient techniques for self-care. Don't put off exercising while you find the perfect program. Instead, just get moving and use your flexibilty to make revisions as you go along. There are energy peaks at the beginning of the year and again in June and July. Use them productively.

Libra

Librans are not enthusiastic about getting fit. It's just not refined enough to suit your sensibilities. You can become motivated when your bathroom scales tell you that things are not in balance, since you're not happy when you don't look your best. The appropriate exercise program is one where your gracefulness can be expressed through movement. This could be through dancing, skating, gymnastics, or even on the tennis court.

Pick a health spa with a tasteful decor and a pleasant clientele. Exercising needs to be a social event. A workout partner will not only make it more enjoyable, but you won't want to disappoint your friend. Don't skimp on your workout clothes either. You'll enjoy exercising more if you like what you're wearing.

Becoming fit is more likely if the more strenuous parts of your workout are balanced with gentle stretches and graceful transitions from one exercise to another.

Libran athletes include Nancy Kerrigan, Max Schmeling, John L. Sullivan, Mickey Mantle, Juan Marichal, Evil Knievel, and dancer Juliet Prowse.

FITNESS FORECAST: Your interest in health may increase in September, as a hidden imbalance comes to the surface. Don't wait until you see problems before you do something. Join a club or team so that you can work out with friends. You may also want to enter a walkathon for charity.

Scorpio

You're not into any fluff workouts, so when you get to the gym, it's because you're seriously into improving your lifestyle. A workout is more therapeutic for Scorpio than for any other sign. It's hard to be so emotionally intense when you're on the stair-climber. You're usually just hoping that you can make it through the program. Once you get started on a fitness routine, you stick to it, but getting things going can be difficult.

Check out a fitness routine that includes the mind as well as the body, and use the physical to transform your psyche. Think about all the endorphins that you will generate. Find a gym where sweatsuits are in the minority and body shaping unitards are more prevalent.

Scorpios are at home in the water, so check out scuba diving and snorkeling. Once your skills are perfected, you could uncover buried treasure. For further adventures, don't rule out hiking into volcanic craters.

Scorpios are not really into team sports, except for baseball, like Roy Campanella, Stan Musial, and Tom Seaver. Other famous Scorpions I found were all in it for themselves and include Boris Becker, Billie Jean King, Charles Atlas, Gary Player, and Ken Rosewall. There's also James Naismith, the founder of basketball.

FITNESS FORECAST:While most Scorpios would agree that their favorite physical activity is sexual, opportunities may be limited at this time. Work off tensions at the gym or in the sea instead. You'll have the most energy for a fitness program in September and October, but you'll miss many opportunities if you wait until then.

Sagittarius

Centaurs tend to be the most physical sign of the zodiac. After all, you're half horse. Outdoor activities captivate you. There, you can commune with the earth, get inspired by the scenery, and ground yourself on the planet.

Naturally Sagittarians are drawn to all equine activities. There's that sense of freedom and expansiveness that comes from galloping on horseback with the wind in your hair. If your favorite pony is not available, roller blading is an urban alternative, and wind surfing is an aquatic one.

If you do join a gym, look for one that has lots of different kinds of equipment. You're more likely to stick to a workout schedule if it has lots of flexibility, and you intersperse your trips to the spa with hiking, biking, and, of course, riding. Look for a facility that has branches all over the world. The Sagittarians I know want exercise that is available wherever they are, and they get around.

Sagittarius is the opposite of shy, and your enthusiam allows you to enjoy a great range of activites. In the course of your travels, you might run into some famous centaurs like Chris Evert, Joe DiMaggio, Monica Seles, Lee Trevino, Ty Cobb, and Larry Bird. Since Sagittarius rules the thighs, its natives are likely to move quickly on the court, gym, or baseball diamond. There aren't more world class Sag athletes because as soon as they master one sport, they quickly move on to something else.

FITNESS FORECAST: Dreams of exotic places are often prominent for centaurs, and this year is no exception. You might want to try mountain climbing in Nepal or horseback riding on the Australian Outback. With Pluto in your sign, you're entering a period of transformation, and you do it by exploring the unknown.

Capricorn

A lot of my Capricorn friends are into fitness. I think it's because they sense they're going to live for a long time, and want their bodies to be prepared. You mountain goats feel right at home in the hills, and enjoy both mountain and rock climbing. You'll enjoy the challenge of scaling the summit. Once you get to the top, be sure to look around, so you can broaden your perspective. There's no anti-depressant better than the exhiliration that comes from scaling those lofty peaks.

You're likely to be able to stick to any fitness program that you begin, but chose a gym with qualified fitness professionals that you can respect. Don't skip the hamstring and quadricep exercises, as they can prevent knee injuries.

Since Capricorn is also the sea goat, many January babies are into swimming, and they prefer doing laps. Remember that you can get just as much exercise if you allow yourself to have fun in the water.

The list of famous and active Capricorns includes Alvin Ailey, Gelsey Kirkland, Robert Joffrey, Muhammad Ali, A. J. Hoyt, George Balanchine, Dizzy Dean, Joe Frazier, Sandy Koufax and Don Shula. As in all other fields, Capricorns make it to the top. I was surprised by the number of dancers on my list, and thought of the tremendous discipline that it takes to make it in the world of ballet.

FITNESS FORECAST: 1995 is a great year for Capricorns to learn about health and fitness and to incorporate this information into their personal program. If you think that you're an expert, you might want to begin sharing what you know with others. Your activity level is likely to be highest in January and June.

Aquarius

When I asked my Aquarian niece what she was doing for fitness, she said, "Cheerleading." My Aquarian mother likes to swim laps in the pool and converse with her fellow condo-commandos. She used to like talking while walking until Saturn conjuncted her Sun and she broke her knee. Water bearers prefer to exercise with other people, making it possible to socialize at the same time.

Once you Aquarians set a fitness goal, you tend to use the most advanced training techniques to facilitate success. You want high tech computerized machines that let you maximize your workouts. You may be too independent to want to join a health club, but if you do, pick the one your friends go to. Consider different options to keep things interesting, like fencing in virtual reality.

You may be drawn to the newest fads in fitness as well as to new age techniques. My favorite yoga teacher was an Aquarius. Your preference is to expand your consciousness while toning your waistline.

Aquarians can have weak ankles, so if roller blading sounds appealing, invest in some special high tech skates that give maximum support.

Aquarians excel in many areas, perhaps because they train with those on the cutting edge, and access state of the art fitness technology. Also, as a fixed sign, their tenacity lets them follow through on their ideas. Famous Aquarians include Mark Spitz, Wayne Gretsky, Gregory Hines, Michael Jordan, Hank Aaron, Roger Staubach, Jim Brown, Bill Tilden, Max Baer, Eddie Arcaro, and Babe Ruth. There are also Red Barber and Joe Gargiola, announcers who talk about sports.

FITNESS FORECAST: Exercising with friends is likely to keep you in shape. The first half of the year also favors working out with a partner. You're likely to feel the most energetic over the summer, so consider a fitness vacation to a foreign country.

Pisces

While fitness is most important for Pisces, there are not many traditional jocks associated with this sign. Instead there are graceful athletes, more at home in the water than on land. Pisces, you are the celestial fish, and like swimming and workouts in the pool. Splashing around in the water gives you opportunities to day dream. Sailing on the ocean relaxes and inspires you.

Since Pisces rules the feet, it's important to keep them moving. You're likely to be drawn to all activities in the dance world, including tap dance, ballet, jazzercise, and country line dancing. Your flexibility makes you a star at gymnastics.

You're likely to engage in any sport in your own Piscean way. Even when you're biking, its more like you're pedaling through water.

Pisces are often too distracted to take care of their bodies. When this occurs you weaken your immune systems and lower your vitality. Then you don't have the energy for the things that you enjoy doing. It's most important to find a fitness program that you can follow.

Make sure that any health club you join has a pool, and look for jacuzzis and steam baths as well. You'll be more drawn to a spa that has soft lights, relaxing music, and yoga classes.

Those rare Piscean sports stars include Ivan Lendl, Mario Andretti, and Knute Rockne.

FITNESS FORECAST: You may be experiencing more than your share of frustration and delays this year. This makes it even more vital to de-stress yourself through exercise. Investing in a personal trainer could really pay off. Your energy is likely to be highest in September and October, so really get into the swim of things in the fall.

CONCLUSION

When you are more fit, you are mastering the material plane of existence. Because we live in a universe where everything is interconnected, fitness enhances mental, psychological, and spiritual well-being. Changing something changes everything. May this be a step in your continuing journey toward enlightenment.

"Getting to Node You"— Astrology's Hidden Grip in Relationships

Noel Tyl

When two people get together, two horoscopes meet. One person's needs and behavioral resources interact with another person's needs and behaviors. Specifically, one person's idealism, say the conjunction of Mercury and Venus, or Mercury strongly focused in Pisces, may be beautifully trine (120 degrees away) the other person's Moon in Cancer, the reigning need for emotional and family security. That would be a "comfortable" blend, a harmonious bond, through the trine aspect that links similar "colors" of being (within the same element family).

One person's Saturn—the awareness of strategy, control, and ambition—may oppose (180 degrees) or square (90 degrees) another person's Mars—energy and drive—suggesting a fight for leadership, a struggle for dominance; conservatism and caution in one person working to subdue spontaneity and volatility in the other. Who makes the decisions? Resolution of anything is difficult.

When one person's Sun or Moon makes *any* aspect with the Sun or Moon in someone else's horoscope, it is a highly reliable indication of harmony. The two find it easy to be together. Marriage is an extreme development out of this basic harmony, of course, but togetherness must begin somewhere and Sun-Moon ties are very natural, easily taken for granted, and always strongly appreciated. Doing business with someone with whom you make such contact is always the best business deal you can make.

Just as you would think, when your Mars and someone else's Venus or your Venus and someone else's Mars whistle to each other through aspect relationships, the tune is not just "Dixie," it's visceral awareness—if age and sociology support potential—and, if Pluto is in the mix, the waters run deep and powerfully—and everything else can be put aside—for the moment, or a lifetime!

Uranus contacts are intense excitement at best and nervous agitation at worst, and the manifestation of the tie depends upon which planet in your chart is getting the "charge" from the other person's Uranus. It's like a "jump start" from someone else's battery to yours.

Neptune contacts are misty, cloudy, perhaps even untrustworthy, so doing business with someone whose Neptune is on your Sun or Midheaven or Mercury presents a long list of cautions!

Jupiter is an uplifting bond between horoscopes, a broad accent of enthusiasm one to another, *for* one another.

When George Bush was heading down the home stretch to election late in 1988, he announced his choice for Vice President: James Danforth Quayle. The nation asked aloud, "Who is this guy Quayle? Where's he coming from?" Many would say that that question was never answered during the Bush presidency. Boyish-appearing Quayle was somehow not congruent with Bush's image of experience, poise, and know-how.

The real question should have been not "Who's Quayle?" but "What brings Quayle together with Bush? That's the question astrology can answer very easily. Would you believe there were/are eight different ties between Quayle's horoscope (born February 4, 1947) and Bush's (June 12, 1924)?

Bush's Moon in Libra is close trine with Quayle's Sun in Aquarius. This is a beautiful, comfortable, no-waves-at-all relationship between the cores of their horoscopes. They genuinely like each other. Bush's Neptune squares Quayle's Sun: Quayle will blindly follow all of Bush's ideas, and Bush will overlook any shortcomings on Quayle's part.

As the synastric (astrology's fancy word for "chart comparison") profile builds, we begin to see that the relationship founded by Moon-Sun contact supports trade-offs at less imposingly fundamental levels of life. That's the way it is getting together with someone else: we like someone fundamentally, and this good feeling colors all other measurements of compatibility and resource exchange. In this case, this was achieved by nebulous, vague, and gossamer Neptune between them.

Bush's Saturn opposed Quayle's Midheaven. This means that the President's ambition and achievement gave Quayle's entire career strong direction. Bush's Mars is square Quayle's Jupiter. This shows a great bond of energy, enthusiasm, and a "we can stand it alone, partner" kind of specialness between them.

Among the other ties between their horoscopes, there emerges a very, very telling one: the link between Bush's Lunar Nodal Axis at 26 Leo-Aquarius ("Getting to Node" You, indeed!) trine Quayle's Midheaven and conjunct/opposed his Mercury. In addition, Quayle's Nodal Axis (8 Gemini) squares Bush's Ascendant exactly, and both those measurements tie in with the United States' Ascendant at 7 Gemini!

This is a powerful cluster of ties, believe me. Whenever there is a tight relationship, usually conjunction/opposition or square between one person's Lunar Nodal Axis and another person's planet, Ascendant, or Midheaven, there is a dimension to the relationship tie that goes very, very deep. The relationship can even be strange, as we will see in some other cases. The relationship can drain someone's resources, even possess someone; and here, there certainly is clear memory of how the "Quayle issue" drained off much stature, energy, time, and verbiage from the Bush camp.

THE LUNAR NODAL AXIS

The Lunar Nodal Axis is defined by two points where the Moon's path in orbit around the Earth intersects the plane of orbit of the Earth around the Sun. These points are symbolically a synthesis of the Sun's apparent motion and the Moon's actual motion, tying together Sun and Moon symbolisms, accentuating relationship, leader and follower, male and female, light and reflection. These dichotomies are certainly the concepts that are extolled in successful relationships of any kind, verging on the poetical paraphrase when love is involved.

There is nothing "wrong" or unwanted here. What we are talking about is something *definite;* something extremely strong and extremely easy to see on the birthdate line in an ephemeris. The Nodal Axis is caught up in the cyclic astronomy of eclipses, the symbolisms of losing light and regaining it, the threat of shadow when the Sun disappears, and so forth.

When the Nodal Axis in one person's horoscope is configured with a planet or angular point in another person's horoscope, the tie is very, very strong, especially in terms of the planet or personal point (Ascendant or Midheaven) configurated. When the Sun or Moon is involved, there seems to be a core recognition, a sense of belonging to one another, if you will. Even under the worst of circumstances, the relationship bond is hard to break. When Mercury is involved, the relationship bond is powerfully focused in the mind, in the thinking process, and in communication. This Mercurial dimension is the bond between Bush and Quayle.

With Venus, the bond is focused in romanticism; with Mars, aggression or defensiveness, and strong sexuality; with Jupiter, enthusiasm, understanding; with Saturn, control, manipulation; Uranus, intense, electrifying magnetism; with Neptune, deception, mistrust, or fantasy and aesthetics; with Pluto, empowerment. The Midheaven involvement links one person to the other in terms of career, even personal destiny; with the Ascendant, the view is of how one is presented to the world.

When the Nodal Axis sets up such a bond between two people—or two nations, as we will see later—can we say that such a bond was bound to happen? That it may come close to being destined? I think so. Nodal contacts carry something primal and inscrutable with them. They are definitely astrology's hidden grip in relationships.

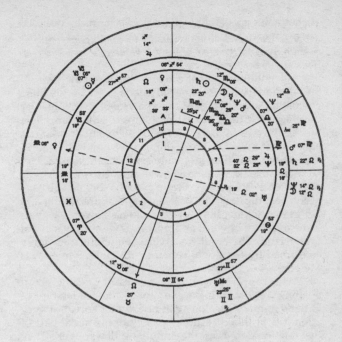

Inner Chart: Adolph Hitler
April 20, 1889, 6:30 P.M. LMT
Braunau am Inn, Austria, 13E02 48N15

Outer Chart: Eva Braun
February 6, 1912, 2:25 A.M. CET
Munich, Germany, 11E34 48N08

Hitler/Braun

Let's look at one of history's most famous *improbable* relationships: Adolph Hitler and Eva Braun, born April 20, 1889 and February 6, 1912, respectively. Hitler was Chancellor of Germany, Der Füehrer (The Leader); Braun was an uneducated and, some say, a distant cousin of Hitler, 23 years his junior. They were tied together from remote levels of the social spectrum, in strange ways, and finally married the day before committing suicide together deep underground in a besieged Berlin bunker, (April 29, 1945). Eva Braun's Nodal Axis

319

at 25 Aries-Libra was exactly conjunct Hitler's Mercury at 25 Aries, *which was positioned in conjunction with his horizon axis, on the cusp of his 7th House, the house of relationships and marriage!*

My goodness, what a bond! Additionally, Braun's Sun in Aquarius was square Hitler's exact Venus-Mars conjunction in Taurus. Many analysts of psychohistory have ascribed deep sexual problems to Hitler, and here we see Braun's involvement with them. Hitler's Saturn, square to his Venus-Mars conjunction, opposed Braun's Sun: they seem tied in a sado-masochistic drama. Her Uranus—the electric shock—was square to Hitler's Sun, exactly. We can also see Braun's Venus conjunct Hitler's Moon and Jupiter, a tie of beauty and appreciation; and her Mars conjunct his Pluto, a tie to his power. This pair came together in ways and purposes we simply can not understand. The bond was overwhelmingly, inexorably confirmed by the nodal contact with Hitler's mind, his Mercury.

Who captured whom, in this case? Did the nodal opening in Braun's psyche invite the leadership of Hitler's mind? Astrology can not say for sure, but very often it is in this direction, i.e., *toward* the nodal part of the relationship that the influence flows. Were they brought together purposefully, though inscrutably, from their extraneous orbits by the fateful crossings of some unknown psychological astronomy? I think we can be sure about that. Was their case exceptional? Here we can say, "No!" Nodal contacts are fulfilled frequently; not necessarily blazingly on the pages of history or in suicide pacts halfway to some netherworld, but in everyday life, in relationships in public business and private bond, when obsession or inscrutability or essentialness marks the tie.

Sirhan/Kennedy

A fascinating example of the touch of fate, if you will, is in the coming together of Sirhan Sirhan (March 19, 1944) and Robert Kennedy (November 20, 1925), on Kennedy's death day, June 6, 1968. The assassin's Nodal Axis was at 4 Leo-Aquarius *exactly square* the candidate's strident and critical Mars at 4 Scorpio! Here, however, it is hard to say that Kennedy's aggressive political nature (Mars) flowed into Sirhan's being (through the "nodal opening," if you will), when it was Sirhan who pulled the trigger. We could say that it was Kennedy's aggressive politics that *did* flow into Sirhan's awareness obsessively before the assassination; indeed, the politics conditioned and framed Kennedy as a target for Sirhan's anger with the world.

Tracy/Hepburn

Another example is the tremendous bond chronicled between actor Spencer Tracy (April 5, 1900) and Katherine Hepburn (November 8, 1909), an unrequited love that became historic in its fervor, importance, endurance, and frustration: Tracy's Jupiter at 10 Sagittarius was conjunct Hepburn's Nodal Axis at 8 Gemini-Sagittarius. This is the same bond (Jupiter-Node) that Benito Mussolini (July 29, 1883) had with Hitler, bringing him together with the German leader in whole-hearted admiration and endorsement, in political and philosophical emulation!

Martin/Lewis

Dean Martin's (June 17, 1917) Nodal Axis at 11 Capricorn-Cancer is not only square Jerry Lewis's Mercury (March 16, 1926) but also conjunct his Pluto as well at 12 Cancer! This is a powerful bond indeed, and the square aspect (90 degrees) adds tension to the bond for sure.

Rodgers/Hammerstein

Richard Rodgers (June 28, 1902), the legendary Broadway musical composer, had his Lunar Nodal Axis at 1 Scorpio tightly conjunct legendary lyricist Oscar Hammerstein's Saturn at 0 Scorpio (July 12, 1895). This tells us for sure that the words came first before the music in their collaboration! Additionally, Hammerstein's Nodal Axis at 15 Pisces-Virgo was square to Rodger's Mars at 14 Gemini! Again, quite a creative, tense and powerful bond, with one nodal contact balancing the other (i.e., Saturn and Mars), that helped this team create the historic musicals: Oklahoma, Carousel, South Pacific, and The King and I.

The Grimaldis

A lovely example is seen between Princess Grace (November 12, 1929) and Prince Rainier of Monaco (October 31, 1923). This was the fairy-tale love bond; European prince and Philadelphia beauty off in their private kingdom. This was love felt and espied across a crowded room. This was "getting to node you" in classic romantic fashion. Princess Grace had her Nodal Axis in 11 Taurus-Scorpio 34 precisely conjunct Prince Rainier's Venus and Jupiter [both] at 11 Taurus 34 and 11 Scorpio 02, respectively! Additionally, her Jupiter at 14 Gemini was square his Nodal Axis at 16 Virgo-Pisces!

Presidential Couples

John F. Kennedy (May 29, 1917) had his Nodal Axis at 12 Capricorn-Cancer and Jackie (July 28, 1929) had her Uranus at 11 Aries, square his axis. *That's* electricity, magnetism, and the bond that kept the two together through so much philandering. Bill Clinton (August 19, 1946) has his Sun at 26 Leo, mighty proud and powerful, and Hillary (October 26, 1947) has her Nodal Axis at 24 Taurus-Scorpio, tightly square his Sun. That's his hookup to the synthesis of her strengths, as well as the bond of tolerance for her in the midst of the stress from all his adventures. We could surmise that his charismatic way to success "fronts" for her deepest professional dreams for herself!

Interestingly, Clinton's Nodal Axis is conjunct Saddam Hussein's Nodal Axis. We don't know what that means in astrology—when there is the conjoining of Nodal Axes—but it *is* something to watch. We can appreciate that one person's network of nodal contacts will also be involved with the other person's nodal contacts because of the conjunction of the axes.

Goldberg/Danson

A final celebrity example defines the hidden grip astrology has, in a most improbable relationship much in the news over the past two years: Whoopi Gold-berg (November 13, 1955) and Ted Danson (December 29, 1947).

It is absolutely no surprise that this extraordinary coupling answers the call of an exact Nodal Axis contact

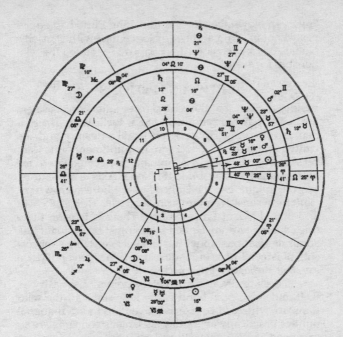

Inner Chart: Whoopi Goldberg
November 13, 1955, 12:48 P.M. EST
New York, NY, 74W00 40N43

Outer Chart: Ted Danson
December 29, 1947, 10:58 P.M. PST
San Diego, CA, 117W09 32N43

between Danson's axis and Whoopi's Sun! She entranced
him; lit up his life. Whoopi's Saturn conjunct her Sun is
pulled into the axis contact with Danson as well, adding
a Machiavellian dimension. We know who ran *that* relationship! Note that Danson's Venus is in broad opposition to Whoopi's Uranus and that his Moon-Pluto
conjunction squares her Moon! This is a very dramatic,
sexual tie between them. The flame began in May 1992
when transiting Pluto was conjunct Whoopi's Sun and,
of course, Danson's Nodal Axis! It was announced

"over" in November 1993 as transiting Pluto had edged past Whoopi's Sun and her major contact with Danson's Nodal Axis and conjoined her Saturn. *She* ended the relationship for sure.

BETWEEN NATIONS

Besides the fact that the central three letters of Jerusalem are "USA", there is another bond as well. There is a hidden astrological grip between Israel's destiny and the United States' place in the sun, its fulfillment of its Cancer-Aquarian birthright as humanitarian caretaker to the world: Israel's (May 14, 1948) Nodal Axis at 13 Taurus-Scorpio is square to the United States Midheaven, a most exultantly sensitive point at 13 Aquarius (July 4, 1776 at 2:13 A.M., LMT at Philadelphia). There is tension there (the square), and the United States must take a lot of flak about its relationship with Israel—its veritable sponsorship of Israel. But as our Aquarian Midheaven and Moon say, *that's who we are as a nation.*

There are dramatic planetary points of synastry as well, but this nodal bond is the tone-setter of the relationship, which, of course, is played out in international politics practically every day, as Israel's concerns are so extremely close to our national activities.

Israel and Its Neighbors

Then we can note that Israel's node is square Iraq's Mars (recall Sirhan Sirhan and Robert Kennedy), an aspect of coming together fatefully antagonizingly, belligerently, aggressively (Iraq: August 23, 1921), with Iraq initiating the onslaughts. Further, would you believe that Kuwait's node (June 19, 1961) is at 29 Leo, *precisely conjunct Iraq's Sun!* The two nations are blood enemies, with Iraq claiming Kuwait as its "province," a part of Iraq (a part of its Sun), not recognizing its sovereignty.

Israel and Egypt were certainly blood enemies for a long, long time. Their ties of hate are clouded in the prehistorical saga of Abraham and the dilemma of which "first born son" was favored of Jehovah—Israel, namesake-son of Isaac (Jacob renamed), grandson of Abraham, or Ishmael, also Abraham's son, key to Arab lineage [see Genesis 32:28; 16:12; 12:7; 26:3; 28:13]. Their astrological contact says it all: the Egyptian Republic's node (June 18, 1953) at 5 Aquarius 51 is conjunct/opposed Israel's Moon at 4 Leo! It is as if they come from the same family, but can not get it together. In the Egyptian kingdom horoscope, founded on its independence from Britain (February 28, 1922), the earlier horoscope for Egypt, we see the Egyptian Neptune square the Israeli State's node at 13 Taurus, which came into being in 1948. This fosters mistrust, deception, and strange animosity.

The Confederacy

The Confederate States of America came into being on February 4, 1861 in Montgomery, Alabama (a delegate assembly from Alabama, Florida, Georgia, Louisiana, Mississippi, and South Carolina). The six states had declared independence from the USA. While five more were to come: Texas, Virginia, Arkansas, Tennessee, and North Carolina, this convention on February 4 marked the formal beginning of the Provisional Congress of the Confederate States of America. Would you believe that the Confederate Pluto—the planet of empowerment, disruption, explosion, metamorphosis—at 7 Taurus was exactly square the *United* States of America node at 7 Leo? This fateful, divisive, power-struggle bond placed brother against brother in our country's bloodiest conflict.

North and ßouth Vietnam

Another interesting national split is in the astrology between North and South Vietnam. The Vietnam states—the North a Democratic Republic, and the South pro-French—were *both* created by the Geneva Accord on July 21 in 1954 (at 3:45 A.M. in Geneva). This would give the same chart to each state, except for one degree difference at the Ascendant for the distance between the two capitals, Hanoi and Saigon. But the French held onto South Vietnam, and true independence did not come to the South until 5:00 A.M. GMT on October 26 1955 in Saigon. This horoscope for South Vietnam has a Mercury at 14 Libra, exactly square to the Nodal Axis of North Vietnam in the Geneva Accord horoscope. With this evidence, it is clear that each state is of the same beginning, but of unalterably different philosophical pursuit.

United States/Central America

Finally, the United States node at 7 Leo was exactly conjunct the former USSR Neptune (mistrust); is conjunct El Salvador's Moon (support) and Nicaragua's Mars (aggression, conflict); the Phillipine's Mercury (meeting of the minds; a U.S. "territory"); the Pluto of Syria and the Pluto of Lebanon (power struggle); and the Cuban Mars (aggression, conflict). The United States controlled the first nuclear reaction on December 2, 1942 at 3:25 P.M., CWT in Chicago. In this horoscope for the beginning of the Atomic Age, Pluto, the symbol of atomic power, was at 7 Leo, *exactly conjunct the atomic-powered United States' Nodal Axis!*

WHO RELATES TO *YOUR* NODE?

One of the questions most asked in social gatherings is "When is your birthday?" Why do people do this, even people without any astrological knowledge at all? Even people who debunk astrology ask!

Everyone knows that birthdates are important dates to remember and celebrate. We ingratiate ourselves with others by giving recognition to birthdays. If there is one song every person knows, it is not the national anthem; it's *Happy Birthday!*

I think we feel we get closer to someone by remarking on one's birthday. *Not* knowing astrology, we exhibit some primal awareness that the day one was born was special, and therefore the person is given special attention in the moment of conversation, is allowed to talk about him or herself freely, can tell stories and share personal data. This brings people closer together.

Knowing astrology, of course, even just the simple fact that the birthday is a reference to where the Sun is on the day of birth, makes the conversation ever so much more meaningful and entertaining. The primal significance of the question takes on sophisticated ramifications and potential.

In our personal lives and business affairs, we seek kindred spirits; people who will feel like "family" and cooperate with us. Every one of us sometime in life has searched for the "soul mate," the significant other who is presumably destined to be our fulfillment, as night is fulfilled by day (an interesting reference to the symbolic significance of the nodes, dealing with the Moon and Sun). Every one of us has had strong personal ties to people with whom we are not involved romantically, but with whom we deal professionally, successfully, or, indeed, not successfully, but compulsively.

We hear stories all the time of people in relationships of many different kinds who stay in those relationships against all odds, under all kinds of stress, for no apparent reason. In these cases, very, very often the Nodal Axis contact between the horoscopes involved is at work. It *is* astrology's hidden grip within relationships.

Locating Your Nodal Sun Contact

One of the most welcome nodal contacts usually is between your Nodal Axis and someone's else's Sun. Let me share with you how to know who has that Sun position that contacts with your node.

An Easy Mental Calculation—First of all, you need to know your node position. In the Ephemeris, the book of planetary positions referred to by astrologers, the "North Node" is listed for every single date, and it just takes a second to spot it; no corrections of position are necessary since the node moves so slowly (backwards about 3', 1/20th of a degree per day). The "South Node" is directly opposite, the exact same number but in the opposite sign, and is not listed. As we have seen, the North and South Nodes create the axis across the apparent path of the Sun where the Moon crosses in its orbit around the Earth. For our discussion here, there is no difference to be made between north and south.

Note the node position as listed in the Ephemeris and also mentally note the same *number in the opposite sign* to establish the axis. If the node position is listed as 5 Capricorn, that's your node position, but it includes 5 Cancer as well, the exact same position in Capricorn's opposite sign. Your Nodal Axis is 5 Capricorn-Cancer.

The signs with their opposites are: Aries-Libra, Taurus-Scorpio, Gemini-Sagittarius, Cancer-Capricorn, Leo-Aquarius, and Virgo-Pisces.

When you know your natal node position, you can do a simple mental calculation to find out *the birthday someone must have to put their Sun on your node, setting up the makings of an extraordinary bond:* we generalize that the Sun travels about one degree every day, i.e., on January 1, the Sun is at 10 Capricorn and on January 2 it is at 11 Capricorn, on the 3rd at 12 Capricorn, etc. Or on June 1, the Sun is at 10 Gemini, on June 11th 21 Gemini, on the 12th 22 Gemini, and so forth.

After thirty degrees are used up (the number of degrees in one sign), the Sun enters the next successive sign in the zodiac. The sign-changes take place around the 21st of every month. For example: on May 1, the Sun is at 10 or 11 Taurus, and on the 20th it is at 29 Taurus. On the 21st, it enters Gemini, on the 22nd it is in 1 Gemini; and then, on June 1st, 9 days later after the 22nd and 10 days after the sign change, the Sun comes to 10 Gemini.

Knowing the order of the twelve zodiacal signs throughout the year (Aries, Taurus, Gemini, Cancer, Leo, Virgo, Libra, Scorpio, Sagittarius, Capricorn, Aquarius, and Pisces), you can organize this specific degree-information in your memory easily: know that *on the first of every month the Sun will always be at 10–11 degrees of its sign for the months January through June, and on the first of every month for the months July through December, the Sun will always be at 8-9 degrees of its Sign.*

"When's your birthday?"

"August 7th!"

On August 1, the Sun will have been at 8 or 9 Leo. Usually, we remember the birthday of someone close to us and their sign as a reference mark, i.e., "Oh, John's born early in August and he's a Leo," to zero in on the appropriate sign quickly. "This person must be a Leo too, since the sign won't change until around the 21st of August."

August 7 then equates to 15–16 Leo (8–9 for the 1st of August plus 7). If your Lunar Nodal Axis is marked by the position 15 or 16 Leo (or 15–16 Aquarius, the opposite sign, not shown in the ephemeris but definitely part of the profile; see above), there's a match: that person's Sun, born on August 7 is conjunct your Nodal Axis . . . and, all things considered, you might want to plan a trip to Hawaii together, quickly!

If you know a little more astrology, you can easily take this process further: you know that each of the three modes in astrology (Cardinal, Fixed, and Mutable) has four signs comprised of opposition axes square (90 degrees) to each other. For example: The Fixed family has in it the signs Leo and its opposite Aquarius, Taurus and its opposite Scorpio. If you're dealing with a birthdate of August 7, the above example, with the Sun at 15–16 Leo, you know immediately that the birthdays of February 6 (Aquarius), and April 6 (Taurus), and November 7 (Scorpio) will all be involved with "noding you!" You will have a strong nodal relationship with the people born on those days, or, indeed, one day either side of the calculated date!

When you know still a little more astrology and see someone's full horoscope or just look up their birthdate in your Ephemeris, you can see the positions of all his or her planets and see instantly which *planets or personal points* relate tightly to your Nodal Axis!

This is powerful information for business and personal relationships. Let me use my own Nodal Axis as a closing illustration: my node is at 23 Sagittarius (born December 31, 1936). Carl Llewellyn Weschcke, President and Publisher of Llewellyn Publications, and I have known each other for 22 years. Llewellyn has published all 18 of my books, some eight-and-still-counting anthologies in the New Age series which I edit, and the extraordinarily well acclaimed *Astrology Now* magazine which I founded and edited for many years in the 1970s—that's probably almost 2 million words of mine published by Llewellyn. Llewellyn has been the foundation of my entire career in astrology. Carl Weschcke has often privately and publicly referred to our bond in a previous life, that I was "his brother." In short, Carl and I are very close to each other professionally; we respect and admire each other considerably.

Carl Weschcke's Midheaven, the high, sharply focused, career, professional point in his horoscope is 23 Sagittarius. My node is precisely conjunct his Midheaven axis, a tremendous bond, a grand relationship graciously created by time.

Sun-Moon Blend Concept Chart
(Excerpt from *Synthesis and Counseling in Astrology* by Noel Tyl)

☉	☽
♈ Energy to lead, to exert force.	♈ Need to be important, to be "Number One."
♉ Energy to build and maintain.	♉ Need to preserve security; to keep things as they are or are supposed to be.
♊ Energy to diversify, to communicate.	♊ Need to be bright, scintillating, informed, intense.
♋ Energy to create security.	♋ Need to be emotionally secure, especially in the family.
♌ Energy to be recognized.	♌ Need to be respected, loved, and honored.
♍ Energy to refine, to discriminate.	♍ Need to be correct, exact, insightful.
♎ Energy to please and gain appreciation.	♎ Need to be appreciated; to be fair, attractive, and popular.
♏ Energy to control by knowing; to plumb depths and reach top.	♏ Need to be in control; to be seen as deep, significant, reliable, self-sufficient, right.
♐ Energy for self-assertion, for what is right.	♐ Need to have one's opinions respected.
♑ Energy to organize, strategize, and deploy resources; ambition.	♑ Need to administrate progress, make things happen.
♒ Energy to innovate, to intellectualize, to all, with others.	♒ Need to be socially significant, unusual.
♓ Energy to feel and understand and sacrifice.	♓ Neeed to identify ideal, understand impressions, work with intangible.

The 1995 Eclipses

Vince Ploscik

Eclipses occur when a New or Full Moon takes place while the Moon is on the plane of the ecliptic (the apparent path of the Sun in the heavens). As the Moon orbits the Earth, it deviates up to five degrees from the ecliptic. Most New Moons occur above or below the Sun's path in the heavens, while most Full Moons occur above or below the Earth's shadow. Hence, when a New or Full Moon occurs and the Moon is right on the ecliptic, a powerful alignment is created that optimizes the energies of the Sun and the Moon. During a Solar Eclipse (New Moon), the Earth is nestled in the Moon's shadow; during a Lunar Eclipse (Full Moon), the Earth is literally caught in the middle between the Sun and the Moon. Since the Moon is the primary reflector of the Sun's energy in our birth charts, eclipses are potent astrological events, and astrologers look to them to time events suggested by natal and progressed aspects, as well as aspects made by the slow-moving outer transiting planets.

It's important to remember that eclipses are heightened lunations. In this respect, a Solar Eclipse will always have the characteristics of a New Moon: as the Sun-Moon conjunction fuses the Sun's vital energy with the nurturing energies of the Moon, an emphasis is placed upon new beginnings or ventures, or on new problems or new concerns (depending upon the aspects the Solar Eclipse receives from the surrounding transiting planets and our individual natal and progressed planets).

A Lunar Eclipse, on the other hand, places the Sun and Moon in opposition with each other. As such, a Lunar Eclipse will always emphasize a need for compromise or cooperation or a major decision, even when it receives favorable aspects. When a Lunar Eclipse receives unfavorable aspects, we often experience outright opposition or confrontation, or are forced to confront major obstacles. Here is where the Full Moon's emotionalism often exacerbates these conflicts.

In the lunation cycle, it's the Full Moon's "job" to finish what the New Moon begins, so Lunar Eclipses often have strong links to the Solar Eclipses that precede them. In this respect, it's always a prudent idea to examine all of the coming year's eclipses. Finally, it can't be stressed enough that although the eclipses provide the tools, it's up to us to provide the labor and to take responsibility for our actions and decisions.

There are four eclipses in 1995, and they will have the greatest impact upon individuals whose birthdays coincide with, or fall within a day or two of their occurrence. The birthdays associated with each particular eclipse's date will be discussed in both "favorable" and "unfavorable" terms, and it will remain up to the individual to determine if their affected Sun degree is free of affliction (if favorably aspected by an eclipse) or receives mitigating positive aspects (if unfavorable aspected by an eclipse). (Note: Llewellyn offers a complete line of professional chart readings if help is needed here.)

Solar Eclipses are said to last for a year, and Lunar Eclipses are said to last for six months, but any eclipse is capable of generating events or situations that may last long beyond these time frames. Since eclipses receive an opening square aspect after about three months, and an opening trine aspect after about four months, their energies are certain to be active during the six months that follow their occurrence. Hence, this article will furnish possible "trigger dates" for each eclipse through a six-month period. These trigger dates all feature a lunation or a transiting planet in aspect with the eclipse, along with the transiting Moon as a possible catalyst, so they may all have the *potential* to generate hard events, whether positive or negative.

The Lunar Eclipse of April 15, 1995

The first eclipse in 1995 is a Lunar Eclipse at 25 degrees Libra 09 minutes on April 15. This Lunar Eclipse may be the most problematical for anyone born around

1/15, 4/15, 7/17 or 10/18 (any year). This eclipse may also generate some degree of mental or emotional stress, or spark potentially difficult adjustments and adaptations for anyone born around 2/28, 3/15, 5/16, 5/31, 9/2 or 12/2 (any year).

The April 15 Lunar Eclipse occurs in a Gemini decanate (every ten degrees of a sign [decanate] has a ruler) and in the eleventh duad of Libra, which is ruled by Leo (every two and one-half degrees of a sign [duad] also has a ruler). This suggests that individuals born around the unfavorable dates cited above may experience *relationship problems* or concerns related to the marriage or business partner, children, neighbors, friends and associates, or brothers, sisters, and other close relatives. Financial or material concerns may figure prominently in these possible conflicts or concerns—this April 15 Lunar Eclipse follows the November 1994 Lunar Eclipse at 25 degrees Taurus and the November 1994 Solar Eclipse at almost 11 degrees Scorpio, both of which may have financial repercussions—and communication problems may also exacerbate matters.

The eleventh duad of a sign always carries an Aquarian inference that suggests the unusual and the unexpected, so there is at least the possibility that old, long-standing issues or hidden problems may suddenly become public. The Lunar Eclipse at 25 degrees Libra opposes transiting Mercury at 26 degrees Aries, and this opposition is T-squared by transiting Neptune at 25 degrees Capricorn, so confusion, misunderstandings, secrets, health concerns and/or drug and alcohol problems may also factor into these concerns. Hence, individuals born around the unfavorably dates cited above should guard their personal/professional reputations and use extreme caution in the writing/signing of contracts and documents, as well as in negotiations and communications.

Again, the eleventh duad of a sign usually suggests sudden and/or unexpected concerns, but the events/situations generated by this eclipse may have quite a bit of history, as well as take a long time to play themselves out, as transiting Uranus first reached 25 degrees of Capricorn from March, 1994, and doesn't leave that degree until October, 1995, while transiting Neptune hovers at 25 degrees Capricorn from March, 1995 through October 1996. These transiting planets are the focal point of the T-square on the date of the eclipse, and 25 degrees Capricorn falls in a Virgo decanate and in the eleventh duad of Capricorn, ruled by Scorpio, so these possible relationship problems may be complicated by work and domestic instability, financial concerns, long-standing anger and resentment or disagreements over joint finances (taxes, insurances, alimony, child support, etc.). Again, with the T-square to transiting Neptune on the date of the eclipse, extreme caution should be used in domestic and business decisions, and all facts and figures should be carefully double-checked with an emphasis upon uncovering information that has been overlooked or based upon faulty assumptions.

Saturn transited 10 degrees of Pisces (which sesquisquares the eclipse) from April 1994 through January, 1995, while Jupiter transits 10 degrees of Sagittarius (which semi-squares the eclipse) from January 1995 through September 1995.

These transits at 10 degrees of Pisces and Sagittarius (which fall in the fifth duad of these signs) again suggest extreme caution in financial investments and partnerships, as well as suggest at least the possibility of these eclipse-related relationship and business partnership concerns escalating into possible legal problems or stress-related health concerns. The fifth duad of a sign also invokes issues related to children, gambling and speculation, and ostentatious displays of wealth or power, while transiting Saturn and Jupiter invoke issues related to career, reputation, in-laws and religious or philosophical beliefs.

With all the above in mind, individuals born around the unfavorable birth dates cited above should watch for the negative potential of this Lunar Eclipse to be triggered around 6/2, 6/18, 7/18, 7/24, 8/29, 9/2, 10/6, 10/18, 12/2, 12/27/1995; 1/2 and 1/13/1996. Around these dates, avoid rash/reckless decisions, carefully double-check facts/figures and try to act upon objective fact/logic rather than upon reactionary emotions.

The April 15 Lunar Eclipse will make favorable aspects for anyone born around 2/14, 6/16, 8/18, 10/18 or 12/17 (any year). Individuals born around these favorable birth dates may enjoy relationship opportunities, involvements with groups/organizations, new avenues of self-expression or perhaps new educational opportunities and business partnerships. However, given the T-square that the eclipse makes with transiting Mercury to transiting Neptune, individuals born around these favorable birth dates may find these opportunities accompanied by much possible confusion, and so, again, extreme caution should be exercised purely as a precautionary measure. Watch for the positive potential of this Lunar Eclipse to be possibly triggered around 5/12, 6/17, 7/1, 8/6, 8/20, 8/29 and 10/4/1995.

The Solar Eclipse of April 29, 1995

The second eclipse in 1995 is a Solar Eclipse at 8 degrees Taurus 56 minutes on April 29. This Solar Eclipse may be the most problematical for anyone born around 1/29, 4/29, 8/1 or 11/1 (any year). This eclipse may also generate some degree of mental/emotional stress or spark potentially difficult adjustments and adaptations for anyone born around 3/14, 6/15, 9/16, 10/2, 12/1 or 12/15 (any year).

The April 29 Solar Eclipse occurs in a Taurus decanate and in the fourth duad of Taurus, which is ruled by Leo. This suggests that individuals born around the unfavorable dates cited above may experience possible financial concerns and/or domestic or familial disputes that may be characterized by much possible stubbornness and emotional inflexibility or anger. The April 29 eclipse makes a very wide, semi-square aspect to transiting Saturn at 21 degrees Pisces (a Scorpio decanate and duad), so once again, extreme caution should be exercised in all material and joint financial concerns related to the home and family, business, insurances, joint finances and alimony or child support. With transiting Saturn in Pisces, there may be health concerns, and finances may be subjected to stressful changes due to behind-the-scenes or unforseen business/economic factors. Hence, careful attention should be given to health insurance, and conservative financial policies may be prudent (especially in June 1995, and in February 1996, when transiting Saturn is at almost 24 degrees Pisces and in an exact semi-square with the eclipse).

This April 29 Solar Eclipse may also have a bit of history behind it, as Jupiter transited 9 degrees of Scorpio in December 1993 and in August 1994, sparking possible financial overextension as well as possibly laying the foundation for legal problems. In light of this, individuals born around the unfavorable birth dates cited above should project a willingness to compromise and show mental or emotional flexibility as well as exercise extreme caution in all financial dealings when the negative potential of the April 29 Solar Eclipse is possibly triggered around 5/23, 6/13, 6/30, 7/31, 8/5, 9/16, 9/20, 10/1, 10/17, 10/30, 11/10, 12/7/1995; 1/20 and 2/3/1996.

The April 29 Solar Eclipse will make favorable aspects for anyone born around 2/27, 4/29, 6/30, 9/1 or 12/30 (any year). Individuals born around these favorable dates may experience possible business or financial opportunities, possible real estate opportunities or conditions that favor family expansion and/or home improvement. However, with the eclipse's semi-square to transiting Saturn in Pisces once again, these opportunities should be thoroughly researched and investigated with an eye toward hidden factors/considerations that may result in some degree of unforeseen stress. Watch for the positive potential of this eclipse to be possibly triggered around 6/14, 6/28, 7/11, 7/15 and 8/26/1995.

The Lunar Eclipse of October 8, 1995

The third eclipse in 1995 is a Lunar Eclipse at 15 degrees Aries on October 8. This Lunar Eclipse may be the most problematical for anyone born around 1/5, 4/5, 7/7 or 10/8 (any year). This eclipse may also generate some degree of mental/emotional stress or spark potentially difficult adjustments and adaptations for anyone born around 2/18, 5/21, 8/23, 9/7, 11/7 and 11/22 (any year).

The October 8 Lunar Eclipse occurs in a Leo decanate and in the seventh duad of Aries, which is ruled by Libra. This immediately suggests that individuals born around the unfavorable dates cited above may experience possible relationship and partnership problems that may be exacerbated by possible arguments/

disagreements, rash/reckless decisions and/or possible difficulties in relating to the needs and emotions of others. These possible relationship and partnership conflicts may in turn generate difficulties in balancing work/career responsibilities with domestic/familial concerns and vice versa, and this may result in much possible intolerance and irritability, as well as emotional frustration. This Lunar Eclipse follows the April 29 Solar Eclipse at almost 9 degrees of Taurus, so a willingness to compromise and cooperate with others may go a long way toward mitigating these possible "people problems."

This October 8 Lunar Eclipse plays against a backdrop of very busy skies, with transiting Venus in Libra squaring transiting Uranus in Capricorn and transiting Jupiter in Sagittarius conjunct the midpoint of this square; on the date of this eclipse, transiting Mercury in Libra also semi-squares transiting Mars (ruler of the eclipse) in Scorpio. Consequently, the conflicts outlined above may be supercharged with emotional tension/resentments, communication problems and/or attempts to steamroll over others that may replace objectivity and sensitivity with innuendo and ultimatums.

In light of the above, individuals born around the unfavorable dates cited above should avoid arguments and confrontations, rash/reactionary emotional responses and egocentricity when the negative potential of this Lunar Eclipse is possibly triggered around 10/19, 10/26, 11/7, 12/19/1995; 1/5, 2/15, 2/18, 2/21, 3/7, 3/31, 4/4 and 4/13/1996. Again, a willingness to consider the needs and point of view of others may go a long, long way toward mitigating these possible relationship and partnership problems.

The October 8 Lunar Eclipse will make favorable aspects for anyone born around 2/4, 4/5, 6/5, 8/7 or 12/7 (any year). Individuals born around these favorable birth dates may experience possible new relationships or partnerships, opportunities for self-promotion or networking, and/or the realization of personal goals and objectives (especially if they involve other people). However, given the rather hostile skies that accompany this eclipse, care should be taken to insure that new partners aren't making themselves available for all the wrong reasons or as a kneejerk reaction to their own relationship problems. Hence, it may be prudent to simply *slow down* in responding to these possible opportunities and try to consider the needs or feelings of others. Watch for the positive potential of this Lunar Eclipse to be possibly triggered around 10/31, 11/9, 11/14, 12/1, 12/7/1995; 1/3, 1/25, 2/4 and 2/26/1996.

The Solar Eclipse of October 24, 1995

The fourth and final eclipse in 1995 is a Solar Eclipse at 0 degrees Scorpio 17 minutes on October 24. This Solar Eclipse may be the most problematical for anyone born around 1/20, 4/20, 7/22 or 10/23 (any year). This eclipse may also generate some degree of mental or emotional stress, or spark potentially difficult adjustments and adaptations for anyone born around 3/6, 3/20, 5/21, 6/5, 9/7 or 12/7 (any year).

The October 24 Solar Eclipse occurs in a Scorpio decanate and in the first duad of Scorpio, which is ruled by Scorpio. This Solar Eclipse also semi-squares transiting Jupiter at 14 degrees Sagittarius 33 minutes, so individuals born around the unfavorable dates cited above may experience emotionally intense conflicts and disputes that may be characterized by unreasonable demands or expectations, emotional subjectivity and inflexibility, and/or attempts to impose their will or beliefs upon others (and vice versa). The control of money and material concerns may factor into these possible disputes (especially joint finances such as taxes, insurances, child support, retirement, or disability funds), and with transiting Jupiter's involvement, these control issues may spill into the legal arena. Hence, once again, conservative financial policies and extreme caution should be exercised.

On the date of this eclipse, transiting Mercury at 13 degrees Libra semi-squares transiting Pluto (ruler of the eclipse) at 29 degrees Scorpio, and this may prompt the possible conflicts outlined above to become even more entrenched in rigid and inflexible thinking or subconscious emotional resentment and anger. Hence, a willingness to show flexibility may offset a good deal of this eclipse's negative potential, and attempts at emotional coercion may only generate increased polarity and subsequent power struggles and tests of will.

With the above in mind, individuals born around the unfavorable birth dates cited above should use extreme care in all financial dealings and try to avoid confrontations with others when the negative potential of this Solar Eclipse is possibly triggered around 11/3, 11/9, 12/6/1995; 1/1, 1/9, 1/20, 1/26, 2/10, 3/5, 3/21, 4/7, 4/20 and 5/2/1996. Be aware that attempts to steamroll over others will likely be met with equal stubbornness and intensity.

The October 24 Solar Eclipse will make favorable aspects for anyone born around 2/18, 6/21, 8/23, 10/23 or 12/21 (any year). Individuals born around these favorable birth dates may experience financial opportunities or opportunities to assert their will and/or emotional desires. However, in light of the semi-square aspects from the eclipse to transiting Jupiter and from transiting Mercury to transiting Pluto, care should be taken so that this possible assertion of personal power or will doesn't create new enemies or trample over the needs and feelings of others. Watch for the positive potential of this Solar Eclipse to be possibly triggered around 11/28, 12/21/1995; 1/4, 1/14 and 2/18/1996.

One final note: between the April Lunar Eclipse in Libra and the afflicted transits in Libra that accompany the two October eclipses (which have been receiving square aspects from transiting Uranus and Neptune for a number of years), it would seem that 1995 may see many long-standing relationship problems erupt into outright confrontations with the help of 1995's eclipses in Cardinal and Fixed signs and their accompanying aggressive and stubborn attitudes. The communication difficulties suggested by these aspects may therefore make it all the more imperative to exercise a willingness to compromise and/or consider the needs and feelings of others, especially with 1996's eclipses (which will all be in Aries or Libra) waiting to extend these relationship conflicts through yet another year. Transiting Jupiter enters Capricorn in 1996, and transiting Saturn enters Aries, so it may be wise to try to settle 1995's conflicts in 1995 so that these problems don't escalate further in 1996.

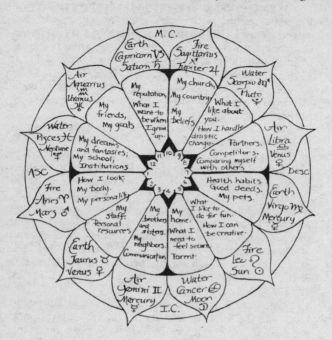

Insights into Children's Needs through the Zodiac

Gloria Star

Astrological insights are not "for adults only." In fact, using astrological guidelines to help understand the needs of your child can offer valuable support. Children are developing into themselves, and at different ages, through different cycles, their needs change and evolve Any parent or teacher will agree that each child has a specific personality and will express unique needs.

For a comprehensive analysis of the needs of your child, you might use a delineation of the child's natal horoscope based upon the date, time, and place of birth. The basic principles used for interpreting the chart of an adult are applied to the chart of a child, but with a difference: a child's chart must be interpreted incorporating the guidelines of developmental growth—physically, mentally, emotionally, and spiritually. A child's astrological chart indicates potential, and it takes time for a child to develop the full potential of the Self. Even if you are not familiar with your child's complete astrological chart, you can gain some insights based upon his or her Sun sign. In children, the Sun sign indicates a gradual advancement into the expression of their personal identities. Generally you will see vestiges of this ego-expression after the child enters into the socialization processes, at about school age. However, you will begin to see the basic characteristics of a child's Sun sign very early in life.

You'll also be able to observe expression of the Ascendant, or rising sign, rather strongly after age seven. (Refer to the Rising Sign Tables on pages 14–15 to approximate the Rising sign.) One of the primary ways the Ascendant manifests from ages seven through fourteen is in the way a child demands attention from the family and from the rest of the world. At a simplified level, the Rising sign shows how others see the child. The difference between the Sun sign and the Rising sign or Ascendant is relative. The Sun sign shows the basic nature of the ego of the individual, whereas the Ascendant indicates the way the child connects with the outside world.

Each of the twelve signs of the zodiac influences a particular array of expressions or affinities. For a child, these levels of expression will evolve over time, from primitive to more complex forms of emphasis. To interpret the meaning of the Sun sign and/or Rising sign, these basic concepts might be helpful:

Aries is exuberant, impatient, and very much in the moment. A child with Aries influencing self-expression is likely to prefer independent action rather than outside control. Encourage physical activity during the early years, and offer this child plenty of room to exercise leadership. The temperament can be quite hot, especially if this child is headed in one direction and you (or someone else) try to steer him or her onto another path.

Taurus is more comfortable with stable, tried and true situations which allow plenty of time to explore the world. A child with strong Taurean energy needs to be encouraged to find ample ways to express their natural loving, creative qualities. Their stubbornness can be frustrating if you're attempting to introduce new situations. You may also run into trouble if you try to take anything away, since Taurus children are very attached to the things and people who are part of their world.

Gemini children are highly curious, and may be quite talkative. The need to connect through social exchange is strong, and mental agility may be accentuated. This child can be easily distracted, and may have a limited attention span, but the ability to grasp new ideas quickly can be amazing. Strive to offer the Gemini child a feeling of consistency and stability while supporting his or her need for a variety of experiences.

Cancer children are emotionally sensitive, and may be most comfortable at home or in close contact to parents (especially mother) and family. Awareness of environment is keen, and there is an easy expression of feelings. Because of their increased intuitive sensibility, these children frequently show a mistrust toward others they do not know. Encourage this child to care for others in healthy ways while staying honest with themselves about expressing and fulfilling their own needs.

A **Leo** child can be highly demonstrative or dramatic, but can also be extremely warm and loving. If given the opportunity, this child may show leadership even in early years. There is strong willpower and a desire to direct their own actions, and you'll also see joy when this child is the center of attention. By stimulating this child to develop creativity and reinforcing self-esteem, you'll help develop a healthy ego. Giving in to emotional blackmail or unreasonable demands, however, may encourage the development of a young tyrant!

Virgo children are mentally creative and may be more emotionally sensitive than they appear to be. This child knows what he or she wants or likes or dislikes. Offering ample opportunities for a Virgo child to further skills or abilities, will help them build a stronger sense of them selves. Excessive criticism will alienate these children and may damage their trust of themselves.

Libra children are socially engaging and have an easy appreciation of the beautiful things life has to offer. This child may appreciate the arts and can show musical or artistic talent. He or she may also be quite sensitive about appearance, and will probably prefer to help make choices about clothes and hair styles. Even at a young age, a Libran will prefer to be in the company of others rather than being alone. Help this child learn to appreciate himself or herself without comparisons to others.

A **Scorpio** child may be charismatic even as a baby, and is always aware of the emotional climate in any situation. This child may demonstrate a keen creativity, and may have a desire to study things at a rather intensive level. Help this child develop perceptive abilities by encouraging a study of nature, and through expressing feelings in comfortable ways. When they ask where they came from, give them an honest answer.

Sagittarius children can be highly energetic, and may be happiest when they are going somewhere. Staying in one place is not a Sagittarian idea of fun—whether at a mental, emotional or physical level! Offer a wide variety of learning experiences to the child with Sagittarian energy, and be ready for a seemingly endless series of questions.

The **Capricorn** child is determined, persistent, and fascinated by things which can be experienced through the senses. There is a cautious nature which can present itself as a reluctance to step into new experiences. By adequately preparing a Capricorn for new learning and patient understanding of their need to feel in control of their life situation, you can help them trust themselves more effectively. Forcing this child is likely to result in a loss of trust and a frustrating struggle.

An **Aquarian** child can be highly independent, and likes things and people that are sensational and unusual. This child is also intellectually curious, and can be quite friendly and outgoing. However, there is a stubborn quality which can manifest in learning and in attitudes. Because this child may feel like a misfit some of the time, find ways to help him or her appreciate his/her unique qualities and abilities.

The **Pisces** child is imaginative, impressionable, and emotionally sensitive. This child may seem to live in another world much of the time, and can be keenly creative and expressive, but there can be problems differentiating between reality and fantasy. Stay connected to the experiences of this child, and help him or her find ways to draw the line between the possible and impossible while still encouraging those wonderful dreams.

1995 CYCLES FOR CHILDREN

During this year, you can use astrological insights to help guide your child's experiences. If you wish to apply the basic information offered in the Sun sign section of this book, it can be helpful. Realize, however, that you are dealing with a child, and that a child's background, needs, and personal expression will be different from an adult's. In "The Year Ahead" section for each of the signs, you will find specific information for each of the signs based upon the date of birth. The following interpretation of the Sun sign cycles for children is geared to their level, rather than to adult experience or expression. If you know your child's rising sign, then you'll also want to incorporate that information for the basic cycles for the year ahead. A professional astrologer will also integrate information based upon the complete chart for your child, and you might find a consultation with an astrologer helpful in gaining a more comprehensive understanding of your child's needs.

The Aries Child

If your child is an Aries, you'll need to offer plenty of opportunities for physical activity and may also see better performance in school. Some type of travel can be rewarding for your child, and may spark a new interest which develops over time. From January through May, Mars transits in strong aspect to the Sun, stimulating increased energy and restlessness. This energy needs a positive outlet for expression. Even if your child has not shown a strong interest in sports or athletics, an increased emphasis may emerge. If attention to school is a problem, it could be because there is a build-up in physical energy which needs to be released!

Additionally, your child may feel more interested in developing creative talents, and may apply more energy to this area than in the past. There could be inconsistent effort, however, unless you emphasize the need for discipline and focus.

Also, Jupiter's cycle this year may spark a curiosity about life which opens new horizons for an Aries child. Very young children may feel more comfortable socializing, and might enjoy interacting with other children. School-age Aries will be more stimulated to interact with teachers, and may find communication with both teachers and peers is easier. However, there can be more distraction than usual, so help your child stay on track. You may sense that there are concerns beneath the surface which your child seems reluctant to share. This is also an important cycle for spiritual growth, and a time when Aries is concerned with some of life's larger questions. Encourage your child to talk about his or her dreams, fears, and hopes, instead of just shrugging them off as unimportant. These inner experiences can either enhance or block your child's progress, depending upon the way they are handled.

During January, your Aries child will enjoy time spent with friends and may also show more interest in becoming involved in group activities or team sports. From February through May, not only will your child seem to be more physically restless, but creative pursuits can bring recognition and rewards which build your child's self-esteem. However, your praise and support are especially important during February and March. Be particularly alert to Aries' psychological needs during April and October, when the Lunar Eclipses may stimulate more emotional sensitivity. Watch for a period of increased impatience and less concentrated discipline during March and April. During May and June, your child may seem to be more interested in spending time with siblings or with neighborhood friends, but cooperative behavior is better in May!

Competitive urges emerge very strongly during July and August, and your child will need a healthy outlet, such as sports, for these energies. Cycles in September and October show indicators that your child may need outside motivation to get things done, and peers can be highly influential. November is an especially rewarding month, and may bring new opportunities for your child to explore frontiers of knowledge which are exciting, interesting and fun. You may experience some discipline problems or power struggles during December, when the rules just don't seem to work very well. You can help your child gain control over this rebellious time by allowing breaks in a busy schedule to play and let off steam, and by rewarding appropriate behavior.

The Taurus Child

Taurus children may be especially geared toward developing friendships this year, and are learning important lessons about sharing. Cooperation with others may be geared toward family, but if your child is in school, he or she will benefit from every opportunity to collaborate with peers. Team sports, group projects, and community activities all serve to help meet these needs. Older Taurus children will also be thinking more about future plans. Work together with them to create a track for realizing their dreams for the future, but also help them set some reasonable short-term goals. Serious and consistent goal setting now will help to shape this ability for a lifetime.

Some jealousy toward friends may emerge if your Taurus child feels that a friend is shunning them for someone or something else. There may be experiences in which a friend does gravitate toward changing interests which are not shared by your child. Conversely, your child's changing focus may also make it more difficult to interact with old friends. These changes can be made gracefully, and may be only temporary. Older children (especially preteen and early teens) may also experience some difficulty from peer pressure and value differences. Your support and understanding can make all the difference in helping your child stay strong about their deeper needs and convictions.

January can be a highly productive month for your Taurus child, and a time when group activities, church-related activities or educational opportunities are positively challenging. Any disruptions in home life between February and May can be quite disconcerting for Taurus, so if you're planning a move, remodeling, changes in the family, or if other situations occur which cut into your regular routine, try to show some understanding toward your child's frustration with these changes. Plan to spend some extra time during the spring and fall months in support of your child's special interests. June and July are more playful and relaxing, and an excellent time to encourage recreation and creative pursuits which may not be possible during the rest of the year. August is a good time to suggest that Taurus add special touches to his or her room, and is a great time to begin a new routine.

September can bring out both a creative and competitive quality which allow your child to show special abilities or participate in activities which stimulate imaginative play. Listen to their concerns, especially in regard to that developing sense of identity during both April and October, when the Solar Eclipses emphasize a need to understand their roots and know who they are. November brings a period of some insecurity, especially in regard to social relationships. December's focus is more soothing and personally satisfying, when sharing family traditions and giving to others is both gratifying and supportive for a Taurean child.

The Gemini Child

Gemini children are struggling to reach a balance between the demands to achieve and the desire to cram as many experiences into their day as time will allow. Setting priorities is crucial, especially for the child in school. Preschool children may seem more clumsy or accident-prone, primarily due to their tendency to be focusing on one thing while they are doing something else. This is accentuated by the tension produced from the cycles of Jupiter and Saturn. You can help a younger child by becoming aware of your own demands on their time or upon their performance. With an older child, talk about their concerns, the areas where they feel overwhelmed or too pressured, and help them find ways to establish priorities which are supported by their abilities and interests.

Social schedules may seem to mushroom, particularly for the school-age Gemini. Young teens may begin to show a stronger interest in developing a "special" relationship, although these are likely to change rather suddenly. Saturn's transit also brings the need to take greater responsibility. For the small child, this may manifest as a reluctance to jump into new situations without your support. Offer support and understanding, and be aware of the things going on in the family which may undermine this child's sense of security or stability (even if it doesn't seem all that important to you!). Make sure children from ages five to eight understand the difference between the things they really can influence, and those things which are beyond their influence or responsibility. Their tendency may be to feel guilty for things which are not their responsibility. However, older children need to be given more responsibilities in accordance with their age and ability, and you need to hold a firm line about those areas in which they need to achieve discipline or focus.

Friction at home can be difficult during January, especially if Gemini feels that parental or family expectations are too high. Increased curiosity about the world and better learning experiences emerge from February through May. Taking a break from routine is necessary for Gemini during June and July, although you may sense that an older child has obligated too much time to situations in which she or he quickly loses interest. Encourage your child to take part in classes or activities which boost creativity or artistry during late July and through August. Allow extra time to support their mental expression during September, October and November. Older children may find this an exceptional time for creative writing, crafts or other activities which require manual dexterity. A competitive

urge is powerful during November, and can be a good stimulus if handled correctly. If that competition is presented in unhealthy ways, then this can be a period of frustration and anger. Social support during December can soothe some hurt feelings, but you may still need to be sure that Gemini has plenty of reasons to feel special and deeply loved.

The Cancer Child

For the Cancer child, this year brings an emphasis upon developing creative talents and becoming more comfortable in educational situations. Very young Cancerians will benefit from interactive play, preschool activities which allow them to explore the world (an emphasis on field trips would be great!), and physical activity which allows them to increase coordination. Older children will be drawn into situations in which they can develop their leadership abilities and through which they learn to share special interests.

Offer Cancer children plenty of opportunities to learn about their own values, including getting them involved in experiences which will develop their self-esteem. In addition, introduce them to an understanding of money and finances, and give them a chance to learn the value of conserving their resources and making the most of what they have. This may also be the year in which your school-age child develops a positive relationship with a teacher, or finds a mentor. If your child has any special talents, finding the right guide or teacher to help develop these talents is crucial, since that person's influence may be more marked now that it would be at another time.

Siblings, neighbors, and favorite companions provide excellent outlets for Cancer's need to connect with others during January. You may see an unusual level of selfishness developing in younger Cancerians from February through May. This can manifest as a case of "I want it and I want it now!" in older Cancer children. Help your child find the best ways to use whatever resources are available, instead of just getting rid of one thing in favor of something which appears to be better. This will be much more appealing to their basic nature, as well. Significant friendships are emphasized during the spring months. Travel, even if only to places nearby, will be exciting and stimulating for your child during June and July. This is also a good time to encourage recreational reading. If you sense that you child is feeling more frustrated than usual during August, there may be some turmoil at home which is not apparently difficult for you, but which is upsetting to your child. If there is family turmoil or change, know that it will be felt in a deeply personal way during this time. Communication about feelings and needs can be inconsistent and may be difficult from September through early November. An older child might benefit by keeping a diary or talking with a family friend. A younger child may just need extra reassurance or a better explanation about what's going on. Creative outlets are fulfilling during November and December, and may provide a special boost to your child's sense of self-esteem.

The Leo Child

Leo children have an especially noteworthy year for expressing their performing or dramatic ability. This can also be a highly active year physically, particularly from January through May when Mars is transiting in Leo. Tempers can be shorter than usual, especially if your child is somewhat impatient by nature. Very young Leo children need extra outlets for expending physical energy, or they may have trouble resting or sleeping.

Jupiter's cycle throughout the year is especially important, and you may find that your child receives greater recognition for their talents than they have in the past. Contests or competition may give your child a chance to show their abilities. Leo children may also be receiving more accolades and experiencing greater popularity with their peers. However, older children may also have some conflicts due to feelings of inadequacy Help them determine the best way to develop themselves without simply comparing their accomplishments or abilities with those of others.

Performance anxiety can manifest for older Leos during January, when your loving support and encouragement offers a real boost to their confidence. A special

 friendship can also be self-confirming during this time. Although Mars transiting in Leo is highly stimulating for Leo children, you may also observe that they are burning the candle at both ends. Very young children are likely to be more short-tempered during this time, while older children seem to be challenging everyone more readily. Your child may also be feeling more emotionally vulnerable during April, May, October, and November due to the influence of the Solar Eclipses.

By emphasizing the positive aspects of your family's roots and traditions and including children in major decisions (whenever possible), you will help them build the stability which is critical to their feeling of security. June is a good time for interaction with friends, involvement with team sports or taking time out for a break. July and August provide an excellent period to get involved in neighborhood activities. Older children will be especially busy with friends, and friends may be around all the time! Some feelings of inner conflict may arise for young Leo during September and through mid-October. Very young children may be more irritable during this time, and older children can be more willful. Encourage cooperation whenever possible, and take time to acknowledge the importance of releasing anger or frustration. Create breaks in daily routine to break up tension, and be prepared for some confusing communication (or lack of communication if your Leo is more sullen!). Creative activities and favorite recreational games add a positive spark of energy in late October through November, and you may also see a contrast involving more cooperative behavior. Recognition by teacher, peers, or others can be forthcoming late in November and into mid-December. Celebrate your child's successes and plan special family events by getting your child involved in all the festivities.

The Virgo Child

Virgo children are very goal-oriented during this year. Even young Virgo may seem to be more determined and focused. Older children may feel more pressure from their own sense of perfection than they normally experience. Some of the pressures may arise from social or peer issues which are in conflict with your child's sense of personal values.

Regardless of age, pay special attention to your Virgo child's physical needs during 1995. Vitality may seem to be a bit lower, and resistance can be lessened. Be attentive to nutritional needs, and make sure your child is getting plenty of rest. The early part of the year may be filled with more anxiety than usual, and if you can explore these fears with your child, you can help alleviate much of this inner tension. Physical strength can actually be increased this year if Virgo children have positive physical challenges. Get them involved in sports or fitness activities, even if they are very young, but be aware of their limitations before you try to push them into anything which is uncomfortable or unfamiliar.

Older Virgos may feel a greater need to embrace the support of family, and may be more comfortable inviting friends to play at home rather than being in new surroundings. Those in preteen or teen years may feel awkward or anxious in social situations in which they sense strong criticism. Positive support from siblings and involvement with groups which offer spiritual and psychological support can be especially helpful to the Virgo child this year. They may also gain special recognition for academic performance.

The year begins with Virgo experiencing a strong drive to achieve. You may also observe some reluctance from your child toward stepping into new directions or taking on challenges. Spend some extra time supporting your child's needs in January by recognizing that she or he is more sensitive to criticism, even though hopes may be high. Older Virgos may feel squeezed between peer pressure and family expectations during February and March. Concentrated efforts in developing creative or artistic skills can provide an excellent source of support. Even challenging projects can be fun if they are approached with a positive attitude. A lower than normal physical vitality may be present from February through May, and your child may need more rest, which

353

should be encouraged. Help your child set reasonable priorities during this time. By late April new interests are likely to emerge which stimulate creative thinking.

The need to gain acknowledgment for intellectual pursuits during May can bring a time of success in school activities, but you still may find that your child tends to take on more than he or she can handle. The need to burn off some physical energy during June can be met by getting Virgo involved in recreational activities which are both physically and mentally challenging. By July, there's more time for friends, and an easier flow of energy with much less emotional and physical stress. Some concerns about appearance emerge during August, and older children should be given a chance to make some important wardrobe decisions. September through October bring a whirlwind of activity and a strong drive to share ideas and learn emerges for young Virgo. November is a busy time, too, and you may spend a lot of time working on important projects with a school-age child. However, a young child may need more of your attention, too, so plan to delegate time for sharing. December is a highly creative time for your Virgo child, when giving of themselves can be both exciting and highly rewarding.

The Libra Child

Libra children may be especially busy exploring their immediate environment and interacting with friends, siblings, and neighbors. This is an excellent time to help your child develop better communicative skills. Young children are likely to become more talkative and will begin to show their charming sensibilities more readily. Older children may become more interested in reading and writing. At any age, a Libra child will find traveling to be a particular delight this year.

New creative talents, interests or abilities may emerge, although you may see some inconsistency from your child in trusting these new experiences. Community support or getting involved in situations where friends show their support may encourage your child to move forward with these interests. Socializing with friends is likely to take a great deal of your older child's attention during the first six months of the year. Team sports can be quite gratifying, if your child enjoys physical activity, although group projects may be the direction a Libra child would follow.

The Lunar Eclipses in April and October are especially challenging for Libra children, who may feel more emotionally vulnerable during these times. Any relationship concerns can be particularly trying if your child feels alone in dealing with them. Find ways to stay in communication with one another, and offer your child an understanding and honest support system.

January brings a busy social period for an older Libra child, and you may see signs of enhanced interests in artistic or creative pursuits for any Libra youth. Learning new skills or improving abilities in areas of special talent is especially encouraging from January through March. Additionally, you may find community programs or group activities which help take the sting out of your budget for such experiences through the end of May! Older children will be especially drawn to social activities which are popular with their friends, and may have little time for you, since their friendships keep them quite busy from February through June!

Keep a careful watch on physical health during February and March. Some competitiveness with friends during March may result in a break-up or disagreement. Before you jump in to resolve it, give your child a chance to work it out. From May through July your child may be fascinated with exploring other cultures or learning more about something which is personally inspiring. This is an excellent period for travel or time away from routine. By late July your child may once again decide to exchange time with family for time with

friends. August is a high-energy month and a time of high optimism. Mercury transits in Libra during September and October, stimulating a period of talkative energy for Libra children. This is an excellent energy for writing, public speaking, or educational activities, and may also be a good period for neighborhood get-togethers. Mental energy continues to be strong during November, and your child is likely to progress beautifully in developing language skills. December brings the concentration to activity within the home for young Libra. This can also be a period of short temper if your child's expectations are not met.

The Scorpio Child

Scorpio children are experiencing a strengthening of spirit and support of their self-worth this year. Even very young Scorpios will feel more confident expressing their creative abilities given adequate support and opportunity to develop their talents. However, there is an impatience and competitiveness present early in the year which may result in a more stubborn and willful attitude on the part of your child.

You may have some health concerns which result from previous illness or injury, but this is a period in which positive ways to overcome these problems lead to recovery or progress from your child. Physical sensitivity is most marked during spring and fall. The Mars cycle, from January through May, can stimulate more rash behavior on the part of your child, which could result in some accidents if your child is taking unnecessary risks. However, the most likely scenario during this cycle is one of high levels of energy, which can drive you to distraction unless you help Scorpio children funnel their restless activity into positive expression.

The most outstanding feature of the cycles for Scorpio children involves the development of talents and abilities. With discipline, guidance, and support, your child may excel in several areas. Very young children will benefit from artistic expression as a means to show their inner thoughts and feelings, and older children are likely to feel more assured of their self-worth by developing their skills.

Extra time spent with friends, in group activities, or involved with special interests can be highly motivating for Scorpio during January. School-age Scorpio may feel mentally frustrated by the introduction of abstract material during January and February. If you help your child with homework, try to use a little humor when dealing with projects or assignments which are new or unusual.

From February through May, Scorpio children may feel driven to achieve the recognition or goals they have set for themselves. Very young children may seem to be more irritable during this cycle, and Scorpios of all ages are likely to have a shorter fuse. Encourage healthy release of anger, and if older children feel highly competitive, help them direct that energy in areas which are more harmonious with their needs and abilities. Creative or artistic activities bring satisfaction and a sense of accomplishment during March and April. Relationships and social activities are an important focus during April and May. However, a child who feels out of place may be especially sensitive during this time, so try to be supportive and seek out good ways to stabilize your child's self-esteem.

June is a busy month for community activities or time spent with friends, although your child may have little patience for inconsistency from friends or family. Optimism and personal confidence increase during July, and a new, supportive friend may be a special feature in the life of your child. Parental support is important during August, and family activities can take precedence. During September and October your child has his/her own agenda and needs to be given a chance to set priorities. Increasing physical activity is highlighted during October and November, and you may also see improvements in self-esteem. Your affirmation of your child's abilities and strengths will be especially well-received during the fall months. An emphasis on writing or developing language skills occurs during December, which is also a good time for most educational pursuits.

The Sagittarius Child

Sagittarius children are experiencing an exciting, confident, and optimistic period while Jupiter transits in their sign all year. Small children will be eager to explore their world, and very active in their pursuits. Older Sagittarian children are likely to develop their communicative abilities and social skills, while feeling more courageous and determined to reach their goals.

However, discipline and taking responsibility are important issues this year, particularly for the school-age Sagittarian. This is one of those cycles during which moving too far away from requirements or expectations will result in immediate discipline or restraint. Small children need to learn about the importance of making and keeping promises. Older children may have difficulty knowing when to say "No" or how to set limits for themselves. By setting up a dialogue with your children, you can become a partner in their decision making and may be able to give them some positive guidance. Older children may resist your interference in areas which they hold sacred, so give them some space to make their own mistakes!

Ambition is strong for older Sagittarius children during January. However, this energy is likely to emerge as a more outgoing attitude and a period of showing off in a very young child. Self-esteem can increase, and your praise and support have a powerful effect. Your child is likely to have little patience from January through July, and will benefit from setting short-term goals and perhaps a limited long-term goal. If you are not offering Sagittarius children the attention they crave during February and March, you're likely to see them acting out behaviors which gain your acknowledgment. Support activities which will lend to development of language and communication skills from January through March. April is an active time which will be well spent in favorite recreational or creative activities.

During May, creative pursuits continue to offer their rewards, but socializing takes a front seat. Young children will prefer to be included in your activities or to be provided with playmates, and older Sagittarius will enjoy being with peers. Although there may be some competitive drive during June and July, it should be friendly competition for the most part. Team sports or group activities are excellent choices.

August is an exceptional month for the adventure of travel, camping, or getting back to nature. September is performance-oriented, with friends and special interests providing the best outlets for focused energy. During October, group activities prevail, but your child may seem to be a bit withdrawn until later in the month. November is active, competitive and exciting, and your child is very likely to gain recognition for an outstanding performance. During December an impulsive energy emerges which is likely to manifest as a need for a variety of experiences. Encourage your child to budget both time and energy.

The Capricorn Child

Capricorn children are more capable of formulating a strong database, and may feel more confident about expressing their thoughts and ideas. This is a good year for Capricorn to develop closer ties to siblings. Very young Capricorn may develop greater trust within their immediate environment, giving them confidence to explore the outside world with greater self-assurance. Older children can be trusted to understand their boundaries and respect their rules more consistently. There is likely to be a tendency to test those limits as frequently as possible, however, particularly for the preteen or teenage Capricorn.

During the spring months be sure to offer your youngsters plenty of chances to show creative talents and excel in areas which are important to them. Older children may gain recognition during the spring and fall, and may even be given an opportunity to guide or lead others. Additionally, this is a time to teach the importance of love, and the relationship between giving and receiving love. If your child shows an interest in exploring sexuality this year, try to offer honest, candid information which incorporates the importance of personal responsibility for their actions and the impact of the emotional changes which occur during such an unfolding.

January offers your child a chance to experience new directions in learning and can be a positive time for education for older children and advancements in development for young Capricorn. Self-esteem improves during February, and the older child may be interested in money matters. Your child may seem to be more easily intimidated by others whose skills, circumstances, or abilities appear to be better than their own from February through May. However, a focus on practical, hands-on learning can increase your children's confidence in themselves. Neighbors and siblings provide good emotional support during March, but your child will also seek your support during April. Misunderstandings or poor communication are problematic in early April, but can be diffused by getting the facts clear. Give your child a chance to showcase their talents and develop skills or interests during late April through mid-June. These experiences will not only help raise your child's sense of personal worth, but may stimulate the development of interests which last for years.

Church activities, travel, or getting back to nature are inspiring for your child during June and July. This could be a good time for a family trip. An older child might also enjoy peer-oriented activities, summer camp, or may be involved in social activities during July. Irritability can run high during August, and you may feel that your child is unusually rash or impulsive. Better judgment returns in September, when a more even temperament and stronger focus emerge for the older child, and when a younger child seems more cooperative. Watch your children's tendency to jump to conclusions or be inconsistent in school performance during October, and help them focus by working with them on assignments or providing necessary structure and support. November's activities bring more friends into the picture, although your child may spend more time playing alone during November. Socializing and increased physical activity bring changes to routine during December. This is a positive time of self-affirmation for your child, who will grow even more confident with your praise.

The Aquarius Child

Aquarius children have special opportunities in regard to developing friendships, and understanding the nature of their needs in regard to their friends. They may also be questioning their values, self-worth, and the importance of material things. Very young Aquarians may be more sensitive than usual, and are likely to resist periods of separation from those they love. Find ways to stay connected, even if you have to spend time away from your child. Older Aquarians may show this sensitivity primarily in regard to their self-esteem, and need to know that you are behind them in every situation, even if they choose to do these things on their own.

Group activities, team sports, special interests and good friends form the primary influence throughout the year, and will provide many opportunities for young Aquarians to offer support to others and find the support they need. However, there is a need to positively direct a strong competitive urge which emerges from February through May. Help your child determine both long-term and short-term goals, and stress the importance of educational pursuits as a means to achieve their aims. Invite your children to develop an understanding of the way money works, and get them involved in family finances if they are old enough. Pressure to meet family expectations is strong during the spring and fall months, and recognition for academic achievements can be one of your child's greatest needs throughout the year. Be sure to find out what older Aquarians want for themselves before you decide to set a path you would desire. Their sense of direction is very strong this year!

Intellectual development is emphasized for Aquarius from January through mid-March, when a young child will become more communicative or interactive, and an older child gains greater satisfaction from developing language skills, writing, or public speaking. Impatience and increased irritability can emerge for young Aquarius through May, and an older child is likely to be more willful and stubborn during this time. Self-esteem improves in March, and opportunities to socialize with school friends or neighbors in April stimulate developing some common interests. If you want to know what's going on in your Aquarius child's head during April, you'll probably get more information from a playmate or sibling than you'll receive from your child! From May through July, creative pursuits gain momentum and you may find that your child is most comfortable expressing ideas, feelings and needs through uniquely creative endeavors.

Cooperative ventures, cultural interests or travel may stimulate an older Aquarian during August. Getting out in natural surroundings is delightful through August, and travel can be favorable if you allow children to do some things that are specifically interesting to them, instead of just following your own agenda. During September and October a powerful stimulus toward academic achievement may encourage your child. A small child can become more talkative. Ambition continues to stimulate young Aquarius during November and December, but most of their encouragement is likely to come from friends or those who share in their daily activities. Recognition for a job well done is forthcoming through mid-December, although your child might prefer a quiet celebration of those achievements.

The Pisces Child

A Pisces child may seek ways to feel more stable and secure during 1995. Structure is extremely important, and consistency is a must. Your influence can be especially powerful now, regardless of your child's age. Older children may also strive to receive greater attention from teachers in addition to their need to please parents. Criticism needs to be balanced, since too much negative criticism will undermine your child's sense of confidence now.

Encourage the development of physical strength and stamina by supporting children's involvement in activities which will benefit their fitness level. Very young Pisces can be extremely restless and may have trouble resting well during the first half of the year unless their activity level is high enough to help them burn off excess energy. Older children may simply be more active, but can also be more accident-prone in situations which are unfamiliar. Proper guidance and training help them avoid these difficulties.

The urge to express ideas effectively and feel a connection to the rest of the world is powerful for Pisces now. Small children will love time spent reading, sharing fantasies, and developing their minds. Older children might prefer to develop their writing, acting or speaking skills and can excel in these areas throughout the year.

Your open support of a Pisces child works wonders in building confidence during January. Even very young Pisces will enjoy time with friends now, but may not like being placed in highly competitive circumstances. Some withdrawal may occur during February, when only close friends or those who have gained your child's trust will be welcome in their lives. March brings a more outgoing energy which continues to manifest as comfort in most social situations through April. Academic endeavors should fare well in March and April, especially in areas of special interest. During May, neighborhood gatherings, interaction with siblings, and daily activities run more smoothly.

Any stress or turmoil at home can have a strong impact on Pisces during June and July, when they may also seem more easily agitated or short-fused. By getting them involved in artistic or creative activities during the summer you may be able to help funnel some of this energy into more positive areas of release. Physical sensitivity increases during August, but this can also be a time when quick recovery occurs if there are any physical ailments. If Pisces children seem to be intimidated by new situations or other children during September, help them find the areas of mutual interest and support their own self-worth instead of getting caught in their vulnerability. Misunderstandings during October can be discouraging, but there are also indicators of enhanced communicative abilities and good outlets for imaginative ideas. Any competitive activities during November can provide a positive challenge. However, you need to be sure your child is fully prepared or conditioned in order to meet these challenges. During December, physical vitality increases and recognition for achievements is finally forthcoming. Friends are especially important during November and December, and you might want to allow your child to invite a special friend to share in family activities during this time.

Note: To discover more about your child through using astrology, you might enjoy reading Gloria Star's book *Optimum Child: Developing Your Child's Fullest Potential through Astrology.* Ask for it at your local bookstore, or order directly from Llewellyn.

Gambling and
Astrology

Edward A. Helin

Astrologers are often asked, "Why would you use astrology in connection with gambling?" The answer should be, "Why not?"

Many very successful gamblers, Nick the Greek, for instance, and stock market gurus have been using the round art throughout history. If they found it achieved their aims, then why shouldn't amateur gamblers use that same information?

On December 9, 1994, Jupiter, the planet of luck, began its transit through Sagittarius. It will remain there until January 3, 1996. Sag says "I like to gamble," and it will demand action during 1995. Prior to Sag, Jupiter was in Scorpio, so "bigger is better" was the motto of the day, and we saw glitter galore in such places as Las Vegas, Reno, and Atlantic City. As bigger and flashier clubs were opened, older and smaller clubs became dinosaurs of the gambling world. Why? Increasing numbers of small communities, Indian reservations, and riverboats got into the action of legalized gambling, and scared the bejeebers out of the big boys. It was fight 'em or join 'em, and it appears the large gambling organizations are doing both.

Jupiter in Scorpio also put people such as Boesky and Milken back in the loop and, since Jupiter is the Sagittarius 12th House, how much other behind-the-scenes activity has been going on? Since Jupiter likes publicity, a lot of those secret deals will find their way into print. Use caution with your stock market gambles!

All phases of the gambling machinery will think Santa Claus has come to town, as the public will crave bigger and better pots for their hard-earned bucks. We must remember that working class people will see smaller paychecks while the South Node moves through Taurus (the sign that rules the earning capability of the public). This is why those in control of games of chance, which also include horse racing, sports, auto racing, magazines' and publishers' grand prizes, have to find new, intriguing and sophisticated ways of getting their hands into our pockets. A cable TV company is even working on a gambling channel. What next?

The major concern has to be with overdoing it as we plunk money down on wagers or lotteries, because over-optimism causes us to take chances that are not wise. The public will tend to put their hearts and souls into gambling, attempting to get rich quick. Jupiter in Sagittarius means we have to study our methods in detail (sorry no quick picks with this combo) whether through classes, lectures, or research. Sag rules the long haul, which includes trucks, buses, and our long-range future, and this is why we must work on more elaborate systems. Remember the plans put into effect now will be around for 10 to 15 years (or longer). Sagittarius spreads things out, which means there will be a push for a national lottery and more enticing deals coming out of Nevada. These lucrative bargains (for Nevada gaming interests) will appear to be too good to pass up. As the old saying goes, "There ain't no such thing as a free lunch."

Other things we can expect to see with Jupiter's transit through its home sign: the public developing a more educated palate in regard to food; a demand that our politicians have brain transfusions to get some common sense between their ears; a more concentrated ban on hunting; more work and business heading south of the border; a larger underground economy; unions losing members and benefits; a demand (especially by minorities) that schools turn out better-educated students; mass rumblings because of hard-to-understand decisions by judges and juries (which could lead to a demand for professional jurors); cold and dry weather still affecting farmlands; real estate markets that can't decide whether to go up or down; health services still under the gun with demands for lower costs (but more and better service); a big increase in the spiritual movement; more accidents during air travel; and increases in legal battles over custody of children due to an acceleration in the divorce rate.

Here are some hints to make it easier for you to come out ahead. Anyone can gamble, but it's kind of nice to win once in awhile. Your 5th House not only shows what type of risk-taker you are, but also the type of gambling at which you might be most successful. However, the 8th House tells you when and how much you collect from those speculative ventures. Planetary hours play an important part in selecting the best time to lay your money down. There are numerous other tricks of the trade which your favorite professional astrologer can work out for you. Research has shown us that roulette follows the laws of astrology more than any other game of chance. Auto and horse racing will take a big jump in popularity, which means that the casino sportsbooks will see more activity. What could be more fun than cruising down the river on a riverboat and gambling in style and comfort?

Sagittarius rules the long road we travel in life, and Jupiter wants to give us a smooth and comfortable ride. The big drawback comes when we try to bite off more than we can chew. The giant planet can also be called "the straw that broke the camel's back."

How about some lucky numbers and dates? These are the ones for everyone, and you will find more detailed numbers and dates located in your Sun sign reading. Eight is the magic number that will put you in control of your destiny. Lucky dates are: February 14, March 4, April 2, October 30, 31, November 5, 6, 11 (the best of the year), 23, December 8, 11. Unlucky dates are February 20, May 5, 12, and October 16. Job losses could occur during the May and October dates. See your Sun sign for a more detailed reading.

ARIES March 20 – April 20

Aries is the sign we usually associate with "here today, gone tomorrow"; however that attitude won't work this year if you want to be a winner. This year's chart shows that Aries will have to be in a concentration mode to line up at the payoff window.

There are two methods that will put Aries in the chips this year, the first being nose-to-the-grindstone study. You have to look at the overall picture, and then make some long-range plans on how you are going to approach the game, race, lottery, etc. What does this mean? How about some down-to-earth study, working out a system, scrutinizing every possible angle, and then coming to a final solution? Don't be afraid to ask questions—or ask for help—because teamwork is the way you will come out on top. This could also mean teaming up to place bets. Now we all know the rams don't like these drawn out procedures, so what is the other way to prevail? Use your psychic and intuitive abilities. That's right; these senses will be working over-time for you this year. However, you can be talked out of winning bets if you don't stick to your guns. Are you talking yourself out of possible wins, or letting others tell you it's a bunch of hokum? Either way, you are missing some sure winners. Your private life is in a con-cluding cycle and partnerships are on a rocky road, and this will have a tendency to effect your gambling instincts. Also, criticism in your work and career area tends to throw you out of kilter and make you feel uncomfortable and rebellious. Fantasize about being a lucky winner, and you could see Ed McMahan knocking on your door.

This is the year when Aries has to pay off old debts (of all types), and, once this happens, rams will take off. Your lucky numbers for the year are 340 and 7. The sin-gle luckiest day is June 21, with other lucky days being February 11, September 16, October 30, 31, November 10, 16, 23, and December 8. The period of March 2 through March 30 puts the four-leaf clover in your cor-ner. The unluckiest day is April 28, so hibernate on this day. Think lucky!

TAURUS April 20 – May 21

Bulls are slow-motion gamblers and don't like to part with their hard-earned bucks. This is why they will look at all angles before laying down their bets. They will do better with one-on-one sports, such as golf, tennis, badminton, bridge, pool, drag racing, etc, the type of game where you play alongside someone, and yet against them. People make a living playing pool or golf, and, stretching the point enough, blackjack and even slot machines could fall into this category. Even legal gambles have an inclination to come out in your favor, but be cautious about being sue happy. Why take a flyer on marriage when you have two strikes against you? Ask yourself, will it last? Only if you have a long leash!

Where will your biggest payoffs come from? New money making schemes that have never entered your mind before can bring some hefty unexpected rewards. Gambles in the career field will be very fortunate; however it wouldn't hurt to shine up to the boss. You will feel strange at times this year, and inspiration will strike at very odd times, more than likely the day after you come home from Las Vegas. Don't try to play both ends against the middle or you will come out on the short end of the stick. Stick with what you know best. When push comes to shove, your creative and gambling instincts should be applied to career matters even if it means taking a back seat for awhile. By opening new doors to the future the bulls can become "king of the hill."

If you must, bet on the above-mentioned games but bet wisely. Your words will seem to have no direction and you will make statements that will cause you to have to mend fences in the future. Keep mum until all of the facts are in. Your lucky numbers this year are 193, 13, and 4. Your luckiest day of the year is February 20, with other good days being March 19, May 25, June 14, September 14, October 29, November 23, December 7, and 31. The period of October 7 to November 15 is a period of time when the Gods want to smile on you. Your unluckiest day is March 25. Think lucky!

GEMINI May 21 – June 21

The twins will feel unloved, left out, shunned and just plain avoided by their peers this year. When people head for the track and leave you home, some of it has been deserved. Well, lucky you! 1995 can be a turn-around year if you play your cards right. Otherwise you will still be left out in the cold.

Your tough luck in love affairs is over, but you now tend to seek out horizontal relationships rather than emotional ones. If you take a gamble on love it could be permanent, so make sure you are on the right track. When it's time to speculate, Geminis will be big time operators and would rather use other people's money than their own. The twins are full of weird and wild schemes this year, and will have an extraordinary ability to sell them to anyone willing to listen.

Once you learn to adjust and fit into the gambling environment, and are willing to put in some hard work, you will see some very happy and surprising results. Since Geminis want to do things on a large scale, you will be attracted to Las Vegas-type casinos, super big lottery pots and even cruise ship gambling. No small time stuff for you! One thing to remember, these types of clubs hand out free drinks. We all know Pisces are the lushes of the zodiac, but Geminis run a close second; and number twos try harder. Don't let the juice impair your abilities! Also, use extreme caution in regard to surgery, as this is one gamble you should not take unless it is absolutely neces-sary. Getting a sec-ond opinion would be wise.

When you collect your vast winnings, keep a tight lip or you will get visits from relatives that you haven't heard from in ages. When you head for the casinos, be sure and pick the days that are best suited to your chart for gambling. By all means, do a compatibility between your chart and the clubs to pick the most favorable location for winning results. Your lucky numbers for 1995 are 216 and 9. Your luckiest day of the year is March 31. Other beneficial dates are February 20, April 26, June 13, July 2, October 28, November 22, and December 4. Your lucky period is from October 30 to December 15. Your bad luck day is April 25.

CANCER June 21 – July 22

Cancers love to gamble, but the major problem is getting the money out of their claws so it can be put down on a wager. Most crabs squeeze a nickel so hard the Indian is riding the buffalo. Cancers can be lucky this year, but still will want to know if the fix is in. They will be thinking "Can I fix it, or is there some way to fudge on the score?" Don't let a Cancer keep score if they bet on the game. They will even try to cash in tickets twice. Cancer's best gambles are in the stock market, however you should stick with old established companies, including government bonds. The dividends are not great, but they are steady.

Mind games will be the challenge you need, even to the extent of trying to outsmart a machine, including all of the electronic machines you find in a casino, as well as keno and lottery games. Chess and bridge are the type of games that offer a challenge, but how much can you win at this type of enterprise? Bobby Fisher put chess in the spotlight, and every newspaper has a bridge column, so money can be made in these areas. Your motto is: "I want things my way." That is why you want to dominate or control any speculation or game of chance with which you get involved. Your real luck comes from how you serve others, and this area should be pursued vigorously. Other areas you should pursue are the occult and philosophy. The more you broaden your insight here, the more you are prepared to handle the future. This insight will help fatten your pocketbook and can help you tune into the psyche of the general

public. This is especially helpful in stock market speculation and also when you head for the casinos. Since
you are a water sign, riverboat casinos would be more
to your liking, but please don't jump overboard if you
lose a few bucks.

Your lucky numbers for the year are 346, 13 and 4.
Your luckiest day of the year is August 27, and the other
fortunate days are April 13, June 5, October 25,
November 4, 16 and December 1. The period of March 8
to April 4 is your lucky month. Go for it and drop a few
bucks once in awhile.

LEO July 22 – August 23

Leo is the sign of the zodiac that rules gambling,
however, the lions can only wish that was the case this
year. It looks as if your partners will be the real winners.
If you feel like things are not going your way, then bet
what they bet, and you will have a jingle in your pocket.
One bug-a-boo is that Leos can fall on hard times in the
love department, and clandestine affairs will get some
unwanted publicity.

Your real luck will be in your career—or it can be
your biggest problem due to lack of attention. Will the
gamble on a secret amour be worth the chance that it
can back-fire? Being forewarned can save you a lot of
difficulty! (This will turn around drastically in 1996.)
Leos have a tendency to wager on emotion rather than
logic, which isn't bad if it's true inspiration. By doing
some solid research before venturing into new and
uncharted areas, you will ensure that your rewards will
be more abundant.

A little research into what type of gambling you
did in your past life will help—if you can go back that
far. Your inclination not to believe in your own ideas
will let too many winning numbers, horses, and sports
teams slip right by you. Shame! If you don't believe in
yourself, then how can you convince others? Some safe
bets for you are real estate, mining stocks, solid objects
from under the ground (minerals, precious metals,
plants/crops, etc.), mail order enterprises, patent medi-
cines, and home video companies. Games of chance that
are up your alley are hockey, boat races, fishing con-

372

tests, the newest game in town, and, of course, riverboat gambling. Lions will be privy to inside information this year, which can make you a sure winner. However, remember that the government frowns on this practice. You will get some sudden unique inspirational ideas at times this year, but can you find anybody to listen to them? Unlikely, since they will be totally out of character for you. Console yourself by thinking of all those winning systems they will miss out on for not believing in the roar of the lion.

Your lucky numbers for 1995 are 91, 10, and 1. Your best day of the year is August 23, and your other favorable days are January 23, February 15, 27, September 6, October 29, November 13, and 18. Your two unfavorable days are March 3 and May 12. Your lucky month is June 23 to July 19. Think lucky!

VIRGO August 22 – September 23

Virgo is one of the three signs (the others are Libra and Capricorn) that will be natural gamblers this year. However, you might lack the enthusiasm to get involved and a lot of winning opportunities could be wasted. Why not hand your good luck over to others who are struggling to be winners? You will be lucky in business ventures, and that seems to be where you are applying your energies. Go for it, but expect slow payoffs as your clients will be tight-fisted.

This is not a year to gamble on major purchases since they could become very friendly with the repairman and you could feel as if he owns them. Check below for your lucky days before acquiring anything major. If you are interested in the stock market, check out the airlines, truck manufacturers, RVs, railroads, telecommunications, the space program, and foreign stocks. Horse racing will be your forté this year, with auto racing, roller hockey, game fishing, and the Olympic sports running a close second. When you go to the track it will seem as if the horses are talking to you, psychically-speaking though, since there are no "Mr. Eds" out there.

Virgoans will seem to lack that natural fire and will run into periods of skepticism, pessimism and depression, especially when discouraging news is received. Using other people's research can save you a lot of time, effort, and energy—and of course, if anything goes wrong, you can blame them. Since horse racing is your bag, remember all of the large casinos have the horse book and you can watch all of the tracks in the country on their monitors. If a casino or track is too far away, there is always the neighborhood bookie. Virgo's will make their own luck in 1995. When you finally take the plunge into a project, the rewards can be plentiful. (That includes life, love, business, speculation, and high-rolling it.)

Your lucky numbers for the year are 250, 25, and 7. Your luckiest day of the year is February 23 and the other extra-good days are March 17, July 17, August 1, October 1, November 1, 11, and 18. The period of December 3 to January 3, 1996 will be your favorable month. March 1 and May 9 are the unlucky days, repeats Aries, and people born May 9 will cause problems for you. Think lucky!

LIBRA September 23 – October 23

You are one of the natural gamblers in 1995, and will want everyone to know of your good luck, to the extent of flaunting it. You will have a way of irritating your colleagues though, and soon will be unable to find an audience to listen to your boasts. Libras will want to be center stage with a lot of pizazz around them, but so much bragging can make loners of you, as others will want to be out of earshot. There are times that you just have to cool it as too much talk can even bring violence toward you. Are they after your winnings? Your pocketbook will need some healing during the next several years, and speculation is one way it can be fattened. One place extra caution has to be exercised is gambling to not have children or you could be in for a rude awakening. Winning strategies are in your grasp if you pay attention. The strange thing about this technique is that it combines research, logic, and intuition, and if any part is left out you are doomed to failure.

Real estate seems to be a good investment; that is, until you start making the payments. Go for the outdoor

door sports, especially visits to the track, since your strong point lies here. That little bug in your ear will clue you in to the long shots, daily doubles, etc. Don't overlook the extra large pot in the lotteries.

Your lucky numbers for the year are 245, 11, 2. The top day of the year is March 4, with other lucky days being April 29, July 11, 28, November 4, 6, 10, and 18. Your lucky month is from November 28 to December 30. Your bad days are February 27, May 9, and July 16.

SCORPIO October 23 – November 22

This is going to be a very interesting year for Scorpios even though you will feel it is a sluggish and tough year. It depends which end of the glass you look through. Plenty of new responsibilities will come your way, and this means you will have to reevaluate old obligations. By being sober and practical, efficiency will set in making everything easier to handle.

How does this affect gambling? It means a complete overhauling of your methods and philosophy about gambling, that is if you want to finish with more money than you started. Scorpios need to personally get involved in any risks, speculations, or gambles they take on. By using your natural resources you can con—or persuade—your friends and opponents to be on the loosing end of the stick.

What kind of games of chance does this entail? First, do not let your cronies (this includes your spouse) in on your plans or they will spill the beans and blow the deal. Poker and all card games are at the top of the list (be sure to bring your deadpan face along), followed by golf, personal competition, and side bets. Use caution

with scams that bend the law, or you may be betting with a judge as to the length of your time in jail. Scorpios sure have had problems in the romance department for the last several years, and 1995 doesn't seem to be much of an improvement. Hold off until next year before jumping into new situations. There will be unexpected opportunities to put down some bets, maybe a joint venture with a friend.

Your lucky numbers are 33 and 6. Your super lucky day is July 28, with other lucky days being June 6, September 14, November 8 through 12, December 12, and 31. Your lucky month runs from April 24 to May 18, with the exception of May 6, which is particularly unfortunate. Other unfavorable days are February 2 and August 3.

SAGITTARIUS November 22 - December 21

Occasionally a time comes along in a person's life that can be a real turning point, and 1995 is it for Sag. Two periods seem to stand out; the end of January and the middle of December. The real gamble is to rise to new heights in your career/success and to go beyond your goals. However, about 95 per cent of Sagittarians will either overlook or ignore this fantastic opportunity. Sag has to unravel things and 1995 is a year of sudden reversals. Being prepared makes your existence a lot easier.

Your sign seems to be the patron saint of horse racing, and this is the year to collect your dues. Your best success comes with group activity; so do your research and betting with the gang and you may have to rent an armored car to bring home the loot. Remember, you can bet in the casinos as well as off-track betting. A good example is the Los Angeles chapter of NCGR which is involved in horse racing and sports gambling using astrology (with very good results we might add). There will be several books out in the near future with the results of this research.

Anything that has to do with group or organizational activities will be very lucky for Sag and the sooner you get involved, the sooner your pocketbook will start to fatten up. With Jupiter passing through your sign, how can you fail? Since Jupiter likes to run with the big boys, though don't go beyond your limits or you will paint yourself into a corner.

Sagittarius has a great awareness potential this year and the more you gamble on knowledge, spirituality, and expansion, the more financial success will be assured. By the way, that group activity includes getting the gang together to purchase a block of lottery tickets or getting a collection of people together for a trip to the gambling meccas. That's right, Jupiter rules travel.

Your lucky numbers for 1995 are 39, 12, and 3. The best day of the year for you is August 5, with other lucky days being January 5, July 9, September 18, October 26, November 6, 19, 21, and December 18. Your lucky month is from April 30 to May 24. Your unlucky days are February 24, May 5, and August 17.

CAPRICORN December 21 – January 20

Capricorn is the third of the signs that are natural gamblers for the year. However, you are probably the worst risk takers of the zodiac. You are the type who, when you go to the track, watch to see which horse won the race and then run over to place your bet. In other words, you only like to bet on sure winners. 1995 will be the year that goats will say, "Money will solve all of my problems," but the world doesn't operate that way. In fact, your mouth can get you into hot water this year and put you on the losing end of lawsuits. This can't be looked on as a good gamble.

Capricorns can be very creative this year, and your energies should be applied in this area because there can be some marvelous payoffs. Believe in yourself! Your best success will come from ventures you can do at home, and since the gambling channel is not in operation yet, you will have to settle for games already in existence. Why not invite the gang over for a poker party? Since you have a rabbit's foot in your pocket, you won't have to use the marked cards. What other games can be played at home? How about bridge, computer games, croquet, scrabble and all games that come over your TV? Stick to one-on-one bets with an opponent, but use jelly beans so that no money is on the table. If you do go out, at least do your homework first so you are completely prepared when you get to your gambling destination. Wear crystals for luck!

Social affairs highlight the year, with an occasional romantic fling thrown in to liven up the proceedings. Is this a good gamble? Yes, if you don't carry it too far. Otherwise you will get nailed with some extra responsibilities. This year is the time for Caps to stir things up and create some excitement, so take a flyer on yourself and adventure.

Your lucky numbers for 1995 are 269, 17, and 8. The luckiest day of the year is April 3, followed by August 8, 10, 21 25, September 20, November 5, 8, and 25. Your lucky month is from December 21, 1994 to January 20, 1995. The unlucky dates are February 27, May 3, and August 25. Think lucky!

AQUARIUS January 20 – February 18

Water bearers, considered by many to be the odd-balls of the zodiac, look for gambles that are unique, different, novel, challenging, and even bizarre. What you will be looking for this year is mental or thinking games, two-handed games, auto racing, or whatever is the new game in town. Pressure on you to perform at work will cause relationship problems, and this will take away from fun-and-games time. Your gambling will have to be squeezed in between work and carrying out personal obligations, thus putting a damper on your humor.

Aquarians will be seeking quickies when it comes to gambling, but will rely too much on the advice of others. You have good aspects to your payoff house and using your own ingenious inspirations and ideas will bring more creative rewards. If you keep your ears open and are a good listener, inside information will flow your way, including everything from stock market to sports betting methods. Your best bet here is to keep mum and then use this knowledge to the best advantage.

Take a gamble on career matters, because under the right conditions you can go all the way to the top. One thing to remember along the way is to be careful how you treat your peers, because the door to your skeleton closet is open and they could let the cat out of the bag.

Aquarians will be on the prowl this year, and will irritate the daylights out of their steadies or partners, potentially leading to permanent separations. Don't be too blunt.

If you have the time, take a flyer on hobbies as they could become future careers; however, watch the sticky fingers because being a pickpocket is not one of them.

Your lucky numbers for the year are 70 and 7. Your lucky days are January 31, February 15, September 7, 18, (the best of the year) 20, November 3, 23, December 1, and 6. The best month is from June 12 to July 5. The unlucky days are March 1, May 1, and August 24.

PISCES February 18 – March 20

Fish should not believe it when people call you airheads or space cadets because you are on the verge of developing a "hard as nails" personality. Before you do, you will have a tendency to scatter energies forty ways to Sunday, but this is what is needed to bring about the hardening.

When it comes to gambling, Pisces will feel very lucky, causing overconfidence to set in, and this can raise the devil with your prosperity. Money pressures will also cause you to take foolish gambles, which could drive you even further into debt.

Old established forms of gambling with a New Age twist will be your strong point in 1995, including such casino games as keno, poker, blackjack, horse racing on computers, and push-button slot machines (no handles please). Speculations on real estate, mining stocks, precious and semi-precious stones and anything solid that comes from under ground will prove profitable.

Also, gambles with words can be productive, providing you are not too much of a reformer, otherwise a few enemies can be made along the way. Weird happenings on the home front could create a strong need to keep your emotions under wraps. If you don't, you could wind up with a flat nose—and let me tell you, that smarts.

Your imagination is in full swing during the year, but if you are not careful your ideas could be ripped off by people you trust. If you play your cards right your brainstorms can pay off handsomely, providing you get patents or copyrights where they are needed.

One risk that will not pay off this year is informing your boss of his/her shortcomings or your real opinion of him or her; that is if you don't want to be checking out a new career.

Your lucky numbers this year are 326, 11, and 2. The fish's best day of the year for the fish is May 31, with lucky days being January 7, September 19, October 9, 17, 25, November 2, 23, and December 5. Your lucky month is February 15 to March 15. Negative days are March 5, April 31, and August 14.

And the Race is On . . .
Joyce C. Wehrman

Picking the winners in horse racing is just as challenging as any other form of gambling. Racing fans often are influenced by the horses' names, and play those hunches. Here are names to look for depending upon the sign that is rising at post time.*

Aries: Names that reflect speed, aggression, early things, soldiers, fire, heads of things, tops, the color red, fighting, daring.

Taurus: Names that reflect stability, stubbornness, art, sweets, banking, money, beauty, investments, bulls, food, music, possessions, reliability, fixity.

Gemini: Names that reflect duality, double names, mentality, writing, travel, communication, books, nicknames, small things, mail, relatives, roads, running, neighbors.

Cancer: Names that reflect home, mother, women, the Moon, domesticity, silver, food, saving, water, families, nurturing, the past, reflections, daily things.

Leo: Names that reflect royalty, gold, importance, pride, high office, authority, the heart, entertainment, crowns, showy things, fire, love, fun, pleasure, sports, the Sun.

Virgo: Names that reflect small things, work, routine, criticism, furnishings, clothing, perfection, aunts and uncles, service, detail, crafts, health, food, animals, math, initials.

Libra: Names that reflect beauty, princes and princesses, society, art, happiness, love, flowers, dancing, fancy things, music, companionship, harmony, balance, girls' names.

Scorpio: Names that reflect depth, sex, regeneration, long-term things, groups, coercion, gangs, the underworld, money, death, searching, magic, eagles.

Sagittarius: Names that reflect travel, pholosophy,

* Excerpt adapted from "On the Fast Track" by Joyce C. Wehrman in *Llewellyn's 1985 Astrological Guide to California*, reprinted by permission from *Winning Zodiacal Timing*.

religion, foreign names, luck, mental things, abundance, carefree optimism, advertising, loyalty, joy, games, and far-reaching things.

Capricorn: Names that reflect responsibility, authority, organization, practicality, methodicalness, caution, class, age, quality, government, rank, time, age, father, proper names and the law.

Aquarius: Names that reflect originality, eccentricity, the unusual, friends, goals, wind, progressiveness, science, arguments, electricity, and unusual names.

Pisces: Names that reflect flying, jets, mists, fog, dreams, sympathy, imagination, sensitivity, art, music, liquids, photography, prison, shipping, the sea, oil, liquor, spies, and silence.

Some of the better days to go to the races (and bet) are when the Moon is in your Sun sign, or the sign directly following it, or when the Moon is trine to your Sun Sign. Find your Sun sign in the list below:

Aries:	Moon in Aries, Taurus, Leo, or Sagittarius
Taurus:	Moon in Taurus, Gemini, Virgo, or Capricorn
Gemini:	Moon in Gemini, Cancer, Libra, or Aquarius
Cancer:	Moon in Cancer, Leo, Scorpio, or Pisces
Leo:	Moon in Leo, Virgo, Sagittarius, or Aries
Virgo:	Moon in Virgo, Libra, Capricorn, or Taurus
Libra:	Moon in Libra, Scoprio, Aquarius, or Gemini
Scorpio:	Moon in Scorpio, Sagittarius, Capricorn, Aries, or Leo
Sagittarius:	Moon in Sagittarius, Capricorn, Aries, or Leo
Capricorn:	Moon in Capricorn, Aquarius, Taurus, or Virgo
Aquarius:	Moon in Aquarius, Pisces, Gemini, or Libra
Pisces:	Moon in Pisces, Aries, Cancer, or Scorpio

Why Astrology Works

Jackie Cavalero Slevin

Since prehistoric times, humankind has attempted to fathom its earthly experience. The first gesture toward this understanding may well have been a cave dweller lifting his or her eyes toward the heavens in wonder and speculation of forthcoming events. The sky could tell stories. It held omens. It foretold weather conditions which in turn affected travel, hunting, and agriculture. Daylight and darkness was measured by the rise and fall of those two majestic objects, the Sun and the Moon. The ancients used the sky as their blueprint for action. The so-called "Wise People" were those who made a thorough study of the patterns of planets and stars, and observed how to use them as signposts. Observations were made regarding how Mother Nature mirrored events in the heavens. Shellfish activity and the rhythms of the tides coincided with phases of the Moon. Seafaring peoples, lacking compasses, used the North Star and other constellations for navigation. The Egyptians repeatedly observed that the Nile flooded every time the star Sirius rose with the Sun. The clockwork that the ancients observed in the sky shaped and defined their annual calendars. This time-honored system of celestial phenomenon worked.

But how did it work? What was the direct correlation between earth and sky? If astronomy was the study of planets and stars, then astrology falls under the definition given to it by transcendentalist Ralph Waldo Emerson. It is "astronomy applied to the affairs of men."

British astronomer Percy Seymour has written a startling book entitled *Astrology, the Evidence of Science*, which states that certain predictions made from horoscopes can be explained logically and tested scientifically. He has wagered his professional standing by espousing such a theory, and has endured much criticism as a result. The science of astrology is no stranger to intolerant criticism and has been often considered a laughing matter. Robert Hand, astrologer, author, and president of Astrolabe, Inc., a company that develops computer software for astrology, claims that "The way the media deal with astrology is to put on the laugh track."[1]

Seymour has earned master's and doctoral degrees in astrophysics and has served as senior lecturer at the Royal Observatory in Greenwich, England. He is currently principal lecturer in astronomy at the Plymouth Polytechnic Institute in southwest England, and director of the planetarium there. "Of course I expected people to take objection to my theory," Seymour concedes, "but I didn't expect the reaction to be so vehement or irrational. Some of my colleagues here at the Polytechnic and at the Royal Astronomical Society simply dismiss the idea without reading the book or even looking at the evidence. Meanwhile, many other scientists, even respected scientists, have evoked the cosmos—in theories that are a little short of bizarre—to explain the extinction of the dinosaurs, or what have you. That's all right. But propose a theory about astrology and people assume you're mad."[2]

Seymour himself looked askance at astrology until 1984 when a BBC crew interviewed him briefly on his opinion of astrology. His reply, which was standard on the question, was that he "knew of evidence to support certain aspects of it, but that I personally could not think of any mechanism to explain how the planets, the sun, and the moon might affect human life."[3]

The media can now cut the laugh track. Seymour began to seriously rethink his pat answer to this perpetual question and discovered the mechanism that could serve as the missing link between the cosmos and humans.

Seymour's theory of astrology is plain and simple: ". . . astrology is not mystical or magical but magnetic. It

1   Patricia King, *Newsweek*, January 15,1990.
2   Sobel, Dava, "Dr. Zodiac," *Omni*, December, 1989, pp. 63-64.
3   Ibid., p.64.

can be explained," he says, "by the tumultuous activity of the sun, churned to a lather by the motions of the planets, borne earthward on the solar wind, and perceived by us via the earth's magnetic field while we grow inside our mothers' wombs."[4]

The initial evidence of the validity of astrology that Seymour embraced was the work of Michel Gauquelin, a French psychologist/statistician, whose rigorous method of testing astrology was to show that the placement of the planets in the horoscope is more conclusive overall than the actual Sun sign. In other words, the components are more important than the sum of their parts. In 1951, armed with the birth data of 576 French doctors who were elected to the Academie de Medecine, Gauquelin made significant headway in his research. "Having (painfully) worked out by hand the position of the planets at the hour of birth of each doctor, I made a statistical compilation of my findings. Suddenly, I was presented with an extraordinary fact. My doctors were not born under the same skies as the common run of humanity. They had chosen to come into the world much more often during roughly the two hours following the rise and culmination of two planets, Mars and Saturn. Moreover, they tended to 'avoid' being born following the rise and culmination of the planet Jupiter. After such a long and fruitless search, here I was, confronted with not one, but three astonishing results—all from observing the daily movement of the planets."[5]

Gauquelin tested this new method further by subjecting to the same scrutiny the charts of 508 doctors who had not yet been elected to the Academie de Medecine. "I calculated the positions of Mars and Saturn. Once again, my doctors 'chose' the rise and culmination of these planets for coming into the world. Once again, they 'avoided' being born when Jupiter was moving through this sector of the sky."[6] The sector Gauquelin is specifically referring to is the quadrant of the horoscope which extends from the 10th through the 12th House.

---

4   Ibid.
5   Michel Gauquelin, *Birthtimes*, Hill and Wang, New York, 1983, p. 21.
6   Ibid.,p. 26.

Gauquelin's discovery led to more research on yet another theory of "planetary heredity," a point which bears resemblance to Seymour's theory that astrology is ". . . perceived by us via the earth's magnetic field while we grow inside our mother's wombs." Sixteen years and over 30,000 charts later, Gauquelin published his results in the book *L'Heredite Planetaire:* "Children have a tendency to be born when a planet has just risen or culminated, if that same planet was in the same regions of the sky at the birth of their parents. Certainly, it is not a very pronounced tendency; yet bearing in mind the great number of births examined, the probability that chance should have produced so many planetary similarities from one generation to the next falls less than a million to one."

Thus, Gauquelin refuted Kepler who, in 1598, tried to convince others of his own theory of astral heredity: "Behold the kinships of births. You have a conjunction Sun-Mercury, so has your son; you both have Mercury behind the Sun. You have a trine from Saturn to the Moon, he has almost a Moon-Saturn sextile. Your Venus and his are in opposition . . ."[8] Kepler could only put forth simplistic propositions because he lacked access to the thousands of birth times that Gauquelin was able to procure.

In discovering his mechanism to explain how the planets, the Sun, and the Moon might affect human life, Seymour claims that Gauquelin's results on planetary heredity "are the most important of all his findings, as far as my theory is concerned. This is because they are based on objectively measurable quantities, like planetary positions and birth times, as opposed to personality traits. They also indicate quite clearly that a physical agency is involved . . . I knew that Gauquelin found the effects he saw to be exaggerated on days with lots of magnetic disturbance, and that seemed very important to me, so I got cracking on it."[9]

Magnetic disturbances are the key to proving the ancient axiom "as above, so below" for disturbance cre-

7   Ibid., p.43.
8   Ibid., p. 39.
9   Sobel, Dava, "Dr. Zodiac," *Omni*, December 1989, p. 66.

ates perceptible action, which, in turn, can be observed and analyzed. After all, Seymour's theory of how astrology works is based on magnetism. The way a womb might perceive magnetic stimulus is through its nervous system. In the same way that a baby resembles its parents in terms of physical characteristics, so its magnetic antennae is similarly wired, and resonates to the mother and/or father's same magnetic frequencies. Seymour reminds us that the very earth itself is a magnet, surrounded by a magnetic field that is 20 to 30 times larger than the actual planet. Therefore, magnetic attractions, or "disturbances," are keenly absorbed. When a baby is ready to be born, it is a magnetic signal from a planet, received by the nervous antennae in the mother's womb, that triggers the actual moment of birth. "Astrology . . . has put the cart before the horse by crediting the planets with the power to predict personality. For Seymour feels certain it is the genes that set the personality on course, and the genes that determine which planetary signal will herald the individual's birth. Astrology merely labels what nature has already ordained, but the effect that astrology describes are not trivial by any means, nor are they limited to the first moments of life."[10]

What is curious about Seymour's theory of magnetism is that, although he fully acknowledges sunspots, solar prominences, solar flares, and solar winds, he never once mentions the work of the patriarch of sunspot research, John H. Nelson. An amateur astronomer since boyhood and radio operator for RCA Communications, Nelson pioneered solar research and forecasting through over 25 years of rigorous experimentation. In 1946 he was given the title "Short-wave Radio Propagation Analyst," and began a course of scientific observation, the results of which ended in unexpected controversy. "We have come to realize that the Sun is doing something to the planets, or the planets are doing something to the Sun that the presently recognized laws of science cannot explain. Though sunspots

10   Ibid., p. 68.

have never been completely understood, I found, through careful observation, that they are predictable. Why the predictions come true is not readily apparent. When future amateurs or scientists find a scientific explanation for what is taking place in the solar system, on the Sun, and in the ionosphere of the Earth, we can take the subject out of the occult and assign it a scientific basis. I am confident this will be done someday."[11]

The Chinese have been recording sunspots since ancient times, but it was Renaissance scientist Galileo Galilei who, after viewing them with his homemade telescope, reported them to scholars in sixteenth century Italy. Scholars at this time were connected to the Catholic Church, whose strict dogmas did not allow for much free thinking. The Church doctrine on the Sun and planets was based on Aristotle, who stated that the Sun was perfect and free of any blemishes whatsoever. After repeatedly insisting that the Sun did show black spots on its surface periodically, Galileo incurred such fundamentalist wrath he was informed that, unless he rescinded his radical statement, he would be punished by torture. Following exasperation and anguish, Galileo finally retracted his statement, but is said to have muttered under his breath immediately afterwards, "but I did see them."[12]

Nelson then doggedly pursued his method of experimentation. RCA constructed a solar map on which Nelson could record sunspots, after observing them with a telescope, just as Galileo did. With this map he was able to make drawings of the sunspots and place them in their proper position on the Sun. At first, research with these maps confirmed that radio frequency requirements would vary according to the number of spots from week to week, and even in some cases day to day. It was also discovered that some types of spots had more influence than others. This information enabled Nelson to develop a system of forecasting frequency changing times on a day to day basis. "This added to

---

11 John H. Nelson, *The Propagation Wizard's Handbook*, 73 Inc., Peterborough, NH 1978, p. viii.

12 Ibid., p. 7.

our efficiency in the handling of messages, because less time would be lost during what are known as 'frequency transition periods.' During normal conditions, it would be about two hours earlier and, during above normal conditions it could be about two hours later. Knowing ahead of time when to change was of value in both the saving of time and the saving of power.

"Getting to understand sunspots in relation to good and bad signals was much more difficult. I mapped and analyzed sunspots for about a year before I dared to try my hand at forecasting what they were going to do to the signals. Progress was made, however, during the winter of 1947–48 when I fastened a solar map on a drawing board and recorded the position of all sunspots each day that the signals were in trouble. After a few months, this map became covered with sunspots but distinctly showed a concentration of spots in one particular area of the sun's surface. This indicated to me that spots in this area were the ones causing our troubles."[13]

What yet proved to be intriguing was that each spot had its own "personality." Some spots made trouble with radio signal qualities whereas other spots "behaved well." Nelson could find no logical reason for this. What Nelson could pinpoint after years of research was that sunspots operate in a cycle of 11 years and correlated with such events as the Sun conjunct or opposite Jupiter, Venus, Mercury and the earth.

Years after his monumental research had been well established, Nelson decided to find out more about the mysterious subject of astrology. He attended astrological meetings in New York and, afterward, decided to keep away from it, stating that "What I have seen in their books indicates to me that astrology is a very difficult subject and frankly, I have enough to do in my own speciality."[14] After one meeting, two astrologers approached him and asked for his birth data, saying they wanted to make predictions for him. "In my business, predicting magnetic storms, I know I can make

13 Ibid., pp. 20–21.
14 Ibid., p. 84.

predictions either forward or backward in time. If for instance, someone asked me to tell them what magnetic conditions were on September 4, 1918, I could analyze the planetary positions on that day and tell them what it was like with considerable confidence. I reasoned that astrologers should be able to do the same thing with their data."[15] Nelson decided on a retrospective reading, asking each astrologer to tell him what he was doing on a particular date two years prior at 12:30 P.M. EST. Three months later, he received a report from each astrologer with a detailed analysis of the date. "They were both right—in fact embarrassingly accurate. It is beyond my comprehension how they could have done this by simply comparing the position of the planets on the day that I was born with the position of the planets on the day that they analyzed. The astrologers themselves have no logical explanation either. This puts them in the same boat with the astronomers who cannot tell why sunspots change polarity each cycle and change latitude as the cycle changes. And, I find myself in a similar situation because I have no reason for the correlation that I have seen for many years between the position of the planets and the behavior of short-wave radio signals."[16]

Astrology can no longer remain a laughing matter. "A 1988 survey from the National Science Foundation found that 38 percent believed astrology to be 'very scientific' or 'sort of scientific.' Six percent confessed to changing their plans to fit their horoscope . . ."[17] The pioneering work of John H. Nelson and the recent theory of Percy Seymour have modern scientists poised to alter their entire perspective on the celestial mechanics of the universe. If the so-called arcane axiom "as above, so below" can be formulated into a rational, proven scientific theory, then the age-old profession of astrology will have its principles vindicated, and the global population will come to comprehend the words of St. Thomas Aquinas, "The celestial bodies are the cause of all that takes place in the sublunar world."

15 Ibid., p. 85.
16 Ibid., pp. 86–87.
17 Patricia King, *Newsweek*, Jan. 15, 1990.

Pluto Enters Sagittarius:
Three Degrees of Change

Kim Rogers-Gallagher

Pluto's a scary kind of guy. Doesn't matter whether you're a seasoned astrologer, or you dabble just enough to stay away from Void of Course Moons when you're scheduling appointments, either. The very mention of the Dark Dude's name is enough to make even the hardiest in our ranks start tapping nervously. It's perfectly understandable, too. He is, after all, the head of some very unappetizing departments—Death, Destruction, and Decay, for starters. None of which are what you'd call "light" topics. 'Course, he's also in charge of Regeneration, Rejuvenation, and Recycling, but nobody much sticks around to hear that part of it—not after they catch the *first* half of his bio.

No, Pluto isn't for the faint of heart. But he's not a *bad* planet, not at all. He's just doing his job. See, every planet in our wonderful, orderly Universe symbolically represents an urge or a need that we humans all absolutely *must* express, once we sign up for a body. The "inner" or "personal" planets, just as you'd imagine, represent our personal needs—the Sun shows our creative urge, the Moon is all about emotional expression, Mercury rules communication, Venus is head of the Department of Love, Mars is in charge of anger, and Jupiter handles growth. Saturn, as the "cosmic line in the sand," draws a line between reality—what we *can* do—and *un*reality—what we can't do. At least, not yet.

That's where the outer planets come in. They're beyond Saturn—so they're symbolically *beyond* reality. Their "job" is to inspire us to look past what we haven't been able to do yet, to push past what we see as our limitations. They prod us to try to do more than what we already can. Needless to say, they're all very fond of change. In fact, if planets had contracts, Uranus, Neptune, and Pluto would all have a mandatory "make things change" clause built right in.

Much as their mission is the same, they've all got very different techniques—different ways to talk us into trying something new. Uranus represents our urge to rebel, to break the rules, forget tradition, fight City Hall, and do it the way we think it ought to be done. Since you've got to be bold to discover new stuff, Uranus is the head of the Blinded Me With Science Department—in fact, he really does head up the Department of Science and Technology, so any new scientific discoveries have to come across his desk first.

Neptune inspires change, too, but much more quietly than Uranus. She's the head of the Department of Wishing On Stars—she encourages us to forget the tedious rules of reality, to dream and imagine. She whispers to us, makes us feel wistful, nostalgic, and romantic. She's in charge of a generation's attitude toward religion, dreams, and drugs. She shows us what we idolize and worship because we see it as perfect. The divine discontent she induces is inspirational, but it's not radical.

Pluto, however, . . . well, Pluto's a whole different trip. He's not shocking or sudden, like Uranus, or soft and subtle, like Neptune. He's extreme and relentless, an expert at control, manipulation, and persuasion—a big, dark, blast of power. He looks a lot like Darth Vader, of *Star Wars* fame—complete with the cape—and when it comes to change, *his* favorite way of handling it is to do a clean sweep—to trash everything and start over from scratch. That includes the baby, the bath water, and while he's at it, maybe even the house the kid bathed in. Complete and total overhaul—that's his style.

Pluto handles the concept of "Process," too. All processes, in fact, are Plutonian—Birth, Life, Death, and Re-Birth, for example. See, Pluto knows that birth and death are really the same thing—just different stages in the process. Picture a sunflower in full bloom, following the sun across the sky every day. At the end of the summer, the flower "dies," and the bloom droops down. The seeds drop into the ground below, where they rest through the winter, waiting to be "born" again in the spring. When spring comes, the seeds from the flower sprout, and the flower grows again—so the sunflower never really "dies"—its energy just takes on different physical shapes during its cycle. The process *changing shape* and *transforming* is the type of process Pluto rules—and it happens all the time.

Costume Changes—And Fads

Now, signs are like costumes for planets. They put a "flavor" or a "filter" of sorts on a planet's expression. So the sign any planet is currently sporting tells us *how that planet will act* out its needs, and the style of behavior it will use to accomplish its goals. 'Course, planets have favorite signs, and not-so-favorite signs, just like you and me, so some mixes work out more comfortably than others. Outer Planets in signs represent collective mindsets. They point to long-term trends, generational fads, and social customs.

Some fads are good, and funny, even. For example, back in '84, Neptune, the planet in charge of *fluids,* entered Capricorn, the sign that establishes boundaries and creates businesses—and we all began drinking *bottled water.* Neptune also rules artificial things, and the state of *confusion*—her stay in businesslike Capricorn also produced a whole rash of oddities we took seriously. The Condo Craze, for example, and the practice of leasing cars, too—imagine *leasing* the *moveable* object and *buying* the *immovable* one? When Uranus, the planet in charge of shocks and rude awakenings, met up with Neptune, (over 1993), who also handles secrets, a wave of unexpected scandals swept through all our institutions—all kinds of fraudulent behaviors came to light—and since the two came together in Capricorn, the sign that rules politics, corporate businesses, and patriarchies in general, it was our politicians, our sports figures, and even our religious leaders who were exposed.

Needless to say, then, when outer planets change signs, our focus shifts, and it shows, big time. The Universe is trying to make a point. It's time for all of us to change our collective way of thinking, so change happens, all kinds of change. The sign the outer planet slips into tells us which area of human life is about to be overhauled. The *nature* of the planet gives us clues about what type of changes we can expect; and let me tell you, friends and neighbors, when any of the Big Three switch signs, it's never boring. Not even a tiny little bit. It is downright invigorating, however, especially if you happen to be an astrologer. See, we have the edge here, gang. We get to prepare for the changes *before* they arrive, because we can see them coming. Makes you grin just thinking about it, doesn't it?

Pluto in Sagittarius

The reason I've mentioned all this is because Pluto is about to change signs, and I want you to understand what's goin' on. Yes, the old Darth-Man himself will leave Scorpio behind this year, and when he steps out of the dressing room, it'll be in something a little less comfortable—Sagittarius. All of which means we ought to be expecting some very big doin's down here on Planet Three.

Now, don't be scared. Don't. Be excited instead. All this really means is that we're all about to change our collective mindset—again—and you're going to be able to understand it. Any planet going from Scorpio to Sag is bound to be somewhat of a relief, anyway. I don't think I need to tell you that we've been living through some pretty intense times, with Pluto all done up in Scorpio. It's his very favorite sign, you know, his power outfit, a basic black suit with red trim that turns invisible at a moment's notice. Yes, in Scorpio, the sign Pluto rules, he found a perfect channel for his considerable energy.

But First, A Review . . .

When Pluto first hit Scorpio, back in November of '83, after 246 long years away, well, needless to say, he was one happy dude. Can't you just picture him, his dark form all done up in that black suit—at last—catching that first glimpse of himself in a mirror? You can just imagine what he sounded like: *"Yesssssss!!!"* Scorpio is the sign that handles deep human experiences—like passion, intensity, sexuality, intimacy, and death. Stepping into this sign gave Pluto the freedom to conduct business as he saw fit—intensely. With no holds barred. Talk about a good time, huh? *Especially* after operating within the confines of a Smilin' Libra outfit for 13 years, a sign that's very *nice*, of course, but not nearly as *deep* as Scorpio, and certainly not as much fun for Pluto.

Yes, when Pluto crossed over the Scorpio State Line 'way back in November of '83, he came out with both barrels blasting. All the unmentionables were suddenly being mentioned—everywhere. The sexual harassment in the workplace that women had been living with silently for years was suddenly talked about. Child abuse and molestation came out of the closet, too, and children were encouraged to talk about it, and not to take blame for it themselves. The news was full of Plutonian topics just like those—in fact, the media gave most of its attention to Plutonian/Scorpionic subjects for the entire decade. Take a look at some of these topics:

The Right to Die—and "Doctor Death"

The right to die became a major issue, especially after Michigan doctor Jack Kevorkian admitted to assisting terminally-ill patients to commit suicide with the aid of a machine he invented and created himself—from parts he bought at garage sales. (*Recycled* parts, by the way). Shortly after he discussed this publicly, nationwide surveys of physicians and nurses showed that he was not alone, and certainly not the exception to the rule—an amazing percentage of health-care practitioners admitted to deliberately giving their terminally-ill patients prescriptions that could kill them, if they chose to take more than the recommended dosage. Many even conceded to having withheld treatment that might prolong the life of a patient in chronic pain, who had no chance of recovery.

Hospice Care

More and more chronically ill people chose to spend their last hours in their homes, and to die with dignity rather than extend their lives artificially. Hospice care allowed the dying the comfort and emotional security of passing over with friends and family at their side.

Genetic Engineering

Another hot debate was born when scientists realized that they could clone human cells in the laboratory. Genetic engineering raised significant questions about what was "right"—and"wrong"—with playing God—a most Plutonian topic.

Abortion Rights

The abortion battle picked up tremendous momentum, too. Laws regarding abortion and pregnancy counseling were so much on our minds, as a matter of fact, that the very first thing President Clinton did after he took office was to sign an order lifting the "Gag Rule," thereby returning the option of discussing abortion to pregnancy counselors who had been banned from doing so. This issue reached such an intense level that a physician was actually shot and killed outside a woman's health clinic in Florida.

Terrorism

Then there was the wave of terrorism that seemed to be happening just about everywhere. The Ayatollah ordered the death of author Salman Rushdie because he had written a book deemed disrespectful to the Islamic faith—and, by the way, the title of the book, if you can stand this symbolism, was *The Satanic Verses*. At the height of Pluto's passage through Scorpio, terrorism even hit "right here in River City"—a bomb was planted in the International Trade Center in New York City.

AIDS

Pluto's passage through Scorpio also marked the beginning of the AIDS epidemic. As we all know now, AIDS is a fatal disease that's passed along through the exchange of body fluids, and especially during sex. AIDS was isolated and identified on April 23, 1984—just four months after Pluto's arrival into Scorpio. After its method of transmission was made public, sex education became more and more available, and another battle ensued: over whether or not to allow the distribution of condoms in our schools.

Ethnic Cleansing, Drugs, and Gangs

The war in the former Yugoslavia went on and on, and the phrase that came up over and again was Scorpionic, too: ethnic cleansing, a systematic purging of an entire race. We also had to deal with an incredible upswing of violence right here at home, via the gangs that came together in our cities during these years. Drug cartels and war-lords also characterized Pluto's passage through Scorpio.

That's Entertainment . . .

Just in case the news didn't provide enough violence, we made up some more. In fact, what we considered "entertainment" reached an all-time violent high. Movie theatres were filled with films that seemed to be trying to outdo each other in their attempts to shock us. "Action film" became an acronym for movies featuring hundreds of deaths. Attorney General Janet Reno even cracked down on television networks, warning them that if they didn't take action themselves about the amount of violence they aired, she would. Reno's warning came after we realized that television violence had escalated to such a point that by eighth grade, the average child had seen 8,000 murders and 100,000 acts of violence. In short, Pluto's trek through Scorpio opened our collective eyes to just how bad we'd become—just how base humanity as a species could be.

Recycling

Of course, the news wasn't *all* bad—but most of it did get "mixed reviews" all except for the idea of recycling, the most Plutonian topic around. Take something that's "dead" as it is, useless in its present form, and turn it into something else. What a great idea—"rebirth" as applied to plastics, metals, papers, and glass. Recycling became common, the rule rather than the exception—most communities now practice it routinely.

The Envelope, Please . . .

But what was the point of all this? What was Pluto trying to say, exactly? Well, it had come time for humanity as a species to face up to just how "bad" we'd become, time to stop covering up our sins and face the basest side of our natures, time to see the real, no-holds-barred truth. Pluto *transforms*, remember. The whole idea behind his trek through Scorpio was to change our collective attitude about The unmentionable topics—like sex and death. 'Course, to change our attitude, Pluto had to first expose it, and that meant bringing all the garbage up from the depths of the cellar. Still, in a nutshell, gang, Pluto in Scorpio was just cleaning house—taking out the trash. And it's not like we didn't need it.

From Scorpio to Sag . . . Looking at the Future Through the Lens of the Past . . .

So what's going to happen now? Now that we've just about peaked out in badness, now that the Scorpionic purging process is just about over, what's the next step? What can we expect from the next leg of Pluto's journey?

Well, the best way to predict the future is to go back to the past and see what happened the last time this happened—to get a feeling for the "flavor" of the time, and the type of impact the planet made on its last pass. The

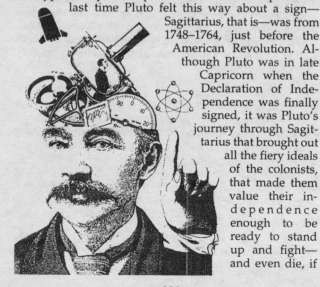

last time Pluto felt this way about a sign—Sagittarius, that is—was from 1748–1764, just before the American Revolution. Although Pluto was in late Capricorn when the Declaration of Independence was finally signed, it was Pluto's journey through Sagittarius that brought out all the fiery ideals of the colonists, that made them value their independence enough to be ready to stand up and fight—and even die, if

398

necessary—for it, for their principles. Remember, this is Jupiter's sign, and Jupiter is an awfully righteous kind of guy, the King of the Gods, the original lawmaker/politician, you might say.

Jupiter is in charge of what you believe in, and he loves to *incorporate*. As Jupiter's agent, then, Sag is *very* interested in organized religions—and the doctrines that hold those religions together. Pluto just loves to raze everything and start all over. So it's not surprising that what was known as "The Great Awakening"came to a fiery close when Pluto was wearing Jupiter's sign. This "great awakening" was a religious revival that began around 1730 in the Colonies, and reached its peak in 1741, when Jonathan Edwards delivered a sermon to his Massachusetts congregation entitled "Sinners in the Hands of an Angry God." At the time he gave that sermon, Pluto was still in All-Or-Nothing Scorpio, "Puritan" was more than just a term meaning "outdated attitude," and folks here in the Colonies were in the process of re-vamping their attitudes about sexuality for the very first time.

Just two years after Pluto entered Sagittarius, however, the colonists were tired of hearing about how sinful they were. In 1750, Reverend Edwards was asked to resign from his position by "liberal members of his congregation who opposed his emphasis on the sinful nature of mankind."[1] Sag is the most "liberal" sign around, and was certainly the technology that inspired these members of Edwards' parish to demand that he step down.

Sagittarius is also famous for just loving to learn. It's the sign that rules higher education—colleges and universities in particular. Pluto in Sag "birthed" several colleges from 1748-1756, not the least of which was Princeton, who awarded its first degrees in 1748. Sag's fondness for absolute freedom is just as well known, and it was also during Pluto's trek through Sag that the inscription for the Liberty Bell was chosen and cast— "Proclaim liberty throughout all the land unto all the inhabitants thereof."

---

1 *What Happened When*, by Gorton Carruth, 1989, Harper & Row.

THAT WAS THEN ... THIS IS NOW ...

Given that our times are very different from the 1700s, what should we expect from Pluto this time around? We've already got a Liberty Bell, and we're a real country, all grown up, with rules and regulations of our very own. Well, that's all true, but Sag's favorite subjects haven't changed any since then, and neither has Pluto's disposition, so let's take a look at each of them and try to imagine how the Dark Dude will re-arrange the furniture once he arrives in Sagittarius.

"Black Humor"

Well, first and foremost, Sag is the clown of the zodiac, the head of the Comic Relief Department. Sag delights in nothing more than laughter, in making light of the situation. So, right from the start, Pluto's entry into Sag will take the edge off the intensity, and make things "feel" a lot lighter around these parts. Putting Pluto in Sagittarian clothes, however, means getting him out of his favorite black suit and dressing him up like a clown, and he's not going to take to that really well. What's going to emerge will be a very dark clown, a lot like Pennywise from Stephen King's *It*, the type of clown that's more like a monster, that scares you and makes you laugh at the same time. The *Nightmare Before Christmas* may have been an early predecessor to what we can expect to see from the entertainment industry.

Now, any type of humor serves a very valuable lesson: it takes all the "bite" out of the stark reality of a situation by making us look at what we're doing and laugh about it. So there's also going to be a big change altogether in what we consider funny, and I'll just bet black humor will make a giant come-back. I mean, picture Pluto laughing—it's kind of scary to think about what might make the Dark Guy grin, isn't it? Monty Python, maybe . . . or Stephen King's rather unusual bent.

Teacher, Philosopher, and Schools in General . . .

But Sagittarius does have a more serious side—it's the sign of the philosopher, too, the sign that's most concerned with the moral of the story, with making sure we learn from all this. Sag is also known for being unbelievably blunt, and Pluto doesn't pull any punches either. Our Sagittarian truths, then, are going to become extremely self-evident when Pluto pulls into town. We'll be delving into the "why's" of everything we do, having deep, penetrating philosophical discussions with strangers on buses. We'll obsess on our opinions, too, with Pluto in already feisty Sag—so expect groups that are already trying to tell you what to do to step up their efforts and become even more persuasive—Pluto always could sell ice-cubes to Eskimos, you know. He's the original salesman. He sees your needs and your weakness, and he knows how to counter your objections by making you feel foolish about voicing them. In short, he's the author of the book on mind control.

As a result, Pluto in Sag will completely change not just our questions, but the answers, too, by doing a major overhaul on our colleges and university systems. Sag wants to know *why*, and as we saw with our trip back to the 1700s, it's very closely tied to colleges and universities—places where we go to get some answers. So first of all, we'll probably see changes in the requirements for a degree. I mean, Sag is fire, so it just loves to cut to the chase—many of the courses that are required by colleges for degrees are useless to the student, since they have absolutely *nothing* to do with the degree itself. What's a chemistry class going to do for an English major who wants to be a writing professor? With Pluto in Sag, then, *unnecessary educational excesses* like those will be cut back—and that may actually make the amount of time spent in school shorter.

The earth changes we've had to learn to live with have also produced a need for new careers—and that means that we'll soon see the need for all new courses to be offered, too, to prepare students for what they'll be doing in this brand-new work force. Recycling, for example, has expanded so dramatically over Pluto's Scorpio stay we're actually *short* of people to fill the demand for skilled workers and consultants in the field.

But it's all schools that will feel the effects of Pluto's transit. Since Pluto does rule crime and violence, it may become standard procedure for schools to send students through metal detectors before they enter. Pluto has a type of x-ray vision, and is the original "detector," after all, and Sag is schooling. The whole concept of education will become more urgent with Pluto's arrival, too, as will the necessity behind learning in order to realize your Sagittarian dreams.

Rules, Rules, Rules . . .

We'll need to re-vamp the laws, too. Sagg is the sign of the lawyer and the politician, and has a lot to do with judges. We're living, right now, with outdated laws, rules that were made for people who don't exist any more. There are blue laws, discriminatory laws, and no laws where there *ought* to be some. At the very least, expect an amendment or two over the next few years. Pluto's passage through Sag will open our eyes to the fact that while we've changed, as a country, and while we've evolved, as citizens, our laws haven't. As we start to realize all this, there'll undoubtedly be major changes in our legal system, too. I'd imagine, what with Sag being as casual a sign as it is, that the changes will be casual, too, that old laws will be made obsolete, that our attitude in general will loosen up considerably.

The Supreme Court may be overhauled, too. Judges may not take their seats for life, but instead be required to take periodic mental acuity tests after they reach a certain age. Several of the judges may leave the bench at this time. Pluto in Sag can certainly be interpreted to mean the end of a judge's career—and a whole new panel of more liberal-minded justices.

Religion

Now, Sag just loves religion. It's a great reason to preach, moralize, and, in general, espouse at length, and Sag is really, really good at all those things. After all,

preaching is really just you talking about how *you* think things ought to go ... in your royal opinion, that is.

I'd expect that modern religions may go the way of Jonathan Edwards, and church leaders may be forced to change church policy on contemporary social issues, too. Outdated practices are already being eliminated on an individual basis by members of each faith. An increasing awareness of overpopulation may force churches to reevaluate their position on birth control, sex education, and pregnancy prevention. *Population excess* is Pluto in Sag, after all—Pluto rules the masses, and Sag is the sign in charge of overdoing it. With Pluto here, we'll have no choice but to pay attention to just how many of us are down here.

Imports and Exports

The trend toward tearing down trade barriers will also continue, and that global economy we've heard so much about will probably become a reality. Sag rules foreigners and far away places, and Pluto won't stand for walls. 'Course, Pluto's also not afraid of a good fight in this arena, so I'll bet the arguments over free trade will escalate before the change finally settles in.

The Problem With Progress ...
Warehouse Syndrome

All growth isn't necessarily good. Some is downright unnecessary, matter of fact, and it falls under the heading of greed, waste, and gluttony. Now, Sag is famous for having a chronic case of grass-is-greener syndrome, for always believing that whatever's over there is probably better than what's here. That "lust," you might say, to try *everything* has given Sag a reputation for never

403

knowing when to quit. That's a wonderful attitude to have about learning, and it's great for exploring and adventuring, too, but it isn't all that great when it's applied to consuming, because it leads to a thirst for bigger, better, and more for less, and *that* takes us to megastores, to chains that Sagittarianly *incorporate*. I'm talking, gang, about the warehouse syndrome that's sprung up like a Plutonian plague of late, the wave of impersonal Cheap-Deals-R-Us shopping that's eaten away a huge chunk of our countryside—and our wage scales, too.

Unfortunately, when stores of that kind arrive, the end result is a lot less forest, a lot more parking lots, and a whole lot of minimum-wage jobs in a town where Joe and Betty are forced to close their corner store after 25 years in business because they can't match the warehouse prices—all so folks could get a good deal on their potato chips. These places also commonly buy goods in an extremely Sagittarian manner—by *importing* products in *mass quantity*. Most of the products are even made by *foreigners*, not all of whom are legally of age to work at all, most of whom work *excessive* hours, and all of whom are paid much less than what they'd make if they were able to work for a smaller company.

Adventure-Travel

Of course, as we just said, all that grass-is-greener syndrome can be great fun if you use it to travel, so expect Pluto in Sag to make boldly going where no person has gone before a very common type of vacation. Cruises will probably be a bit less popular over the next few years. Folks will be looking for *intense adventure*—with a rather rugged edge to it—and that may mean that organizations like Earthwatch and Wildlife Conservation see a huge upswing in the number of people willing to make their vacations working ones. At the very least, we'll be trekking through Nepal, back-packing the Andes, and doing photo-safaris to Kenya. In short, we'll be looking for an adrenalin rush from our travels, for "expeditions" rather than "holidays." So buy your hiking boots now—and don't forget the ice-clamps and the mosquito-nets.

Meet Rosy, Rabbit, and Buzz . . .

'Course, Sag is nothing if not casual . . . After all, it's the only sign that's got a nickname. You sure don't walk around calling formal Capricorn "Cap," do you? Or Scorpio "Scorp"? Not if you want to stay on their Christmas card list, you don't . . . anyway—with Pluto in Sag, just watch what kinds of nicknames we'll come up with for situations. Everybody and everything will have a nickname, a pseudonym, and an alias that's darkly humorous. You can just imagine what this will do for political cartoons, the first of which, by the way, was published in 1754, the *last* time Pluto was in Sag.

Then There's The U.S. Chart . . .

Now, when Pluto gets to 7 or 8 Sagg, he's going to be right on top of what some folks consider to be our Ascendant, and what others consider to be our Descendant. How's that going to affect us? Either way, it's going to change our way of relating to the world. And we can only hope it *doesn't* mean War. Pluto, however, is not world-famous for his patience and tolerance, and frankly, I don't think I'd just *love* to be the President when he arrives—early 1998-ish.

And In Conclusion . . .

So this is it, then. We're on the edge of a giant evolutionary step. Although Pluto will officially leave Scorpio behind on January 17, 1995, he'll have to stop back in from April 21–November 10 (of this same year) to pick up a few things he may have forgotten. After November 10, however, he'll be outta there permanently. His Scorpio costume will be back in the mothballs for another 245 years or so. It's going to be amazing, and the changes will be everywhere. One thing's for sure—Sag is the sign of the Eternal Optimist, with the ability to see the silver lining in every cloud. It's certainly one heck of a lot more laid-back than Scorpio. Whatever changes are en route are necessary—Pluto doesn't deal in maybes, he handles what *must* be done. Keep your eyes open—and your mind, too.

Signs of the Presidents

You're in good company if you were born under the same sign as these leaders of our country:

Aries	♈	Thomas Jefferson, John Tyler
Taurus	♉	James Monroe, James Buchanan, Ulysses S. Grant, Harry Truman
Gemini	♊	John F. Kennedy
Cancer	♋	John Quincy Adams, Calvin Coolidge, Gerald Ford
Leo	♌	Benjamin Harrison, Herbert Hoover, William Clinton
Virgo	♍	William H. Taft, Lyndon Johnson
Libra	♎	Chester Arthur, Dwight Eisenhower, James E. Carter
Scorpio	♏	John Adams, James K. Polk, James Garfield, Theodore Roosevelt
Sagittarius	♐	Zachary Taylor, Martin Van Buren
Capricorn	♑	Millard Fillmore, Andrew Johnson, Woodrow Wilson
Aquarius	♒	William Henry Harrison, Abraham Lincoln, Franklin Roosevelt
Pisces	♓	George Washington, James Madison, Andrew Jackson, Grover Cleveland

New Headliners Close the Millenium

Noel Tyl
(March 1994)

China's horoscope immediately presents a contradiction to western observers. With the Sun in Libra and the Moon in Aquarius, rising at the Ascendant, we see China as a true "People's Republic!" On one hand are the Sun-Moon signs of the true romantic, the humanitarian, loving and affectionate. Conversely, there is Venus in Scorpio squaring the conjunction of Mars and Pluto in the 7th House, an aspect formation so involuted and twisted that it suggests violence. Reinforcing this is the subtle but undeniable measurement of the Aries Point equaling the midpoint of Saturn/Node, a loner position, a serious and secretive appearance; and Saturn in Virgo making no aspect within the horoscope, running away with symbolic potentials!

This picture is going to change, climaxing at midnight on July 1, 1997 when China takes possession of Hong Kong. The shape of this Earth-shaking astrology, the process, plan, and growth, will have begun formation in 1995.

I believe China will make a tremendously important business announcement or deploy a major international promotion program to increase trade and to attract foreign investment, starting off 1995 with a high profile. It is entirely possible that China will have changed leadership; that new, younger leaders with high business/marketing sophistication will have taken over the country's energies, poised for grand leadership in the transition to the 21st century (as its Sun arcs to its Midheaven!), in response as well to unrest among its

people. These developments will have begun May–July 1994, with the leadership changes most likely then, or in October–December 1994. This country-wide shift to capitalism and individualism is a counter-counter revolution of enormous importance and significance for China's next century.

China as a nation is emerging into modern history with an extraordinarily new and different image: the world's largest population and an economy growing at double-digit rates! China exhibited tremendous poise early in 1994 when the nation stood up to the United States on several issues—and won. It was no accident in early 1993 when China made headlines regarding the United States' concern about human rights and trade status, or as an intermediary with North Korea and the nuclear weapons issue. China has a plan of reemergence, of making history, of expanding economically as far as it can, with a philosophy marked by gradualism (Saturn in Virgo, peregrine!).

The research of British astrologer Nicholas Campion (see his *The Book of World Horoscope*, The Aquarian Press: England, 1988) provides us with many national birth dates and times, now catalogued and available for serious testing by Mundane astrologers, i.e., astrologers studying the affairs of nations and history. For example, we know that the Chinese Peoples' Political Consultative Conference opened in Peking on September 21, 1949 and established the Peoples' Republic of China. During the following week, the Conference debated and drew up a new constitution and system of government for China. On September 30,

Mao Tse-Tung was elected Chairman. The process was completed on October 1, 1949 with a massive rally in Peking amid proclamations and broadcasts of national music. Charles Carter, the great English astrologer-scholar, is credited with determining a time of 3:15 in the afternoon in Peking, for the "birth" of Communist China, which time is holding up well with astrologers' study of events for modern China.

China will look past its own New Year to the New Year for the West and market its new capitalist thrust in ways that will startle other nations. Response by foreign investors within the world community will be highest in July 1995. There will be a curious development, probably on October 8 or 9, 1995, which will be financial in strategy but inscrutable or deceptive in long-range significance. I can't help but see the United States misled, perhaps while preoccupied at that time with armed force-support on the Israel-P.L.O. front. I believe the United States and China do not and can not get along. What else will be forming in China's grand plan at that time, as the United States is distracted by its own problems (see below)?

Korea

My prediction in the December 1993 issue of *New Worlds of Mind and Spirit* (Llewellyn; call 1-800-THE-MOON for magazine availability) stated simply, "North Korea has the BOMB!" I cited western conjecture about that status as very strong around "March 12" (actual newsdate focus was March 22). Further projections were made for international strategic positioning between April 16 and 24, 1994, and in the third week of August.

The certainty of this explosive news is based on transiting Pluto (the symbol for Atomic energy) being exactly conjunct Korea's national Ascendant (27 Scorpio 19) and, in the national chart (September 12, 1948, Noon in Pyongyang), Pluto squares the exact midpoint of Sun and Moon (and Mars is exactly conjunct the Mars of the "Atomic Energy" horoscope, December 2, 1942 at 2:25 P.M., Chicago). It is fascinating to see why China is so involved as well since its Midheaven (27 Scorpio 09) is almost precisely the Ascendant of North Korea!

Where will North Korea have gone with all of this nuclear tension throughout 1994 and into 1995? With its collapsing economy, North Korea desperately needs a better market position to be taken seriously in the future. The country knows where China is heading with its long-range grand plan and wants to be right beside its inscrutable ally. These two countries and their combined resources for weaponry and stoic diplomacy are formidable.

North Korea surely will have dominated the news April 14-24, 1994, and throughout the month of May, staying on the safe side of real trouble (they are not yet ready). Then, between August 15 and through December, 1994 (especially October 20–November 1 and the third week of December), this small country will have been "clarified." Their idealized outlook will have been exposed, and the rest of the world will know how to deal with them. In my opinion, they will be very closely allied to the plans being made by China (see above). Look at a map of the Far East: China, then Nationalist China (Taiwan) probably in May 1996 en route to formal annexation of Hong Kong (July 1997) with North Korea in an embrace of power, all facing Japan—with its increasing political and economic disarray (watch March–May 1995 especially)—across the Sea of Japan. The Korean peninsula is of critical importance to whomever wants dominance of the "Japanese Basin."

I do not foresee a clash between North and South Korea. Much will depend on how the world receives North Korean developments in October–November 1994. There is a peacefulness developing in the midst of this conjectural maelstrom late in December 1994. Then, North Korea begins rebuilding its economy, achieving new stature in the world: watch the last week of January 1995, the first weeks of April, and especially the first two weeks of June 1995 for a major development. China will not let North Korea break up its identity. The entire year of 1995 is a tough, tough year for North Korea. Rebuilding efforts will start to produce results in the spring of 1996.

India

The Republic of India (January 26, 1950 at 10:15 A.M. in New Delhi) faces an extraordinary upset, which will have begun and made news probably in July–August 1994, and which we can anticipate a major focus in March 1995, with most conspicuous development probably March 18–19 (SA

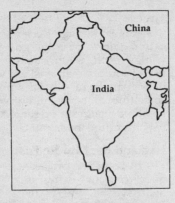

Uranus conjunct Pluto and transiting Saturn conjunct Saturn cycle chart Mercury at the Ascendant in New Delhi; see "Iran" section below for "Cycle Chart" explanation). India likes to stay as it is, to be remote within, unchanging, persisting in a weakened but inscrutably self-rationalized state. This will now become impossible at the brink of the approaching Millennium, the national changes everywhere, and, specifically, with its exploding population and its extreme insecurity on every front, including health, housing, and income per capita. The revolt could very easily be triggered by a health crisis such as tuberculosis or some form of paralysis.

The spring of 1995 is the first phase, probably involving the youth of India, a student force, perhaps, protesting social conditions and the government in power. The students will perhaps block transportation routes and communications networks to dramatize their position. The situation will involve a tremendous upset of the status quo. This will have definite repercussions in November–December 1995.

The next phase of this extraordinary unrest in India will be in the spring and summer of 1996, March through July, when national elections will probably occur. The build-up of a year of protest will reorganize India in ways impossible to predict at this time.

Greece

August through December 1994 will be a period of extreme upset with the government in Greece. There will be revolt, an uprising of the people, with probable use of force. Great tensions will accompany dramatic new goals framed by the populace. Resolution will come through some kind of written document, amendment, or manifesto presented to Greek leaders for the nation's future in May 1995.

Iran and the Middle East

In Iran, we can expect that an outburst against the party in power will have occurred strongly (even with firepower) May 18–21, 1994. This is a beginning of a show of the people's discontent.

The astrology here is most interesting, based on firm rules involving what is called a "cycle chart," drawn for the moment a particular planet enters Northern Declination from the South. In the Mars cycle chart (April 17, 1994 at 8:27 P.M., GMT), we can see that the Sun is almost precisely at the Nadir (fourth cusp) of the chart drawn for Teheran (-3:30 hours), and it is squared by Uranus-Neptune rising (and the Moon is in Cancer in the 7th). When the planet that "owns" the particular cycle chart (in this case, Mars) transits particular planet positions in the cycle chart in real future time, we can expect major occurrences on earth where these planets are placed.

Transiting Mars conjoins the cycle chart Sun in 27 Aries on May 20, 1994, suggesting an uprising against the party in power (the 4th House against the 10th). Public involvement is suggested by the Moon in Cancer in the 7th. Many other measurements then rush into play. The cycle chart stays in force until the next one; the cycle charts for Mars, Jupiter, and Saturn are most revealing in Mundane astrology.

Extending transits from the Mars cycle chart further into the world and into future time, we see Mars conjoining cycle chart Moon in the first week of September 1994 in Dar Es Salaam in Tanzania and in Yemen. Working with the eclipsed Full Moon on April 15, 1995 (12:08 P.M., GMT), we can put Tanzania on revolutionary alert from April 15 through August 1995. A similar alert in the same span of time is registered for Ethiopia, Turkey (an eruption of civil rights issues and the pressures to abandon old ways and join the European Community), Panama, and San Salvador.

Italy

The elections in Italy have been hailed as the burial of the corrupt Fourth Republic (June 10, 1946, at 6:00 P.M. CED, in Rome). Public media tycoon Silvio Berlusconi has won, but he represents a conservative three-party alliance and is not an out-and-out victor. With the bitter, quarrelsome air among his coalition partners, the tensions are not yet resolved. Italy still is in a tremendous period of change, beginning some 10 years ago, with financial double-dealings from top to bottom in its society, reaching an apex four years ago (with SA Neptune upon the Ascendant).

Resolution of the discord depends on who will be named new Prime Minister by Italy's president Oscar Luigi Scalfaro. This will have taken place around April 28, 1994, and will probably be Berlusconi. Between then and August 1994, there will be much wheeling and dealing in Italy's extremely complex political machinery. Another crank of the gears will have taken place November 16–December 15, 1994. The plans that settle things down then among all the factions should be strong in June, late August, and early October 1995. It will take just about that long for the volatile atmosphere to stop smoldering. Just before Christmas 1995, a more mature Italy will emerge, with "post-fascist" voices quieted, with the leader of the right-wing National Alliance, Gianfranco Fini, working well within the coalition. Government policy will be altered with regard to the Mafia: campaign promises to crack down on illegalities and crime will be high on the agenda for the new government.

France

France (The Fifth Republic, October 5, 1958 at 00:00 A.M. in Paris) is flirting again with revolution. The youth are very powerful in France (Moon in Gemini; Mercury conjunct Sun), and early in 1994 students successfully forced the government to drop plans to change the guaranteed minimum wage. It resurrected memories of successful(!) student riots in the past. Astrologically, this was a symptom of a revolt and force in France growing now to adjust the strictures of government, to trade in the old and conventional for the new and more individualistic. Many measurements forming now in 1994 echo those that dominated the French chart in 1968, during that year's student uprising.

In May, June, July, and October 1994, all of this should have become known. New individual perspectives with characteristic French emotionalism will be aimed at reform of the bankrupt social structure of that country.

May 1995 is the target date (when the Solar Arc picture Uranus=Sun/Mars sums it all up): high excitability, sudden impulse and events; forceful adjustment of new circumstances, militarism, overexertion causing a breakdown of efficiency, troubles with authority, etc. There will be demonstrations, government corruption

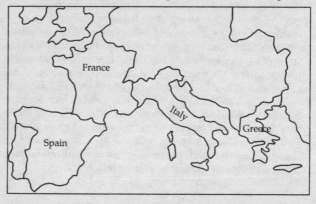

unmasked (how the public has been duped; transiting Neptune on the Descendant), and deceptive tactics run amok. International policies will suffer until all of this settles down. Fuel prices will soar.

France's national elections will take place in May 1995. The laws under consideration will be pivotal in those elections, with the outcome of the elections doubted and mistrusted; there will probably be a rebellious outburst again October 13–16, 1995 (transiting Mars conjunct cycle chart Pluto; see "Iran" above), and it will take one month to be resolved.

Spain

Spain returns to the headlines, this time projecting a modernized national image, beginning late in 1994 and extending for three years of strong, focused development. The changes could affect the very organization of the government, the king/parliament alliance.

Spain needs to "catch up," to the rest of Europe. Franco's revolutionary regime rescued Spain from medievalism; Juan Carlos' restoration of monarchy and parliamentary democracy rescued Spain from dictatorship. Now, the Spanish chart's Saturn-Uranus square (November 22, 1975, 12:45 P.M., Madrid) presses again: get into the world market, catch up with the plans being made by the rest of Europe, regain the glory of their Olympic prominence in 1992.

A new national goal and projection of image should formulate itself strongly around October 1994 (SA Jupiter Opposed Uranus; transiting Pluto conjunct the Sun) and then gain structured development prominently in late April and/or July 1995 with major recognition to the people and their voice, to international commerce, and to major housing starts domestically. September 1995 is another key time in these developments, with a grand thrust to culminate throughout 1996 and into January 1997. I would suggest that major change "at the top" is indicated, a shift in the Spanish king's position.

These developments in Spain do not appear bellicose. There is a calm prevailing throughout the country, but the scope of change is undeniable.

Mexico

When Mexico's leading presidential candidate was assassinated on March 23, 1994, Mexico showed its national profile at its most distressed in 60 years. The chart of the Mexican Constitution appears to be valid for January 31, 1917 at 4:05 P.M., LMT in Queretaro, Mexico. March 1994 shows Solar Arc Saturn opposed the Midheaven, SA Midheaven conjoining Pluto, SA Neptune square the Ascendant, and transiting Uranus opposed Saturn—a very difficult position, with total reform on the horizon.

I do not see clear progress out of the reorganization confusion until early 1995: perhaps on January 16 or 17, major plans will be made public, a New Year, a new regime, a new projection into a better future. Education will be an extremely important tool to improve the Mexican people's standard of living. Mexico will resurrect a most dramatic national pride. There will be firepower pockets of revolt in May–June 1995, and in June and/or August 1995, the worst time of all during the conflict, with all the revolutionaries put down. There will be every effort then to put aside militarism as a form of government, and peace will soon prevail.

Israel and the P.L.O.

Every prediction I've made in these pages and in Llewellyn's bi-monthly *New Worlds* magazine about Israel and its interaction with the P.L.O. has come to pass. In *New Worlds* (June–July 1994), I will have explained and presented a profile of violence based on 20 years of research through the reliability of the Israel chart (May 14, 1948 at 4:00 P.M., EET in Tel Aviv). Those dates throughout 1994 were around February 25 (the Hebron massacre occurred), March 4, May 14, June 24, July 17, August 21–30, October 27–November 9, and December 1–4. These are times of extreme vulnerability to violent eruption.

I hesitate to project these times into 1995 because of the extreme nature of the activities that will have closed 1994. For Israel, the civil turmoil among its own people objecting to government liaison with the P.L.O. and the fight against the civil dissidents on the P.L.O. side of all issues is a threatening specter in June 1994 and, finally, in December 1994. From November 18 through December 1994, the fighting is at its worst.

A major proclamation by Israel will probably be made between January 14–28 1995. This should be a major pronouncement of Israel's new position in the Middle East chaos, after the dust has settled: it will involve an enduring pact with the P.L.O., the emergence of peaceful accords with Syria, and all the internecine violence that plagues every step of development.

Still another cloud arises around March 15, 1995, but again Israel's might will prevail and stabilize in May at its 45th birthday (a very important time of the accumulated Solar Arc semisquare, exact to the month).

Predictions in these pages were exact as well with the specifics of the signing with the P.L.O. (September 13, 1993 at 11:43 A.M., EDT in Washington D.C.), the various announcements coming out of the talks, the interruption by the Hebron violence, and will have noted the resumption of talks in "early April 1994." August 1994 represents a major time of success in the talks, but we come crucially again from this measurement perspective to the bombast and chaos of December 1994. This extends with great difficulty into April 1995, and coincides with Israel's identity adjustment in May 1995. The likelihood is great that the talks will break down completely if they cannot survive the militarism at the close of 1994 and in April 1995. The next steps of the talks are most at risk in September 1995 and January 1996.

Arafat's nature (August 27, 1929 at 2:00 A.M. in Cairo) is to keep his word. His horoscope parallels the violence schedule seen above but shows extreme agitation, threat, and breakdown May–August 1995. At this time, his control of his people is at its lowest, most dangerous (SA Pluto square Saturn, ruler of his 7th) point. I believe Arafat will prevail in mid-October.

United States

The United States horoscope (July 4, 1776 at 2:13 A.M., LMT in Philadelphia) is tightly bound to the chart of Israel. There is little doubt that the United States will be involved between September and the end of 1994, with militarism to aid Israel in the Middle-East crisis involving implementation of the peace pact with the P.L.O. for Palestinian self-rule. This will have prompted again an American outcry to keep U.S. attention at home, to stop policing the world. Clinton will have exerted the military power as a way to flex presidential muscles once again.

The people will have their way, and I feel that the United States will adopt formal policies of non-intervention, framed in April–June and between September and October 1995.

Bill Clinton is under siege almost constantly throughout 1994, as predicted long ago. His wife will have been dragged into the arena with him, especially in May–June 1994. As I predicted a year ago, the Health Program was pronounced dead in the water in February–March 1994. Bill Clinton will wonder why anyone would want the job he has during his worst times June–September 1994. The application of force within the Middle East violence actually rescues his success profile!

Hillary Clinton (October 26, 1947 at 8:00 P.M. in Chicago) has extraordinary astrological upheaval from September 1995 through November 1996. She will propel her husband's drive to be reelected in the campaign of 1996, as if she, herself, will want to run for reelection.

Hillary's power is so great throughout the second half of 1995 and into the spring and summer of 1996, that we must speculate about how she will use her energies and resourcefulness. With the Health Plan basically defeated as she and the president have designed it, there will be a new and different health plan adopted. This will have to be the vehicle for her to express the 6th House power (with transiting Pluto conjunct Jupiter in Sagittarius) in her horoscope. As long as the cause Hillary serves remains "noble," the greater winner she will be. It is important to point out here that Hillary Clinton's self-emphasis throughout 1995 is so strong that it would threaten to disrupt a marriage under conventional circumstances.

Bill Clinton's horoscope calms down in 1995. Indeed, he will have really been "through it," with all the investigation of his personal finances (the ending of

Pluto's transit of Clinton's 2nd House), and I think we can anticipate a maturation, an aging if you will, evident in March 1995. The success of his militarism at the end of 1994 will have buoyed him with a reinforced confidence and optimism in the light of the nation's demand for attention to domestic problems. Clinton will mellow in the spring of 1995. He will consider that he need not run for reelection in 1996 to fulfill himself further, but in September and November 1995, Clinton will indeed resolve to run in 1996 for another term as President.

As poised and affable as Bill Clinton is, it is important to point out that Hillary's growing power can become a burden to him: while it fuels his energies, invigorates his strategies, and makes decisions for him, her power can begin to intimidate him as well. On a personal level, Clinton needs to be adored, never challenged, especially in terms of personal emotions and ego considerations. Bill and Hillary are going to have to come up with some codes of conduct to keep their relationship as apparently efficient as it is.

Long term: Bill Clinton will run again and will enjoy an enormously positive April and May 1996, the key months of his campaign. Late in 1996, however, there are two powerful measurements that need more time beyond this present moment to give them an interpretive base (SA Saturn square Uranus and SA Neptune square Sun). In all the bravura of the reelection campaign, Bill Clinton is hypersensitive about ego matters and this may have a basis in his marital relationship.

Republican Senator Robert Dole (July 22, 1923 at 00:10 A.M. in Russell, KS) will be there too! I believe Dole will announce his bid for the presidency, campaigning against Bill Clinton, early in October 1995, perhaps on the 8th. Throughout 1995 Dole is on fire, so to speak, with particularly grand times of success in June and July. All of this will be a turnaround from the confused times Dole will have experienced from August to November 1994, coming out of the strange quandary of self-doubt through his positioning against the United States' involvement with military support to Israel in the Middle East late in the year.

Astrological Dictionary

Ascendant. Rising Sign. Cusp of the 1st House. The degree of the zodiac on the eastern horizon at the time and place for which the horoscope is calculated. Each sign takes approximately two hours to rise above the horizon. An *ascending planet*, or *rising planet*, is one which is between 12° above and 20° below the Ascendant.

Aspect. The angular relationship between planets, sensitive points, or house cusps in the horoscope. Lines drawn between the two points and the center of the chart, representing the Earth, form the angle of the aspect.

Direct Motion. Proper Motion. Proceeding in the order of the signs, from Aries toward Taurus, etc. Denoted in the ephemeris by a "D". Opposite of retrograde motion.

Elements: Triplicities. The signs symbolized by the four elements: Fire, Earth, Air, Water. See chart, p. 18.

Ephemeris. A listing of the Sun, Moon, and planets' places and related information for astrological purposes.

Geocentric. Earth-centered.

Greenwich Mean Time. GMT. Universal Time. The time at the prime meridian of 0° longitude. The standard for navigation, astronomy, international communications, and astrology. Ephemerides are usually calculated for either noon or midnight GMT.

Heliocentric. Sun-centered.

Houses. Division of the horoscope into 12 segments beginning with the Ascendant. The dividing lines between the houses are called house cusps. Each house corresponds to aspects of daily living or earthly affairs.

Modes. Quadruplicities. Qualities. Three groups of four signs, one of each element. See chart, p. 18.

Retrograde Motion. Apparent backward motion of a planet in the reverse order of the signs, from Aries toward Pisces, etc, an illusion caused by the relative motion of the Earth and the other planets in their elliptical orbits.

Transit. The ephemeral or ongoing movement of the planets. The movement of a planet over or in aspect to a sensitive point, planet, or house cusp in a horoscope.

Zodiac. Tropical Zodiac. The circle or band following the path of the ecliptic, ending about 9° on either side of it. Distance along the zodiac is measured in terms of zodiacal longitude, divided into 12 signs of 30° each.

LLEWELLYN'S 1995

SUN SIGN BOOK

PRODUCTS

and

SERVICES

Sensual Products

**How to order them without embarrassment.
How to use them without disappointment.**

Today, people are interested in improving the quality of their lives and exploring their own sensuality with options from the **Xandria Collection**.

What is The Xandria Collection?

It is a very special collection of sensual products. It includes the finest and most effective products available from around the world. Products that can open new doors to pleasure (perhaps many you never knew existed)!

Our products range from the simple to the delightfully complex. They are designed for the timid, the bold or for anyone who has ever wished there could be something more to their sensual pleasures.

The Xandria Collection has had the same unique three-way guarantee for nearly 20 years.

First, we guarantee your privacy. Everything we ship is plainly packaged and securely wrapped, with no clue to its contents from the outside. All transactions are strictly confidential and we <u>never</u> sell, rent or trade any customer's name.

Second, we guarantee your satisfaction. If a product seems unsatisfactory, simply return it for a replacement or refund.

Third, we guarantee the quality of our products for one year. If it malfunctions, simply return it to us for a replacement.

Send for the **Xandria Gold Edition Catalogue**. It's price of $4.00 is applied, in full, to your first order.

Write today. You have absolutely nothing to lose, and an entirely new world of enjoyment to gain.

Now <u>You</u> Can Own
The Ultimate Talking Board Set!

Enjoy the "Cadillac" of Talking Boards at an affordable price! This board is designed like no other to enhance the enjoyment and ease of your sessions. Use the board to access information about yourself, your life, and your personal growth from the "realms of non-form." Ask about (or even talk to) deceased loved ones. Inquire about your past lives. Obtain answers to questions on virtually any subject! The redesigned version of this ancient device comes with a complete booklet of instructions and a <u>30-day unconditional money-back guarantee.</u> Order today and you too will see why thousands feel that they would trade this board for no other!

Constructed from 1/8 inch reinforced oak plywood beautifully silk-screened and varnished; the round 18" board and 4" indicator make use uniquely effortless.

ORDER TODAY! CALL 24-HOURS TOLL FREE: 1-800-650-0065, or send $35 plus $4 s/h (Check/ MO/ VISA/ MC) to TEC, Dept A, PO Box 9338, Tacoma, WA 98409-9338

NEVADA HUDSON
Astrological Consultant

"Reach for the Stars"
SPECIAL HOROSCOPES

Natal Charts ✧ Gambling ✧ Career ✧ Lectures
Comparisons ✧ Business ✧ Investments
Workshops ✧ Relocation ✧ Health
Future Trends ✧ Parties

Accomplishments

President Southwestern Parapsychology Assoc.
President Texas Astrological Assoc.
President Dallas Chapter of NCGR
Vice President Astrological Society of Fort Worth
Psychic Operator Certified by Silva Method

Telephone conferences with MasterCard or VISA
Seven days a week 10 a.m. - 10 p.m.

P.O. Box 531168, Grand Prairie, TX 75053

(214) 988-1168
Call for confidential and private appointments.

Life Flavored by Planets and Stars

The Prophet Elijah

Abbe Bassett
Personal Astrology Services

Vocational Guidance: Explores your birthchart to reveal your potential. Very effective for those beginning work, making career changes, or stuck in dead end jobs. Describe what you enjoy, your talents, training, and job experience. $50

Complete Natal Report: Discusses your birth chart in response to your specific concerns and provides insights to their resolution. Defines your transits and progressions and solar arc directions for one year and introduces spiritual lessons contained in them. $85

Compatibility: This is a useful tool for discovering the relationship dynamics between you and a lover, partner, friend, or enemy. Send birth data for both people. $65

Child Guidance: Provides a useful tool in discovering the emerging personality of your child. Shows how your child relates to you, his or her environment, school, and friends. Illuminates interests and talents. $65

Solar Return: Gives a clear picture of what to expect in the coming birthday year. Deals with trends and influences for the year as well as personal dynamics and what the year will bring. $65

Horary: Cast for the moment of an inquiry, reveals issues related to the question and trends pertaining to the matters involved. Deals with influences concerned with the resolution of the question. $65.

Detailed Natal: Deals with a specific set of questions in view of transiting influences, solar arc directions and progressions for the year. Provides answers which are specific in nature. $65.

Speculation Reading: Provides lucky numbers and dates based on your horoscope and name. (Please give full name!) Discusses lucky trends, influences and investments in your life. Gives an outline of luck in your life. $65

Send a detailed letter with your birth data: month, day, year, time of day, city, state, country where you were born, with check to:

Abbe Bassett
Personal Astrology Services
P.O. Box 17, Essex Junction VT 05453-3030

Please allow 3-5 weeks for your order to be completed.

Master the Power:

© 1993

For most it works the first day, but if you need help, phone us toll free

Chi is the Chinese word for the electrical energy that powers your body. Mostly used by Master Martial Artists, methods for building and using chi power have been kept very secret. Chi power is mostly used for healing, but on occasion when great strength is needed, this Chi Power Plus is called forth. They can easily break a stack of bricks, or move with blinding speed to avoid harm or to capture a weapon.

Now, YOU can, too.

SPC•USA Chi Power Plus is being made available to all who wish to learn it. Chi Power Plus is based upon Christian teachings. Even a child can learn the following: ❖ Move objects with Chi Power without touching them ❖ Extinguish a candle flame with your eyes only ❖ For speed faster than a cat, try this test ❖ **Attract** fish, birds, animals, people, with Chi Power Plus ❖ **Or repel them** ❖ Your health will improve by adjusting your internal organs so there is a balanced blood flow ❖ Your muscular balance will also improve ❖ With regular practice, a protective ion shield will form around your body ❖ You will learn how to see visions meant especially for you through your "Third Eye". *This is the way the prophets of old saw visions.*

SPC•USA Chi Power Plus™ $47.95 + $3 P&H.

Package includes: poster of internal organs, instruction booklet, audio demo tape including how to create a Chi Power Voice. **You will be heard with this special voice.**

• • • • • •

SPC•USA Pressure Points will eradicate all muscular pain quickly and completely. Then by following a few simple stretching exercises, the pain permanently

disappears -- all without drugs or surgery. We believe these are the same methods Jesus taught to His disciples. Even the terrible backache or kneeache can be cured simply and safely. This is the latest technology in medical treatment. It is not ordinary acupressure. It works everytime on everyone. This is lifetime knowledge for pain free survival. Used for protection, a sharp strike on certain points quickly disables an enemy.

SPC•USA Pressure Points™ $29.95 + $3 P&H.

Package includes: poster of muscle structure with vital points, instruction booklet with secret method to learn Chinese or American splits. No equipment of any type required.

Internationally copyrighted, and practiced in over 60 nations and in nearly every city in the U.S. Accept no substitutes. Nothing at any price works as well or as fast.

Worldwide Guarantee:

All claims are true. Test them for 90 days and this practice will change your life.

If you have trouble learning the practice, ask a friend to help you. Or phone us for free technical help. If not satisfied, return for a prompt refund.

NOTE FOR ALL PRODUCTS:

Order both at once and save $3.00 P&H. Ohio orders add 6% sales tax. Orders from foreign countries must prepay in U.S. dollars, payable thru a U.S. bank, plus $1.00 for extra handling.

FOR FAST C.O.D. DELIVERY
CALL 800 334 7353

No credit cards accepted. $4 extra per order. All orders sent Air Mail.

Or mail to:
SPC•USA; Dept. 46
P.O. Drawer 10
Middletown, OH 45042

Gifted Psychics

Provide Inspired Counsel
--
Love. - Money - Health
Career - Relationships
The Future

1-800-405-0MEN
(405-6636)

En Español   1-900-745-1193

NO CREDIT CARD NEEDED TO CALL
$3.99/Minute - APE San Rafael CA - 18+Years

Horoscope by BURTON

FREE Love Sign Reading

Here's Your Chance to Have Your Horoscope Cast by a World Class Astrologer

The mystic known as Burton accurately predicted the precise time and date of the disastrous Los Angeles earthquake. Now, after 25 years of successfully casting horoscopes for some of the most famous people in the world, Burton is prepared to personally forecast your future!

HERE'S WHAT BURTON COULD DO FOR YOU:

Your astrological chart will be analyzed to its finest detail, with no potential windfall or pitfall overlooked or disregarded. The positive will be highlighted, and you will receive specific guidance on how to neutralize the negative.

BURTON'S OFFER

"Let me prepare your forecast and bring you up-to-date on your future. I will cover the areas of your life that are most important to you: relationships, love, luck, friendship, money, financial security and much more."

FREE INTRODUCTORY OFFER: Order today and Burton will include his famous "Love Sign" Reading (16 pages) —absolutely **FREE**! This exciting and informative study of your Venus sign will reveal your specific compatibility with all other signs. Now you can learn the secrets of improving relationships with everyone you know or want to know.

☐ I am enclosing $16.95 + $2.00 shipping for my **HOROSCOPE BY BURTON** and my free **LOVE SIGN READING.** Send to: C.A.A., Dept. LS-5, P.O. Box 8005, Canoga Park, CA 91309

Name _____

Address _____

City _____ State _____ Zip _____

Birthdate: Month _____ Date _____ Year _____

Place of Birth: City _____ State _____

Time of Birth: __ AM __ PM (If time unknown we'll use sunrise)

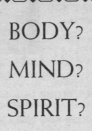 

Classifieds

Ancient Teachings

FREE REVEALING REPORT. How to get almost everything you ever wished for. Amazing, ancient secrets, magickal spells, rituals. Wizeworld-LA, P.O. Box 1337, Huntington Beach CA 92647

Astrology

NO BULL! The Real Astrological influences daily for real people by a real astrologer! Janice Scott-Reeder's Cosmic Corner℠ 1-900-680-7779. Touch Tone needed! $1.79/min. 18+. Catalogue $2.00, Box 499-SS, Deerfield FL 33443

JAN MOODY, CERTIFIED astrologer. Horoscope readings. No wild predictions. Calm, problem solving approach. MC/Visa. 207-363-1238

Audio/Video

I'M A FREE person, are you? Non religious material, 120 min. tape $10.00. Action, c/o P.O. Box 1568, Overgaard Arizona 85933

Books

LIFE AFTER DEATH. An alternate view. Write for transition. $2.00 (mailing and materials). Hastings, 874 N. Park Ave., Pomona CA 91768

HOW TO BECOME a son, or daughter, of God. 60-page booklet includes Biblical verification. Send $5.00 to: Mr. B.E. Stewart, 771 Belland Ave., St. Paul MN 55127

Business Opportunities

LET THE GOVERNMENT finance your small business. Grants/loans to $500,000.00. Free recorded message: 707-448-0270 (GC8)

Crystals

CRYSTALS, FREE GIFTS! $1.00 refundable for details and price list. Ariels' Crystals, Box 387L, Marcy NY 13403

Health & Healing

PERSONALIZED MUSICAL HEALING tapes for your mind, body & soul. $15.00. Harmony Ministries, Box 1568, Overgaard Arizona 85933

FACELIFT NATURALLY! "Youth-Skin Secrets/Image Games Revealed." Infopak $1.00. AAP, P.O. Box 14189, Coral Gables FL 33114

HERBAL HEALER ACADEMY offers you alternatives to chemical drugs! Medicinal Herbology correspondence courses/natural medicine supply catalog/newsletter- $4.00. HC32 97-B, Mountainview AR 72560

Instruction

THE most complete & advanced metaphysical, magical & psychic power development correspondence course ever offered. Ancient secrets finally revealed by 5000-year-old magical order. Our simple to understand, and easy to apply methods can make your dreams into reality. Free brochure. Very reasonable rates. Priesthood, 2301 Artesia Blvd., 12-188A Redondo Beach CA 90278 310-397-1310

Magick

MAGICAL GOODS, FREE catalog, mystical oils and incense, Isle of Avalon 800-700-ISLE. In California: 714-646-4213

Personals

FREE PERSONALITY TEST. Your personality determines your happiness. Know why? Call 1-800-334-LIFE

Products

UNIQUE DESIGNS "BORN Again Pagan" or "Howl at the Moon" - button $1.50, bumper sticker $2.00, 8" diameter iron on transfer $5.00. Catalog $1.00, free w/order. KLW Enterprises, 3790 El Camino Real, #270S, Palo Alto CA 94306-3314

Publications

FELLOWSHIP OF ISIS and Wiccan Correspondence Courses. Crystal Moon International Metaphysical Digest: quarterly, 70+ pages. Sample/information U.S. $6.50. Astrology/Occult Catalog, US $3.00 refundable. Box 802-LB, Matteson IL 60443-0802

EXTRAORDINARY PSYCHIC COUNSELOR, Randal Clayton Bradford, will tell you the best possible future in any situation, and how to make it happen. "Cuts straight to the truth"...accurate, detailed and specific." Established worldwide clientele by telephone. AMEX/MC/Visa 310-823-8893 or 213-REALITY.

Readings

CLARIFY YOUR LIFE! Anna Victor Hale—Psychic-Astro-Intuitive counseling. $1.99 per min. MC/VISA/M.O., 1-800-438-1266

PSYCHIC PHONE READINGS, incredibly accurate. Need answers on love, health, finances? JoAnna, 516-753-0191, $35

KNOW THYSELF. SIMULACRA of your soul. For free information write to: P.O. Box 776, Mesilla Park NM 88047

ACCURATE TELEPHONE READINGS by experienced clairvoyant counselor. By appointment. Susan 301-645-1226

JOIN OUR PSYCHIC Calling Card™ family for the reading of your lifetime. Live! 24 hours. 1-800-549-7337 or 1-900-773-7374 ext. 5772. $3.99/min. 18+. Neat Stuff Catalogue $2.00 The Psychic Network® Box 499-SS, Deerfield FL 33443

LIVE READINGS! 90% ACCURATE psychic astrological answers. Walk through other's minds! $2.40 per minute. Checks by phone, Mastercard/VISA 800-488-3786

PSYCHIC SPIRITUALIST REUNITES all lost loves. Lamarr Dell, a natural-born gifted psychic, has abilities to restore love, happiness, business, health. One phone reading will give you peace of mind. 900-287-7924 or 818 760-8424, $2.49/min.

Reincarnation

THE TWO CRUCIFIXIONS Poster-size illustration of the star figures and configuration of the heavens which was the first Bible and the common ancestor of almost all religion. Included is a booklet of explanation. $15.00. 675 Fairview Drive, #246, Carson City NV 89701

Free Catalog!

LLEWELLYN'S

New WORLDS
OF MIND AND SPIRIT

**Call 1-800-THE-MOON
for your free issue of
New Worlds!**

Llewellyn's Computerized Astrological Services

Llewellyn has been a leading authority in astrological chart readings for over thirty years. Our professional experience and continued dedication assures complete satisfaction in all areas of our astrological services.

Llewellyn features a wide variety of readings with the intent to satisfy the needs of any astrological enthusiast. Our goal is to give you the best possible service so that you can achieve your goals and live your life successfully.

When requesting a computerized service be sure to give accurate and complete birth data including: exact time (a.m. or p.m.), date, year, city, county and country of birth. (Check your birth certificate for this information.) *Accuracy of birth data is very important.* Llewellyn will not be responsible for mistakes made by you. An order form follows for your convenience.

Computerized Charts

Simple Natal Chart
Before you do anything else, order the Simple Natal Chart! This chart print-out is programmed and designed by Matrix. Learn the locations of your midpoints and aspects, elements, and more. Discover your planets and house cusps, retrogrades and other valuable data necessary to make a complete interpretation.
APS03-119 . . . . **$5.00**

Personality Profile
This is our most popular reading! It makes the perfect gift! This ten-part reading gives you a complete look at your "natal imprint" and how the planets mark your destiny. Examine your emotional needs and inner feelings. Explore your imagination and read about your general characteristics and life patterns. Very reasonable price!
APS03-503 . . . . **$20.00**

Life Progression

Discover what the future has in store for you! This incredible reading covers a year's time and is designed to complement the Personality Profile Reading. Progressions are a special system with which astrologers map how the "natal you" develops through specified periods of your present and future life. We are all born into an already existing world and an already existing fabric of personal interaction, and with this report you can discover the "now you!"

APS03-507 . . . . $20.00

Transit Report

Know the trends of your life—in advance! Keep abreast of positive trends and challenging periods for a specified period of time in your life. Transits are the relationships between the planets today and their positions at the moment of your birth. They are an invaluable aid for timing your actions and making decisions. This report devotes a paragraph to each of your transit aspects and gives effective dates for those transits. The report will begin with the first day of the month. Be sure to specify present residence for all people getting this report!

APS03-500 – 3-month report $12.00
APS03-501 – 6-month report $20.00
APS03-502 – 1-year report $30.00

Biorhythm Report

Ever have one of those days when you have unlimited energy and everything is going your way? Then the next day you are feeling sluggish and awkward? These cycles are called biorhythms. This individual report will accurately map your daily biorhythms. It can be your personal guide to the cycles of your daily life. Each important day is thoroughly discussed. With this valuable information, you can schedule important events with great success. This report is an invaluable source of information to help you plan your days to the fullest. Order today!

APS03-515 – 3-month report $12.00
APS03-516 – 6-month report $18.00
APS03-517 – 1-year report $25.00

Compatibility Profile

Find out if you really are compatible with your lover, spouse, friend or business partner! Do you have the same goals? How well do you deal with arguments? Do you have the same values? This service includes planetary placements for both individuals, so send birth data for both. Succeed in all of your relationships!

APS03-504 . . . . **$30.00**

Personal Relationship Interpretation

If you've just called it quits on one relationship and know you need to understand more about yourself before you test the waters again, then this is the report for you! This reading will tell you how you approach relationships in general, what kind of people you look for and what kind of people might rub you the wrong way. Important for anyone!

APS03-506 . . . . **$20.00**

Tarot Reading

Find out what the cards have in store for you! This reading features the graphics of the traditional Rider-Waite card deck in a detailed 10-card spread, and as a bonus, there are three pages explaining what each Tarot card means for you. This report is also custom made to answer any question you might have. Order this exciting tarot reading today!

APS03-120 . . . . **$10.00**

Lucky Lotto Report
(State Lottery Report)

Do you play the state lotteries? This report will determine your luckiest sequence of numbers for each day based on specific planets, degrees and other indicators in your own chart. Provide your full birth data and middle name, and specify the parameters of your state's lottery: i.e., how many numbers you need in sequence (up to 10 numbers) as well as the highest possible numeral (up to #999). Indicate the month you want to start.

APS03-512 – 3-month report **$10.00**
APS03-513 – 6-month report **$15.00**
APS03-514 – 1-year report **$25.00**

Numerology Report

Find out which numbers are right for you with this insightful report. This report uses an ancient form of numerology invented by Pythagoras to determine the significant numbers in your life. Using both your given birth name and date of birth, this report will accurately calculate those numbers which stand out as yours. With these numbers, the report can determine certain trends in your life and tell you when the important periods of your life will occur.

APS03-508 – 3-month report $12.00
APS03-509 – 6-month report $18.00
APS03-510 – 1-year report $25.00

Ultimate Astro-Profile

This report has it all! Receive over 40 pages of fascinating, insightful and uncanny descriptions of your innermost qualities and talents. Read about your burn rate (thirst for change). Explore your personal patterns (inside and outside). The Astro-Profile doesn't repeat what you've already learned from other personality profiles, but considers often the neglected natal influence of the lunar nodes plus much more.

APS03-505 . . . . $40.00

SPECIAL COMBO OFFER

Buy both and save!
APS03-214 . . $40.00

Personality Profile & Compatibility Profile
Learn about the real you and discover what the
future holds with that special someone!

Astrological Services Order Form

Include all birth data plus your full name for all reports.

Service name and number _____

Full name (1st person) _____

Birthtime _____ ❑ a.m. ❑ p.m. Date _____ Year _____

Birthplace (city, county, state, country) _____

_____

Full name (2nd person) _____

Birthtime _____ ❑ a.m. ❑ p.m. Date _____ Year _____

Birthplace (city, county, state, country) _____

_____

Include letter with questions on separate sheet of paper.

Name _____

Address _____

City _____ State _____ Zip _____

Make check or money order payable to Llewellyn Publications, or charge it!

❑ VISA   ❑ MasterCard   ❑ American Express

Account Number _____

Exp. Date _____ Daytime Phone _____

Signature of Cardholder _____

❑ **Yes!** Send me my **FREE** copy of **New Worlds!**

Mail this form and payment to:

Llewellyn's Personal Services, P.O. Box 64383-K901, St. Paul, MN 55164-0383. Allow 4-6 weeks for delivery.

LLEWELLYN ORDER FORM

Llewellyn Publications
P.O. Box 64383-K901, St. Paul, MN 55164-0383

You may use this form to order any of the Llewellyn books listed in this publication.

Give Title, Author, Order Number and Price.

_____

_____

_____

_____

_____

_____

_____

Shipping and Handling: We ship UPS when possible. Include $3 for orders $10 & under; $4 for orders over $10. Llewellyn pays postage for all orders over $50. Please give street address (UPS cannot deliver to P.O. Boxes). Next Day Air cost—$16.00/one book; add $2.00 for each additional book. Second Day Air cost—$7.00/one book; add $1.00 for each additional book.

Credit Card Orders: In the U.S. and Canada call 1-800-THE-MOON. In Minnesota call 612-291-1970. Or, send credit card order by mail. Any questions can be directed to customer service 612-291-1970.

❏ Yes! Send me your free catalog!

❏ VISA   ❏ MasterCard   ❏ American Express

Account No. _____

Exp. Date _____ Phone _____

Signature _____

Name _____

Address _____

City_____ State_____ Zip_____

Thank you for your order!

SUPER DISCOUNTS ON
LLEWELLYN DATEBOOKS AND CALENDARS!

Llewellyn offers several ways to save money. With a four-year subscription you receive your books as soon as they are published. The price remains the same for four years even if there is a price increase! We pay postage and handling as well. *Buy any 2 subscriptions and take $2 off! Buy 3 and take $3 off! Buy 4 and take an additional $5 off!*

Subscriptions (4 years, 1996-1999)

- ☐ Astrological Calendar ···································· $40.00
- ☐ Sun Sign Book ·· $19.96
- ☐ Moon Sign Book ·· $19.96
- ☐ Daily Planetary Guide ·································· $31.80
- ☐ Organic Gardening Almanac ························· $23.80

Order *by the dozen* and save 40%! Sell them to your friends or give as gifts. Llewellyn pays postage and handling on quantity orders.

Quantity Orders: 40% OFF
1995 1996

- ☐ ☐ Astrological Calendar ···························· 12/$72.00
- ☐ ☐ Sun Sign Book ·································· 12/$35.93
- ☐ ☐ Moon Sign Book ································ 12/$35.93
- ☐ ☐ Daily Planetary Guide ······················ 12/$57.24
- ☐ ☐ Magical Almanac ····························· 12/$50.04
- ☐ ☐ Organic Gardening Almanac ··············· 12/$42.84
- ☐ ☐ Myth & Magic Calendar ···················· 12/$72.00

On single copy orders, include $3 p/h for orders under $10 and $4 for orders over $10. We pay postage for all orders over $50

Single copies of Llewellyn's Almanacs and Calendars
1995 1996

- ☐ ☐ Astrological Calendar ···························· $10.00
- ☐ ☐ Sun Sign Book ·································· $4.99
- ☐ ☐ Moon Sign Book ································ $4.99
- ☐ ☐ Daily Planetary Guide ······················ $7.95
- ☐ ☐ Magical Almanac ····························· $6.95
- ☐ ☐ Organic Gardening Almanac ··············· $5.95
- ☐ ☐ Myth and Magic Calendar ················· $10.00

Please use order form on last page.